Sixteenth-century Antwerp and its Rural Surroundings

SEUH

14

Studies in European Urban History (1100-1800)

Series Editor

Marc Boone

Ghent University

Sixteenth-century Antwerp and its Rural Surroundings

Social and Economic Changes in the Hinterland of a Commercial Metropolis (ca. 1450 – ca. 1570)

Michael Limberger

BREPOLS

This book forms part of the IAP-project 'City and society in the Low Countries', 1200-1800, phase VI, n° 32.

This book has been published with the financial support of the Catholic University of Brussels (K.U.Brussel – Hogeschool-Universiteit Brussel).

Cover illustration: Frans Huys, Panoramic view on Antwerp (1557), published by Bartolomeus de Momper, Paris, Bibliotheque Nationale de France

D/2008/0095/12
ISBN 978-2-503-52725-3
Printed in the E.U. on acid-free paper

Table of Contents

List of Maps, Graphs and Tables

Maps

Tables

Graphs

Acknowledgments

This book is a revised version of my PhD. thesis, which I defended in 2000 at the University of Antwerp. The revision of the manuscript took essentially place during the period 2001-2002, during my postdoctoral assistantship at the University of Antwerp. During this period, I received useful comments on the occasion of presentations at various European Universities (Facultés Universitaires Notre Dame de La Paix, Namur, University of London, University of Vienna, University of Padova) as well as in the framework of the Recent Dissertations in Economic History Session at the Economic History Congress at Buenos Aires in 2002 and during the ESTER seminar 'Long-term development of rural economies and societies, 13th-19th centuries, at Gent, in 2002. The original text has also been edited by Tom Johnston for style and errors in English.

I would like to thank all collegues for their suggestions and comments, especially the members of the jury of my PhD.-defence, Raymond Van Uytven, Herman Van der Wee, Bruno Blondé, Peter Hoppenbrouwers and Erik Thoen. Furthermore I would like to mention Derek Keene, Stefan Epstein, Salvatore Ciriacono, Peter Feldbauer, Erich Landsteiner and Herbert Knittler as well as the contributors to the ESTER seminar Bas van Bavel, Markus Cerman, Paolo Malanima, Tine De Moor, Thijs Lambrecht, Tim Soens and Dries Tys.

Finally, I would also like to thank the editors of the series Studies in European Urban History for accepting the manuscript for publication and the Katholieke Universiteit Brussel for the financial support.

Introduction

Theoretical Background: Sixteenth-century Antwerp and its Rural Surroundings – A Case Study on Economic Transitions in a Metropolitan Hinterland

Sixteenth-Century Antwerp and its Historiography

Sixteenth-century Antwerp occupies a prominent place in the economic history of Europe. For nearly a century it was the major commercial centre of the Low Countries, just as Bruges was in the fifteenth century and Amsterdam during the seventeenth and eighteenth centuries. Moreover, its spectacular rise around 1500 was one of the impulses leading to the shift in the commercial centre of gravity of Europe from the Mediterranean to the North Atlantic. As a consequence, Antwerp has also played a central role in studies on the rise of a so-called world economy during the early modern period. F. Braudel considered it one of the first *urban poles* of his *économie monde*, and I. Wallerstein similarly devoted particular attention to its role in both the political and financial developments of the first half of the sixteenth century.[1]

The vision of a European financial and commercial network with Antwerp as a major node is not a creation of the 1970s, however. As early as 1925, R. Ehrenberg's treatment of Antwerp as one of the leading financial markets of Europe formed one of the focal points in his *Das Zeitalter der Fugger*.[2] Nevertheless, Braudel went further than Ehrenberg in emphasising the importance of Antwerp. For Braudel, the Age of the Fugger was "actually the Age of Antwerp, during which the town at the Scheldt formed the centre of the entire international economy."[3]

In keeping with Antwerp's significance in economic history, the abundance of historiography dealing with its *Golden Age* is exceptional. In his *Histoire de Belgique*, H. Pirenne stressed the town's liberalism as being one of its main assets, along with the opening of its waterway to the open sea during the fifteenth century, the advantages of its harbour, the rise of the English trade and the arrival of the southern Germans.[4] In the decades that followed, the major theme of interest among scholars was the role of the foreign merchant colonies in Antwerp. J.A. Goris' *Etude sur les colonies marchandes méridionales*[5] was the model for a series of case studies concerning particular groups of merchants and their commercial activities.[6] Among these studies, W. Brulez' analysis of the continental trade

1 F. Braudel, *Le temps du monde, Civilisation matérielle, économie et capitalisme, XVe–XVIIIe siècle*, tome 3, Paris, 1979, pp. 118–129; I. Wallerstein, *The Modern World System. Capitalist Agriculture and the Origins of the European World-Economy in the Sixteenth Century*, New York, 1974.

2 R. Ehrenberg, *Das Zeitalter der Fugger, Geldkapital und Kreditverkehr im 16. Jahrhundert, vol. 2: Die Weltbörsen und Finanzkrisen*, Jena, 1922.

3 Braudel, *Temps du monde*, p. 118.

4 H. Pirenne, *Histoire de Belgique*, vol. III, Bruxelles, 1923, p. 271.

5 J.A. Goris, *Etude sur les colonies marchandes méridionales (portugais, espagnols, italiens) à Anvers de 1488 à 1567. Contribution à l'histoire des débuts du capitalisme moderne*, Louvain, 1925.

6 J. Craeybeckx, J.A. Van Houtte, "Les Français et Anvers au XVIe siècle" in *Annales* E.S.C., 17/1962, pp. 542–554;

between Antwerp and Italy was perhaps the most influential.[7] Brulez was particularly interested in the spread of commercial techniques and the resulting democratisation of trade. Besides examining the organisational and social aspects of the foreign colonies in Antwerp, these studies provided rich quantitative material on the Antwerp trade. On the basis of this new evidence, J.A. Van Houtte wrote a general synthesis of the rise and decline of the commercial metropolis in which he introduced the classic concept of the three pillars of the first wave of commercial growth, from ca. 1490 to ca. 1520.[8]

The broadest and most complete study on sixteenth-century Antwerp published so far (but in fact also including the fifteenth and part of the fourteenth century) is H. Van der Wee's *The Growth of the Antwerp Market.*[9] It forms a synthesis of the economic rise and decline of Antwerp in both a European and a regional context. Starting from a study of prices and wages in both Antwerp and the nearby town of Lier, this synthesis encompasses the commercial, financial, industrial and agricultural developments of Antwerp and its Flemish and Brabantine hinterland. *The Growth of the Antwerp Market* set a new standard for the historiography on sixteenth-century Antwerp. Most of its results still form the backbone of the economic history of the town and that of Flanders and Brabant of the fifteenth and sixteenth century.

In subsequent studies, Van der Wee himself went on to elaborate the major topics of the book, such as the industrial development of the Low Countries and the innovations of financial techniques.[10] Other questions were taken up by other historians and would become the subject of scholarly discourse in subsequent years. These include the views that W. Brulez put forth concerning the commercial developmentof the region[11] and the questions H. Soly raised about the social benefits of the rise of Antwerp. In contrast to Van der Wee, Soly stressed the strong polarisation between wealthy merchants and other entrepreneurs on the one hand and the masses of poor workers on the other, rather than the importance of the relatively well-to-do middle class.[12] H. Soly, for his part, wrote a brilliant study on the urban and industrial activities of G. van Schoonbeke, who turned the town upside down in the middle of the sixteenth century. In this study, he literally shows Van Schoonbeke and many other real-estate speculators, building entrepreneurs and industrial monopolists at work.[13]

O. De Smedt, *De Engelse natie te Antwerpen in de 16e eeuw (1496–1582).* 2 vols. Antwerp, 1950–54.

7 W. Brulez, *De firma Della Faille en de internationale handel van Vlaamse firma's in de 16e eeuw*, Brussels, 1959.

8 J.A. Van Houtte, "La genèse du grand marché international d'Anvers à la fin du Moyen-Age" in *Belgisch Tijdschrift voor Filologie en Geschiedenis/Revue Belge de Philologie et d'Histoire,* XIX (1940), pp. 87–126; J.A. Van Houtte, "Anvers aux XVe et XVIe siècles. Expansion et apogée" in *Annales* E.H.C., 16/1961, pp. 248–278. Other major syntheses of the Golden Age of Antwerp of that period are: E. Sabbe, *Anvers. Metropole de l'Occident (1492–1566),* Bruxelles, 1952; and S.T. Bindoff, "The Greatness of Antwerp" in *The New Cambridge Modern History II. The Reformation*, ed. G.R. Elton, Cambridge, 1958, pp. 50–69.

9 H. Van der Wee, *The Growth of the Antwerp Market and the European Economy (Fourteenth – Sixteenth Centuries).* 3 vols. Den Haag, 1963.

10 See for example: H. Van der Wee, "Industrial Dynamics and the Process of Urbanisation and De- Urbanisation in the Low Countries from the Late Midle Ages to the Eighteenth Century. A Synthesis" in *The Rise and Decline of Urban Industries in Italy and in the Low Countries (Late Middle Ages – Early Modern Times),* Leuven, 1988, pp. 307–381; or H. Van der Wee, "Antwerp and the New Financial Methods of the 16th and 17th Centuries" in *The Low Countries in the Early Modern World,* (Aldershot: Variorum, 1993), pp. 145–166.

11 W. Brulez, "De handel" in *Antwerpen in de XVIe eeuw*, Antwerpen, 1975, pp. 109–125.

12 See for example H. Soly, "Social Relations in Antwerp in the Sixteenth and Seventeenth Centuries" in J. Van der Stock, ed., *Antwerp, Story of a Metropolis (exhibition catalogue, Antwerp, Hessenhuis, 25 June – 10 October 1993),* Gent, 1993, pp. 37–48.

13 H. Soly, *Urbanisme en kapitalisme te Antwerpen in de 16e eeuw. De stedebouwkundige en industriele ondernemingen*

Another topic from Van der Wee's book that was subsequently taken up for discussion was the extent to which the impact of the metropolis of Antwerp on the economy of the southern Low Countries was either generative or parasitic. For the duchy of Brabant this question was first raised by R. van Uytven. His intimate knowledge of the history of Brabant, and the town of Leuven in particular, led him to the revisionist conclusion that the Leuven area, rather than witnessing a stimulating impact of the economic growth of the Antwerp market, was literally overshadowed by the glory of that metropolis.[14] Case studies on other Brabantine towns furthermore showed that the stimulating effects of the export facilities via Antwerp were limited to specific industrial sectors, while other sectors were drained by the attraction of Antwerp or could not keep up with the heavy competition on the international market. The economic dominance of Antwerp, rather than being all generative or all parasitic, therefore had a polarising effect on the economy of the southern Low Countries.[15]

Metropolitan Cities and their Impact on the Economy of their Rural Hinterland

While a whole range of aspects of the Golden Age of Antwerp has been treated in great detail and by many historians, Antwerp's influence on the surrounding countryside still remains a subject that has received little attention. The economic influence that other major commercial centres exerted upon their respective rural hinterlands has been studied extensively. D. Beltrami dedicated many years of research on the impact that Venice had on the surrounding mainland, the so-called *Terraferma*, from the sixteenth to the eighteenth century,[16] for example, while R. Gascon has studied sixteenth-century Lyons and its hinterlands.[17] Similar work has been done for the major capital cities of Europe,[18] Among those in particular, London, Paris and Madrid have received much attention.[19] The recently

van Gilbert van Schoonbeke, Brussel, 1977.

14 R. VAN UYTVEN, "In de schaduwen van de Antwerpse groei: het Hageland in de zestiende eeuw" in *Bijdragen tot de Geschiedenis*, 57 (1974), pp. 171–188; and R. VAN UYTVEN, "De sociale krisis der XVIe eeuw te Leuven" in *Belgisch Tijdschrift voor Filologie en Geschiedenis/Revue Belge de Philologie et d'Histoire,* XXXVI (1958), pp. 356–387.

15 This discussion is summarised in B. BLONDÉ, R. VAN UYTVEN, "De smalle steden en het Brabantse stedelijke netwerk in de Late Middeleeuwen en de Nieuwe Tijd" in *Lira Elegans,* 6 (1996), pp. 139–143. See also B. BLONDÉ en M. LIMBERGER, "De gebroken welvaart" in *De Geschiedenis van Brabant van het hertogdom tot heden,* R. VAN UYTVEN, ed., Deel II: Nieuwe Tijd, Hoofdstuk 1. Nieuwe geluiden en sterke tegenstellingen (1531-1629), Zwolle 2004, pp. 307–330.

16 D. BELTRAMI, *La penetrazione economica dei veneziani in terraferma. Forze di lavoro e proprietà fondiaria nelle campagne venete dei secoli XVII e XVIII* (Venice–Rome, 1961) summarised in S.J. WOOLF, "Venice and the Terraferma: Problems of the Change from Commercial to Landed Activities" in B. PULLAN, ed., *Crisis and Change in the Venetian Economy in the 16th and 17 Centuries,* London 1968, pp. 175–203.

17 R. GASCON, *Grand commerce et vie urbaine au XVIe siècle. Lyon et ses marchands,* 2 vols. (Civilisations et sociétés 22) Paris, The Hague, 1971.

18 For an overview of the studies of European Capital cities and their surroundings, see: P. CLARK and B. LEPETIT, eds., *Capital Cities and Their Hinterlands in Early Modern Europe,* Aldershot, 1996 (Historical Urban Studies; 1996:1); and E. AERTS and P. CLARK, eds., *Metropolitan Cities and Their Hinterlands in Early Modern Europe* (Proceedings, Tenth International Economic History Congress Leuven, August 1990, Session B-6), Leuven, 1990.

19 The most important studies on London are: F.J. FISHER, "The Development of the London Food Market. 1540–1640" in *The Economic History Review,* V 1934–1935, pp. 46–64; and E.A. WRIGLEY, "A Simple Model of London's Importance in Changing English Society and Economy 1650–1750" *in* P. ABRAMS and E.A. WRIGLEY, eds., *Towns in Societies: Essays in Economic History and Historical Sociology, Cambridge, 1978 (Past and Present Publications, 10), pp. 218–309.* On Paris, see J. JACQUART, *La crise rurale en Ile-de-France. 1550–1670,* Paris, 1974 (Publications de la Sorbonne : nouvelle série : recherches, 157). On Madrid, the most significant is: D.R. RINGROSE, *Madrid and the Spanish Economy, 1560–1850,* Berkeley, 1983.

published volume on towns and countryside in Europe, edited by S.R. Epstein, likewise provides interesting insights on the impact of large cities on the economy of the surrounding areas. Epstein nevertheless remarks that "*more conclusive answers about the causes and consequences of urban primacy in the pre-modern world require further systematic study open to a comparative European perspective.*"[20]

For the Low Countries, the most important work treating the urban impact on the rural economy is still J. de Vries' *The Dutch Rural Economy in the Golden Age.*[21] In this study, de Vries set up a general model of the economic transformation of rural Holland and Friesland from the sixteenth to the eighteenth century from a peasant economy to a specialised farming region. For the county of Flanders, the only major study specifically dealing with the relation between town and countryside is D. Nicholas' *Town and Country in Medieval Flanders.* It concentrates on the political supremacy of the great Flemish textile centres and their protectionist measures against rural competition rather than on market ties, however.[22] More recent studies by E. Thoen deal with the economic influence of the urban economy on the countryside as an aspect of the rural economy.[23] The town-countryside relationship is also mentioned in P. Stabel's work on the urban network of Flanders.[24]

There is no study on Antwerp corresponding to those mentioned for Venice, Lyons, and the Dutch towns and their surroundings. The most significant contribution in this regard can be found in the chapters on agricultural evolutions in *The Growth of the Antwerp Market.* Van der Wee devoted a significant part of his book to agricultural evolutions and their link with the urban economy. He did not concentrate exclusively on the immediate hinterland of Antwerp, however, but chose for a larger focus: Flanders and western Brabant. The sources he used for his study of the agrarian developments nevertheless refer primarily to the greater surroundings of Antwerp.[25] His analysis therefore contains many elements pertaining to the urban impact on the economy of the surrounding countryside. The main factors were the local farmers' access to a major urban market for agrarian products and the rise of a variety of forms of wage labour, which helped to compensate for the tiny agrarian income that small peasants earned.[26] The picture Van der Wee sketches therefore forms a good starting hypothesis for a case study on sixteenth-century Antwerp and its economic interaction with its rural surroundings. Besides attempting to verify the impact of the growth

20 S. R. Epstein, ed., *Town and Country in Europe, 1300–1800,* Cambridge, 2001 (quote from p. 29).

21 J. De Vries, *The Dutch Rural Economy in the Golden Age, 1500 – 1700,* New Haven, 1974.

22 D. Nicholas, *Town and Countryside: Social,Economical and Political Tensions in Fourteenth-century Flanders,* Bruges, 1971.

23 E. Thoen, *Landbouwekonomie en bevolking in Vlaanderen gedurende de late middeleeuwen en het begin van de moderne tijden. Testregio: de kasselrijen van Oudenaarde en Aalst* (*Publications du Centre Belge d'Historie Rurale*; 90), 2 vols., Gent, 1988; and E. Thoen, "A "Commercial Survival Economy" in Evolution. The Flemish Countryside and the Transition to Capitalism (Middle Ages–19th century)" in P. Hoppenbrouwers and J.L. van Zanden (eds.), *Peasants into Farmers? The Transformation of Rural Economy and Society in the Low Countries (Middle Ages -19th Century) in Light of the Brenner Debate, Turnhout, 2001* (CORN Publication Series, 4), pp. 102–157.

24 P. Stabel, *Dwarfs Among Giants: the Flemish Urban Network in the Late Middle Ages,* Leuven, 1997; P. Stabel, *De kleine stad in Vlaanderen: bevolkingsdynamiek en economische functies van de kleine en secundaire stedelijke centra in het Gentse kwartier (14de–16de eeuw),* Brussel, 1995 (Verhandelingen van de Koninklijke Academie voor Wetenschappen, Letteren en Schone Kunsten van België: Klasse der Letteren, 156).

25 The major sets of data refer to the area of Lier, 15 km south-east of Antwerp, the Campine (Kempen), 30–50 km east of Antwerp, the polders of Zandvliet, 15 km north of Antwerp and the village of Schoten, 8 km north of Antwerp. See Van der Wee, *growth,* vol. I, Appendix 42. I will refer to this material at different points throughout this study.

26 *Ibidem,* vol II, pp. 295–302.

of the Antwerp market on agriculture and on the rural labour market, this case study will also have to include the aspect of investments made by urban citizens in the countryside – the so-called "*emprise bourgeoise sur la campagne*",[27] – and their consequences on rural property relations.

The studies mentioned in the preceding paragraphs illustrate the strong impact that urban centres had on the agrarian structure of their hinterland, reaching in many cases beyond the immediate surroundings of the town in question. In particular, J. de Vries' work on early modern Holland and Friesland contains a far-reaching hypothesis on the economic development of the United Provinces. According to de Vries, not only did market factors transform the rural economy of Holland into a specialised agrarian economy, but at the same time the rural economy formed an integral part of the economic development of the northern Low Countries during the early modern period. Based on the work of de Vries, along with the evidence provided by B. Slicher van Bath,[28] the northern Low Countries have been assigned a unique position in the agrarian history of Europe. According to many authors, including I. Wallerstein, F. Braudel, R. Brenner and P. Kriedte, the so-called Dutch case forms the great exception to the general trend in economic development elsewhere in rural Europe. The northern Low Countries were the first European region to specialise in commercial farming while abandoning the production of grain for bread almost entirely, leaving the supply of the latter to international trade.

The Low Countries in the Debate on the Transition from Feudalism to Capitalism

This brings us to a major topic in the economic history of early modern Europe: the transition from a feudal, peasant economy to a system of capitalist agriculture, which took place during the long period between the late Middle Ages and the industrial revolution. In this so-called transition debate, which has been going on since the 1950s, two major positions can be distinguished. The first is the Neo-Malthusian approach, which takes as its point of departure the equilibrium between the size of a population and the resources available to it. Population growth beyond the limits of this equilibrium leads to crises of underproduction. This approach is normally linked to a Neo-Ricardian explanation, in which the concept of diminishing returns is applied to the additional land cultivated as a result of increasing population. Another theoretical approach that is influenced by classical economics, i.e. by the ideas of Adam Smith, sees the intensification of trade and the rise of a commercial network on a European and later a worldwide scale and the resulting international division of labour as a way out of the Malthusian trap. The Marxist explanation, on the other hand, is based on the primitive accumulation of capital that helped to replace the feudal class relations between lords and peasants with the relation between capitalist landlords and tenant farmers who ran their farms by means of landless labourers. R. Brenner's influential articles from the 1970s sum up the Marxist position and challenge the Neo-Malthusian, Ricardian and Smithian explanations. He puts forward a hypothesis based on the local

27 A.-M. PIUZ, "Les rélations économiques entre les villes et les campagnes dans les sociétés préindustrielles" in *Revue européenne des sciences sociales, XV* (1977) pp. 195–231.

28 B. SLICHER VAN BATH, *De agrarische geschiedenis van West – Europa (500–1850)*, Utrecht, 1960.

property structures that in his view determined the degree to which peasants got involved in the market and thus became dependent on economic forces instead of on extra-economic lordly power.[29] Brenner refers to an argument already used by Marx, who maintained that landowning peasants tended toward subsistence farming and would therefore resist market integration. Only by separating the peasants from their direct access to land they would be forced to increase productivity.

It is striking that, until recently, precisely the most urbanised areas of Europe during the late Middle Ages and the early modern period, the two European core-regions northern Italy and the Low Countries, have been neglected within the Brenner debate. The various contributors have concentrated on the areas that Brenner treated in his article: England, France, and Eastern Europe. In contrast, the rural structures of the Low Countries have played only a very marginal role, although the area is generally seen as having been the industrial core of the rising world economy and therefore having stood at the basis of the international division of labour. Holland has been considered an exceptional case, where feudal structures were already very weak in the Middle Ages and hence never had to be overcome. The southern Low Countries, or more precisely Flanders, has been admitted to have been an exceptionally progressive farming area during the late Middle Ages. Its economy failed to develop into a capitalist system however, due to the small-scale of peasant property ownership, which led to a system of subsistence farming. For the early modern period, the major interest of those taking part in the debate went toward the rise of rural textile industry and its role as a first step towards industrialisation.[30] This neglect of the most commercialised areas of Europe has to do with the marginal role of the market as a factor of influence in the model Brenner proposed. According to him, market forces alone were incapable of transforming the prevailing social property systems. A transformation could only take place if the power relations were changed, which normally happened through class struggle. From this perspective, the northern Low Countries formed the great exception because of the weak extra-economic power of the landlords.

Since the publication of de Vries' book on the Dutch rural economy, a series of regional case studies have been published that make it necessary to revise some of the points put forward by de Vries. For Flanders, too, insufficient information was available at the time the Brenner-debate was taking place. In the meantime, E. Thoen's thesis on late medieval South-east Flanders and F. Mendels' work on the rise of proto-industrial structure during the seventeenth and eighteenth century, followed by a series of contributions on the rural textile industry, provide a much more complete picture than was available thirty years ago.[31] Based on this new evidence, a number of Belgian and Dutch historians have begun discussing the role of the Low Countries in the transition debate. Their common starting point was that both the "Dutch case" and the "Flemish case" as described by Brenner and other contributors

29 R. Brenner, "The Agrarian Roots of European Capitalism" in *Past & Present*, 97 (1982), pp. 16–113; A good synthesis of this discussion is W. Hagen, "Capitalism and the Countryside in Early Modern Europe: Interpretations, Models, Debates" in *Agricultural History* 62 (1988) p. 37. See also: P. Hoppenbrouwers and J.L. van Zanden, "Introduction, The Brenner debate and its Historical Fate" in *Peasants into farmers?*, p. 13.

30 F. F. Mendels, *Industrialization and Population Pressure in Eighteenth-century Flanders*, New York, 1981; see also the criticisms of his work in for example C. Vandenbroecke, "De proto-industriële ontwikkeling van België in het kader van de internationale historiografie" in *Belgisch Tijdschrift voor Filologie en Geschiedenis/ Revue Belge de Philologie et d'Histoire*, LXIII (1985), pp. 310–323.

31 Thoen, *Landbouwekonomie*; Mendels *Industrialization*.

to the debate are based on a simplified vision of the economic structures of these regions. The Dutch case is based almost exclusively on de Vries' findings on the maritime provinces Holland and Friesland, which have been generalised for the whole of the northern Low Countries. In particular, L. Noordergraaf and more recently B. van Bavel have made critical remarks on this position.[32] As two of the major weaknesses of Brenner's approach, van Bavel mentions his tendency to generalise for very large entities, such as France and England, and, second, his neglect of the market as an influence factor. When it comes down to urban markets and their influence, these two points merge, because the latter can only be observed on a regional level and not on a macro-level like that used by Brenner.

The Flemish situation has recently been summarised by E. Thoen in a general synthesis. He defines the Flemish agrarian system as a combination of subsistence farming and market farming. This system had its origin during the so-called long thirteenth century and persisted until the eve of the industrial revolution. Although this structure hampered the development of capitalist agriculture, it nevertheless allowed agrarian innovation and a high degree of arable productivity. As argued by F. Mendels, the rise of proto-industrialisation on a large scale in the countryside near Ghent was only possible in these conditions, as they provided not only a strong potential for rural cottagers but at the same time sufficient agrarian supplies for the urban market. The urban market played an important role in preserving this system during the late medieval and early modern period but, according to Thoen, was not the prime mover in terms of its coming into being.[33]

The Central Questions

Antwerp and its Countryside: A Case Study Comparing the Flemish and the Dutch Cases

The ambiguous role of the urban market as a factor in the transition from feudalism to capitalism has been described convincingly by R. Merrington in his contribution to the *first* transition debate between M. Dobb and P. Sweezy.[34] He argues that commercial capitalism's failure to break the boundaries of the feudal system was caused by its inability to get beyond the limits of the urban economy, *except in north-western Europe*. He appears to be referring to the two exceptions admitted also by Brenner: England and the northern Low Countries. Brenner also maintains that market integration was incapable of creating a system of capitalist agriculture as long as it could not separate the peasants from the possession of their land and hence make them dependent on market forces for their subsistence.[35] Recently, however, the role of towns and commercial activity in agrarian development has been reconsidered in several studies on medieval England.[36] For early modern Italy, S. Epstein has stressed the

32 L. Noordergraaf, "Het platteland van Holland in de zestiende eeuw. Anachronismen, modelgebruik en traditionele bronnenkritiek" in *Economisch en sociaalhistorisch Jaarboek* 48 (1985), pp. 8–18. And B.J.P. van Bavel, *Transitie en continuïteit: de bezitsverhoudingen en de plattelandseconomie in het westelijke gedeelte van het Gelderse rivierengebied, ca. 1300 – ca. 1570*, Hilversum, 1999 (Werken uitgegeven door Gelre, 52) p. 21–22.

33 Thoen, "Commercial Survival Economy", p. 102–157.

34 J. Merrington, "Town and Country in the Transition to Capitalism" in R. Hilton, ed., *The Transition from Feudalism to Capitalism*, London, 1976, pp. 170–195.

35 Brenner, "Agrarian Roots", p. 17.

36 See for example: R.H. Britnell, *The Commercialisation of English Society, 1000–1500* (Manchester, 1996), and G.D.

importance of towns for the rural economy. His approach is oriented not so much towards commercialisation however, but rather on the towns' institutional impact on the countryside that shaped their opportunities for market-integration.[37] In monographs by E. Thoen, P. Hoppenbrouwers, and B. van Bavel on three distinct areas of the Low Countries, the urban factor is repeatedly stressed as being important. However, with the exception of the Aalst and Oudenaarde area, which lay very close to the town of Ghent, the areas they considered in their respective case studies were not among the most urbanised areas within the Low Countries. Both Heusden, the major place of Hoppenbrouwers' area of research, and the Meuse area towns studied by Van Bavel were relatively insignificant towns in comparison to Amsterdam, Ghent or Antwerp. The urban influence therefore remained relatively weak in these areas. As the merchant class of the local towns was not as numerous and wealthy as it was in the larger Dutch and Flemish towns, investments in their surroundings remained on a lower level. Also in terms of the urban demand for agrarian products, these small towns had less of an impact than a large centre like Antwerp.

In contrast, the Antwerp area during the fifteenth and sixteenth centuries offers very interesting perspectives for a study on the potential of the urban market to change the rural economy. Unlike the towns mentioned above, Antwerp was an outstanding commercial centre, while at the same time the largest town in the Low Countries, in many ways comparable to Amsterdam in the seventeenth century. Like Amsterdam, it was an international staple market where commodities like Baltic grain and other foodstuffs were traded in large quantities. Like Amsterdam, it was a meeting point of wealthy merchants and hence formed an extraordinary concentration of capital. Consequently, its potential for influencing the economy of its rural surroundings was essentially comparable to that of Amsterdam on the Dutch countryside. In contrast, the social and economic background of Antwerp's hinterland was comparable to Flanders or other areas of the southern Low Countries, rather than to that of the provinces of Holland and Friesland.

It is precisely this duality that makes Antwerp a most suitable area for a case study within the theoretical context discussed above. In the case of Holland, the commercial factors leading to the commercialisation and specialisation of the rural economy did not have to overcome either strong feudal bounds or a centuries-old agrarian system. Antwerp, on the other hand, was surrounded by a rural economy that is in many ways similar to the system Thoen described for late-medieval Flanders. It is therefore intriguing to see if the mechanisms described by de Vries for Holland can also be detected in the case of Antwerp, or to determine to which extent the different economic and social but also geographic conditions led to a totally different reaction of the rural economy. It is my intention in this study to apply a theoretical approach similar to the one de Vries applied to the Brabantine context and to detect the degree to which commercial expansion in the urban centres led to similar transformations of the rural economy to those in Holland or Friesland. Naturally, I will also be discussing the obvious differences in the economic development of the two areas.

Snooks, "The Dynamic Role of the Market in the Anglo-Saxon Economy and Beyond, 1086–1300" in R.H. Britnell and B.M.S. Campbell, eds., *A Commercialising Economy: England 1086 – c. 1300* (Manchester, 1995), pp. 27–54.

37 S.R. Epstein, "Cities, Regions and the Late Medieval Crisis: Sicily and Tuscany Compared" in *Past & Present,* 130 (1991), pp. 3–50; and "Town and Country: Economy and Institutions in Late Medieval Italy" in *Economic History Review*, XLVI, 3 (1993), pp. 453–477.

From a Peasant Economy to a Specialised Economy?

The central features of the economic change that took place in the rural economy of Holland and Friesland during the sixteenth and seventeenth centuries were the occupational specialisation of the peasants, the technical change as a result of specialisation and a strong integration of markets for agricultural produce.[38] De Vries presents these factors within the framework of a theoretical explanatory model. This so-called specialisation model takes as its basic assumption a self-sufficient peasant society with a stable population. If this society is faced with a rising population and "*open trading opportunities*", the peasant will concentrate on intensive farming. This makes him able to produce a regular surplus for the market. The specialisation in goods, "*for which he is best suited, given the factors of production at his disposal and his acquired skills*" results in a favourable situation on the market. The population increase can be absorbed in part by new labour-intensive agriculture and stimulated local trade; the rest of the population is not admitted to the agricultural sector and has to find non-agricultural employment. "*Loosened from any ties to the land, these workers can migrate to the cities, which are in a position to grow because of the development of rural-urban trade.*" The result of the *specialisation model* is a strong group of market-oriented farmers and a stimulated exchange of urban and rural production.[39]

De Vries also describes the opposite development in the so-called *peasant model.* If a stable rural society is faced with a rising population and "limited trading opportunities", it can react by dividing the land and increasing the intensity of agriculture within smaller productive units. As the marketable surplus diminishes due to the ever-growing number of people living from the same amount of land, the peasants cannot profit from growing urban demand by selling their products on the market. The smallholdings are often too small to feed even the peasant himself, so that he has to try to obtain additional income by working as a day labourer or producing manufactured goods through home handicraft. The peasants in this model try to avoid market dependence and to live from their own production as far as possible. The social effect of this economic change is a differentiation into the small peasant holdings of small *cottars* on the one hand, and the large landholdings of the bourgeois, noble and clerical landowners who profit from high food prices and the weak peasant class on the other hand. Urban growth is not stimulated by this reaction, since town-country relations are reduced to the minimum necessary exchange.[40] These concepts allow us to identify some central variables of possible change. De Vries focuses on the physical, legal, sociological and economic factors affecting the peasant household's response to changing opportunities.[41] Nevertheless, urban demand and commercial relations, the farming system and social stratification are the central features of his analysis. These three will also be major elements in my analysis of the economic influence of Antwerp on its surroundings.

38 De Vries, *Dutch*, pp. 119–173.
39 *Ibidem*, pp. 7–10.
40 *Ibidem*, pp. 4–7.
41 *Ibidem*, p. 16.

Concept and Organisation of the Study

In accordance with the theoretical background described in the previous sections, this book will focus on four types of influence that Antwerp had on its surroundings: a) the demographic influence, b) the increasing urban demand for agrarian products, being the major change in market opportunities for the peasants of the Antwerp area during the sixteenth century, c) the impact of the urban economy on non-agrarian types of labour in the countryside and d) the purchase of land as well as other investments made by Antwerp citizens. The choice of these elements as the main topics of my study was influenced primarily by the decisive role they played in the theoretical literature cited in the earlier sections. Furthermore, a number of specific case studies on large cities and their hinterlands, as well as the literature on sixteenth-century Antwerp itself, contained various elements on the basis of which I decided to specialise on these particular issues. Finally, some of the current theoretical models of town-countryside interaction were applied on the relationship between town and countryside in the case of western Brabant in the *fifteenth* century.[42] The major issues were specified by combining this empirical study with the theoretical background of the general literature. Within the framework of these three fields of interaction between town and countryside, three essential questions have to be answered: First, how can we characterise the urban influence in each of these three fields? Can it be considered a stimulus for the rural economy or rather an obstacle? Second, what was the economic response of the rural economy to the urban impact? Did it respond by specialising, according to the model presented above, or rather by retreating from the market, hence falling into marginality? Third, what role did the medieval legacies play in the interaction between the "capitalist" metropolis and the feudal countryside?

The Research Area

In contrast to de Vries, I have limited my study to the immediate rural hinterland of Antwerp, instead of trying to cover the whole of Brabant. On the one hand, such a limitation was made necessary by the great internal differences among the economic conditions within Brabant but also by the absence of adequate literature on the rural economy of Brabant.[43] On the other hand, the economic relations between a town and its rural surroundings were in many ways focused on a narrow area. The diameter within which urban citizens had landed property was therefore generally not greater than 20-30 km. Also, the market area of towns was generally relatively limited. Especially in highly urbanised areas such as Brabant, there was a strong competition for urban hinterlands. Hence, 20 km south of Antwerp one was already in the middle of the territory of Mechelen, and another 15 km further south in the sphere of influence of Brussels.[44] The study on the relationship between a town and its rural

42 See Chapter 2.

43 In my M.A. thesis *Die Metropolenstellung Antwerpens im 16. Jahrhundert. Aspekte der Antwerpener Zentralität auf verschiedenen Wirtschaftsebenen: Weltwirtschaft, nationaler und regionaler Markt* (unpublished M.A. thesis, University of Vienna), Vienna, 1990, pp. 110–200; I tried to sketch the interaction of the Antwerp growth with the economy of Brabant in general, on the basis of the available literature. The results of this study convinced me to focus on the closer surroundings of Antwerp for a more detailed study.

44 See below, Chapter 2. For the eighteenth century, see B. Blondé, *Een economie met verschillende snelheden, Ongelijkheden in de opbouw en de ontwikkeling van het Brabantse stedelijke netwerk (ca. 1750 – ca. 1790)*, Brussel, 1999 (Verhandelingen

surroundings can therefore best be analysed within a limited geographical area, where the urban impact was most concentrated.

Considering these points, a definition and geographical description of the rural hinterland of Antwerp can only be made in connection with the specific aspects to be studied. As a first point of departure, I therefore used a relatively ample definition, that is, the fiscal district (*kwartier*) of Antwerp.[45] This rudimentary limitation has been further specified by means of literature and empirical data concerning demographic patterns, the range of urban landed property and immigration.[46] Departing from the results of these preliminary studies, I focused on a considerably smaller area, forming a semi-circle of ca. 20 km east of Antwerp. This closer *umland* roughly coincides with the administrative units of *Waterland*, *Land van Rijen*, and *Land van Arkel* (also *Land van Mechelen)* and the west of the *Kempen* area (in particular, the south of the *meierij* of Zandhoven) (see Map 1).[47]

---

van de Koninklijke Vlaamse Academie van België voor Wetenschappen en Kunsten, Klasse der Letteren, Jaargang 61, 1999, no. 166), p. 119–164.

45 See J. CUVELIER, *Les dénombrements de foyers en Brabant (XIVe – XVIe siècle)*, Bruxelles, 1912, appendix., and M. MARTENS, *L'administration du domaine ducal en Brabant au moyen âge, 1250–1406*, Brussels, 1954.

46 LIMBERGER, *Metropolenstellung*, passim.

47 For an overview of the administrative limits, see A. BOUSSE, "De verhoudingen tussen Antwerpen en het platteland" in *Bijdragen tot de Geschiedenis*, 58 (1975) p. 139–150. They are mapped in C. KERREMANS, *Etude sur les circonscriptions judiciaires et administratives du Brabant et les officiers placés à leur tête par les ducs, antérieurement à l'avènement de la Maison de Bourgogne (1406)*, Bruxelles, 1949.

Map 1: Administrative Map of Brabant (extract)

Source: Kerremans, C., *Etude sur les circonscriptions judiciaires et administratives du Brabant et les officiers placés à leur tête par les ducs, antérieurement à l'avènement de la Maison de Bourgogne(1406)*, Brussels, 1949.

The Organisation of the Study

"*Give me a point to stand on and I will move the earth*" (Archimedes).[48] A reliable point of reference is not only necessary to move the earth, but it is also a basic requirement

48 Cited from E.J. Dijksterhuis, *Archimedes*, Princeton, 1987, p. 15.

for the study of economic change. In order to distinguish the changes the rural economy of western Brabant underwent as a result of the growth of Antwerp, we need to have a clear idea about the economic and social situation *before* Antwerp's rise began. The specialisation model takes as its point of departure "a self-sufficient peasant society with a stable population". These conditions were not met in either the Dutch or the Brabantine countryside. The peasantry of the Low Countries was anything but self-sufficient at the dawn of the sixteenth century, and population was anything but stable. My study begins therefore with an overview of the rural economy and the major social patterns of the area under consideration shortly before the rise of Antwerp.

The period in which Antwerp's Golden Age actually began – roughly around 1490 – was nevertheless characterised by a severe political and economic crisis in the southern Low Countries, which makes it a bad period to serve as the basis for such an overview.[49] This is why this book begins some decades earlier, i.e. around the middle of the fifteenth century. Hence, the demographic survey, for example, starts with the first Brabantine household census of 1437. For some aspects, certain sources and other kinds of evidence made me go back in time even further. Where the landed property of Antwerp citizens is concerned, for example, I used the data of F. de Nave's exhaustive study on the period 1394-1402. When concentrating on the food trade in late medieval Antwerp, I used, among other things, the testimonies of merchants referring to the decades before 1433.

One of the major obstacles for this study has been the lack of a general synthesis concerning the agrarian history of late medieval Brabant, upon which one could base a sketch of the situation in the fifteenth century. Most of the historical territories of the southern Low Countries have been the subjects of such a study. L. Génicot devoted a magisterial study to the county of Namur,[50] G. Sivéry wrote an important synthesis on Hainaut,[51] and E. Thoen did the same for the southeast of the county of Flanders in a very convincing way.[52] Until now, no such attempt has been made with respect to Brabant. I therefore thought it necessary to undertake an elementary study of the basic features of the rural economy of western Brabant myself, based on the primary sources and the available literature dealing with individual places or particular aspects of its rural history. Hence, a separate chapter will deal with the economic interaction between Antwerp and the other major Brabantine towns and their respective rural hinterlands in the fifteenth century. This chapter is to be seen as a theoretical introduction to the question of town-country relations, and to the specific economic and institutional background of late medieval Brabant. It treats the economic links between the Brabantine countryside and the large cities of Brussels, Mechelen and Antwerp. For a classification of the rural economy of western Brabant somewhere between a peasant economy and a specialised economy, the degree of market integration is a crucial factor. The economic interaction between the Brabantine towns and their closer environs will therefore be discussed at length. The main factors in this interaction are first presented

49 W.P. BLOCKMANS, G. PIETERS, W. PREVENIER, A.W. VAN SCHAIK, "Tussen crisis en welvaart: sociale veranderingen 1300–1500" in *Algemene Geschiedenis der Nederlanden* IV, (Haarlem, 1980), pp. 42–86. R. VAN UYTVEN, "Politiek en Economie. De crisis der late XVe eeuw in de Nederlanden" in *Belgisch Tijdschrift voor Filologie en Geschiedenis/Revue Belge de Philologie et d'Histoire,* 53, (1975), pp. 1097–1149.

50 L. GÉNICOT, *L'économie rurale namuroise au bas moyen âge*, 4 vols., Louvain-la-Neuve, 1960–1995.

51 G. SIVÉRY, *Structures agraires et vie rurale dans le Hainaut à la fin du moyen-âge*, 2 vols., Lille, 1977–1980.

52 THOEN, *Landbouwekonomie.*

schematically and then dealt with systematically. The most detailed section is on the urban market for agrarian products and the role of the closer environs for the provisioning of the large Brabantine towns. The most space is devoted to the question of which share the immediate hinterland had in supplying the towns with grain. Other features discussed in this chapter are the town's role as supplier or distributor of industrial products, the purchase of land by urban citizens, and the town's attraction to migrants from the countryside. Besides providing a categorisation of the degree of urban integration of rural western Brabant during the late Middle Ages, this discussion is also a first step toward an analysis of the influence of sixteenth-century Antwerp. By applying the theoretical approaches to the economic interaction between late-medieval towns and their surroundings to the case of western Brabant, this chapter introduces some of the major themes that will be discussed later on in the study.

Before getting to this theoretical introduction, however, I will first briefly introduce the research area: western Brabant, and the surroundings of Antwerp in particular. Although common knowledge among specialists in Brabantine history and for most Antwerpers, I nevertheless thought it useful to explain some general features of the natural and human geography during the fifteenth and sixteenth centuries that may have influenced the economic development of the area.

Chapter 3 is titled "Demographic Changes". Using the first Brabantine household census, taken in 1437, I was able to calculate the number of households per square kilometre in the western part of the district of Antwerp and in the district of Brussels and map these out. I then discuss the principal common patterns and local differences on this map, paying special attention to the surroundings of the large cities and their demographic profile. In a second step, I analyse the percentage of poor households per village in the same way. This allows initial conclusions concerning the relation between the factors of population density, poverty rate and distance from the town, within the area under consideration. After that, I present the evolution of the population density in the Antwerp area between 1437 and ca. 1570. Departing from the simplified hypothesis that demographic growth goes hand in hand with economic expansion, these basic demographic figures provide a first indicator for the positive or negative character of the economic changes taking place during the sixteenth century. In this demographic overview, the crisis of the late fifteenth century and its results in the Antwerp area are also briefly discussed, as it seems to have had a strong impact on the regional divergences in economic development during the sixteenth century.[53]

One aspect of the economic influence of the growth of Antwerp on its rural surroundings that will be discussed thoroughly is the role of the urban demand for agricultural products and its effects on the agrarian system of the surrounding countryside. The increasing demand for food, fuel and building materials corresponds in large part to the factor of "changing market opportunities" within the specialisation model. In Chapter 4, I focus mainly on urban demand in Antwerp, because its enormous increase during the sixteenth century was the most significant change in the market opportunities for the peasants of the area under investigation. While Antwerp grew to be the major market of consumption of the Low Countries, the interregional trade with agrarian products from its surroundings or even

53 R. Van Uytven, "Crisis als cesuur, 1482-1494" in *Algemene geschiedenis der Nederlanden* V, (Haarlem, 1980), p. 434f.

the export of agrarian products was insignificant in comparison. A first question to answer in this context is to which degree Antwerp still relied on its immediate hinterland for its increasing supplies of food, fuel and other raw materials. Was there still a strong demand for local bread-grain or dairy products, or had the Baltic or the northern provinces taken over the role of major supplier? Only with a basic notion of the changing patterns of the urban demand can we turn to the central question of this chapter concerning the degree to which the agriculture of the Brabantine countryside responded to the changing market opportunities with specialisation and commercialisation.

To provide the basis for doing this, the agrarian system of western Brabant in the late Middle Ages will be analysed briefly in Chapter 5. This analysis is based primarily on lease contracts, as these provide qualitative data concerning the organisation of agriculture, agrarian techniques, and the main agrarian products. The central question in this chapter is the extent to which the area of Antwerp – on which only very little research has been done from this point of view – was an intensive farming area, comparable with the area of Brussels. According to the work done by M.J. Tits-Dieuaide, F. Daelemans, and P. Lindemans, the latter area can be characterised as highly productive and progressive. To obtain an answer to this question, I compare lease contracts from both areas as well as some documents that allow a rough quantification of the productivity of the land. On the basis of this survey of the late medieval situation, the changes of the agrarian system near Antwerp during the sixteenth century will be evaluated in Chapter 6. Following a general sketch of the rural economy by means of descriptions of the individual villages by the local authorities, the changes in the product mix, agrarian techniques, and lease prices are analysed.

A second central topic is the urban stimulus for non-agrarian forms of labour. While the urban demand for agrarian products and the investments in landed property by urban citizens primarily had an influence on the agrarian sector, the rise of a large town, and in particular of a commercial and industrial centre like Antwerp, also had effects on the non-agrarian sector of the rural economy of its surroundings. In Chapter 7, I will investigate whether there was an increase in non-agrarian employment as an alternative to agrarian labour, especially for the victims of the processes described above. The greatest part of this chapter consists of the presentation of different non-agrarian occupations with a significant economic importance in the neighbourhood of Antwerp. For each of these occupations, the influence of the rise of Antwerp and their potential as labour supply for landless or land-poor peasants is evaluated.

Finally, the impact of urban land ownership on the rural property relations, which I consider to be one of the central problems of the historical study of towns and their hinterlands, is treated. Chapters 8 through 10 can therefore be taken together under the common title of property structures. Considering the crucial importance of the social property system in the transition debate and the complexity of the subject, the question of the distribution of landed property among the different social groups will need to be discussed at length. The extensive treatment of this topic has also methodological reasons. The lack of comprehensive sources or literature on the distribution of landed property in Brabant compels us to give a detailed account of various sources concerning the different types of property. I therefore decided to divide the argument into two chapters, one dealing with the landlords, that is to say those individuals or institutions receiving any form of land rent, and the other with the tenants, or immediate land-users, who paid a land rent or lease. The landlords and their share in the landed property are the subject of Chapter 8. These landlords hardly formed a homogenous group: the term landlord applies to the sovereign, noblemen, major and minor ecclesiastical and charitable institutions, rich citizens and other individuals, all of whom levied either incomes from jurisdiction, manorial rights, tithes, or land rents of various types. Measuring the share of different types of land rent, i.e. copyhold, hereditary lease or similar types of rents, in the total land is difficult, not only for lack of a consistent body of sources, but also for the ambiguous character of the term property itself.

Chapter 9 is dedicated to the tenants in the most general sense. The term *tenant* is the counterpart of *landlord*, although it is not identical with the more general term *peasant,* which lacks any reference to a lord-tenant relation. Parallel with the different kinds of landlords, I make a distinction between different sorts of tenants: the *fief-holder*, the *tenure-holder* or *copyholder*, and finally, the *lessee* or *leaseholder*. The last group differs from the others, because a lease is not a form of landed property, but rather a temporary form of landholding. For each of these groups, it is possible to estimate approximately the distribution of the land within the same group. The central problem in both chapters concerning landed property, however, is the difficulty in calculating the quantitative importance of each of these groups and therefore to obtain an overall figure of the distribution of landed property within western Brabant.

Finally, Chapter 10 deals with the purchase of land by Antwerp citizens and their influence on the property structures in the surrounding countryside. The high concentration of wealthy merchants meant that this "conquest of the soil" attained exceptional dimensions. The competition between townsmen and peasants for landed property had important implications for the ties of the peasantry to the land – a crucial feature in the transition debate. An increase of urban landowners led to a rise of leaseholds, and hence to a (forced) market orientation for the tenants. In contrast, peasants with a specialised production could better resist expropriation by urban citizens than peasants who did not specialise. The study of the resulting changes in the rural property structures cannot be reduced to duality of citizens versus peasants, however. I will therefore attempt to provide a sketch of the rural land market in the area under consideration, in order to identify other actors among the different social groups who played a role in the distribution of the land. Finally, the distribution of the land among the different social groups around 1570 is analysed for a number of villages in order to determine the position of the peasants and townsmen in comparison to that of other groups of landowners.

The goal of this study of the various fields of economic relationship between Antwerp and its rural surroundings – i.e. demography, agrarian supply, labour market and, finally, land market – is to characterise the role that large cities played in the early modern economy, outside the sphere of international trade and finance, on the regional economy and in particular the rural economy. In the foregoing discussion of the theoretical literature, the "commercialisation models" proposed by de Vries, Van der Wee, Wrigley or Hoffman have been confronted with property-relation-based models such as that provided by Brenner and more recently by van Bavel. If property relations play only a secondary role in the classical studies on the commercialising effects of large cities, commercial factors are almost completely left out in the models based on property relations. Instead of choosing between either the one or the other, the analysis of the case of Antwerp should include both elements and should lead to a model in which commercial elements and property relations are closely related. This integration of the question of property relations into the commercialisation models forms the major theoretical challenge I hope to confront in this book.

CHAPTER 1

The Air of Brabant: A General Description of the Brabantine Landscape

"Goed lant es Brabant dat es waer...
van beemden, van wijngaerden, van foreesten,
vol goeds lands, vischen ende beesten."
(Hennen van Merchtene, Cronicke van Brabant, 1414[1])

"L'aria di Brabante è veramente buona per tutto & salubre: il paese è piano, & per la maggior' parte fertile, & fruttifero, quantunque il suo paese di Campigna sia molto sterile: è accomododato oltre a laghi, stagni, & altre acque di belli & utilissimi fiumi. I principali sono la Mosa, & Schelda di sopra mentionati, & descritti. E ornato di selve & di boschi sufficcientemente, i principali sono Sonien, Zaventerloo, Groetenheist, & Meerdael.

Ma sopra ogni cosa è nobilitato di bellissime & famose citta, terre, castella, villaggi,& d'altre Signorie di conditione, che truovo primieramente comprendercisi ventisei terre murate."
(L. Guicciardini, *Descrittione di tutti I paesi bassi...*, 1567[2])

"The air of Brabant is really very good and healthy: The land is flat and for the largest part fertile and fruitful, although its Kempen area is very barren..." Thus begins the chapter on Brabant in Ludovico Guicciardini's *Descrittione de tutti i Paesi Bassi.* I cite this passage in the original Italian version in order to reflect the sound of the Florentine merchant speaking of the area surrounding his residence, Antwerp, at the summit of its Golden Age. Guicciardini is known as an attentive and analytic observer of the sixteenth-century Low Countries. While the extract from Hennen van Merchtene's early-fifteenth-century chronicle gives only a very brief, idealised picture of Brabant, Guicciardini's description goes beyond the level usually found in accounts made by foreign travellers and represents a highly reliable source of information on the socio-economic situation of his period.[3] Although dating from the late sixteenth century, this brief summary on Brabantine geography contains some important features that are also valid for the late Middle Ages.

I begin this study of sixteenth-century Brabant with a short sketch of its geographical features, which is intended to serve as an introduction to its social and economic life. While the geography of the area surrounding Antwerp may be obvious for those who know the

1 Cited in P. Lindemans, *Geschiedenis van de landbouw in Belgie,* Antwerpen, 1952, II, p. 125.

2 L. Guicciardini, *Descrittione di tutti i Paesi Bassi, altrimenti detti Germania Inferiore,* Antwerp, 1567, p. 61.

3 His data have for example been used by W. Brulez to draw up an economic map of the Low Countries during the sixteenth century. See: W. Brulez, "De economische kaart van de Nederlanden in de 16e eeuw volgens Guicciardini" in *Tijdschrift voor Geschiedenis,* 83 (1970) pp. 352–357. For the historical value of Guicciardini's *Descrittione,* see also P. Jodogne, ed., *Lodovico Guicciardini (1521-1589): actes du colloque international des 28, 29 et 30 mars 1990,* Louvain, 1991 (Travaux de l'Institut interuniversitaire pour l'étude de la Renaissance et de l'Humanisme, 10).

area, it needs some explanation for non-Brabantine readers or those less familiar with past of the Brabantine countryside. The natural conditions can explain many aspects of economic life in the countryside. The differences in soil fertility, the profile of the country, the existence of rivers, etc.: all these features played a role in the agrarian development, the density of settlement and the degree of commercialisation of an area. While this book does not aim to analyse the links between nature and economy, the landscape of Brabant nevertheless forms the background and the basis for the economic activities and transformations that will be analysed in the following chapters.

Brabant is indeed a flat land, without any mountains, as Guicciardini remarks. Its soils are generally fertile. It is also true that the sandy Kempen area in the northeast of the duchy forms the major exception to this. The duchy had a dense network of navigable rivers and some considerable forests, and it boasted a large number of cities, towns and villages, as well as castles (*castella*) and seigneuries (*signorie*). The latter point to the feudal aspect of the Brabant countryside, where the seigniorial system was still in full vigour in the sixteenth century.

Some of these features can essentially be generalised for the whole of the Low Countries, such as the flatness of the land (except for the Ardennes in the south) and the presence of "very useful" rivers. Another feature typical for the Low Countries in general is the great number of cities, towns and villages. Even more so, these features were among of the geographic characteristics of the Low Countries as a whole. To W. Prevenier and W. Blockmans, in their synthesis on the Burgundian Low Countries, the presence of a multitude of means of communication was one of the major ecological links of the Low Countries, while the high degree of urbanisation is one of the main features of their human geography.[4] Nevertheless, these generally very good connections had their limitations. They did not reach every part of the Low Countries in the same way. Extensive forests and heaths formed barriers for communication. In general, this was the case for the eastern parts of the Low Countries, such as the county of Namur, the duchies of Luxembourg and Limburg and parts of Guelders, Veluwe and Drenthe, which therefore formed areas of sparse settlement and little economic activity. In Brabant, the *Zoniënwoud* (Fr.: *Soignes*), near Brussels, and the Kempen area (Fr.: *Campine*), mentioned by Guicciardini, can be counted among these areas.[5] The latter reached to only few kilometres from Antwerp and contrasted sharply with the densely settled southern part of the duchy, as we will show later in this chapter. In the following sections, taking Guicciardini's observations as our point of departure, we will specify some of the major geographical aspects for our research area: the surroundings of Antwerp.

4 W. Prevenier and W. Blockmans, *De Bourgondische Nederlanden*, Antwerp, 1983, p. 16.
5 *Ibidem*, p. 25.

1.1 Natural Features

1.1.1 "...flat and for the largest part fertile..." – The Topography and Quality of the Soil

As there were no major differences in elevation or climate within the duchy of Brabant, two geographical features were decisive for the different patterns of settlement and economic activity on the Brabantine countryside: the type of soil and the presence or absence of rivers. In terms of soil, the southern part of Brabant was generally a fertile plain with clay and mixed sand-and-clay soils. As in the south of Flanders, these soils enabled the cultivation of very demanding sorts of grain, such as wheat. The latter two areas were also the first areas of the Low Countries to be reclaimed. In the north of Flanders and Brabant, reclamation dated from later, and also in the late Middle Ages the cultivation of bread grains was limited to rye instead of wheat.[6]

Map 2: The Agricultural Areas of Belgium

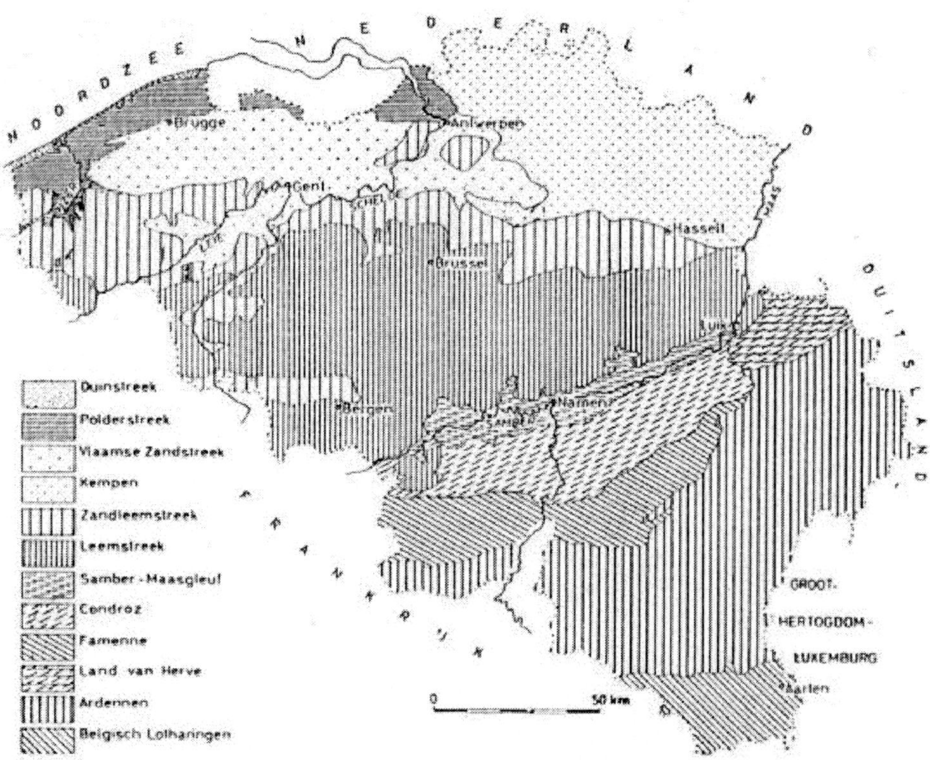

Source: A. Verhulst, Het landschap in Vlaanderen in historisch perspectief, Antwerpen, 1965.

6 *Ibidem*. In the northern provinces, the grain production was even more limited and specialised in oats and barley, the latter becoming important mainly for brewing beer. Further specialisation went toward dairy products and depended strongly on interregional trade. See also below.

Map 2 shows the different agricultural areas in Belgium. The line dividing the central Belgian clay area from the Flemish sand area along with the Kempen, is a narrow zone of mixed soil that runs right between Antwerp and Brussels, separating Brabant into two distinct zones. In the surroundings of Brussels, the soil still consists largely of clay, covered with a fertile layer of limon (loess). This made th "*a lightly wooded area, relatively easily cleared and settled, and the quality of the soil with alternating limon and alluvium, (...) capable to support a dense, rural population*".[7] The further one moves north, however, the more the proportion of sand increases. Whereas the transition from clay to sand-clay soils going northwards from Brussels is rather linear, the different types of soil around Antwerp form irregular patterns. North of Antwerp, along the banks of the Scheldt, a strip of very fertile polders, the result of an offensive movement of dike-building from the twelfth century onward.[8] To the east, the Kempen forms a homogenuous area reaching as far as the Meuse valley and the border of the Netherlands. Today, the Kempen has the connotation of being a deserted and infertile area, covered mainly with heath – an image that in any case held true for the period from the eighteenth century on. The area had been covered by forests until the High Middle Ages, but was then cleared and subsequently abandoned after relatively short time, which led to the formations of heaths.[9] Proof that this was already the case in the sixteenth century can be found in Guicciardini's observation: "*only the area of the Kempen is very infertile*". This view, however, was modified in a later edition of his *Descrittione* with the following addition: "*but the labour & diligence of people, together with much manure, make it fertile and good*".[10] South of Antwerp, the lowlands of the Flemish sand area (*Vlaamse Zandstreek*) reach deep into Brabant with only two islands of very fertile soil: one along the left (west) bank of the Scheldt and the other between Antwerp, Lier and Mechelen in an area known these days as the Antwerp vegetable region (*Antwerpse groentenstreek*). The presence of clay in this small area along the rivers Scheldt and Rupel also made it an important zone for the production of bricks.[11]

Hence, in spite of the generally flat landscape and fertile soil that Guicciardini observed, the surroundings of Antwerp show some major internal differences as to the fertility of the soil. The proportion of sand in the soil's composition increases as one moves northwards, reaching its maximum in the Kempen. The polders north of Antwerp, on the other hand, were characterised by their exposed location near the river Scheldt. As we will see, these differences would have a strong impact on the intensity of settlement and the economic activity in the different zones.

7 N.J.G. Pounds, "Population and Settlement in the Low Countries and northern France in the Later Middle Ages" in *Belgisch Tijdschrift voor Filologie en Geschiedenis/Revue Belge de Philologie et d'Histoire XLIX* (1971), p. 376.

8 K.A.H.W. Leenders, "De Antwerpse polder in de Middeleeuwen. Ontginning, bedijking en overstromingen" in *Tijdschrift van de Belgische Vereniging voor aardrijkskundige studies,* 1985/1 (1985), p. 57.

9 Pounds, "Population", p. 377; based on F.J.Monkhouse, *The Belgian Kempenland*, Liverpool, 1949, pp. 5–54.

10 "*ma il travaglio et diligentia de gl'huomini sopplisce di sorto con molto bestiame che lo fanno fertile et buono*' – L. Guicciardini, *Descrittione di tutti i Paesi Bassi, altrimenti detti Germania Inferiore*, Antwerp, C. Plantin, 1588, p. 65.

11 H. Gysels, *De landschappen van Vlaanderen en Zuidelijk Nederland. Een landschapsecologische studie*, Leuven, Apeldoorn, 1993, for the production of bricks in the Rupel area, see chapter 7.

1.1.2 "... beautiful and very useful rivers.." – Hydrology

The second feature in the pre-modern landscape that had a decisive economic impact was the presence of rivers. A major precondition for the exceptional economic position the Low Countries achieved during the late Middle Ages and the early modern period was their easy access to the Sea. In comparison with the counties of Flanders, Zeeland or Holland, the duchy of Brabant did not have a long coastline. Its access to the North Sea was limited to the estuary of the river Scheldt, and its only ports of any importance were Bergen op Zoom and Antwerp. The accessibility of Antwerp from the North Sea improved considerably around 1400, when heavy floods expanded the shallow river Honte, which thereafter became a wide estuary known as *Westerschelde.*[12] Bergen op Zoom was situated nearer to the open sea, but it was quite remote from the larger towns of the duchy, all of which were situated in the south. From Antwerp, a dense network of navigable rivers reached far inland. The Scheldt formed an important traffic route, peering far into Flanders and even to northern France.[13] Its Brabantine effluents – the Rupel, the Zenne, the Dijle, the Demer and the Gete – made river traffic possible far into the south of the duchy: to Brussels and Leuven and even as far as Zoutleeuw in the very southeast.[14]

Besides its worse-quality soil, the north of the duchy also lacked the favourable density of navigable rivers found in the south. The Kempen and Pee areas had hardly any significant rivers except the Nete, which was navigable only up to Herentals. This was also a major reason why the main urban centres of the area, such as 's-Hertogenbosch, Bergen op Zoom and Breda, were situated on the periphery, near the great rivers Scheldt and Maas or their effluents.[15]

River transport had a particular importance not only for the urban sector, but also – and even more so – for the rural economy, as many roads proved to be impracticable for large parts of the year.[16] The flatness of Brabant, as for the Low Countries in general, strongly favoured river transport. A large range of different products was transported on the Brabantine rivers, the most important of which were grain, salt, peat, stone, and wood.[17] The comfort and speed of river transport should not be overestimated, however. The valleys of most Brabantine rivers were shallow and sandy and bent in numerous meanders. That meant that the journey from Brussels along the Zenne up to the Rupel could take as long as a month, but certainly at least several days, according to Alphonse Wauters.[18]

12 G. Asaert, "Antwerp and the Sea" in Van der Stock, ed., *Antwerp, Story of a Metropolis*, pp. 33–35.

13 G. Asaert, R. Berger, B. Delmaire e.a., *Valleien van Schelde en Scarpe,* Brussel, 1991, (Albums de Croÿ, 25).

14 G. Asaert, *De Antwerpse scheepvaart in de XVe eeuw (1394-1480). Bijdrage tot de ekonomische geschiedenis van de stad Antwerpen* (Verhandelingen van de koninklijke Academie voor Wetenschappen, Letteren en Schone Kunsten van België, Klasse der Letteren, XXXV (1973), no.72) Brussel, 1973, p. 325.

15 R. Van Uytven, "Brabantse en Antwerpse centrale plaatsen (14de-19de eeuw)" in *Het stedelijk netwerk in België in historisch perspectief (1350-1850). een statistische en dynamische benadering/le reseau urbain en Belgique dans une perspective historique (1350-1850), une approche statistique et dynamique*, (Handelingen 15de Internationaal Colloquium /Actes 15e Colloque International, Spa, 4-6 sept. 1990), Bruxelles, 1992, p. 35.

16 Cuvelier, *Dénombrements* p. XII, cites in this context a document concerning the construction of a canal along the river Nete "because of the bad shape of the roads". See also: R. Van Uytven, "Landtransport durch Brabant im Mittelalter und im 16. Jahrhundert" in F. Burgard, A. Haverkamp, *Auf den Römerstraßen ins Mittelalter. Beiträge zur Verkehrsgeschichte zwischen Maas und Rhein von der Spätantike bis ins 19. Jahrhundert*, Mainz, 1997, pp. 471–499.

17 Asaert, *Scheepvaart*, p. 326-333.

18 A. Wauters, *Documents concernant le canal de Bruxelles à Willebroeck précédés d'une introduction contenant un résumé de l'histoire de ce canal*, Bruxelles, 1882, p. IV, Van Uytven gives more detailed figures on the traffic between Mechelen and

Rivers not only served for transporting goods. They also were important as a water supply and for propelling mills and irrigating the land. Finally, they also had an impact on the micro-topography of their respective valleys. The strips of land along the southern Brabantine rivers formed excellent pastures, which were in high demand for cattle farming and feeding.[19] In these respects, too, the northern Brabantine plains were very unfavourably situated in comparison with the south of the duchy and the area along the Scheldt.

It is mainly due to these two geographic features, i.e. the quality of the soil and the hydrology, that the duchy of Brabant was divided in two zones with very distinct patterns of settlement and economic activity. Antwerp was situated exactly at the border of the two areas. This geographic location between an area of intensive agriculture and a relatively unproductive region had an important impact on the economic ties Antwerp had with each of the two areas.

1.1.3 "...sufficiently adorned with forests and woods..."

This passage is rather surprising, if one knows the actual landscape of Brabant. The part of Brabant covered by forests has diminished drastically since the eighteenth century. Together with peat, which was cut mainly in the Northern provinces but also in the north of Flanders and Brabant, wood was the major fuel in late medieval Brabant.[20] In the fifteenth and sixteenth centuries, Brabant still had some considerable forests, such as the ones mentioned by Guicciardini: *Sonien, Zaventerloo, Groetenheist* and *Meerdael,* which formed a substantial part of the income of the duke and other local landlords.[21] So, for the forest of Zoniën, the reconstruction of settlements suggests that it had about the same dimensions as today.[22] In the area surrounding Antwerp, instead of large forests there were only isolated woods belonging to individual landowners. The appearance of these woods is not to be confused with that of central or northern European forests. Ducal accounts, but also toponyms mention beeches and oaks, but also poplars and alders, which grew on the wet soils. The latter sorts grew very quickly and could be cut very frequently for firewood, whereas the more precious sorts, such as oaks and beeches, mainly served as building materials.[23]

Leuven; van Uytven, "Landtransport"; see also: B. Blondé and R. van Uytven, "Langs land- en waterwegen in de Zuidelijke Nederlanden. Lopend onderzoek naar het preïndustriële transport" in *Het transport en het stedelijke netwerk in de Zuidelijke Nederlanden Bijdragen tot de Geschiedenis,* 82 (1999), pp. 135–158.

19 For example along the river Zenne, between Vilvoorde and Brussels: De Waha, "Het landelijke leven" in A. Smolar-Meynart and J. Stengers, *Het Gewest Brussel: van de oude dorpen tot de stad van nu*, Brussel, 1989 (*Historische uitgaven: reeks in-4°* = Collection Histoire: série in-4°, 16), p.80. This practice was also common in other Western European areas. See for example: G. Fourquin, *Les campagnes de la région parisienne a la fin du Moyen Age (du milieu du XIIIe siècle au début du XVIe siècle),* Paris, 1964, p.29.

20 J.A. Van Houtte and A. Verhulst, "L' approvisionnement des villes dans le Pays-Bas (Moyen Age et Temps Modernes)" in *Troisième conférence internationale d'histoire économique.* Munich, 1965, (Paris, The Hague, 1968) Vol I, pp. 76–77.

21 F. Goblet d'Alviella, *Histoire des bois et forêts en Belgique*, 4 vols., Paris, 1927-1930; for the forest of Zoniën/Soignes: S. Lefèbvre, "The City and the Forest: a Privileged Relationship? Some Remarks on the Case of the Soignes Forest, 16th-18th Centuries" in B. Blondé, E. Vanhaute, M. Galand, eds., *Labour and Labour Markets between Town and Countryside (Middle Ages - 19th Century* (Corn Publication Series, 6), Turnhout, 2001, pp. 236–249.

22 Pounds, "Population", p. 382.

23 De Waha, "Landelijk leven" p. 84. See also: A. de Cuyper, *Coutumes de la ville de Bruxelles* (Coutumes du pays et duché de Brabant. Quartier de Bruxelles, tome premier) Bruxelles, 1869. p.170-172: "*Item enen tochtenaar mag afhouwen allerhand opgaende hout, als abeelen, elzen, espen, popelieren, roode kerselaren, wilgen, ende diergelijke, met ook allerhande schaerhout, mitsgaders de verdroogde boomen, zonder enigzins te mogen raken aen enige opgaende of andere bomen van herd hout, als eycken, buken, herzelteren, olmen, esschen, ende diergelijke haeghout afhouwen in zijn saisoen, (met akse ende houwmes)*".

1.2 Human geography

Guicciardini's description continues with an aspect that has less to do with the purely physical conditions of the landscape than with the human geography: the towns, castles and villages as well as field patters, etc. Geography naturally had an impact on the patterns of settlement. Some natural surroundings are more favourable for human settlement than others in terms of climate and topography, such as a ford in a river, a seaport, the top of a hill or another particularly well-protected place. In the fifteenth century, the period in which our investigation starts, human settlements such as towns, villages, farms and castles had themselves already become an integral part of the landscape, and there were no more considerable changes in the location of those settlements. Hence, our major interest lies not so much in their origins as in their position and importance in the Brabantine landscape.

Generally, the human geography is much more subject to changes within time than is the case with the natural features. The quality of the soil, the geographical relief and the courses of rivers hardly ever change within a few decades.[24] Human influence, on the other hand, can quite drastically change the outer appearance of an area, whether by building towns, roads or canals or by cutting down forests, draining land and so on. For a reconstruction of the late-medieval and early-modern landscape of Brabant, we are therefore dependent on contemporary sources.

1.2.1 "...beautiful and famous towns..."

If the flatness of the land, the dense network of transport routes and the easy access to the sea were the natural features typical of the Low Countries, the great number and size of cities within the limited area were one of the main aspects of their human geography. They formed another distinctive feature at least of the coastal area of the Low Countries.[25] In Brabant, towns were particularly densely spread over the southern part of the duchy, the actual Brabantine core area. In 1567, Guicciardini counted twenty-six fortified places within the duchy of Brabant, not all of which could meet the standards of a town. Still, according to approximations, thirteen of them had more than 5000 inhabitants in 1437.[26] In demographic terms, the multitude of big towns meant that, in 1437, 34% of the Brabantine population lived in cities larger than 5000 inhabitants.[27] The principal cities among them – Brussels, Leuven, Antwerp, and Mechelen – were among the major towns of the Low Countries in that period.

The four leading centres in the urban hierarchy of Brabant were situated exceptionally close to each other. One could literally look from one to the other, as Guicciardini mentions. From Antwerp, travellers on horseback could easily reach Brussels within a day and Mechelen

24 Physical geography was also sometimes subject to important changes, as the changes in the Scheldt estuary around the fourteenth century show. Such radical changes were nevertheless rather exceptional.

25 For regional differences within the Low Countries, see: Blockmans, Pieters, et al., *Crisis en welvaart*, p.43.

26 The population of the towns is calculated from the data given by Cuvelier on the basis of a factor of 5.5 persons per household, applied by P.M.M. Klep, *Bevolking en arbeid in transformatie. Een onderzoek in Brabant 1700-1900*, Nijmegen, 1981, p. 354.

27 P.M.M. Klep, "Urban Decline in Brabant. The Traditionalization of Investments in Labour (1374 -1806)" in H. Van der Wee, ed., *The Rise and Decline of Urban Industries in Italy and in the Low Countries (Late Middle-Ages – Early Modern Times)*, Leuven, 1988, p. 274.

even within half a day.[28] On their way, they would pass yet another town, Vilvoorde, which with only 3000 to 3500 inhabitants in 1437 would have been a secondary centre.[29]

The situation in the north of the duchy, on the other hand, did not correspond to this pattern, due to its natural features. There, we do not find the same density of urban centres that was so characteristic for the Southern Netherlands in the late Middle Ages. In the district of Antwerp, besides the metropolis itself, only a number of secondary centres along the waterways to the west and south ever establish themselves. Among them, Turnhout and Hoogstraten, but also the ancient town of Herentals, can hardly be considered towns by virtue of their size or economic function at that time.[30] The two towns situated closest to Antwerp were Mechelen and Lier, at 24 and 17 km, respectively. Going from Antwerp to Lier or Mechelen, one moved without noting it from the hinterland of one town to that of the other. While the villages of Wilrijk, Mortsel and Edegem were clearly oriented towards Antwerp, Rumst, situated on the Rupel, was strongly influenced by Mechelen.[31] Antwerp itself, being the main exception in this area, owed its exceptional importance mainly to its situation along the Scheldt. It served as the main port for the southern Brabantine hinterland with its dense network of cities, among which the Brabantine capital cities (*hoofdsteden*) Brussels and Leuven and the enclosure of Mechelen. For the economy of that area, this dense urban network, and especially the high concentration of large towns, had particular consequences.[32]

1.2.2 "...lands, castles, villages and other seigneuries..." – The Rural World

Towns, with their fortifications, towers and prestigious buildings, were the pride of every country. In a sense, they formed the diamonds on their rulers' crown. In spite of their exceptional multitude and importance in the Low Countries, however, they formed only a part of the country, albeit the economic focus. In his short description, Guicciardini therefore also includes lands, castles, villages and seigneuries. By doing so, he touches on the other side of sixteenth-century Brabant, the world beyond the splendid towns, which followed a logic different from that of the towns.

Although he gives a very general description, Guicciardini uses expressions that clearly refer to a feudal context. This is not so much the case for the terms "villages" and "lands", although "*terre*" can also refer to holdings or properties in addition fields in general. The terms castles and seigneuries, however, refer to a world that might not fit in with the image one generally has in mind when thinking of the Low Countries during the sixteenth century. One is more likely to think of a society under a strong urban influence, with merchants possessing large landholdings, a quasi non-feudal island, as suggested by studies like J. De Vries' *The Dutch Rural Economy*. The feudal regime was nevertheless still vigourous, at least formally speaking.

28 In the seventeenth century, the Antwerp deputies to the Estates of Brabant traveled from Antwerp to Brussels in less than a day: "*Vannacht van Antwerpen vertrokken en tegen de middag in Brussel gearriveerd*" (Pensionary Melchior Haeckx to the Antwerp burgomasters 7 nov. 1668, SAA Pk. 2428: Correspondence of the Antwerp representatives at the Estates of Brabant, 1664-1669); according to G. Fourquin, *Les campagnes* p. 248; a medieval seigneur from Paris could go as far as 50 km and return in a day.

29 Cuvelier, *Dénombrements*, p. 475.

30 Van Uytven, "Centrale plaatsen", p. 35.

31 This is illustrated by the involvement of townsmen from Mechelen in the brewing business in Rumst, see Chapter 7.

32 We will discuss these characteristics of the interaction between the major western Brabantine cities and their surrounding countryside in Chapter 2.

The jurisdiction of most villages was partly the prerogative of the duke, and partly that of a *seigneur* or landlord. Peasants had to pay seigniorial rights and land rents as well as tithes. Although many seigniorial rights may have become uncommon by the sixteenth century and land rents may have become purely symbolic in some cases, the seigniorial system nevertheless persisted and formed part of the economic and social reality.

While the major physical characteristics of the landscape of Brabant were its flatness and the fertility of the soil, the cultural landscape was dominated by fields and meadows. Paintings by Bruegel, Jacob Grimmer and others give an image of a copious peasant landscape with rich fields of grain, small farms and heavily laden hay wagons. These drawings and paintings can be seen as illustrations of country life, but to a certain extent they also serve as contemporary sources.[33] P. Lindemans, the author of the two-volume *History of Belgian Agriculture*, used the etchings of village scenes from the series "Praediorum villarum" to explain particular agrarian practices, for example.[34] These etchings are some of the earliest realistic scenes of the countryside near Antwerp and hence useful for reconstructing the size and form of fields and meadows, as well as other aspects of sixteenth-century villages. These "Small Landscapes" are far more than topographic records, however. They offer a visual testimony to the complex associations relating to rural land in Antwerp at the middle of the sixteenth century. "The prints, depict the countryside as the dependent part of this perfect order and naturalise the implicit hierarchy in which the city and its socio-cultural values transform the rustic landscape into an artefact".[35] Some representations of towns also offer a general view on their rural surroundings, but it would be precocious to draw conclusions without corresponding written sources. Frans Huys' panoramic view of Antwerp from 1557 gives a good impression of the countryside outside the city walls of Antwerp, for example, or rather of how the artist perceived the town and its surroundings.[36] Antwerp and its outlying areas are also represented in a very detailed map from the seventeenth century (Map 3). It reflects some of the major agrarian characteristics of the area. While the plains north of Antwerp are shown as meadows with cattle grazing on them, the east and especially the south were covered by a variety of different plants, cultivated in small fields. One can distinguish the villages of Berchem and Borgerhout, as well as the garden areas outside the *Rodepoort* and the *St. Jorispoort* with their vegetable gardens and fruit trees.[37] This map nevertheless reflects the period after the Golden Age of Antwerp. The agrarian situation depicted on this map cannot therefore be automatically projected into the fifteenth century. We will have to analyse the evolution of specialised farming near Antwerp in order to determine the period in which intensive gardening and cattle farming originated.

---

33 Although he does not use them in a strictly documentary way: as all iconographic sources, they are filtered through the artists lens, designed for the (urban) buyers' taste. I am grateful to Alexandra Onuf for her comments on this section.

34 "Multifarium casularum" and "Praediorum villarum", Antwerp, H. Cock, 1559 and 1561. Lindemans falsly attributed the etchings, which were based on drawings by an anonymous artist known as the Master of the Small Landscapes, to Peter Bruegel (the Elder).

35 Cited from Alexandra Onuf, *The Small Landscape Prints and the Discovery of the Local in Sixteenth-Century Antwerp* (PhD thesis, Columbia University, manuscript).

36 Frans Huys, Panoramic view on Antwerp (1557), published by Bartolomeus de Momper, Paris, Bibliotheque Nationale. This print has been used for the cover illustration.

37 Marchionautus Sacri Romani Imperii (J.C. Visscher, 1587-1652)" Antwerp, Museum Plantin Moretus, Prentenkabinet, see also in *Kaert-Boeck van de XVII Nederlandstsche Provinciën,etc.*, Amsterdam 1684, reprinted " in D. R. DUNCKER and H. WEISS, *Het hertogdom Brabant in kaart en prent: zijn vier kwartieren Leuven, Brussel, Antwerpen*, 's-Hertogenbosch, Tielt, 1983, pp. 86–87.

Map 3: *Marchionatus Sacri Romani Imperii* (J.C. Visscher, 1587-1652)

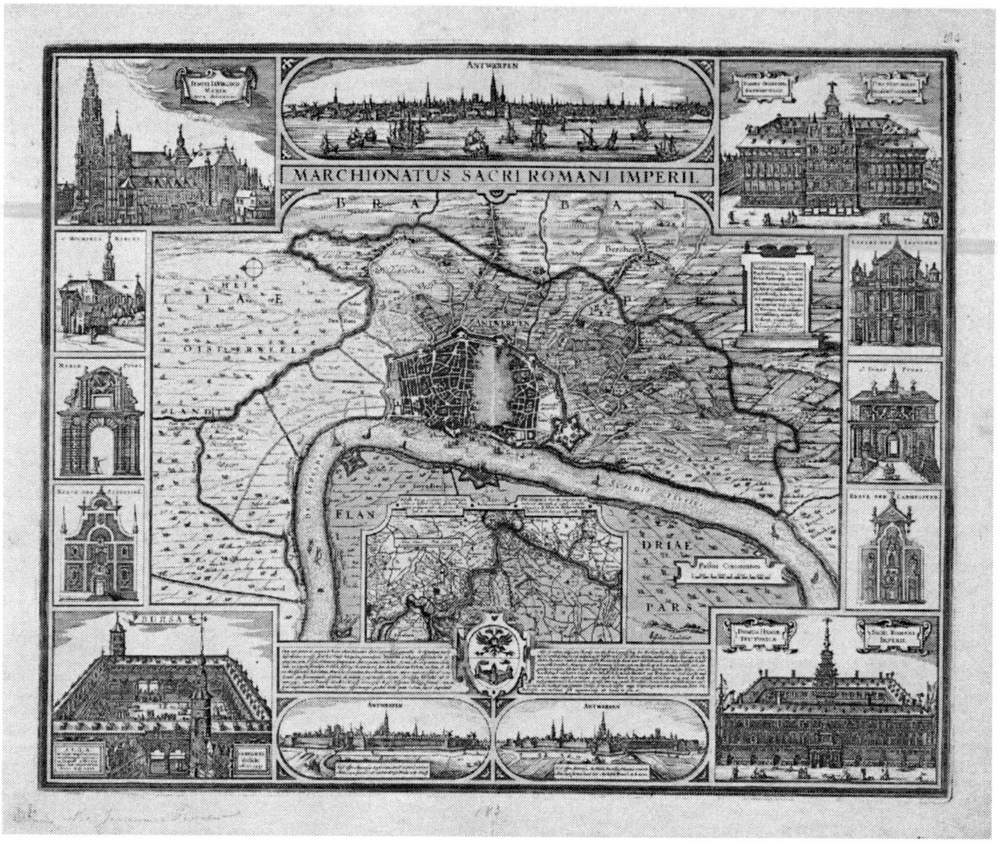

Source: Museum Plantin-Moretus/Prentenkabinet, Antwerp - UNESCO World Patrimony

As far as villages are concerned, it is difficult to make a clear distinction between towns and large villages. Guicciardini uses the term "fortified place" (*terre murate*) to define the towns, but there are many other criteria. As was the case for cities, Brabant also had a great number of villages: 695 in total. The size of a Brabantine village could vary from twenty to several hundreds of houses. Hence, in Waarloos, between Mechelen and Antwerp, there were only 24 households in 1526, while neighbouring Kontich had more than ten times as many (245). Most of the villages had a clearly distinguishable village centre along a river or road, where a church stood, and whose centre was formed by a square. This was where the small common meadow and a pond for the cattle were originally situated, around which lay the common fields, which had been divided into individual fields by the late Middle Ages. The farmhouses and most of the houses in the villages were low and mainly constructed of wood. Some, however, were larger and more imposing than the others. They distinguished themselves from the average country house by virtue of the fact that they were built of brick and were sometimes given names, as well as by their higher price. These houses were generally situated near the market square and tended to be taverns, breweries or the residence of a local merchant. Mention of such stone-built houses can also be found in the written sources concerning larger villages.[38] Outside the village, there were single farms, which were sometimes grouped into hamlets.[39] Villages also formed the social basis of rural life: they did not exactly correspond with but were highly similar to the boundaries of a parish, and partly with the boundaries of seigneuries.

Beside its division into villages or parishes, which determined the actual living context of the rural population, the rural world was also divided in feudal units, i.e. seigneuries. The size of seigniorial demesnes varied considerably. There were large estates containing more than fifteen different villages, for example, but also small ones, with only a handful of farms, on which the landlord levied rents.[40] Most of the estates had a residential building: a castle or a large manor where the seigneur – or, in his absence, a bailiff representing him – would stay. In many cases, the seigneur would not constantly reside at his seigneurie, either due to his duties at the court or simply because he had several demesnes. Finally, lords also had a tendency to live in town.[41] Behind the feudal façade, however, some fundamental changes were taking place. Many of castles became the country residences of rich merchants during the sixteenth century, for example, and urban entrepreneurs became landlords of whole clusters of villages.[42]

As represented both in the work of contemporary authors and on maps and paintings, The Brabantine landscape illustrates some major economic features of the rural surroundings of Antwerp during the sixteenth and seventeenth centuries. One can get an impression of the topography, the rivers and the woods, as well as of the dominant role of the towns. The surroundings of Antwerp were anything but homogenous in geographical terms. To the west, the Scheldt formed a highway downstream to the Atlantic and upstream to a large commercial hinterland. At the same time it was a natural barrier between Antwerp on the one hand and its Brabantine hinterland and Flanders on the other. The polders to the north formed good grazing land, which was nevertheless constantly threatened by the risk of inundations and hence had to be protected by expensive dikes. East of Antwerp, the Kempen was rather infertile and less suited for agriculture than the south of Brabant. Finally, the area to the south and southeast of Antwerp was much more fertile and offered good possibilities for intensive farming. Furthermore, the availability of clay, together with the transport facilities of the Scheldt, led to the establishment of a cluster of brick ovens along the banks of the river. The city's economic relationship with its surrounding countryside was affected by these physical patterns, as we will see throughout the chapters that follow. Iconographic sources also show the major agrarian activities, i.e. the cultivation of grain, cattle farming and, in the immediate surroundings of the towns, gardening. It is possible to estimate the size and the structure of some villages and in some cases to detect specialised

38 See the description of Walem in Chapter 9 and the references to breweries and taverns in Chapter 7.

39 See the description of Edegem in R. VAN PASSEN, *Geschiedenis van Edegem*, Edegem, 1974, p.73-75 and of Kontich in Idem, *Geschiedenis van Kontich*, Kontich, 1988², pp. 645–652.

40 See Chapter 8.

41 See M. BOONE, "La terre, les hommes et les villes. Quelques considérations autour du thème de l'urbanisation des propiétaires terriens" in *La ville et la transmission des valeurs culturelles au bas moyen âge et aux temps modernes: actes*, (Crédit communal. Comité d'histoire. Colloque international 17: 1994: Spa) (*Historische uitgaven: reeks in-8°* = Collection histoire: série in-8°, 96), Bruxelles, 1996, pp. 153–173.

42 See Chapter 9.

occupations such as river shipping, carting, and brick making. Another feature that manifested itself in the landscape of the Antwerp surroundings were the villas and parks of some wealthy Antwerp merchants. Unluckily, this picture is not at all precise. The wealth or poverty of the peasants cannot be estimated merely by looking at Breughel's village scenes. The efficiency of the agrarian system cannot be evaluated that way either. Nor can we detect changes in a chronological dimension, due to the absence of detailed iconographic material concerning the fifteenth century. For a more systematic analysis of the social and economic structure of the Brabantine countryside, and one that meets the requirements of the theoretical questions put forward in the introduction, we cannot limit ourselves to a study of the landscape or its representations, we must therefore to turn to written sources related to the actual economic transformations.

CHAPTER 2

The Urban impact on the Rural Economy: Antwerp and its Surroundings in the Late Middle Ages

2.1 Introduction

The role a town plays in the economy of the surrounding area is one of the central topics of economic history. Citing Karl Marx, one could even say that "the whole economic history of society is summed up in the antithesis of town and country". According to Marx, the separation of town from country is "the foundation of every division of labour which has attained a certain degree of development and has been brought about by the exchange of commodities".[1] Especially since the 1970s, economic and social historians have studied the topic of the economic relation between town and countryside by means of concepts deriving from urban geography. The two major theoretical concepts that they have applied are Von Thünen's model of concentric circles and the Central Place theory, introduced by Walter Christaller in 1932.[2] These geographic models have been used by historians not only to study urban networks but also to analyse the relationship between town and countryside – a discipline called *Stadt-Umland-Forschung* in German-language historiography.[3] It is based on the assumption that within an economic area a number of special functions were concentrated in a central place, which formed the basis for a town. On the level of production, this led to a principal division between agricultural and non-agricultural labour between towns and countryside (although there was of course some agriculture in the towns and some non-agricultural activity in the countryside). As a result of this division of labour, both remained strongly interdepend: the town depended on the agrarian surplus of the countryside and the rural area depended on the secondary and tertiary sectors of the towns. This helps to establish a basic typology of the economic town-countryside interaction:

The countryside provides the town with:
- foodstuffs
- raw materials and fuel
- immigrants (labour force)
- land (control over raw materials, opportunities for investment, country residences).

1 K. Marx, *Das Kapital,* 1976, p. 472 cited " in R. Hodges, *Primitive and Peasant Markets,* Oxford, 1988, p. 63. Cf. S. R. Epstein, "Introduction. Town and Country in Europe, 1300-1800" in *Town and Country in Europe,* p. 1.

2 J. H. von Thünen, *Der isolierte Staat im Beziehung auf Landwirtschaft und Nationalökonomie*, 3rd edition, Stuttgart, 1842; W. Christaller, *Die zentralen Orte in Süddeutschland,* Jena, 1932.

3 See for example: *Stadt-Land-Beziehungen und Zentralität als Problem der historischen Raumforschung.(Veröffentlichung en der Akademie für Raumforschung und Landesplanung: Forschungs-und Sitzungsberichte* vol. 88, *Historische Raumforschung,* 11), Hannover, 1974; or H. K. Schulze (ed.) *Städtisches Um- und Hinterland in vorindutrieller Zeit,* Cologne, 1985.

On the other hand, the town provides the countryside with:
- industrial products
- specialised labour
- market functions (local consumption, export, import)
- employment opportunities
- capital.

This scheme limits itself to the purely economic aspects of the town-countryside relation. Administrative and juridical aspects, such as the protective function of the town for the rural population, are excluded here, although they too had a strong impact on the economy. The different points are closely related with each other, as, for example the supply of foodstuffs and raw materials and the supply of land. Whereas the one refers to the transfer of products such as grain, livestock, wood and bricks, the other refers to the fields, meadows, woods or limekilns where these products were made and which could be the property of townsmen. Urban functions for the countryside and rural functions for the town were in many cases reciprocal. The urban labour market provided opportunities of employment for countrymen, while immigrants from the countryside formed a necessary source of population and labour force for the town. The same is true of the relation between supplies of rural products and urban market functions. Whereas the one refers to the town's need of supplies from the countryside, the other has to do with the opportunities that the urban markets offered to the rural population.

In principle, this reciprocity suggests that we have to do with an equal exchange which is beneficial for both town and countryside, or in the words of A. Smith, "we must not...imagine that the gain of the town is the loss of the country. The gains of both are mutual and reciprocal".[4] Many authors, however, lean towards the Marxist vision, in which the exchange is considered to have been based on unequal terms causing a transfer of the rural surplus to the town and an accumulation of capital in the hands of the urban bourgeoisie.[5]

In the following sections, we will be concentrating on some of the major aspects of the interaction between town and countryside: the supply of the town with food, raw materials and fuel, the immigration from the countryside to the town, urban landownership and, on the other hand, the supply of urban products, specialised labour, and capital for the countryside. These points shall be analysed for the concrete circumstances of fifteenth century West Brabant, with the focus on Antwerp as well as the other two major towns of the area, Brussels and Mechelen. The aim of this analysis is to sketch a picture of the relationship between Antwerp and its rural surroundings shortly before its spectacular rise as world metropolis. Considering these mechanisms in a comparative perspective will moreover help us distinguish between the general patterns of the town-country relationship in Brabant and the specific case of Antwerp.

4 Cited in R. Hodges, *Primitive and Peasant Markets*, Oxford, 1988, p. 63.
5 Ibidem.

2.2 The Provision of the Town with Food and Raw Materials

A first dimension of the relationship between town and country is the fact that a town had to be supplied with a number of basic goods to satisfy the material needs of its population. These included basic foodstuffs (bread, dairy products, meat, fish, salt, vegetables, fruit, water and other beverages); building materials for the construction of houses, shops, administrative buildings and fortifications; raw materials for industrial production; and fuel for the heating of houses and for industry (brewers, smithies, etc.).[6]

All these goods had to be supplied primarily by the wider surrounding areas of the town in order to guarantee its existence, which meant the size of a town was restricted by the availability of these essential goods.[7] The specific characteristics of these supply goods, for example in terms of transportability, influenced the production structure of the urban Umland, which in the ideal case would be structured in concentric "Von Thünen circles" of specialised production.[8] Von Thünen's theoretical model has been adapted to the medieval situation by F. Irsigler. He places horticulture in the centre of the urban sphere of provision, separating the second circle into sectors including the municipal forest, pasture, hydraulic energy and material deposits. In zone three, we find improved three-field agriculture, in zones four and five less-developed agriculture and specialised zones of mining and metal industry, and in zone six livestock farming and forestry.[9] He admits, however, that "the real constitution of each town is different, in function of its dimension, means of communication, the quality of the soil and other geologic and geo-morphologic conditions".[10]

Let us take a closer look at the supplies of the major towns of western Brabant in the late Middle Ages, as far as the available information makes this possible. First in importance was the supply with grain for the major basic foodstuff, the "daily bread". Besides for baking bread, grain was also needed for brewing beer and as fodder for different sorts of animals.[11] The main bread grain in late medieval Brabant was rye, which was also the main agrarian product of the area. Wheat was less common and therefore reserved for the wealthier parts of the population and for special occasions, such as Sundays and holy days.[12] Other grains current on the urban market were oats, barley, peas, beans, and vetches.[13]

6 F. Irsigler, "L'approvisionnement des villes de l'Allemagne occidentale jusqu'au XVIe siècle" in *L'approvisionnement des villes de l' Europe occidentale au Moyen Age et aux Temps Modernes.* Centre Culturel de l'abbaye de Flaran. Cinquièmes Journèes internationales d'histoire, 16-18 septembre 1983, Auch, 1985, p. 119.

7 P. Bairoch, cited in Piuz, "Rélations"., p. 199, note 16.

8 Cited in Irsigler, "Approvisionnement", p. 143f. The Von Thünen model is based on the assumption of an isolated flat area with homogenous soil quality and one single town in the middle. According to this model, we would find free agriculture in the centre, forests in the second circle, intensive agriculture in the third, mixed enclosure farming in the fourth, extensive grain production in the fifth and livestock farming in the sixth circle.

9 *Ibidem*, p. 144.

10 *Ibidem*, p. 137.

11 An account of the Infirmary of the Great Beguinage of Leuven from the fifteenth century lists the use of the different sorts of grain: wheat (for bread, pasteries, soups and beer), rye (for bread, pigs and young animals), barley (for beer, capons, fattening, and pigs), oats (for geese, cattle, calfs and horses), M.J. Tits-Dieuaide, *La formation des prix céréaliers en Brabant et en Flandre au XVe siècle, Bruxelles, 1975,* p. 121, note 9.

12 See Van Uytven, "R., L'approvisionnement des villes des anciens Pays Bas au Moyen Age. " in *L'approvisionnement des villes de l' Europe occidentale au Moyen Age et aux Temps Modernes.* Centre Culturel de l'abbaye de Flaran. Cinquièmes Jornèes internationales d'histoire, 16-18 septembre 1983 (Auch, 1985), p. 96; Van der Wee, *Growth*, vol I., p. 183.

13 Beans and vetches were counted among the grains although being legumes rather than grains. See for example the declarations of Antwerp cornmongers during a process between Mechelen, Antwerp and Brussels, in 1433, SAA, T 584, fols. 241-280.

Grain found its way to the urban market in different ways. First, the immediate producer of a farm – the tenant or farmer – could sell his surplus at the market. In fact, we can assume that most tenants were to some degree obliged to do so in order to pay their manorial dues in cash.[14] Evidence for this most obvious transaction is scarce, if not absent, for the simple reason that tenants did not keep records of their sales. Local ordinances refer to the suppliers of grain in only very general terms, so that we cannot identify them as peasants, lease farmers or landlords. We are therefore limited to information from urban registers. One example of what could be such a transaction is documented in the registers of the Antwerp aldermen from 1465 and 1467, when a certain Jan Schollemont from Edegem sold 200 viertel (15,400 l.) of wheat and 200 viertel of rye from his farm to Joris Ysnoutssone from Gouda. In this case, the grain was not used for local consumption, but rather exported. Moreover, it is not clear if Schollemont cultivated his farm himself or had leased it out.[15]

Yet, the immediate producer only disposed of part of his production. Beside keeping enough for his own consumption and for the necessary seed, he needed to pay different sorts of seigniorial dues, taxes and leases up to almost half of his gross production. Although not being sold by the tenant, some of these dues also made up part of the flow from the country to the town. A large quantity of leases, land rents, tithes and other dues that were payable in kind, mainly in grain, also formed a substantial part of the food supply of the town, although not necessarily via the market. Although land rents and leases increasingly became payable in money in the fifteenth century, a large proportion was still payable in kind. The leaseholders of farms or single plots of land were supposed to deliver the leases at the house or barn of the lessee, as we can read in many lease contracts or documents of aldermen concerning rents.[16] Van Uytven observed that, in the case of Leuven, 25% of the total transport volume coming to the towns consisted of such dues in kind.[17]

The different sorts of revenues in kind from land rents or leases were partly used for the consumption of the individual landlord or institution that levied them. But landlords, both individuals and institutions, also sold parts of these incomes in kind. The bailiff (rentmeester) of the lord of Grimbergen (the count of Nassau), for example, regularly sold large quantities of rye in Mechelen.[18] Urban institutions, too, sold their surplus at the urban market. Hence, a considerable proportion of the town's grain supply arrived through the feudal rents, as suggested by Kriedte.[19]

Rye, wheat, oats and barley were produced in great quantities within western Brabant. Grain was the major agrarian product of the area, and yields per hectare were high. Still, even with a gross yield as high as 1,500 litres of rye, the total yield of a farm was only about 500 litres per hectare as a result of three-field rotation. Moreover, considering that the

14 P. Kriedte, *Spätfeudalismus und Handelskapital. Grundlinien einer europäischen Wirtschaftsgeschichte vom 16. Jahrhundert bis zum Ausgang des 18. Jahrhunderts*, Göttingen, 1980, p. 22, See also Hagen, "Capitalism and the Countryside", p. 17.

15 Van Passen, *Geschiedenis van Edegem,* p. 792.

16 See Appendix 1.

17 R. Van Uytven, *Stadsfinanciën en stadseconomie te Leuven van de XIIe tot het einde der XVIe eeuw*. (= Verhandelingen van de koninglijke Academie voor Wetenschapen, Letteren en Schone Kunsten van Belgie / Klasse der Letteren Jg. XXIII/1961, 44) Brussels, 1961, p. 441, and Idem., *Approvisionnement,* p. 96.

18 ARA MW I 796 accounts 1449/50, 1455/56, and I 797, account 1474/75.

19 Kriedte, *Spätfeudalismus*, p. 17; according to him, this shows that the rise of towns in the Middle Ages was conditioned by the feudal mode of exploitation.

farmer and his family consumed at least 250 litres of grain per person each year, only farms with more than 2.5 ha. would have been able to produce a marketable surplus.

On the basis of these assumptions, R. van Uytven calculated that to supply a town of 20,000 inhabitants, like Antwerp or Mechelen in the fifteenth century, with rye, the production of 150 villages was needed.[20] If we apply this calculation to western Brabant, Antwerp would have absorbed the grain production of an area larger than its fiscal district, or kwartier (118 villages, not including the seignieuries of Breda and Bergen-op-Zoom).[21] Moreover, the potential dimensions of a city's supply areas were limited by those of the neighbouring towns. Within the kwartier of Antwerp, the towns of Lier (ca. 6,000 inhabitants intra muros), Herentals (ca. 4,500), and Turnhout (4,500) will have required some of the countryside for their own food supply. But the most striking obstacle was Mechelen, with more than 20,000 inhabitants, situated right in between the towns of Antwerp and Brussels. Its supply area overlapped that of both these towns, but because its juridical hinterland was restricted to a very small area, its claim to the grain supplies from its larger surroundings was very limited. Its situation was therefore quite precarious. This was the reason for the serious conflicts regarding the supply of grain that arose repeatedly with Brussels and Antwerp.[22] The Brabantine towns imposed grain embargoes against Mechelen several times during a long-lasting conflict concerning the staple on oats.[23]

This – admittedly very rough – approximation of the necessary grain supply areas of the large Brabantine towns shows that the towns literally had to compete with each other for their food supplies, as early as the late Middle Ages. From a very early stage, they therefore had to take recourse to imports from other areas. These imports came especially from the less urbanised areas south of Brabant: Walloon Flanders, Hainaut and Cambrai, and, to a lesser extent, by ship, from Artois, Picardy, Normandy and Brittany. There were also already regular grain imports in the fifteenth century from Northern Germany, Prussia and Poland (the area that would become so important in the sixteenth century), but these only became really important after 1480.[24] Holland and Zeeland, on the other hand, were major suppliers of oats and barley, which were important as fodder and for brewing.[25] This explains why the brewers' guild from Brussels regularly purchased wheat, barley and oats in Antwerp or

20 Van Uytven, *Approvisionnement,* pp. 78–79. For France, the provisioning area of a town with ca. 20,000 inhabitants was calculated as covering a circle with a radius of ca. 15 to 18 km; see R. Chartier and H. Neveux, "La ville dominante et soumise" in E. Le Roy Ladurie, *La ville classique*, Paris, 1981 (Histoire de la France urbaine, ed. G. Duby, III), p. 15-286, 57-62.

21 In Chapter 4, we will try to find out to what extent this estimate can be applied for the case of Antwerp. See also M. Limberger, "Feeding Sixteenth-Century Antwerp. Food Imports, Local Supply, and the Agrarian Structure of the Town's Rural Surroundings" in P. van Cruyningen and E. Thoen eds., *Food: Production, Demand and Trade. Aspects of the Economic Relation between Town and Countryside (Middle Ages-19th Century)* (CORN Publication Series no. 9, forthcoming).

22 Tits-Dieuaide, *Formation,* p. 144.

23 R.Van Uytven, "Het sociaal economisch leven" in Idem, ed., *De geschiedenis van Mechelen: van heerlijkheid tot stadsgewest,* Tielt, 1991, p. 43; M. de Laet, "Mechelen versus Antwerpen. De strijd om het bezit en het behoud van de stapel voor vis, zout en haver (1233 – 1467)" in *Handelingen van de Koninklike Kring voor Oudheidkunde, Letteren en Kunst van Mechelen,* 90/ 1986, (Symposium De sociaal- economische geschiedenis van Mechelen in de Bourgondische tijd (1384 – 1530)), pp. 57–90.

24 M. van Tielhof, *De Hollandse graanhandel 1470-1570: koren op de Amsterdamse molen,* Den Haag, 1995, (*Hollandsche historische reeks,* 23), p. 11, R. Van Uytven, "Politiek en Economie. De crisis der late XVe eeuw in de Nederlanden" in *Belgisch Tijdschrift voor Filologie en Geschiedenis/Revue Belge de Philologie et d'Histoire,* 53, (1975), p. 1113, see also H. Neveux, *Les grains du Cambrésis. Vie et déclin d'une structure économique: (fin du 14e-début du 17e siècle),* Paris, 1980 (*Civilisations et sociétés,* 64).

25 Tits-Dieuaide, *Formation* p. 144.

Mechelen.[26] Even the St. Elisabeth hospital in Antwerp made large purchases of barley at the Antwerp corn market, despite its own high agrarian incomes from land rents.[27]

The river Scheldt and its Brabantine effluents formed a convenient transport network for shipping grain. Antwerp, moreover, as a seaport, was the first staple market for grain reaching Brabant from the sea. The major import axis from the South went via Leuven, from where the grain was shipped to Mechelen and Antwerp. Mechelen also received grain from Liege in periods of famine, when the Brabantine towns did not "export" grain to the enclave.[28] The Brabantine rivers were also used for the distribution of grain from Antwerp into the interior.[29]

Grain supplies being of vital importance to them, the towns devised strict regulations for the market. It is by means of these regulations that we can catch a glimpse of the way the Antwerp grain market actually functioned. The farmers or landowners generally brought their grain to the weekly markets, which took place on Saturday, by boat, cart, or on horseback.[30] At the same time, grain merchants brought in grain from more distant areas by boat or ship, or from smaller local marketplaces. The declarations of numerous cornmongers and shippers made during the great legal proceedings that Antwerp and Brussels brought against Mechelen in 1431, concerning the staple for oats, salt and herring shed some light on the grain trade in fifteenth-century Brabant. Grainmongers either sold grain at the weekly markets of their hometowns and delivered it at the place of destination, or they went to a promising market with a shipload of grain and tried to sell it for a profitable price. Once there, they generally tried to find a return cargo for the trip home. Antwerp played an important role as a transit market of oats and barley from Holland and Zeeland on the one hand, and wheat and rye from Flanders, Northern France and Southern Brabant on the other. We regularly find mention of grain cargoes on the Scheldt coming from Dordrecht or Gent, and along the Brabantine rivers Zenne, Rupel, Nete, Demer and Dijle between Antwerp and Lier, Brussels, Leuven, Diest or even Zoutleeuw. Grain merchants were probably also involved in the local marketing of grain, although the sources remain silent on this item, and the urban legislation forbade this practice. In many cases they will have already bought the harvest on the field, as was common in Flanders[31] or Holland.[32] The aim of urban regulations was to keep prices down by forbidding intermediaries, such as grain merchants or millers, to buy and resell grain at high prices before the larger public had a chance to buy directly from the producer. Therefore, all grain had to pass through the market place, and be offered first to the common citizens, before millers, bakers and grain merchants were allowed to buy the remainder.[33] Hence, there were different ways of transferring grain between its producers

26 G. Des Marez, *L'organisation du travail à Bruxelles au 15e siècle,* Brussels, 1904, p. 227.

27 Van der Wee, *Growth,* I, p. 189.

28 Tits- Dieuaide, *Formation,* p. 145, R. van Uytven, "Sociaal-economisch leven" p. 43.

29 Antwerp, SAA, T 584, fols. 241-277.

30 De Cuyper, *Coutumes,* p. 80.

31 Thoen, *Landbouweconomie,* II, p. 678-79.

32 D.E.H. De Boer, "Vanden Corencopers". Veertiende-eeuwse graanspeculatie door een dichterlijke bril" in *"Proeve 't al, 't is prysselyck" Verbruik in Europese steden (13de – 18de eeuw). Consumption in European Towns (13th -18th century). Liber Amicorum Raymond van Uytven* (Bijdragen tot de Geschiedenis, 81 (1998)), pp. 127–143, 98.

33 G. De Longé, Coerboek de la ville d'Anvers (14th c.) " in *Coutumes de la ville d'Anvers* (Coutumes du pays et duché de Brabant. Quartier d'Anvers, tome premier) Bruxelles, 1870. p. 22-26. On the principles of regulation of the urban grain market in the Ancien Regime, see also S.L. Kaplan, *Provisioning Paris, Merchants and Millers in the Grain and Flour Trade during the Eighteenth Century,* Ithaca, 1984, especially Chapter 1.

and the urban consumers: via sales directly by the producer or owner of a farm at the local market, in the form of land rents or leases in kind, or via imports from other regions. The lively traffic in grain and the strict regulations between the towns of the Low Countries shows the strong demand for this vitally important product.

For other foodstuffs, the general situation was similar. The immediate surroundings of the towns produced a considerable part of the necessary products, but due to the great urban demand, especially for higher quality products, they had to be supplemented by means of imports. Meat consumption, for example, increased strongly during the fifteenth century.[34] The most important sources of meat were cattle, pigs and sheep. The meadows along the Brabantine rivers formed particularly rich pastures for cattle and sheep grazing. These meadows were used not only by peasants and farmers, but also by cattle merchants and butchers from the towns, who used them for fattening oxen. In Brussels, butchers and other citizens were allowed to hold 300 sheep in the meadows along the river Zenne near the town of Vilvoorde. The butchers also had the right to let their cattle graze along the fortifications of the town.[35] Among the landowners in Oosterweel, situated in the polders north of Antwerp, were many butchers and cattle breeders from the town.[36] Many people, including urban citizens, kept pigs for their own consumption. Millers and brewers fed their pigs with the residues from their respective activities.[37] In addition to the local production, however, oxen were also imported from the northern provinces of Guelre, Overijssel and Friesland, and sometimes from Normandy and Brittany. These imported oxen lost much of their weight on the journey to Brabant and therefore had to be fattened in the closer surroundings of their final destination before being sold at the regional oxen market.[38] Pigs, on the other hand, were a speciality of Hainaut. They were sent to Brussels and sold there on the market.[39] An almost entirely local resource of meat, finally, was poultry. Chickens, capons, geese and even swans appear in almost every rental register as payments in kind. They served as a cheap source of fresh meat, and were relatively readily available.[40]

Brabantine farmers also produced dairy products, like cheese and butter. An order from Brussels, dating from 1360, forbids merchants to buy butter, eggs, and cheese from villagers coming to the market, within two miles from the town.[41] Religious institutions regularly bought fresh butter from the surrounding countryside in order to salt it for

34 VAN UYTVEN, "Approvisionnement", p. 100.

35 DES MAREZ, *Organisation*, p. 230.

36 F. PRIMS, "Antwerpen in het 'land van Oosterweel'" in *Antwerpiensia*, 21 (1950) pp. 25–28.

37 The Antwerp '*kuere*' limits the number of pigs that a baker was allowed to keep to twelve. G. DE LONGÉ, *Coerboek*, p. 22.

38 LINDEMANS, *Landbouw* II, p. 432., R. BAETENS, "De lokale markten te Antwerpen (16e-18e eeuw)" in *Antwerpen in de XVIIde eeuw*, Antwerpen, 1989, H. VAN DER WEE and E. AERTS, "The Lier Livestock Trade in the Low Countries from the 14th to the 18th Century" in E. Westermann (ed.), *Internationaler Ochsenhandel (1350-1750). Akten des 7th International Economic History Congress Edinburgh 1978*, Stuttgart, Bamberg, 1979 (Beiträge zur Wirtschaftsgeschichte, 9), pp. 235–254; K. WILDIERS VAN DER WEE, "De Geschiedenis van het Lierse veemarktprivilegie" in *Land van Ryen*, XVI, p. 124 –136 and XVII 33 – 52.

39 VAN UYTVEN, "Apprivisionnement", p. 100f. The lord of Grimbergen regularly bought pigs (from Hainaut?) in Brussels during the fifteenth century, in order to have them sent to his estates in Breda (47 pigs in 1434/5, 41 in 1438/9 and 40 in 1440/41); ARA MW I 796.

40 The lord of Grimbergen had sent 404 chickens, 101 capons and 61 geese from his manor to his residences in Brussels and Rode in 1464/65 for his provision; ARA MW I 797 Account 1464/65.

41 DES MAREZ, *Organisation*, p. 339.

conservation. Their annual purchases could reach as much as 1,000 lb.[42] On the other hand, the towns also imported cheese and butter from Flanders, Holland and other parts of the Low Countries, and even from England and Denmark.[43] Antwerp had had the staple right for Dutch dairy products since 1358.[44] In the early fifteenth century, merchants from Nieuwpoort, Dunkerk, and St. Omer in western Flanders regularly came to Antwerp to sell butter and cheese there.[45] Young Flemish cheese was the kind that religious institutions bought most at the Antwerp market during the fifteenth century.[46]

For seafish and salt, on the other hand, the Brabantine towns were dependent on the import from the maritime regions of Zeeland and Holland and from the estuary of the Scheldt. The places Steenbergen, Zevenbergen and Reimerswal were major providers of salt in the early fifteenth century.[47] Other important centres in Zeeland were Tholen and Zierikzee. In northern Flanders, the town of Biervliet and the places Oostburg, Axel and Sluis were major salt-refining centres.[48] Salt and herring were transported via the Scheldt and the inland rivers and formed major staple products for Antwerp and Mechelen. The staple right of salt, herring and oats was heavily disputed between Antwerp and Brussels on the one hand and Mechelen on the other. This shows their importance for the urban economy and the provisioning of the towns. River fish, on the other hand, came from the local rivers and ponds.[49]

In terms of beverages, beer had become the major drink for mass consumption. The brewing of beer strongly expanded in the late Middle Ages, with beer replacing wine as the most popular drink. While beer had originally been imported from Holland in great quantities, the local production developed strongly from the fifteenth century on.[50] The countryside provided the necessary grain, but the brewing itself took place in town. In contrast, wine production diminished sharply in the late Middle Ages, until is was all but abandoned. Wine, from then on, became more and more a luxury drink.[51]

Fruit and vegetables formed an exception to this pattern of supply. As they were not suited for transport over long distance, they were grown almost exclusively in the immediate surroundings of the towns, and in many cases in the towns themselves. Gardeners, who were organised in their own guilds, were numerous in the Brabantine towns. From the late Middle Ages on, the adjoining areas of the large towns were characterised by countless gardens of a relatively large size.[52] In Antwerp, hundreds of gardens with a total area of more than

42 Van der Wee, *Growth*, I p. 210.

43 Brussels ARA, A no. 583, cited by Lindemans, *Landbouw* II, p. 378.

44 Van Uytven "Approvisionnement", p. 82, J.F. Mertens and K.L. Torfs, *Geschiedenis van Antwerpen sedert de stichting der stad tot onze tyden*, Antwerpen, 1845, p. 280 and 553.

45 Antwerp, SAA, T 584 fo. 281 r., declaration of the innkeeper and dairy merchant Willem Beys.

46 Van der Wee, *Growth*, I p. 217.

47 Antwerp, SAA, T 584 declarations of Jan van Nedervenne, merchant from Leuven (fo. 247 v.) and Dankart Peterssone, from Antwerp (fo. 268v.).

48 J.A. Van Houtte and R. van Uytven, "Nijverheid en Handel 1300-1482" in *AGN*, IV. Haarlem, 1980, p. 100.

49 For fishing and fishponds in medieval and early modern Brussels, see: C. Deligne, *Bruxelles et sa rivière. Genèse d'un territoire urbain (12e – 18e siècle)* (Turnhout, 2003), (Studies in European Urban History (1100-1800), 1), p. 131-178.

50 Van der Wee, *Growth* I, p. 229.

51 R. van Uytven, „Le combat des boissons en Europe du moyen âge au XVIIIe siècle" in S. Cavaciocchi (ed.), *Alimentazione e nutrizione secc. XIII-XVIII, Atti della „Ventottesima Settimana di Studi" 22-27 aprile 1996*, Firenze, 1997, pp. 53–88 (Istituto Internazionale di Storia economica „F.Datini" Prato, serie II – Atti delle „Settimane di Studi" e altri Convegni, 28).

52 Lindemans, *Landbouw,* II, p. 173-174.

50 ha. can be identified within and outside the city walls as early as the fourteenth century.[53] There was also some regional trade in fruit, however: apples and pears from Brabant were shipped down the Scheldt toward Bergen op Zoom,[54] and cherries from Mechelen were sold in Brussels.[55]

Besides food, the countryside provided the town with a broad range of other primary materials used for building, industrial production and fuel. As far as building materials were concerned, the Brabantine towns could rely on a relatively ready supply of bricks and stone. Both of these materials were available in the closer surroundings. The brick ovens of the Scheldt and Rupel areas provided more than sufficiently for the local needs. The ammanie or district of Brussels comprised a dense network of limestone and sandstone quarries. Sand and lime were also available in sufficient quantities. A material that was more difficult to obtain was high-quality wood. The south of Brabant was wooded in the late Middle Ages, but larger quantities of timber for the construction of roofing and beams were very difficult to retrieve. These were regularly brought by ship from Scandinavia and the Baltic region.[56] Antwerp was a centre of distribution for wainscot, i.e. the boards for lining walls and floors.[57]

Not only was wood used as building material, but it was also the major source of fuel in the late medieval Brabantine towns.[58] In contrast to wood for building purposes, firewood was available in relatively large quantities. The trade in wood was a major activity, conducted by professional woodcutter-merchants. There were fewer forests in the Antwerp area than in the south of Brabant, and firewood was cut especially along the Scheldt, south of Antwerp. Wood was a very precious resource and had to be supplemented with peat, which was retrieved in the north of Flanders and in various parts of the Northern Provinces.[59] Peat was also dug in the area between Antwerp and Mechelen, although on a very modest scale. The lord of the Land of Mechelen, for example, had a seigniorial right to the peat that was cut in his forests.[60]

Finally, raw materials were also needed for the urban industries. The proportion of such materials that the closer surroundings of Antwerp and Brussels could provide those cities was smaller than in the case of food. Wool, flax and a number of plants used for dyes were produced in some parts of Brabant,[61] but with the growing dimensions of the urban textile industry, these primary materials had to be imported in even greater quantities. For the area around Leuven, this increasing import of raw materials and the decline of the local

53 F. PRIMS, "Historische teksten II. Hoven en hoveniers te Antwerpen in 1338" in *Bijdragen tot de Geschiedenis*, 23 (1932), pp. 150–156; IDEM, *Geschiedenis van Antwerpen*, vol. III, pp. 85–88.

54 A fruitmonger from Zoutleeuw shipped apples and other products toward Antwerp; SAA T 584.

55 DES MAREZ, *Organisation* p. 339f., cit. in VAN UYTVEN, "Approvisionnement", p. 86.

56 J.P. SOSSON, *Les travaux publics de la ville de Bruges 14e-15e siècles*, Bruxelles, 1977, pp. 102–112

57 For example in 1462/63, wainscot (*wagenschot*) was brought from Antwerp to Londerzeel, in the *ammanie* of Brussels, to line the roof of a mill. ARA, MW I 796.

58 For medieval London, compare: J.A. GALLOWAY, D. KEENE AND M. MURPHY, "Fuelling the City: Production and Distribution of Firewood and Fuel in London's Region, 1290-1400" in *Economic History Review*, 49 (1996), pp. 447–72.

59 K.A.H.W. LEENDERS, *Verdwenen venen, Een onderzoek naar de ligging en exploitatie van thans verdwenen venen in het gebied tussen Antwerpen, Turnhout, Geertruidenberg en Willemstad 1250-1750*, s.l. 1989.

60 ARA, Rk. reg. 11898- 11915 (1474/75-1589/90).

61 In the fourteenth century, madder and thistles (for combing the wool) were cultivated in and near the Antwerp. PRIMS, "Hoven en hoveniers"; and IDEM, *Geschiedenis*, vol. III, pp. 85–88. For example, welt (NL: *wouw*) was grown in the area of Asse, near the Flemish border. LINDEMANS, *Landbouw*, II, p. 254. Also in the East of Brabant, near Diest, dyeing plants (*wee*) were grown in the late Middle Ages; see R. VAN UYTVEN, "In de schaduwen van de Antwerpse groei: het Hageland in de zestiende eeuw, " in *Bijdragen tot de Geschiedenis*, 57 (1974), pp. 171–188.

industries may have been a reason for the economic decline of the area.[62]

Can we distinguish the spatial patterns as proposed in Von Thünen's model in our research area? It seems that we can, especially for the inner zones of the Von Thünen circles. Gardening was concentrated within the towns themselves and in their immediate surroundings, and there were some woods in the closer surroundings of the town, which were regularly cut in order to provide the towns with firewood. Although these woods were not comparable with the large Zoniën forest, Brabant was one of the few areas of the Low Countries that had woods in the immediate surroundings of the large towns. In contrast, Flanders and Holland were almost entirely dependent on imported wood and peat.[63] Besides these areas with specific functions, agriculture followed a pattern that was similar throughout the whole of western Brabant: improved three-field agriculture. Local differences were due to different natural conditions rather than to the distance from the town.

The reason for this lack of clearly visible areas corresponding with the outer Von-Thünen circles can be explained by the fact that western Brabant was not an "isolated state" with one urban centre, but an area in which urban spheres of influence were situated next to each other and tended to overlap. The short distance between the relatively large towns shaped a pattern of small immediate urban supply areas, covering almost exclusively the inner circles of the – adapted – Von Thünen model. The outer circles, i.e. the zones of extensive agriculture, livestock breeding and forestry, and mining and metal industry, were generally located outside western Brabant, and in some cases at a great distance from the Low Countries in general. In the late medieval period, the southern Low Countries had already become integrated in a system of interregional division of labour. For the rural economy of western Brabant, this location in the centre of the urban supply areas meant a strong demand for grain and other kinds of foodstuffs. This situation was very favourable for the rise of intensive husbandry in the area.

2.3 The Provision of the Countryside with Industrial Goods and Imported Products

The town received a great deal of – mostly primary – goods from the countryside, but it also furnished its surroundings with goods that were not available there. The peasant who sold his grain on the market often returned home with goods that he had purchased there. These were primarily manufactured products, such as farming tools, household goods or clothes, but could also be imported foodstuffs like salt and fish (both sea fish and freshwater fish).[64] While the Brabantine countryside could itself provide part of the basic products it needed, by the late Middle Ages, it was far from being an autarkic economy. Agriculture produced a broad range of grains, vegetables and meats. But for salt, sea fish, and more exclusive products such as spices, Brabant had to take recourse to imports. Antwerp and Mechelen, the staple markets for salt and herring, dominated the Brabantine trade for all these products.

---

62 Van Uytven, "In de schaduwen".

63 Van Houtte & Verhulst, "Aprovisionnement", p. 76.

64 D.L. Farmer, "Marketing the Produce of the Countryside" in E. Miller, ed., *The Agrarian History of England and Wales*, 3: 1348-1500, Cambridge, 1991, p. 328.

Building materials of local origin, such as lime and bricks, were generally distributed via the urban markets, although a local landlord sometimes decided to have them produced on the spot.[65] Crafted products were not made exclusively in the city, as of course there were weavers, tailors, smiths and coopers in many villages. Not all primary materials were available on the spot, however, and for many standardised goods, as well as for high-quality products, the countrymen increasingly relied on urban craftsmanship. The degree of specialisation of the urban craftsmen was already very high in the late Middle Ages. Among many other professions in towns like Antwerp or Brussels in the fifteenth century, we find: weapon smiths, locksmiths, belt makers, spooners, bridle makers, knife makers, glove makers, saddlers, etc.[66] We have no documents concerning the provisions of common tenants, although the inventories of some farms do reveal a considerable number of industrial products.[67] Whether these products were all of urban origin is not sure, however. Explicit references to urban products and craftsmen do occur regularly in the accounts of rural manors or religious institutions, on the other hand. Metal wares were one type of product that was regularly purchased in town. The receiver of the Land of Grimbergen, for example, bought an iron hoop for the mill of Londerzeel in Mechelen, nails and a hammer in Brussels, and 400 lb. of lead in Antwerp.[68] Other products of craftsmanship that were bought at the urban market were either imported or the result of specialised artisans.

Urban craftsmen were employed in the countryside for technically complicated work, when the local know-how was thought to be insufficient. Local carpenters, smiths and other craftsmen were employed on such occasions for less specialised tasks. It is striking that landlords relied on expensive materials and specialists from the town especially for such technically complicated tasks as the repairing mills. High-quality millstones were imported from the quarries of Meyen in Germany and shipped down the Rhine, via Dordrecht, to Antwerp, which formed the major centre of distribution for the duchy of Brabant. It is not surprising, therefore, that such an "*Andernaersche*" millstone was almost worth its weight in gold. A pair of them cost about 22 Brabantine pounds, or 460 times a mason's daily wage! The traffic in these "precious stones" was considerable, throughout the ancien régime, as the hundreds of references in various different accounts prove.[69] Especially for luxury products for the wealthier part of the rural population, i.e. the nobility, the gentry or the clergy, urban craftsmen were employed. Seigniorial accounts show that noblemen relied on urban craftsmen for many specialised services.

Besides imported goods and craftsmanship, the town also offered other services to the countryside in exchange for its agrarian surplus. These can be summarised as administrative and judicial functions, as well as financial ones. Some aspects of these functions, i.e. the role of the (voluntary) jurisdiction of the urban aldermen, the institution of urban citizenship,

65 ARA, MW, I 796, account 1438/39.

66 See for example the lists of new citizens of Antwerp later in this chapter, which indicates their professions. For the professional structure of Mechelen, see e.g. R. van Uytven, "Sociaal economisch leven", p. 45-47.

67 On the 60-ha. farm of Boutersbrugge in Bogaarden, 20 km. southwest of Brussels, we find, among other goods: five harnesses, two carriages, two ploughs, two harrows, 100 lb. of tin pots, 100 lb. of pottery, 100 lb. of ironware, etc. J. Verbesselt, "Inboedel van het hof te Boutersbrugge in 1436, in *Eigen Schoon en de Brabander*, p. 450-451.

68 ARA, MW, I 796 accounts 1435/36, 1450/51, 1454/55.

69 M. Limberger, "De prijs van het water- en wegtransport in de vijftiende en zestiende eeuw. Het vervoer van molenstenen in de rekeningen van het hertogelijke domein Tervuren-Vilvoorde (1450-1572)" in *Het transport en het stedelijke netwerk in de Zuidelijke Nederlanden, Bijdragen tot de Geschiedenis,* 82 (1999), p. 215-234.

and the growing importance of constituted rents as a means of credit, will be treated in the following sections. For more exhaustive treatments of this topic, we refer to the existing literature.[70]

2.4 Urban Landownership

An important area of interaction between town and countryside involves the ownership of land outside the town by townsmen or urban institutions. Via leases, land rents and other payments, they received a large part of their incomes from these lands. A group of urban landowners that is difficult to identify in the rural sources are the urban citizens, ranging from the rich merchant down to the small craftsman. Their individual holdings were less impressive than those of the urban elites and often consisted of only a few plots of arable land or some meadows. Taken together, however, they formed a great part of the urban landed property in the countryside.

The holdings of Antwerp townsmen in the countryside around 1400 have been analysed in detail by F. de Nave.[71] In an exhaustive study of the landed property of Antwerp citizens between 1394-1402, she situated almost 4,000 rural holdings, including land, rents, tithes, seigniorial rights, etc. The goods were all situated within a radius of 35 km. This is a relatively great distance in comparison with other medieval towns. Leuven, for example, one the most important towns of Brabant at that time, only had landed property within a distance of 12 km, while for French towns like Arras or Toulouse, such properties were located within a radius of ca. 20 km. Nevertheless, more than 83% of the holdings of Antwerp citizens were situated within 13 km from the town (Map 4).[72] This pattern did not change fundamentally during the fifteenth century. In 1496, the farms of Antwerp citizens were still situated almost exclusively within the same distance.[73]

70 In particular, the Contributions to the fourth conference on the Brabantine towns, on the interactions between town and country between imperialisme and self-defence, "De Brabantse stad. Colloquium Brussel 29-30 maart 1974" in *Bijdragen tot de Geschiedenis* 58 (1975), pp. 5–166. For the role of the urban aldermen in the surrounding countryside: F.F.X. Cerutti, "De schepenbank in de Brabantse stad en de overdracht en bezwaring van onroerende goederen" in *De Brabantse stad. Tweede colloquium, 23-24 nov. 1968*, 's-Hertogenbosch, 1969, pp. 47–87.

71 F. de Nave, *Antwerpen, stad en land (1394-1402). De innerlijke vervlechting van stedelijk en landelijk milieu in de late middeleeuwen op basis van het privé bezit aan gronden en renten en andere soorten van goed, 5 vols.*, (unpublished thesis) Brussels, 1978.

72 De Nave, *Antwerpen*, pp. 315ff.

73 Cuvelier, *Dénombrements*, p. 498-532. See also: Limberger, „Feeding Sixteenth-Century Antwerp".

Map 4: Landed Property of Antwerp Citizens, 1394-1402

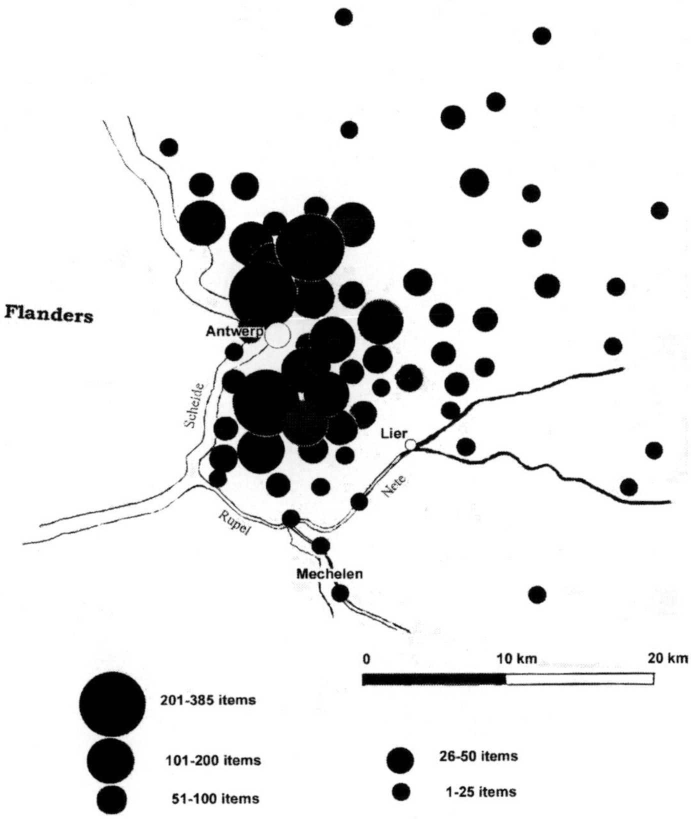

Source: De Nave, Antwerpen, stad en land, pp. 309–313.

More than 60% of the holdings of Antwerp citizens around 1400 consisted of landed property properly speaking, i.e. farms, houses, land, meadows, forests, woods, etc. The most frequent type of holding was a plot of farmland or a small to mid-sized farm of up to 10 hectares, the average size being 1-2 ha[74] (Table1). Annuities (renten) were a type of property that was already important in those days. They formed a very popular form of investment for townsmen, with a high degree of flexibility and security. For the owner of a plot of land, on the other hand, the sale of a rente formed a convenient possibility of obtaining credit against the payment of relatively low annuities. The inconvenience of annuities – for the debtor – was their originally perpetual character. In fact, only the yearly interest was paid, but nothing of the capital. By the fourteenth century, however, they had become re-buyable, which gave the debtor the chance of cancelling his debt.[75]

74 De Nave, *Antwerpen*, pp. 522ff.

75 Ph. Godding, *Le droit privé dans les Pays-Bas méridionaux du 12e au 18e siècle*, Bruxelles, 1987, p. 174.

Table 1: Rural Property Owned by Inhabitants of Antwerp, 1394-1402

Type of property	Number	%
Land, farms, houses etc.	2,318	60.7
Annuities	1,283	33.6
Hereditary leases (erfpacht)	159	4.16
Customary tenures (cijns)	19	0.5
Tithes	15	0.39
Seigniorial rights	6	0.157
Fishing rights	5	0.13
Fiefs (lenen)	3	0.078
Tolls, etc.	3	0.078
Feodal courts	2	0.052
Costumary-tenure courts	2	0.052
Incomes from jurisdiction	1	0.026

In comparison with these very frequent types of urban property, the others were relatively insignificant. Lands given out as hereditary leases and customary tenures were rather atypical in comparison with immediate landownership or leases. Tithes and seigniorial rights in the hands of urban citizens were also rather uncommon.[76]

The Antwerp townsmen obtained their landed property in different ways, most frequently by purchasing them. More than half (56.22%) of the holdings were acquired in this way. It is remarkable, however, that in most cases, these purchases concerned property situated within 8 km of the town. Properties located farther out were either inherited or acquired through marriage, if not already owned by immigrants who had moved to the city in the meantime.[77]

De Nave's study also provides some explanations in terms of the motives of townsmen to acquire landed property. First, landed property offered regular incomes. Direct exploitation of land by townsmen was common in the late Middle Ages. Many townsmen had small plots of land in the immediate surroundings of the town. This is also evident from the fact that urban legislation entitled citizens to leave the town for a period of 40 days at harvest time.[78] Indirect exploitation, i.e. via copyhold, hereditary lease or temporary lease, was more frequent, however. According to de Nave, the dues were payable in kind in more than 60% of the cases. Money rents were almost exclusively limited to the immediate surroundings.[79] This underlines the importance of landed property in the countryside as a means of immediate supply – mainly of food, but also of raw materials – which was not

76 De Nave, *Antwerpen* p. 330.
77 *Ibidem*, p. 384.
78 De Longé, *Ceurboek*.
79 De Nave, *Antwerpen*, p. 406, 427.

subject to price shifts. Therefore, the total area of landed property owned by urban citizens is a good indicator of the urban supply area, considering that citizens were likely to purchase land within the supply area of the town.[80] On the other hand, immovable goods formed a good investment, offering a high degree of security. In comparison, trade or crafts were more profitable, but offered only little security. Furthermore, landed property offered the possibility to obtain credit via the sale of rents. Landed property therefore began to form a common complement to trade and industrial activities as early as in the late Middle Ages.[81] Together with these economic motives, owning real estate also had social functions. Wealth consisting of landed property, or even seigniorial rights, was the major symbol of social status in late medieval society.[82]

For the rural population, the ownership of land by townsmen had different implications. First, the townsmen were competitors on the land market. Through their purchases, part of the land was put beyond the control of the village community and came into the hands of outsiders. Hence the land available for the rural population, which was already subject to intensive parcellation, diminished further. Once bought by a townsman, this land would only be available to the peasants via hereditary lease, or temporary lease, which meant a loss of property rights. On the other hand, the increasing frequency of transactions led to an opening of the land market. Land was bought and re-sold not only by townsmen, but also by local tenants. Real-estate transactions with townsmen also intensified the contacts between the peasants and the townspeople. The transactions were generally registered before the aldermen of the town, which meant that the peasants increasingly went to town to settle their affairs. The aldermen's deeds gave legal guarantees to the holder of a plot of land or a rent, which he always could claim in case of a conflict. *Schepenbrieven* from Brussels, for example, attracted contracting parties from all over Brabant, who went there "for more security". Even the local merchants profited from the attraction of the legal guarantees the town offered, since the visiting parties would buy their provisions from them.[83] The payment of leases or land rent, too, resulted in regular contacts with the urban market when the rents were delivered. A derivative effect of urban landed property was therefore an increase in the links between the urban market and the countryside.

Constituted rents were an ambiguous innovation for the tenants. On the one hand, they stimulated capital input and the availability of credit in the countryside, but on the other hand, they often were the first step toward the loss of property as a result of debt. It is striking to see how heavily mortgaged farms and plots of land already were in the fifteenth century. This leads us to the crucial question of whether the urban landowner was simply an economically passive *rentier* or if he invested in his possessions and tried to specialise production. Through lease contracts, the owner could steer not only the production on his farms, but also the techniques applied there. Yet he could also merely be content with the regular income from rents or leases without concerning himself with the production process.[84]

80 Van Uytven, "Approvisionnement", p. 95.

81 H. Soly, "The Betrayal" of the Sixteenth Century Bourgeoisie: A Myth? Some Considerations of the Behavior-Pattern of the Merchants of Antwerp in the Sixteenth Century" in *Acta Historiae Neerlandica* 18/1975, pp. 31–49.

82 Boone, "La terre, les hommes et les villes".

83 Ph. Godding, *Le droit foncier à Bruxelles au moyen âge*, Brussels, 1960, p. 273, and Idem, "Impérialisme urbain ou auto-défense: Le cas de Bruxelles (12e – 18e siècles)" in *Bijdragen tot de Geschiedenis*, 58 (1975), (De Brabantse stad. Colloquium Brussel 29. – 30. march 1974), p. 132.

84 For a further discussion, see: M. Limberger, "Credit, Land Market and the Connection between Rural and

2.5 The Flow of Migration from the Countryside to the Town

The influx of migrants was similar to the flow of goods from the countryside to the town. A mass of immigrants was actually needed to provide the towns with a labour force, because the natural reproductive potential of the urban population was not sufficient to replenish itself, and even less so to create demographic growth.[85] Especially in a region with such a high percentage of urban settings as Brabant, the urban population placed a heavy burden of replenishment on the relatively small rural sector.[86] Preindustrial society was highly mobile: 'Large numbers of people moved, repeatedly in search of spouses, work, skills, and sometimes religious freedom, physical security or sheer survival.'[87] Basically they moved from the countryside to the next town, but also from town to town. Many people from the highly populated countryside came to the town to make a living there, but there were also cases of people who left the towns to live in the countryside.[88] Besides the migrants who moved to the town for good, there was also short-term migration. This could be the case in times of war, or during a famine or an epidemic. On the other hand, there were seasonal migrants who came to town during the winter. The latter left hardly any traces in the records, however.

The lists of new citizens are a very useful resource for the study of the immigration into a particular town. They indicate the names of the new citizens, their places of origin, and their professions. Nevertheless, they contain only a fraction of the new immigrants, i.e. those who purchased the rights of urban citizenship. In contrast, citizens by birth, i.e. the legal children of citizens, were not included. While citizenship, or poorterij, as a right was not necessary in order to live in a town, it nevertheless offered a series of legal advantages and was required in order to exercise certain types of professions.[89] Furthermore, the new citizens were generally not newcomers, but those who decided to become citizens of a town only after some years of residence. As a result, the new citizens constituted a limited group of better-off immigrants, who succeeded in settling in the town and who could afford the price of registration. The masses of unskilled workers who moved into towns are therefore not included in the lists. If the lists of poorters cannot provide concrete quantitative data about the immigration into town, they still reflect the area from which the immigrants were recruited. Even so, the recruitment area of the new citizens was not identical with the total immigration area of a town. Skilled workers or members of a higher social rank would travel further to get to town than unskilled workers. Therefore, the new lists of poorters enable us to sketch the outer limits of a town's area of attraction, rather than its core area.

Urban Economy. The Use of Perpetual Annuities in Aartselaar (Brabant), 14th – 16th centuries" in T. Lambrecht and P. Schoffield, eds., *Credit and the Rural Economy in Europe, c.1100-c.1800.* (CORN Publication Series, forthcoming).

85 The pre-industrial cities showed a natural decrease since the mortality rate was higher than the birth rate. A discussion of the law of urban decrease can be found " in J. De Vries, *European Urbanization 1500 – 1800*, (London, 1984), pp. 179 –198.

86 Klep "Urban Decline", p. 276.

87 M.P. Gutmann, *War and Rural Life in the Early Modern Low Countries*, (Assen, 1980) (*Maaslandse monografien*, 31), p.133.

88 De Nave, *Antwerpen*.

89 For a critical analysis of the '*poortersboeken*' as source for immigration, see for example: C. Bruneel, "Bijdrage van de poortersboeken tot de historische demografie. Kritische bedenkingen bij het voorbeeld van Antwerpen" in *Gemeentekrediet van België. Driemaandelijks tijdschrift*, 44 (1990), pp. 101–110. Idem, "Les migrations entre ville et campagnes. L'exemple des pays-bas méridionaux" in *Le migrazioni in Europa secc. XIII-XVIII. Atti della "Venticinquesima Settimana di Studi" 3-8 maggio 1993*, Prato, 1994, p. 501-532; M. Carlier, "Migration trends in the towns of Flanders and Brabant (15th-18th century)", *ibidem*, pp. 355–370.

Apart from these structural problems, we are confronted with problems related to the incompleteness and the preservation of the sources. For Antwerp, two registers from the fifteenth century, covering the period between 1390 and 1443, have survived.[90] They contain the names of the new citizens, and in many cases their professions and places of origin. New citizens belonging to the nobility or the gentry were listed with the titles of lord, knight or squire. Furthermore, a new citizen had to have a guarantor, whose name was also indicated. Unfortunately, the occupations and places of origin were not systematically, but only partially included. A lack of clarity also exists in terms of the precise status of the new citizens. The documents do not distinguish between resident citizens (binnenpoorters) or external citizens (buitenpoorters). The former were obliged to reside in town during at least part of the year, whereas the external citizens could live outside the town without losing any of their rights as citizens.[91] This distinction is crucial, however, as we can only speak of immigrants in the first case.

The main recruitment area of new Antwerp citizens between 1409 and 1414 stretched ca. 40 km to the north and to the east of Antwerp. It is clearly limited by the rivers Scheldt and kleine Nete. 91.3% of the new citizens of Antwerp came from this area, which can be roughly defined as the Antwerp Kempen plus the polder area along the Scheldt. For the rural immigrants, the percentage coming from that area is even 96.4%. Only three new citizens came from places farther away than 50 km,[92] while three others originated from the left bank of the Scheldt, which belonged to the county of Flanders. Remarkably, however, the attraction of Antwerp was not strongest in places situated closest to the town. Most candidates came from places between 30 and 40 km from Antwerp (44%), whereas only 17% came from places closer than 10 km. Some larger places show a very high concentration of migrants, as for example Brecht and Rijkevorsel in the Kempen, with 17 and 20 new citizens respectively. This is due in part to the particularly large area of these villages, but perhaps also to the fact that we are dealing here with new citizens and not all the immigrants, as mentioned above.

Drawing conclusions about the professional profile of the new immigrants is a daring enterprise. The profile of the professions of the new citizens was not necessarily identical with that of the town in question. First, it only partially covers the professions of a town, namely those for which citizenship was necessary. Second, it includes only newcomers, albeit with some delay. This latter limitation, on the other hand, adds a dynamic character to the picture we obtain by analysing the lists. By listing the occupations of established immigrants in a town, they might indicate the expanding sectors, which were able to absorb new labour-force.

The construction and transport sectors were on top among the occupations of the new Antwerp citizens, for example. These were followed by crafts and cloth production. This fits very well with the established picture of fifteenth-century Antwerp as a growing commercial centre with a strong cloth-finishing industry. Luxury industries and money exchanging, sectors that would become so important in the sixteenth century, still seem to have been less

90 SAA, Vierschaar, no. 1980, Geberderd Daechceeelboeck de Anno 1389 tot 1414, (published " in F. de Nave, "De oudste Antwerpse lijsten lijsten van nieuwe poorters (28 januari 1390-28 december 1414) " in *Handelingen van de Koninklijke Commissie voor Geschiedenis,* 139 (1973), pp. 67–309), and no. 1981, Geberderd Daechceeelboeck 1414-[1443], fos. 133-179 v°.

91 De Nave, "Oudste lijsten", Introduction, p. 74-80.

92 From Boxtel and Hilvarenbeek (near 's Hertogenbosch) and Retie.

important (Table 2). The ducal residence Brussels offers a totally different profile: 24% of the new citizens there were active in the luxury industries, followed by the food and clothing sectors, which still cover more than 20%, and crafts (14%).[93] The administrative functions of the rising capital were also directly reflected by the registration of two secretaries and a clerk. The immigration areas of Brussels and the other Brabantine towns therefore seem to have been complementary: Brussels attracted especially highly qualified artisans, whereas boatsmen preferred to go to Antwerp and Mechelen. For brewers or bakers, who seem to have been in equal demand in all three towns, the closest town was probably the most obvious place to go. The specific conditions of one's place of origin were also of some importance. Boatsmen generally came from places along navigable rivers with something of a shipping tradition, for example, while woodcutters came from more or less wooded areas and weavers probably came from areas where weaving was a common activity.

Table 2: Professional Profile of Antwerp's New Citizens, 1409-1414

Category	Number	%
Construction	45	18.9%
Transport	36	15.1%
Crafts		14.0%
Metal	14	(6%)
Leather	10	(4%)
Wood	5	(2%)
Others	4	(2%)
Cloth production	32	13.4%
Food	22	9.2%
Clothing	19	8.0%
Commerce	16	6.7%
Agriculture and fishing	13	5.5%
Luxury industry	12	5.0%
Health care	5	2.1%
Church, nobility, etc.	3	1.3%
Others	3	1.3%
Administration	2	0.8%
Military sector	1	0.4%
Total	**238**	**100%**

93 The percentages do not include the noblemen and illegitimate sons, who comprised more than 50%.

In the absence of sources covering the totality of the phenomenon of migration from the country to the town, we are confined to the conclusions that can be deduced from the lists of new citizens. Antwerp attracted rural immigrants from a well-defined sphere of influence of some 50 km. Most of them came from within the duchy of Brabant, however. The immigrants who finally established themselves in their new homes had a wide variety of occupations, depending in part on the specific economic structure of the town of destination, but also on their local backgrounds. The growing towns absorbed these newcomers, who formed a necessary source of labour. For the people of the country, the towns provided good opportunities for employment and an alternative to the agricultural or industrial activities of their place of origin.

2.6 Conclusion

This rough account of the interaction between the rural and urban economies shows that the Brabantine countryside was strongly oriented towards the urban market. Peasants came to town both to pay their land rent and to sell their agricultural surplus. In exchange, they bought urban and imported products for their farms and for personal use. Peasants also came to town in order to work there, either temporarily or for good. Here, too, there was a (quantitatively limited) movement in the opposite direction, in form of urban specialists going to work in the countryside. There was also a close interaction as far as real estate was concerned. Townsmen bought land in the surrounding countryside, providing capital in exchange. This was not only the case for investments in farms or in drainage, but also in the form of credits, as shown by the fact that many townsmen bought annuities on rural property. If we have characterised the rural economy of western Brabant as a peasant economy with a feudal framework, we still need to reiterate that it is a peasant economy with strong market ties. Surplus from the surrounding countryside is a prerequisite for the rise of large urban centres.

The fact that western Brabant could afford a dense urban network with three very large towns within a radius of less than fifty kilometres was only possible on the basis of a massive rural surplus of food, fuel, building materials and of labour, although in fifteenth century the urban demand exceeded the local production. These rural surpluses were directed towards the town not only by economic means. To ensure their physical survival, the towns had to include their surroundings within their juridical and fiscal market area. F. Braudel describes this situation as follows: 'No town that does not impose upon its hinterland the amenities of its market, the use of its shops, its weights and measures, its moneylenders, its lawyers, even its distractions. It has to dominate an empire, however tiny, in order to exist'.[94] Nevertheless, the dependency between town and countryside in Brabant was mutual, and except for the payments of rents and leases, the towns stimulated the peasants to go to the market rather than obliging them to do so.[95]

94 F. Braudel, *Civilization and Capitalism 15th – 18th Century, vol. I, The Structures of Everyday Life. The Limits of the Possible* (London, 1981), p. 481f.

95 Recently, the voluntary character of market involvement has been increasingly stressed. Peasants had an interest in taking the opportunities that the market offered them. Hodges, *Primitive,* p. 14f.

CHAPTER 3

Demographic Changes (1437–1570)

An initial indicator for possible influences of the growth of Antwerp on its rural surroundings is the demographic structure of the area. Important changes in the population density near Antwerp can indicate the nature of the urban influence. Population levels, along with population movements, lie at the very centre of any agrarian economy.[1] An increase in population in a rural economy is likely to coincide with economic growth, while sharp drops in population are indications of unfavourable circumstances.[2] Therefore, by improving the economic opportunities in the area in question, the town contributed at the same time to a rise in population. This could be either by stimulating labour-intensive agriculture or by offering alternative sources of employment, such as any number of proto-industrial activities.[3] On the other hand, the local centre absorbed a considerable part of the rural population surplus via emigration and could therefore also contribute to a stagnation or even decline in population.

Hence, by measuring changes in population density in the countryside near Antwerp, we can detect economic transformations and their geographic dimensions. Demography is only a rough indicator, however. It does not give any qualitative explanation for the nature of the economic changes taking place but simply indicates their possible presence. Of course, other factors of demographic change also have to be taken into consideration. In particular, demographic decline on a local or regional level could be caused by a variety of factors, ranging from war to epidemics or natural catastrophes.

We will be approaching the demographic development in two different ways. First, an overview of the structures of settlement in 1437 will situate the Antwerp area within a European context in general and the southern Low Countries in particular. Moreover, it will show the internal differences within the area under consideration. In that way, the economic significance of the geographical features and the internal structure of the Antwerp area will become visible. The longitudinal study will then focus on the demographic changes the area underwent during the fifteenth and sixteenth centuries and on its relation with Antwerp. By means of a series of household censuses dating from the period 1437–1526, the evolution of the population of the Antwerp countryside can be analysed on the village level, and in comparison with that of the duchy of Brabant in general. During this period, Brabant witnessed a serious decline of its population due to a combination of war, plague and economic crises.[4] It is crucial to see how the environs of Antwerp were affected by this

1 P. Musgrave, *Land and Economy in Baroque Italy. Valpolicella, 1630-1797*, Leicester, 1992, p. 48.

2 See for example: Kriedte, *Spätfeudalismus und Handelskapital*, p. 12-13. This positive relation between population and economic growth is not necessary, however. Population may continue to grow even if the economic basis becomes weaker.

3 Klep, *Bevolking, p. 38*-39 sees a direct relationship between population density and the predominant economic activity in an area. As an example, he mentions the demographic impact of proto-industrialisation in the county of Flanders.

4 See below.

crisis and how quickly they recovered from it in comparison with other parts of the duchy. In the context of our study, the evolution during the period after 1526 is also highly interesting. In 1526, Antwerp was still in the first phase of its economic rise, the peak of which was only reached in the 1560s.

To make a full assessment of the demographic consequences of the growth of Antwerp, figures for the second half of the century, shortly before the beginning of the Revolt, are necessary. Unfortunately, the demographic evidence for the second half of the century is much less reliable than the household censuses of the fifteenth and early sixteenth centuries.[5] We will have to rely on dispersed data, including numbers of communicants and declarations concerning the local situation but without the uniform overview as provided by the censuses or *dénombrements*.

3.1 The Patterns of Settlement in Western Brabant in 1437

The Low Countries, and the southern provinces in particular, were among the most densely populated areas of late medieval Europe, comparable only with northern and central Italy, and the Île-de-France.[6] Indeed, the maximum figures for Flanders in the fourteenth century reach up to 78 persons per square kilometre.[7] The Netherlands were not a homogenous area with equal population development, however. Rather, according to Blockmans, et al., there were three zones, forming concentric circles – depending on their distance from the sea and the estuaries of the big rivers. The duchy of Brabant belonged to the second zone, together with Hainaut, northern Holland, Liège and Namur, without however achieving the same level of population density as southern Holland and Flanders.[8] A major reason for Brabant's apparent lag in this regard has to be sought in the low degree of settlement, as well as of urbanisation, in the northern part of the duchy. This distinction between a sparsely populated northern part and a highly populated and urbanised southern part is a significant feature of the Brabantine geography and has already been discussed by Joseph Cuvelier in his 1912 edition of the Brabantine household counts.[9]

This pattern is also confirmed by a comparison of the size of communities.[10] The distance between village centres provides an initial indication of settlement in an area. The average community size in the districts of Brussels and Leuven, in the south of the duchy, was 9 and 7.7 km^2 respectively. In the northern districts Antwerp and s'-Hertogenbosch, communities tended to be much larger, i.e. 21 and 24 km^2, respectively.[11] This implies that the villages there were in very close proximity to each other (ca. 2–3 km in southern Brabant), whereas in the north, the distance between two neighbouring villages could be as much as 7 to 10 km.

5 See for example: Klep, *Bevolking*, pp. 31f.

6 For the latter, see : G. Fourquin, "La population de la région parisienne aux environs de 1328" in *Le Moyen Age*, 1956, 1-2, pp. 63–91 and Idem, *Campagnes*, p. 11.

7 W. P. Blockmans, "Die Niederlande vor und nach 1400. Eine Gesellschaft in der Krise? " in F. Seibt, ed., *Europa 1400. Die Krise des Spätmittelalters*, Stuttgart, 1984, p. 119.

8 Blockmans, Pieters et al., "Crisis en welvaart", p. 45f.

9 Cuvelier, *Dénombrements*, p. IX-X.

10 The size of the communities in the late nineteenth century as mentioned by Cuvelier, *Dénombrements*, pp. 432–487, is closer to the historical reality than the modern communities, which have been subject to fusions.

11 Cuvelier, *Dénombrements*, p. 432-483.

3.1.1 The Brabantine Household Censuses

The Brabantine household counts, or *dénombrements*, contain not only global values that confirm the rather obvious differences between the north and the south of the duchy of Brabant, but also much more detailed information. As the major base of fifteenth- and early sixteenth-century ducal taxation, they contain precise information on every Brabantine village for seven distinct years between 1437 and 1526.[12] Joseph Cuvelier's collection and thorough edition of these counts from different fiscal documents, published in 1912, have made the *dénombrements* a precious source for the study of Brabant, probably one of the most important for the fifteenth century. The figures have been used by many local historians writing the history of their village or town, while for researchers specialised in historical demography they have provided an irresistible challenge.[13] Cuvelier recognised the usefulness of the fiscal counts as a source of proto-demography, as it were, relating to a period for which other demographic sources are scarce. With an eye to reconstructing the movements of the Brabantine population between 1437 and 1526, he analyses each census in detail, providing not only its fiscal but also its political and social background.

The Brabantine *dénombrements* first came into being around 1437, when Philip the Good introduced a system for distributing of the tax-burden based on the number of households. This system was the common form of direct state taxation in the fourteenth and fifteenth centuries in the Low Countries but also in other Western European countries.[14] The States of Brabant had conceded taxes in form of *beden* (aids) to the duke before 1437, but only then was the number of houses seen as the most fitting way to distribute the payments among the towns and rural communities of the duchy. We have the data of a census from 1374, for example, which is based on 'taxed' individuals, however without defining precisely who exactly was included in this taxation. In contrast, the household censuses formed a primitive form of census based on 'hearths' or 'households', rather than on individuals or taxable persons. In contrast with other areas, where households were a rather artificial key of distribution, the Brabant household counts were actual censuses of real households.[15] There are explicit texts which show that the term hearth can be equated with 'house' in Brabant and that, for the Brabantine countryside, 'house' is equivalent to 'household', considering the negligibly low proportion of houses that included more than one household.[16] It was the ducal administration itself that raised the question of a distinction in 1491: "If there were several households in one house, they should be counted separately".[17] Even if we

---

12 For an evaluation of this source, see also: M.A. Arnould, *Les relevés de feux* (Typologie des sources du Moyen Âge occidental, 18, A-IV.1), Turnhout, 1976.

13 This can be illustrated by a series of articles by P.M.M. Klep. See for example: 'Urbanization in a Pre- Industrial Economy. The Case of Brabant, 1374 –1930'" in *Belgisch Tijdschrift voor Nieuwste Geschiedenis*, 7 (1976), p. 153–168; Idem, "Regional disparities in Brabantine Urbanization before and after the Industrial Revolution 1374-1970. Some aspects of measurement and explanation" in P. Bairoch, M. Lévy Leboyer (eds.), *Disparities of Economic Development since the Industrial Revolution*, London, 1981, p. 259–269. Idem, "Urban Decline",

14 Cf. A. Zoete, *De beden in het graafschap Vlaanderen onder de hertogen Jan zonder Vrees en Filips de Goede (1405-1467)* (Verhandelingen KAWLsK, Klasse der Letteren 56 (1994), 149), Brussel, 1994, pp.31–36.

15 Cuvelier, *Dénombrements* p. L; see also: J. C. Russel, "Population in Europe 500-1500" (C.M. Cipolla, ed., *The Fontana Economic History of Europe*, vol I, chapter 1), London, Glasgow, 1971, pp. 7f.

16 Very detailed figures of the number of houses with more than one household in 1496 are presented in Cuvelier, *Dénombrements*, pp. 255–261.

17 *"Item, of t' gebeurde dat bevonden worden bynnen eenre wooningen oft bijvange diversche luyden wonende, houdende verscheyden huysraden ende hertsteden, sullen dieselve viersteden getelt worden elc besunder."* 29 Dec. 1491, cited in Cuvelier,

do not have any similar documents for the period before 1491, those texts that explicitly concern the problem of houses inhabited by more than one family point in the same direction. The distinction would not have caused any problem, if 'hearth' had meant 'family' per definition, rather than house. The organisation of these censuses was a very costly and complicated enterprise, but since they were the most precise key of taxation available, they were undertaken with extreme care. Although the inhabitants of the villages had the right to protest in the event that the results did not conform with the real number of houses, and also had a strong interest in interfering, there were only few claims against the results of the counts. This can be seen as another proof of the reliability of the census.[18]

Being the first census of its kind in the duchy of Brabant, the *dénombrement* of 1437 was carried out with much care by the appointed officers. Later counts, such as those of 1464 or 1472, are less complete and are consequently not as useful sources for a demographic overview. The census of 1437 not only included the number of houses, but also made a distinction between the total number of the inhabited houses and the houses of the poor, i.e. of the people who received assistance through poor relief, the so-called Tables of the Holy Spirit. The total tax burden per village was calculated on the basis of the total number of households, with a 20% reduction for the poor hearths, a percentage that came quite near to the real average percentage of 23.4%.[19] It is nevertheless interesting that the poor households were counted in each village, even though they did not serve as a basis for the calculation of the tax. The real numbers were only relevant for the internal distribution within the village. As a matter of fact, only the 'wealthy' families – i.e. those families that did not receive any assistance from poor relief – had to contribute, but then on the basis of the total number of households, as mentioned above, that is for the whole of the village community.[20]

3.1.2 The Towns

Some of the Brabantine towns had attained a considerable population by 1437. Brussels was at the top of the urban hierarchy, being the main residence of the dukes of Brabant and the seat of the court, as well as of the ducal administration.[21] Brussels had 6,376 households or ca. 33,000 inhabitants in 1437, which made it one of the largest towns in northwestern Europe at that time.[22] The second largest town was Mechelen, which was legally no part of Brabant but rather an enclave within Brabantine territory, with about 21,000 inhabitants.[23] Antwerp had only 3,579 households, which would result in a population of ca. 17,000 inhabitants. P. Klep estimates the population to have been about 20,000, however.[24] The other two capital cities were Leuven and 's-Hertogenbosch. Leuven, which had ca. 19,000 inhabitants, lay about 15 km east of Brussels and formed the centre of

Dénombrements, p. LXI.

18 *Ibidem*, p. LIX.

19 *Ibidem*, p. CXII.

20 *Ibidem*, p. XLIX.

21 The role of the first town of the duchy had already shifted from Leuven to Brussels during the fourteenth century. See J. Baerten, "Brussel, hoofdstad van een hertogdom: politieke en economische aspecten" in J.Stengers, ed., *Brussel, Groei van een hoofdstad*, Antwerpen, 1979, p. 56.

22 Cuvelier, *Dénombrements*, p. 446.

23 Klep, *Bevolking*, p. 354.

24 Cuvelier, *Dénombrements*, p. 462; Klep, *Bevolking,*, p. 354.

the ancient Brabantine core area.[25] It was surrounded by a group of secondary towns, such as Diest, Tienen, Zoutleeuw and Aarschot. 's-Hertogenbosch, with ca. 13,000 inhabitants, was a frontier town in the northeastern part of the duchy, near the river Meuse.[26]

Among the smaller towns, Diest and Tienen, situated in the district of Leuven, were the largest, with ca. 10,000 and 7,000 inhabitants, respectively.[27] In the district of Antwerp, Lier was the largest secondary town, with 1,550 households or ca. 6,000 inhabitants, followed by Bergen op Zoom (5,500 inh.), Breda (5000 inh.), Herentals (5000 inh.) and Turnhout (ca. 4,500 inh.).[28]

With Antwerp and Mechelen, two towns of similar size were situated quite close to each other. In the late fourteenth century, Antwerp was still the smaller of the two, with only 7000 inhabitants compared to Mechelen's 13,000. But within several decades, Antwerp almost tripled its population, whereas Mechelen had 'only' grown by 54%. With Lier, another town of considerable size was situated within the short distance of just over 10 km. The other towns in the Antwerp district were all more than 30 km away from Antwerp. The two major centres of the western Kempen, Turnhout and Herentals, were rather small and could hardly be considered towns at all, but rather central villages.[29]

3.1.3 The Patterns of Settlement in the Countryside

For a study of rural settlement it is insufficient to compare the absolute number of inhabitants per village. The community areas generally differed considerably from village to village, and in many cases the number of inhabitants was due to the geographical extension of the village rather than to the concentration of people within it. Consequently, we have to estimate the population density, or rather the household density per village. In its totality, the duchy of Brabant had a density of 27.3 inhabitants per square kilometre in 1437, which was considerably lower than that in Flanders (44.9 inh. / km^2) and Holland (47 inh. / km^2).[30] In his general demographic survey of the Low Countries, De Vries makes a distinction between the northern districts of Antwerp and 's-Hertogenbosch, which had very low figures, and the two southern districts of Brussels and Leuven, which had a very high population density. Thus, in his demographic map of the Low Countries around 1500 (Map 5), he shows that the southern part of the duchy comes very near to the figures of Flanders and that there is a sharp gap towards the northern part of the duchy, the latter being among the least populated areas of the Low Countries as a whole.[31]

25 Cuvelier, *Dénombrements*, p.432.
26 *Ibidem*, p. 475.
27 *Ibidem*, pp. 434, 436.
28 *Ibidem*, pp. 462, 470, 472.
29 Van Uytven, "Centrale plaatsen", pp. 58–59.
30 Blockmans, Pieters et al., "Crisis en welvaart", p. 46.
31 De Vries, *Dutch Rural Economy*, p. 83.

Map 5: Rural Population Densities in the Burgundian Netherlands, ca. 1500

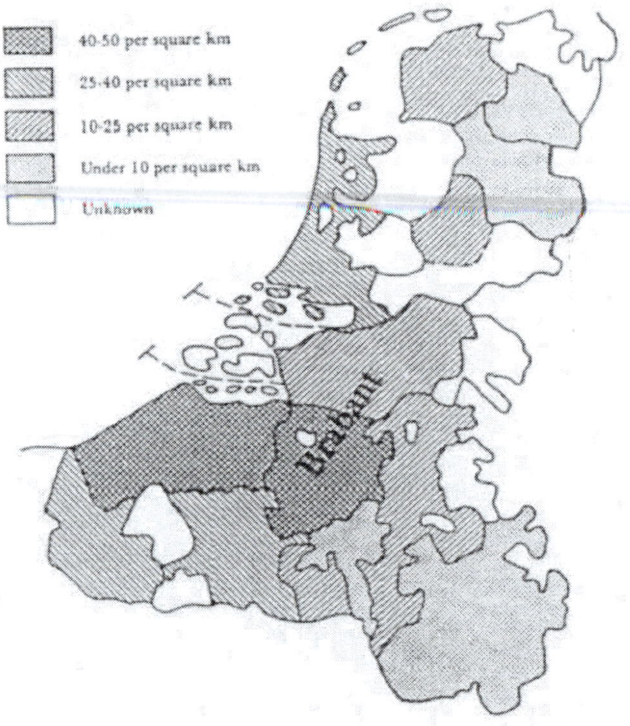

From: De Vries, *Dutch rural economy*, p. 83.

Aside from some local studies concerning only one or very few villages,[32] the most detailed analysis of the *dénombrements* was done by N.G. Pounds, who drew up a demographic map of the southern Low Countries and northern France in the mid-fifteenth century (Map 6).[33] He discovered that the population density was highest within a belt between Picardy and southern Brabant, with more than 40 persons per square kilometre. The area between Brussels and Liège, in particular, was very densely settled and was equalled only by two other areas in Europe, namely, Picardy and Artois, and perhaps Tuscany.[34] On Pounds' map, southern Brabant indeed shows higher values than Flanders.

32 See, for example: A. Bousse, *Geschiedenis van Schilde. Van heidenschommig dorp tot woonforensengemeente*. Schilde, 1983. J.B. Stockmans, *Geschiedenis van de gemeente Berchem*, Brussel, 1975² (orig. 1886). Van Passen, *Geschiedenis van Edegem*; Idem, *Geschiedenis van Kontich*; or Idem, *Geschiedenis van Wilrijk*, Wilrijk, 1982. An exception to this is F. Nooyens, *Geschiedenis van Deurne I (tot 1648)*, Deurne, 1981, who calculated the population density of the whole district of Antwerp for 1464.

33 Pounds, "Population", p.401, Fig. 8.

34 Ibid., p. 386f.

Map 6: Population Map of the Southern Low Countries and Northern France in the Mid-Fifteenth Century

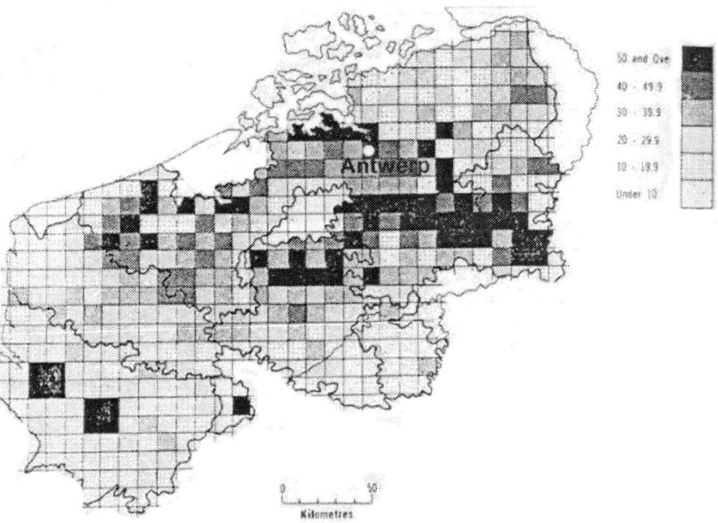

From: Pounds, "Population", p. 400.

To obtain figures for the Antwerp area that are more precise than the rather general results cited above, I have mapped out the household density of 58 communities of the district of Antwerp that lay within 25–30 kilometres from the city. This entailed a number of methodological problems. We have no certainty regarding the exact dimensions of the fiscal villages referred to in the tax lists. As a basis for the calculation of the village area, I therefore used the community areas from the nineteenth century, as cited in Cuvelier's study. These numbers refer to the old communities before the reorganisations that took place in the twentieth century. They are generally closer to the situation of the fifteenth and sixteenth centuries than the modern data.[35] In spite of these deviations, there is a strong continuity as to the names and limits of the villages. Almost all the villages cited in the *dénombrements* still existed in the nineteenth century, and all can be situated quite clearly. In order to be able to use the community areas with a geographical database, I tried to reconstruct the corresponding nineteenth-century areas on a digitised map.[36] This method may have its imperfections and may give deviating results in some individual cases. Within very close distances, there can be extreme differences in the population density of adjoining villages. These irregularities are due in part to the extreme differences in the

35 Instead of community areas, some authors, including Van der Woude, prefer using the areas of cultivated land per village. This method has the advantage that it directly reflects the agrarian land - labour ratio. However, the absence of sources indicating the cultivated area in the fifteenth and sixteenth centuries prevented me from using this method. See: A. van der Woude, "Demografische ontwikkeling van de noordelijke Nederlanden, 1500-1800", in *Algemene Geschiedenis van de Nederlanden* 5, Haarlem 1980, pp. 126–128. See also: B. van Bavel, *Transitie en continuïteit*, p. 77.

36 This work was carried out in autumn 1993 at the Computer Laboratory of the European University Institute, with the program Atlas-Gis. The digitised map of the Belgian communities (A historical GIS for the Belgian territorial structure 1800-2000: http://www.flwi.ugent.be/hisgis/) was not available at that time.

size of communities, especially in the southern part of the duchy. A village with very small territory may have had a higher density than a larger village because of the relative preponderance of its village centre. The number of villages in the sample compensates for this methodological weakness, however, and allows us to see general trends for each area, even if the values for individual places must be treated with care. The method of using rectangular cells like Pounds' has the advantage of being indifferent to these deviating frontiers. On the other hand, by using a strong focus, as in our case, the projection of one village in one cell or another would result in the same imprecise result as we would obtain by using the modern village areas.

3.1.4 The Household Density in the Surroundings of Antwerp

Map 7 provides a general survey of the household density per square kilometre in the western part of the district of Antwerp. The focus chosen is relatively broad in order to determine the existence or non-existence of structural differences that could help to delimit the immediate area of influence of Antwerp. Going from north to south, one should first note the low population density of the communities north of Antwerp with their vast extensions. Many of these communities do not achieve a density above five houses per square kilometre. Here, the main Brabantine break-line, as indicated by Cuvelier and De Vries, is visible. These low figures are due to geographical features: as described at the beginning of this chapter, the Kempen region had probably the most unfavourable natural preconditions for settlement within Brabant.

Map 7: Household Density in Western Brabant, 1437
(households per square kilometre)

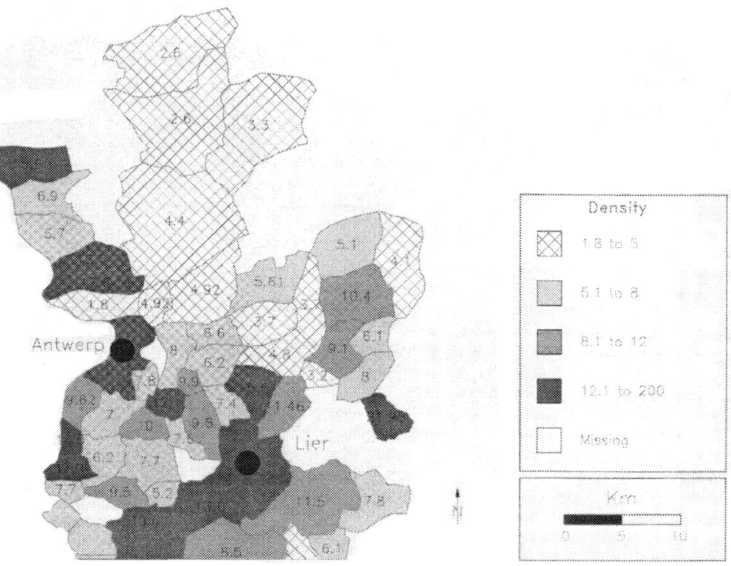

Source: Cuvelier, *Dénombrements*, pp. 432–483.

The most obvious exception to this pattern are the communities along the Scheldt (on the western edge), which attained much higher figures than the neighbouring communities farther inland. The population density of some polder villages reaches values of 15.9 (Zandvliet) and even 17.6 (Wilmarsdonk) houses per square kilometre. The significant differences among these polder villages may be due to the unclear frontiers between them. Thus, the average value of ca. 10 houses per square kilometre is probably more appropriate here than the strongly contrasting values that figure on the map. As in the case of the Kempen, this strong settlement can be explained to a great extent by natural features. The polders along the Scheldt were both more fertile than the latter and better situated in terms of transport.

South of Antwerp, the average density of settlement was considerably higher than to the north. There were internal differences, however, i.e. relatively low figures (5–8 h. / km^2) within 10 km around Antwerp and a homogeneously densely settled area north of Mechelen. The latter area, situated along the major Brabantine inland rivers Rupel, Dijle and Nete, was not known for having exceptionally fertile soil, but nevertheless witnessed intensive economic activity, also in non-agrarian sectors. Its favourable position along the major inland rivers and the frequent traffic there may have played a decisive role in this case. This is confirmed by the fact that south of Antwerp, the villages situated directly along the river Scheldt also had a higher density of settlement than places further east.

The major internal differences in the patterns of settlement were directly or indirectly linked with natural conditions, such as the fertility of the soil or the proximity of a river. Besides the quality of the soil, navigable rivers also had a remarkable impact on the patterns of settlement. The places along the rivers Scheldt, Rupel and Nete formed a corridor of dense settlement. This may be due in part to the higher level of fertility of the soil near the rivers, but also to transport factors. In fact, population density also tended to be higher along some important roads than at places farther off. We can observe this phenomenon for example in the villages along the road between Antwerp and Lier. In contrast, Antwerp did not yet have a strong impact on the density of settlement in its immediate surroundings, that is to say in the villages within a radius of five or ten kilometres. The whole research area is, of course, an urban area. Within its limits, however, the impact of rivers and other major transport routes was stronger than that of the distance from the city. The late medieval city apparently did not yet influence the surrounding villages to the same degree that it did from the sixteenth century on.

3.1.5 The Social Dimension: The Percentage of Poor Households

The social definition of poverty in the late Middle Ages is obviously difficult to determine. It could range from people living at the minimum level of biological subsistence on the one hand to people with no land or other taxable property on the other. Blockmans and Prevenier attempted to answer this question on the basis of sixteenth-century surveys of the Lille area, which give the size of the landed property of each inhabitant of a village. In the village of Capinghem, the boundary between the smallest taxed holding and the largest untaxed was around 38 are. This is a vague estimate, however. Examining other villages, or using different criteria, such as the yearly rent or the value of the landed property, will yield quite different results. Therefore, this estimate can only serve to give a global idea about the relation between landed property and the degree of poverty.[37]

The poor households indicated in the census of 1437 refer to those families who were considered poor by the local authorities and hence received poor relief. Although the criteria applied to define the poor could differ from village to village – also depending on the potential of the community to sustain the poor – these numbers allow a survey of the degree of poverty in Brabant in general and in the environs of Antwerp in particular.

According to the 1437 census, the total poverty rate in Brabant that year was 23.4%. This means that about every fourth household was sustained by poor relief. The poverty rate was lower in the towns than in the countryside and tended to be even a bit lower in small towns than in the four capital cities Brussels, Antwerp, Leuven, and 's-Hertogenbosch. The degree of poverty differed strongly between the districts of the duchy, however: the poverty rate was the lowest in the Antwerp district with 18.3%. The figures for the districts of Leuven and Brussels, in the south of the duchy, were slightly higher, with 24.4 and 24.2% respectively. In contrast, the district of Den Bosch had a much higher rate of poor hearths (29.4%) than the southern part, as a result of a severe famine that had hit the area in 1437.[38]

A closer analysis of urban and rural poverty rates shows significant structural differences within Brabant. The rate of poor households in the towns was similar throughout the duchy and lay between 7.6 and 13.5%.[39] In the countryside, the differences between the districts were remarkably large, with the highest figures being found in the Walloon part of the duchy, within the rural districts of Leuven (56%) and Brussels (41.5%). It was also high in the Flemish part of the district of Leuven (33.9%) and in the district of 's-Hertogenbosch (35.8%). The rural district of Antwerp displayed the lowest figures (20.7%), followed by the Flemish part of the district of Brussels (26.4%).[40]

The local differences in the poverty rate can be explained in various ways. The first explanation is methodological and refers to the different criteria used in each village to define the poor. Poor tables could work in very different ways in different communities or towns, and they may have had quite different means too. Some may have adopted more severe criteria for accepting people, while others may have had a more open policy. This argument is of secondary importance as long as we analyse a larger area with a sufficiently high number of villages, in order to establish a reliable average value. In the following section, I will nevertheless focus on the local level in order to find out if considerable differences of poverty rates within the surroundings of Antwerp can be detected.

A survey of the percentage of poor households in the villages of the research area can be seen on Map 8. In the Kempen area, the poverty rate was generally high (> 25%), and in some places even very high (> 33%).[41] In contrast, remarkably low figures were registered

37 W.P. Blockmans and W. Prevenier, "Armoede in de Nederlanden van de 14de tot het midden van de 16de eeuw: bronnen en problemen" in H.F.J.M. van den Eerenbeemt, P.C. Jansen, R. van Uytven eds., *Armoede en armenzorg, Tijdschrift voor Geschiedenis,* 88 (1975), p. 510.

38 Blockmans and Prevenier, "Armoede" p. 517; The census of the district of 's-Hertogenbosch took place between November of 1438 and January of 1439, i.e. shortly after the famine. Cuvelier, *Dénombrements*, p. CVII-CIX.

39 Only the small towns of the district of 's-Hertogenbosch had a higher poverty rate. Being rather large villages instead of actual towns, they displayed a more rural pattern than an urban one. But the high percentage of poor hearths was also the result of the famine of 1437.

40 Blockmans and Prevenier, "Armoede", p. 517.

41 Ekeren-Kapellen-Brasschaat: 34.3 %, Brecht: 36.7%, Westmalle-Zoersel: 35.4%, Zandhoven: 33.3%.

in the villages to the southeast of Antwerp – in the direction of the towns of Lier and Mechelen. Here, the average percentage of poor households was as low as 9.2%. The villages along the Scheldt showed higher poverty figures than the neighbouring inland villages. The low figures between Antwerp, Lier and Mechelen are exceptional and can be explained by various factors. First, we have seen that this area had particularly favourable topographical features. It forms a small island of exceptionally fertile soil. Second, its location between three big towns, together with a good transport network, is very likely to have favoured the area economically. We will focus on this area in our analysis of the economic impact of Antwerp in order to see what made the economic situation there so special.

MAP 8: Percentage of Poor Households in Western Brabant, 1437

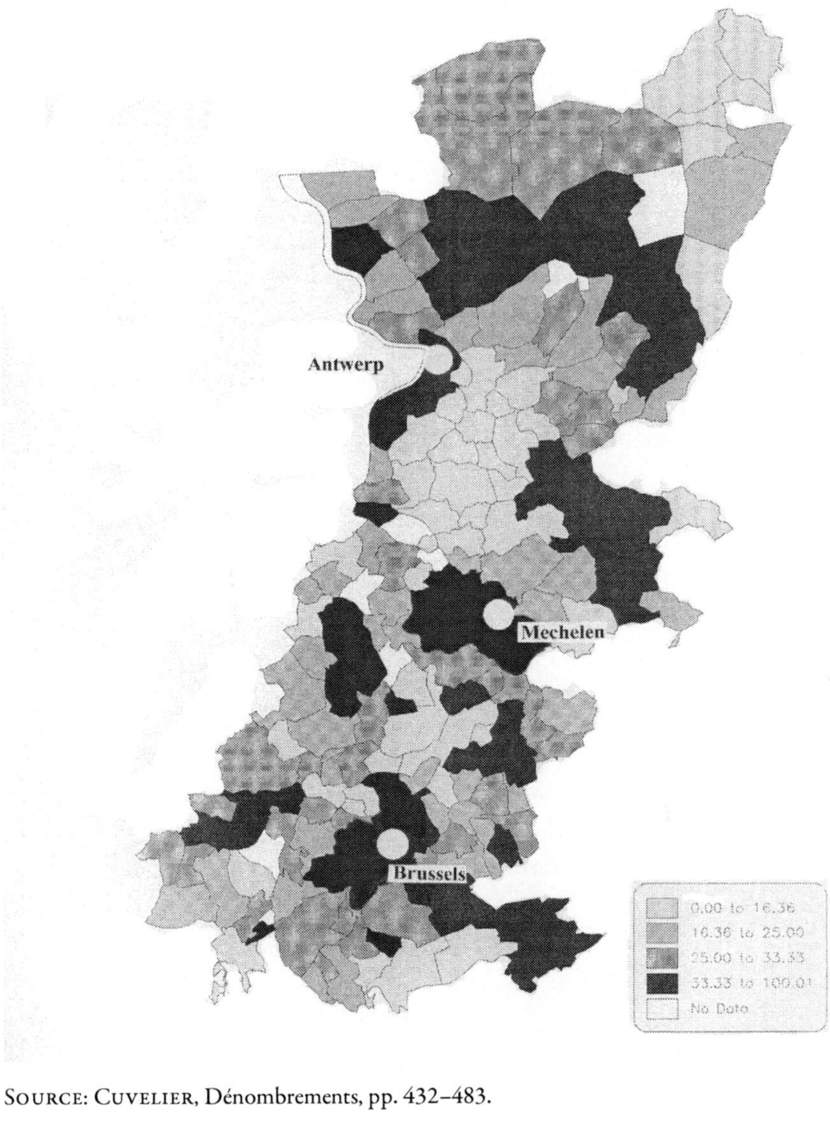

SOURCE: CUVELIER, Dénombrements, pp. 432–483.

3.2 Demographic Changes between 1437 and 1570

Between 1437 and the end of the sixteenth century, the demographic structure of Brabant underwent significant changes. The most dramatic moments in this development were the deep population crises of the seventies and eighties of the fifteenth century and of the last decades of the sixteenth century. While the first crisis was caused by multiple factors, among which plague, famine and civil war, the second was mainly a result of military destruction. In contrast, the period between these two crises, i.e. from ca. 1492 to ca. 1575, was marked by a recovery and even growth in the population.

3.2.1 The Demographic Crisis of the Late Fifteenth Century

The period after the death of Philip the Good, and especially the years between 1480 and 1492, was characterised by a number of subsequent wars that caused severe damage, especially in the countryside. The wars between France and Charles the Bold, and later Maximilian of Habsburg, the civil wars in Liège, as well as in Flanders and Brabant, and repeated years of plague and famine had caused a deep economic and demographic decline.[42] The number of households in Brabant decreased from ca. 92,000 in 1464 to 75,000 in 1496. That is a loss of almost 20%.[43] There was however a big difference in the development between the southern part of the duchy and the north. The whole of the duchy witnessed a significant drop in the population between 1464 and 1472. While the districts of Leuven and Brussels were suffering the worst losses in population between 1480 and 1492 due to the civil war against Maximilian of Habsburg, the district of Antwerp was not immediately affected and even witnessed a slight population growth during the same period. This recovery, however, was limited to the towns, and especially Antwerp itself, which grew strongly during that period. The rural population of the district, on the other hand, still diminished until 1496, although not as sharply as in the south of the duchy.

Antwerp, which was still the third town in western Brabant in the early fifteenth century, witnessed an extraordinary demographic growth. The increase of the town's population, which had already begun in the late fourteenth century, was not interrupted by the crises of the late fifteenth century. From ca. 20,000 inhabitants in 1437, the population increased to 33,000 in 1480 and 55,000 in 1526. In the following decades, however the growth became spectacular. Around 1565, the population probably exceeded 100,000 inhabitants. Mechelen, the former rival of Antwerp and Brussels, stagnated between 1480 and 1526 and only slightly increased its population afterwards to reach 30,000 in 1565. Mechelen had been the juridical and administrative centre of the Low Countries during the reign of Charles the Bold, but after his death in 1477, it lost most of its central institutions. It nevertheless remained of some importance as the residence of Margaret of York, the duke's widow, and through the Great Council of Mechelen, the highest court of justice.[44] Furthermore, in 1539 Charles the Fifth moderated its staple rights for salt in favour of

42 Van Uytven, "Politiek".

43 Cuvelier, *Dénombrements*, p.486-487.

44 Van Uytven, "Centrale plaatsen", p. 37-38.

Antwerp, which undermined its former key position in the Brabantine trade network.[45] Brussels, although having become the capital of Low Countries, with the court and a great part of the central administration, was not as lucky as Antwerp and Mechelen. During the civil wars at the end of the fifteenth century, the town had suffered severe population losses, from which it recovered only slowly. In 1526, the capital had 32,000 inhabitants, that is still almost 7000 fewer than in 1480. It would take until 1565 until Brussels would once again have 40,000 inhabitants.[46] Leuven, which had claimed the title of "the best town of Brabant" in the Middle Ages, had gradually lost inhabitants over the course of the fifteenth century, reaching a minimum of ca. 15,000 inhabitants in 1496. It recovered in the early sixteenth century but – in contrast with the other large towns – stagnated after 1526.[47]

The smaller towns were affected more strongly by the demographic crisis. The towns with the heaviest losses were Tienen, Diest and Zoutleeuw, situated in the south-east of Brabant. But also the smaller towns in the environs of Antwerp, Lier and Herentals lost inhabitants between 1437 and 1496. In contrast with the Leuven area, however, the sharpest decrease in population took place there not between 1480 and 1496 but between 1437 and 1472.[48]

3.2.2 The Demographic Evolution in the Antwerp Countryside

Also in rural Brabant, there were strong regional differences in the demographic development.[49] The total loss between 1472 and 1496 was no less than 26%. The worst-hit area was the district of Leuven, where the population decreased by 57% between 1437 and 1496. After a period of decline between 1464 and 1472, the civil war caused an authentic catastrophe in the 1480s. Villages, farms and great parts of the harvests were destroyed. The district of Brussels was also severely hit. Most of the villages were sacked or burned at least once, many several times. The total population losses were about 32%; that shows that the situation was catastrophic, though less than in the area around Leuven, at least in quantitative terms.

In the district of Antwerp, the demographic development was less disastrous than in the southern part of the duchy. But also within the district itself the development was anything but homogeneous. Some areas suffered more from the political unrest of the late fifteenth century than others. In order to detect demographic developments on the local level, we have subdivided the district of Antwerp into several zones according to geographic and demographic criteria: the first zone is the western Kempen, characterised by its sandy soil and low population density. The second zone is the so-called Waterland, that is, the polder area north of Antwerp; this zone was fertile and had a relatively high population

45 E. AERTS and F. DAELEMANS, Sociaal economische aspecten van het 16de-eeuwse Brussel" in *Tijdschrift voor Brusselse Geschiedenis* 1/ 1984, no. 1-2, pp. 20–22.
46 KLEP, *Bevolking*, p. 413.
47 R. VAN UYTVEN, "De sociale krisis der XVIe eeuw te Leuven" in *Belgisch Tijdschrift voor Filologie en Geschiedenis/Revue Belge de Philologie et d'Histoire*, 1958, p. 356–387.
48 The economic decline of the smaller Brabantine towns during the sixteenth century is discussed in B. BLONDÉ & R. VAN UYTVEN, "De smalle steden en het Brabantse stedelijke netwerk in de Late Middeleeuwen en de Nieuwe Tijd" in *Lira Elegans*, 6 (1996), p. 129-182.
49 CUVELIER, *Dénombrements*, pp. 432–487. The number of rural households was calculated by subtracting the households of the towns from the total numbers. See VAN DER WEE, *Growth*, vol. I, Appendix 49/2, pp. 546–647.

density. The third zone is the area south of Antwerp, which was more fertile than the Kempen, and which had a high population density. In terms of economic activity, this area differed strongly from the other two.

3.2.2.1 The period between 1437 and 1464

The period between 1437 and the *dénombrement* of 1464 did not bring about any dramatic changes in the settlement of the surroundings of Antwerp. The average change in the different sub-areas lay between a slight growth of ca. 2% and slight decline of about 5%. The population rose to some extent in the Kempen (+1.7%) and in the suburbs of Antwerp (+4%). In the rest of the area, the trend was slightly negative. The only area in which these losses were more pronounced was the polder area north of Antwerp, which lost about 15% of its population. These losses were mainly due to a drastic decline in the two adjacent villages of Oorderen and Wilmarsdonk, however, whereas other places, such as Oosterweel, Lillo and Berendrecht, had growing figures. In the southern part of the district, which had a higher population density, the trend was more or less uniform. Here, the population declined by 2.3% on average.

Table 3 : Household Density in 1437 and 1464: District of Antwerp

	Kempen	Polders	South of Antwerp
Density 1437	6.66	8.35	9.11
Density 1464	6.8s	7.16	8.9
Index (1437=100)	101.7	85.8	97.7

In 1464, the contrast between the two northern zones was therefore smaller than in 1437. The mean density of the Kempen had risen slightly from a 6.66 to 6.8, and in the Waterland area, the value had decreased from 8.35 to 7.16. Also in the area south of Antwerp, the mean population density remained almost unchanged, although here, too, local differences can be distinguished. Between 1437 and 1464, the household density of the villages in the immediate vicinity of Antwerp rose above that of the villages farther away from the town. The places along the rivers Scheldt and Rupel nevertheless maintained their relative advance (Table 3.2).

Table 4: Household Density in 1437 and 1464: South of Antwerp

	Suburbs	Scheldt-Rupel	Centre	South-East
1437	8.9	12.3	9.04	7.32
1464	9.26	11.77	8.63	7.23
Index	104	95.7	95.44	98.7

It seems that the impact of the growth of Antwerp, where the population had increased by ca. 6000 inhabitants or about 30% since 1437, had yet to be felt very strongly outside the town. Only in the villages immediately outside Antwerp and the very thinly settled area in the very north of the district was there a slight increase in population. In contrast, the most densely settled parts of the district – and most of all the polder area north of Antwerp – witnessed considerable losses.

At the same time, the population of the area surrounding Brussels increased by 15%, although the density there was considerably higher than in the surroundings of Antwerp. The population density achieved there in 1464 was exceptionally high and formed the absolute maximum within the fifteenth century. For many places it remained unparalleled in 1526, when the last *dénombrement* took place.[50] The major exception was a small island of places near the small town of Vilvoorde, where population decreased. Vilvoorde itself witnessed a constant decline during the late Middle Ages.[51]

3.2.2.2 The period of demographic decline: 1472–1496

The *dénombrement* of 1472 marks a drastic change in the general situation. While during the 27 years between 1437 and 1464 the development had been rather stable, the picture suddenly changed within only eight years. In the district of Antwerp, even the areas where population had still been increasing until 1464, the figures were now negative. The decrease reached the greatest dimensions in the Waterland area, where it reached as much as 20% in comparison to 1464 (29% in comparison to 1437). In the south of the district, near Antwerp, the losses amounted to about 10% in most places. This negative development also continued after 1472. In 1480, the Waterland area had lost almost half its population in comparison with 1437. In Oorderen and Wilmarsdonk, the loss of inhabitants was as much as 70%! In the rest of the district, the losses were less dramatic but still amounted to 15–20%.

In the district of Brussels, too, the positive trend was broken. The most densely settled area, around Grimbergen, lost 7.5% of its population in 1464. The western part, which had seen a considerable increase in households even in 1464, lost about the same quantity, falling back to the level of 1437. In the Tervuren area, the loss was as much as 13%.

Cuvelier gives two major reasons for this decrease: the political turmoil at the beginning of the reign of Charles the Bold on the one hand, and unfavourable natural circumstances on the other, including the very severe winter of 1464 and the heavy rainfall in 1467 and 1468, which led to flooding along the river Nete[52]. Van der Wee, too, stresses the drastic worsening of the situation in the countryside under Charles the Bold. While the economic situation had already been bad in the towns at the middle of the century, the countryside had been somewhat better able to resist this. After 1467, however, agrarian rents and incomes from large farms dropped and wages stagnated. The fiscal policy of Duke

50 Only the area near Tervuren, east of Brussels, and the area near Willebroek, in the north, lost some of their population (-3.35 % in the Tervuren area, -0.62 % in the Willebroek area).

51 Cf. J.P. Peeters, *Bloei en verval van de middeleeuwse stadsvrijheid Vilvoorde*, Tielt, 1975.

52 Cuvelier, *Dénombrements*, CLXIV ff. Herentals was flooded in 1468 – see also the incomes of the Anderstad farm in the accounts of the ducal demesne Land van Mechelen, ARA, Rk., reg. 11897.

Charles further increased the pressures on the population.[53] The reason for the dramatic losses of population in the polder area north of Antwerp must be sought in the floods that frequently hit the North Sea coast. A Flemish chronicle refers to the flood of 17 September 1477 as follows: "The same day of St. Cosmas...the sea flowed so high and became so stormy from the wind...like it had not done in a hundred years. In Antwerp, the ships were thrown up on the wharf... many dikes broke in Holland, Zealand and Flanders...". But there were also other contributing factors, such as a plague that broke out in 1469 and the rebellion against Maximilian of Habsburg.[54]

In 1496, the demographic figures for Brabant reached their nadir. War, famines and plague had reduced the population of the duchy by more than 20%. As the district of Antwep was not directly hit by military destruction it was therefore spared the demographic catastrophe. The population figures stabilised in most places, and in the Waterland, the immediate environs of Antwerp and in the Scheldt-Rupel area, there were even considerable increases. The Waterland area grew the most. It not only recovered from the losses of the previous decades, but some places such as Stabroek and Oosterwiel even surpassed the number of inhabitants they had in 1437. Zandvliet, Oorderen and Wilmarsdonk recovered a great part of the losses they had suffered but still did not reach the dimensions they had had in 1437.

In the immediate surroundings of Antwerp, the population increased strongly but did not reach the level of 1437. Some places showed an astonishing growth, like Berchem, which increased its population by 45.8%, and Aartselaar, whose population grew by 43%. Only Deurne suffered strong losses. Even more remarkable was the increase of population in the Scheldt-Rupel area. While the villages along the rivers had suffered losses of population in the previous period, they now recovered those almost entirely, increasing their population by an average of 37%. In contrast with the south of Brabant, the environs of Antwerp had already reached the peak of the late-fifteenth-century demographic crisis in 1480. By 1496, most villages were already recovering, and some were even growing significantly. P. Klep attributes this extraordinary increase to the migration within Brabant. As potential sources for the supply of immigrants, he suggests the two southern districts and the Kempen.[55]

53 Van der Wee, *Growth*, II, p. 65f.

54 A charter of the archdukes Maximilian and Philip from 1484 referring to the land rents of the Antwerp abbey St. Michaels in Zandvliet and Berendrecht refers to the latter two: "*binnen 25 jaren herwaerts, soe mits der pestilentien die daar geweest heeft, soe mits der ingesetenen rebelligheyt*" "*na welcken tijde, vele beruerte onder die gemeynten geweest heeft*" N. Cartularium S. Mich. VII 120-122, edited by P. Goetschalckx and F. Prims in "Lillo en Zandvliet in de XVde eeuw" in *Bijdragen tot de Geschiedenis*, reeks III, V (1953) p. 98; also Antwerp, Leuven and Mechelen were hit by the plague between 1470 and 1474; see Van Uytven, "Politiek", pp. 1100–1103.

55 Klep, *Bevolking*, p. 50-51.

3.2.2.3 The situation in 1526

After 1496, it would be another thirty years before a new household count was made. The duchy was busy recovering, and nobody seemed to have an interest in a new *dénombrement*. A new count was only organised in 1526.[56] The population in the environs of Antwerp increased strongly during the first quarter of the sixteenth century. Deurne, which had been reduced to only 46 households in 1496, not only recovered its loss but even increased its number of households to 322 – seven times as many as in 1496 and still more than thrice as many as in 1437. The other villages in the immediate neighbourhood of Antwerp, such as Wilrijk, Berchem, and Merksem, all underwent had a similar development. The polder area north of Antwerp and the villages along the rivers Scheldt and Rupel still increased their population by 15 and 20%, respectively, achieving figures that were ca. 10% higher than in 1437. This is remarkable, especially considering the polder villages had been hit so hard during the fifteenth century. In the Kempen, the population growth was also quite high. In the north, it could reach nearly 50% in some villages and in the south as much as 60% in comparison with 1496.

As a result, the settlement patterns of the countryside surrounding Antwerp had changed significantly since the fifteenth century. The effects were especially noteworthy in the triangle formed by the rivers Scheldt and Rupel and the line between Antwerp and Lier. This had become a compact area of particularly dense settlement, with more than 12 households or 54 inhabitants per square kilometre. This is comparable to the most densely settled parts of Brabant near Brussels and Leuven, and can be considered a top European value. The places situated along the Scheldt south of Antwerp and some of the villages along the rivers Rupel and Nete, such as Rumst, Duffel and Walem, reached an even higher density. In the polder area north of Antwerp, the figures were not as homogenous but also reached an average level of ca. 8.5. In the Kempen, there was some increase north of Antwerp (Ekeren, Kapellen, Brasschaat, Essen, Kalmthout and Wuustwezel), and in some villages east of Antwerp (Wijnegem, Wommelgem and Oelegem), whereas the surroundings of the small town of Turnhout lost some of its population (see Map 9).

The demographic map of the surroundings of Antwerp in 1526 therefore shows some traces of the expansion of Antwerp. The population had increased visibly within a distance of ca. 20 km from the town, in what we can consider to be the immediate sphere of urban influence. This area formed a homogenous block of considerably high population density. In some places, especially in the closer environs of Antwerp, but also along the rivers Scheldt and Rupel, population density reached levels of more than 70 inhabitants per square kilometre, which are very high values for purely agrarian communities.[57] In fact, these villages were the centres of non-agrarian activities that had already existed in the fifteenth century, but which appear to have undergone a strong expansion at the beginning of the sixteenth century.

56 The organisation of the *dénombrement* of 1526 cost more than 26,000 guilders. It was carried out with much precision and this time included houses with more than one household. Furthermore, the *dénombrement* from 1526 also included the number of full fiefs, farms and clerics. Unfortunately, these figures are not available for the marquisate of Antwerp. See CUVELIER, *Dénombrements*, Introduction, pp. CCXLVII–CCXLIX.

57 A.H. HAWLEY, *Human Ecology. A Theory of Community Structure*, New York, 1950, estimates the typical population density of agrarian societies between 25 and 75 inhabitants per square kilometre (cited in KLEP, *Bevolking*, p. 39.).

Map 9: Household Density in the Western Part of the District of Antwerp, 1526

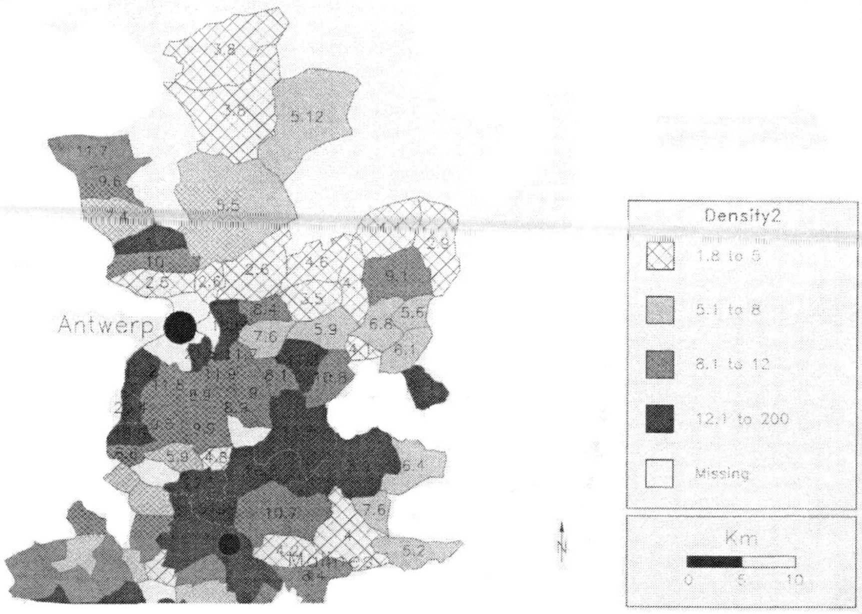

Source: Cuvelier, *Dénombrements*, pp. 432–483.

3.2.2.4 The demographic evolution after 1526

The Brabantine household counts only extend to 1526. For the rest of the sixteenth century, only dispersed data concerning local populations are conserved. These are some numbers of communicants, numbers of houses or families that figure in taxation lists, or testimonies of local aldermen. This group of sources dates from the end of the sixteenth century and constitutes part of the declarations of the village authorities concerning the state of the villages before and after the religious troubles. Declarations of this type are, of course, highly subjective. Village aldermen probably presented the state of their village in very dramatic terms, using passages such as: "the houses are inhabitable; the inhabitants have to live in the castle of Cantecroy, in the church or in the house of Peter van Bergen. The corn has to be threshed on the field."[58] The same reservations have to be made with regard to the description of the villages before the war. If it was in the interest of the village authorities to present the present state of their village in a very negative way, it was also in their interest, by way of contrast, to exaggerate the welfare before the beginning of the war. Nevertheless, the fantasy of those who made such declarationswas limited by the tax officials' knowledge of the state of the villages around 1570, when detailed lists of immovable property were made for levying the 100th-penny tax. Although many of these documents have long since disappeared, they were known to the central administration at that time. In spite of their

58 SAA, VG 14, Declaration concerning Mortsel and Luithagen from 17 Sept.1593.

subjective character, the declarations concerning the pre-war state of the Brabantine villages are therefore probably more reliable than the descriptions of the destruction caused by the war. Nevertheless, the figures concerning the second half of the sixteenth century are less reliable than the household counts and can only give a general impression of the demographic situation in the Antwerp countryside at the dawn of the Revolt.

For calculating the population by means of the numbers of communicants, various coefficients are applied. Essentially, they include the total of the population without children younger than twelve years of age. The total population can be therefore be calculated by multiplying the number of the communicants with a factor ranging from 1.3 to 1.6.[59] From the declarations of village aldermen of 1593, some other population figures can be ascertained. The combination of numbers of communicants, couples, and inhabitants in the 1593 declarations enables a comparison between the different factors. In some cases, the numbers of communicants multiplied by 1.4 give similar results to those of the numbers of couples multiplied by 4.5. This was the case for Mortsel, where there were 400 communicants (inc. servants) and 126 couples before 1582. By applying the factors 1.4 and 4.5, we obtain a number of inhabitants between 560 and 567.[60] In Deurne-Borgerhout, the number of communicants shifted between 2000 and 3000 between 1564 and 1576, and the number of houses before the beginning of the Revolt is estimated to have been between 500 and 600. Its population can therefore be estimated to have been between 2500 and 3000 inhabitants.[61] In some cases, however, the sources contain contradictory indications. There were 500–600 couples living in Rumst and Boom around 1568, for example. Boom had about 400 to 500 inhabitants at that time, and there were 800–900 communicants in Rumst. According to the number of couples living there, Rumst would have had 1750 to 2300 inhabitants, whereas the number of communicants in Boom indicates it had only 1120–1260 inhabitants.[62]

On the basis of these indications, we can make rough estimates of the population for a number of villages in the period between 1567 and 1575. For two villages in the immediate surroundings of Antwerp, Deurne-Borgerhout and Berchem, which have become part of the city in the meantime, the population increase between 1526 and 1570 was spectacular: Berchem had 500 households, which is nearly four times as many as it had in 1526 and more than ten times as many as in 1437.[63] Deurne-Borgerhout had increased its number of households from 322 in 1526 to ca. 500–600 in 1570, which is still a rise of 55 % and as much as 85% if related to 1437. The average increase in the area to the south of Antwerp was 36.6%. Along the Scheldt and the Rupel, there were similar increases: the cloth-making villages Duffel and Walem grew by 33 and 28%, respectively. Schelle, situated at the Scheldt, still had 18% more households than in 1526. In the Kempen, the growth was much more modest. In six places for which figures are available, the average increase was 6.25%.

59 The actual percentage of communicants varied considerably. Around 1600, the average in Flanders can be estimated at between 60 and 62%. Cf. J. DE BROUWER, "Het belang van de kommunicantencijfers en de verhouding ervan tot de bevolking (uitgewerkt op de dekenij Aalst van 1621 tot 1795)" in *Handelingen van de Koninklijke Maatschappij voor Taal- en Letterkunde en Geschiedenis*, 17 (1963), p. 67-80.

60 SAA, VG 14 Mortsel and Luithagen 17 Sept.1593.

61 NOOYENS, *Deurne*, I, p. 495-504.

62 SAA VG 5, fo. 84 –89: Rumst and Boom.

63 The register of the 100th-penny tax from 1570 contained 460 houses; J. B. STOCKMANS, *Geschiedenis van de gemeente Berchem*, Brussel, 1975, p. 15.

We do not have any comparable sources concerning the villages in the polders north of Antwerp. Their population probably fluctuated throughout the sixteenth century. The area was hit by a series of heavy floods, the most serious of which were those of 1530, 1532 and 1570. The polders were inundated during the siege of Antwerp in 1584, and a large part remained flooded until well into the seventeenth century.[64] The flooded area reached from Antwerp until Berendrecht and Zandvliet. Only the villages of Oorderen and Wilmarsdonk were above the water level.[65]

Hence, the trend of population growth that started between 1480 and 1496 continued throughout the sixteenth century. The population figures for the fifteenth century, which remained unattained for a long time in the south of Brabant, were soon surpassed and in many cases left far behind. The densely settled area south of Antwerp, and especially the places along the rivers Scheldt, Rupel and Nete, further increased their population, reaching an average density of 17.6 households or almost 80 inhabitants per square kilometre. As a result, they reached the level of the southern part of the province, which had been much more populated than the Antwerp area in the late Middle Ages. We do not know if 1570 formed the actual peak in this development or if that had already been reached earlier. The contemporaries who described the damages of the war in the early 1590s referred to the period between 1570 and 1575 as "the good times before the troubles".[66] Some authors, on the other hand, propose that the economic situation was already in decline at that moment.

Although it is not absolutely clear if the period around 1570 was the demographic peak of the sixteenth century, it is nevertheless the last moment that we can see the effects of the demographic growth the area had witnessed throughout the preceding decades. The years to come were marked by war and destruction. The inquiries concerning the situation of the Brabantine villages in 1593 reflect a picture of total destruction, empty villages and burned houses. In the 1480s, the Flemish civil war had caused similar effects in the south of Brabant. Then, the Antwerp area had been spared the worst effects and may even have received immigrants from the south of the duchy. Now, it was fully hit by the direct and indirect effects of war. The population of the villages was drastically reduced. Many people were killed, others fled to a safe town or moved to the south of the duchy. Some villages were totally empty for a period of some years,[67] while the population of others was diminished by 80 to 90%.[68] Many of these statements may be exaggerated. However they reflect a clear break in the demographic development. If there had been a period demographic growth in the Antwerp area between the late fifteenth century and ca. 1570, it definitely came to an end with the beginning of the Eighty Years' War in the 1570s. Even in 1615, the population in the *arrondissement* of Antwerp was still 22% lower than it had been in 1565.[69]

64 The area south of Lillo and Stabroek was probably re-diked in 1587, the polders of Lillo, Stabroek, Zandvliet and Berendrecht only in 1650; P. Guns, *De Antwerpse Noorderpolders in de 16de en 17de eeuw*, Antwerpen 1972, p. 23-29 and 44-52.

65 Guns, *Noorderpolders*, p. 23-29.

66 For example: SAA VG 14, Mortsel, Luithagen.

67 For example: Kalmthout in 1587 or Boechout 1582-1587. A. Cosemans, "Het uitzicht van Brabant op het einde der XVIde eeuw" in *Bijdragen tot de Geschiedenis*, XXVII (1936), p. 344 and 346.

68 Cosemans, "Uitzicht", pp. 345–47.

69 Klep, *Bevolking*, p. 399, Table B-36.

The demographic development of the rural environs of Antwerp correlates with the economic development of the metropolis. The population increased, especially in the places immediately outside the city and along the major transport axes, although not to the same degree as in Antwerp itself. The demographic figures also illustrate very clearly the impact of political and military events, especially on rural society.[70] The crisis of the late fifteenth century, the result of civil wars, plagues and famines, formed the point of departure for a period of economic expansion. Hence the even more severe character of the demographic crisis in the south could have hampered economic development there during the sixteenth century.[71] The surroundings of Antwerp were spared from destruction and underwent a much milder population development during the late fifteenth century. Hence, instead of merely recovering the losses suffered during that period, its population would grow beyond the late medieval level during the sixteenth century.

70 E. THOEN, "Warfare and Countryside: Social and Economic Aspects of the Military Destruction in Flanders during the Late Middle Ages and the Early Modern Period " in *Acta Historica Neerlandica* XIII (1980) p. 25–40. GUTMANN, *War.*

71 On the other hand, crises could be turning points of development, i.e. moments of structural change. Brenner, for example, states that class struggle was necessary to break through structural bonds of feudalism. Military crises or other fundamental crises could have a similar impact.

CHAPTER 4

Urban Demand and the Agrarian System of the Antwerp Hinterland

4.1 Introduction

The rise of an urban centre with the dimensions of sixteenth-century Antwerp was very likely to cause changes in the agrarian structure of its surroundings. The demand for agrarian products increased enormously, which in normal circumstances would form a stimulus for local farming.[1] Studies concerning early modern metropolitan cities and their hinterlands have shown that large urban centres had a great influence on the agrarian structure of their surroundings via their demand for agrarian products.[2] A striking example for this process is London, a very large city with a vast agrarian supply area already in the Middle Ages.[3] During the early modern period, however, the town underwent a major expansion, exercising a great influence on the agriculture of the surrounding counties in the process. The main changes that occurred were an increase of the supply area of London, a rapid spread of market gardening, increasing local specialisation, and intensive farming on enclosures. Finally, London's increasing demand encouraged wholesalers to engage directly in the production of food or to sink capital in the improvement of productivity.[4] London merchants bought land in the country, which also hastened agricultural change. These agrarian changes went hand in hand with changes in the organisation of the food market and of transport.[5]

Likewise in the surroundings of Paris, P. Hoffman has observed a strong increase in agrarian productivity during the early modern period due to urban demand. Hoffman stresses particularly the importance of urban fertiliser and transport. Paris provided good conditions in both respects: as a concentration of hundreds of thousands of inhabitants, it represented an extraordinary supply of manure, especially in form of horse dung. The great concentration of horses in the capital created also a high demand for fodder, which on its part gave rise to a specialised sector of agriculture: artificial meadows. Second, the French transport network was concentrated on Paris, which meant that the Paris Basin was extraordinarily well furnished with both waterways and paved roads. The organisational factor is also an important feature in Hoffman's argument. He considered the problem of moral hazard to be a major obstacle for the rise of long-distance trade networks. Large towns such as Paris or London seemed more likely to overcome this barrier through an improved commercial organisation, which was backed by monopolies in both cases.[6]

1 This is the premise for the specialisation model of J. de Vries. See also: J. Langton & G. Hoppe, *Town and Country in the Development of Early Modern Western Europe*, Norwich, 1983.

2 Aerts & Clark, eds., *Metropolitan Cities* and Clark & Lepetit, eds., *Capital Cities.*

3 Cf. B.M.S. Campbell, J.A. Galloway, D. Keene, M. Murphy, *A Medieval Capital and Its Grain Supply: Agrarian Production and Distribution in the London Region, c.1300*, London, 1993 (Historical Geography Research Series, 30).

4 Fisher, "London Food Market", pp. 46–64.

5 Wrigley, "A Simple Model", pp. 229–234.

6 P. T. Hoffman, *Growth in a Traditional Society: The French Countryside, 1450–1815*, Princeton, 1996, pp. 170–184.

These studies on London and Paris provide a series of arguments in favour of a beneficial influence of very big cities on the countryside surrounding them. In many cases, however, the requirements for agrarian specialisation were not met. On the contrary, many towns drained the rural surplus and failed to invest in the agriculture of their environs. This was the case for Madrid and most of the great towns of northern Italy. This failure was mainly due to institutional circumstances that limited the peasants' access to the urban market.[7]

Antwerp differed in several respects from the examples discussed thus far. As in the case of London, the demographic rise was particularly sharp. The impulse of the urban demand was nevertheless counterbalanced by the great supply of imported food offered at the Antwerp market. In contrast with London, the pressure to increase the output of regional agriculture was therefore moderated by massive imports. Another difference between Antwerp and towns like London or Paris was its relatively short period of economic prosperity. Whereas the changes in these other towns took place over a period of two or three centuries, the Golden Age of Antwerp lasted only about 70 years. The link between the long-term development of Brabantine agriculture during the early modern period and the rise of Antwerp is therefore more complex than in the case of towns that continued to expand. The Golden Age of Antwerp was initially followed by a period of 50 years that is generally characterised as an "Indian summer", and finally by a long period of economic decline.[8] The urban expansion therefore was short lived and followed by a phase of contraction. Although the impact of this period of decline on the rural economy would be interesting to trace, we concentrate only on the sixteenth century in this study.

A final, and perhaps the major difference between sixteenth-century Antwerp and early-modern London and Paris concerns their respective sizes. Antwerp reached about 100,000 inhabitants at the top of its expansion, whereas London and Paris were almost four times as large at theirs. In this case, size does matter, of course. The importance of many of the factors referred to in the discussion of the commercial influence of metropolitan cities on their surroundings multiplied in correlation with the size of those cities. Hence, the impact on the environs of Antwerp can be expected to have been more modest than that on the Paris Bassin or on the surroundings of London.

Seventeenth-century Amsterdam is therefore a better point of comparison. Both Antwerp and Amsterdam were port cities and commercial centres rather than capital cities, and their dimensions were also more modest than those of London or Paris. In de Vries' work on the specialisation of Dutch agriculture between 1500 and 1800, urban demand plays a major role. In contrast with the London area or the Paris basin, Holland and Friesland abandoned grain production as a major agrarian activity, specialising instead in cattle-raising, dairying, horticulture and the cultivation of industrial crops.[9] As de Vries puts it, those who were once peasants became specialised farmers.

On the other hand, J. Jacquart, "Paris: First Metropois of the Early Modern Period" in P. Clark & B. Lepetit, *Capital Cities and their Hinterlands*, p. 112–113; stresses rather the negative terms of trade between Paris and its hinterland.

7 E. A. Wrigley, "Metropolitan Cities and their Hinterlands: Stimulus and Constraints to Growth" in Aerts, Clark, eds., *Metropolitan Cities*, p. 15.

8 A. Thijs, "The River Scheldt Closed for Two Centuries, 1585–1790" in Asaert, G., De Vos, A., Thijs, A., Veraghtert, K., *Antwerp, a Port for All Seasons*, Antwerpen, 1986, pp. 165–212; For the 17th century afterglow of the prosperity of Antwerp, R. Baetens, *De nazomer van Antwerpens welvaart. De diaspora en het handelshuis De Groote tijdens de eerste helft der 17e eeuw*. 2 vols., Antwerpen, 1976.

9 De Vries, *Rural Economy*, p. 72–73.

So how did the extraordinary urban growth of Antwerp influence the agrarian structure of its surrounding countryside? Did it lead to specialisation as has been shown in the case of London or the Dutch towns? Or did the increasing influx of imported grain and other foodstuffs lead to a withdrawal of the peasants from the Antwerp market and to a stagnation of the peasant economy? Indications for the latter development exist for the area of Leuven, for example, where the formerly advanced agriculture encountered a serious blow during the sixteenth century.[10] A crucial question in this context is the role of the local agriculture in supplying the town. Was the local production competitive in comparison with Baltic grain or Danish oxen? Or was its contribution rather marginal and therefore not subject to important market-induced changes?[11]

4.2 The Urban Demand for Agrarian Products

As a result of the demographic growth of Antwerp, the demand for all sorts of agrarian products increased significantly during the sixteenth century. The population of the metropolis increased from ca. 20,000 inhabitants in 1437 to almost 100,000 around 1565, which made it one of the largest towns in Western Europe. Hence, the demand for food, fuel and raw materials of its population had also multiplied by almost five. Providing sufficient food and other basic commodities for such a large town was a difficult task for the agrarian hinterland of Antwerp, especially if one considers the great density of major towns in the southern Low Countries. Brussels, only 40 km south of Antwerp, had over 50,000 inhabitants by 1526, while Leuven and Mechelen each had between 20,000 and 25,000. Regional agriculture was not capable of providing enough grain and other foodstuffs to feed such a giant. We have already seen that the southern Low Countries already depended on food imports for their provisioning in the fifteenth century. In the case of sixteenth-century Antwerp, this dependence was even stronger. Yet, one hardly gets the impression that Antwerp was short of food when reading what sixteenth-century visitors like L. Guicciardini wrote of it: "*The food supply is excellent. Victuals are being imported from abroad and from the countryside every day. So much is brought by boat or with horse and cart that the ingredients for a simple meal are always at hand. And what is more: there is always a broad choice of more refined food and drinks.*"[12] Obviously, the massive importation of a broad range of foodstuffs, together with the local production, provided plenty of food for the Antwerp population in normal years. In the following sections, we will consider the major types of food and their provisioning areas in order to find out how local production, regional trade and imports related to each other.

10 VAN UYTVEN, "In de Schaduwen".

11 Other factors also played a role, of course, such as the fact that townsmen were both investors and competitors in the land market. We will treat this subject in the final section of the book. On the other hand, the town was also a provider of seed, farming tools and especially urban waste as fertiliser. Although we do not underestimate the importance of these aspects of the urban impact on the agriculture of its surroundings, we will not be treating them as a separate topic in our study.

12 GUICCIARDINI, *Descrittione* (1567), P. 82.

4.2.1 Grain

Grain was imported in great quantities to feed the urban population. The Baltic, which had already been important in the fifteenth century, became the major foreign supplier of rye, the bread grain for the masses from the final decades of the fifteenth century onward.[13] Northern France, the major supply area for grain during the late Middle Ages, continued to remain important during the sixteenth century as well, although the imports were repeatedly hampered by war. Especially for wheat, the big cities of the Low Countries continued to rely in great part on the traditional granaries of northern France and the southern Low Countries themselves. The actual ratio of imports to regional agricultural products as resources that met the demand for food in Antwerp is unknown and would be very hard to calculate. Not only are there insufficient quantitative sources for making such an estimate, but it must also be remembered that Antwerp was not only a market of consumption but also a transit market. In other words, the fact that not all the food arriving in Antwerp by ship was consumed in that town makes it even more difficult to make such an estimate.[14]

One way to find out if the Antwerp market was supplied by means of imports and regional trade or by its immediate hinterland is to estimate the agrarian potential of the urban surroundings. In R. van Uytven's estimate, the area necessary to provide a town of 20,000 inhabitants in the southern Low Countries with bread grain was equal to ca. 150 villages.[15] This may be somewhat overvalued in the concrete situation of Antwerp, however. Due to greater village areas, the number of farms per village in the district of Antwerp was greater than the 10 large farms with an average size of 10 ha that van Uytven used the basis for his estimate. In the village of Edegem, situated south of Antwerp, for example, there were no less than 30 farms with an average size of 28 ha – thus almost five times as many as the model suggests.[16] If we also include land rents, lease payments and tithes that went to the town, and the farms between two and five hectares in size, which were not taken into account in the calculation, the agrarian output available for the town would have to be estimated much higher. The number of villages necessary to provide Antwerp with bread grain may therefore be reduced to some extent, at least for those years that had a good or normal harvest. Instead of 150 villages, the area of 70 villages would be more accurate, and this coincides more or less with the area in which Antwerp townsmen owned landed property. Even if we assume that the agrarian hinterland of Antwerp, i.e. a radius of ca. 30 km east of Antwerp, had produced enough rye to feed Antwerp in the early fifteenth century, the situation had changed fundamentally by the middle of the sixteenth century, when the quantity of bread grain required was about five times greater than in the fifteenth century. The dependence on grain from other areas was therefore much stronger than in the fifteenth century.

---

13 Van Uytven, "Approvisionnement", p. 97 and "Politiek", p. 1111.

14 H. Soly, for example, shows how the major garrisons in the south of the Low Countries, including those of Luxemburg and Cambrai, were supplied with food via the Antwerp market in 1556–1558. H. Soly, "Een Antwerpse Compagnie voor de levensmiddelenbevoorrading van het leger in de Nederlanden in de zestiende eeuw" in *Bijdragen en Mededelingen betreffende de Geschiedenis der Nederlanden* 86 (1971) p. 350–362.

15 See Chapter 2, section 2.

16 SAA, VG 14, 100th penny Edegem.

If we approach the question from the import side, one of the few quantitative estimations available is that of E. Scholliers concerning Baltic grain. According to his estimates, the imports via the Sound covered about 13 to 14% of the Low Countries' total annual demand for bread grain. The highest percentage was probably reached in the period between 1562 and 1569, with ca. 23%.[17] This very general finding is nevertheless too vague to use as a basis for assumptions dealing with Antwerp in particular. Baltic grain was distributed all over the Low Countries, in particular to the larger towns, where the demand was greater than elsewhere, and to a greater extent in the northern provinces than in the south. Antwerp, by far the greatest town, will therefore have received a larger share than other places. M. van Tielhof, for example, assumes that a considerable part of the grain that was transported from Amsterdam to the south via Gouda went to Antwerp.[18] The toll accounts of Gouda also indicate another important feature, however, namely that the percentage of Baltic grain in those transports varied very widely between years with a good harvest and bad years. While the percentage of grain from the east was very low in years with low grain prices, the picture changed completely in years of very high prices, as for example in 1557. Therefore, the importance of grain from the western part of Europe for the provisioning of Antwerp is not to be underestimated. Only in years when the western supplies were insufficient did the Low Countries depend for a large part on grain imports from the east.[19] For grain imports from other areas, such as northern France, the main supplier of wheat, the bread grain of the well-to-do, there are no quantitative estimates. In spite of the frequent wars between the France and the Low Countries, the traffic of French grain toward the north seems to have continued during the first decades of the sixteenth century, albeit with interruptions.[20] After the 1530s, however, this trade diminished in importance.[21]

Grain did not necessarily have to be imported from abroad. Indeed, it was also transported to Antwerp from the southern part of Brabant and from Zeeland. Theoretical models of town-hinterland relations in the Low Countries start from the assumption that the towns absorbed most of the grain surplus from their immediate surroundings, and that there was therefore little or no grain left for the regional or interregional trade. For some areas, such as Zeeland, this was not the case. The islands north of the estuary of the Scheldt were not as densely urbanised as Brabant or Flanders, and hence produced a net surplus. The type of grain that Zeeland exported was not so much rye or wheat, however, but mostly oats and barley. The Rupelmonde toll register of 1541/42 shows that great quantities of oats and barley were shipped toward southern Brabant, to Brussels, Leuven and Mechelen, among other places.[22]

There also appears to have been a lively internal grain trade within Brabant, at least in normal years. Grain and flour were shipped up and down the Brabantine rivers. Antwerp was the major destination for grain coming downstream from southern Brabant. Throughout the whole year, hundreds of sacks of grain and almost a thousand

17 E. Scholliers, *Loonarbeid en honger. De levensstandaard in de XVe en XVIe eeuw te Antwerpen*, Antwerpen, 1960, p. 61. See also: Kriedte, *Spätfeudalismus*, p. 38.
18 Van Tielhof, *Graanhandel* p. 209.
19 *Ibidem*, p. 207.
20 Van der Wee, *Growth*, vol. II, p. 171.
21 Van Tielhof, *Graanhandel*, p. 18–30.
22 ARA, Rk. Reg. 22739 Toll register of '*het wiel*' near Rupelmonde Oct. 1541 – Sept. 1542.

sacks of flour were registered at the Rupelmonde toll. Although shipping flour had its advantages, the fact that the quantity of flour coming from central Brabant should have been considerably greater than that of unmilled grain is somewhat surprising. In medieval London, the flour trade was of only little importance, and in Paris it only became predominant by the eighteenth century.[23] Grain was also shipped in considerable quantities along the Scheldt to Antwerp from Dendermonde and other places in the county of Flanders,[24] Hence, besides local provisioning and imports from northern France and the Baltic, Antwerp could also rely on regional supplies from southern Brabant and eastern Flanders. Studies of the Dutch grain market have shown that grain from different origins was normally traded simultaneously in most towns, although for different prices.[25] These price differences were related to differences in quality. Local grain was most expensive, while eastern grain was cheapest. Besides the natural differences between the different sorts of grain, the long transport probably also contributed to the deterioration of the imported commodity. This difference in quality was an advantage for local producers on the urban grain market, in addition to the cheaper transportation costs.

Hence, grain prices in Antwerp were dependent on multiple factors. The shifts in the regional grain supply, together with the inelasticity of demand, were the reason for the typical fluctuations, especially in the price of bread grain. Generally speaking, grain prices tended to be high in years of bad harvests and low in years with favourable harvests. On the other hand, the interregional grain trade meant that there was no direct correlation between the local production and price of grain. By the fifteenth century, an interregional market area had developed within which grain prices were highly interrelated.[26] Other things that influenced grain pricing included psychological factors, such as the prospects for the grain supply during the following season, and storage.[27]

There was nevertheless still a correspondence between the local production and the level of grain prices. This can be illustrated by the sales of rye by Antwerp's St. Elisabeth Hospital, which sold part of its rye surplus every year. The hospital had relatively little surplus to sell in years of high prices, although the profits would have been much higher. For wheat, on the other hand, the opposite phenomenon can be observed. The purchases of the hospital were higher in years of high prices than in years of low prices.[28] On the other hand, the relatively easy access to imports from the Baltic meant that rye prices in Antwerp in years of shortage were somewhat lower than in other towns of the Low Countries.[29] In contrast, wheat was expensive in Antwerp due to the high demand combined with the low

---

23 B.M.S. Campbell, et al., *A Medieval Capital*, p. 79. For the advantages of the flour trade in comparison to the grain trade, see: S. Kaplan, *Provisioning*, p. 339 ff.

24 In the toll register of Rupelmonde from Oct. 1541 – Sept. 1542, about 1500 sacks of grain were listed as going from the area of Dendermonde toward Antwerp: ARA, Rk. Reg. 22740.

25 M. Van Tielhof, "Grain Provision in Holland, ca. 1490 – ca. 1570" in Hoppenbrouwers & van Zanden, eds., *Peasants into farmers*, p. 212–215.

26 G. Sivery, „Les profits de l'éleveur et du cultivateur dans le Hainaut à la fin du moyen age" in *Annales E.S.C.*, 31 (1976), p. 605, even insists that harvest fluctuations were only decisive in years when trade was blocked by wars or similar factors.

27 The relation between the annual shifts in production and the formation of the grain price has been explained very accurately for the fifteenth century by M.J. Tits-Dieuaide, *Formation de prix*. Although the importance of imports became greater in the sixteenth century, the principles of price formation remained similar. A detailed account of the interdependence of grain prices between distant markets can be found in Neveu, *Vie et déclin*, p. 115–189.

28 Scholliers, *Loonarbeid*, p. 20.

29 *Ibidem*, p. 23.

production in the Antwerp area.[30] Imports and regional production hence formed the two components of the Antwerp grain supply. Depending on the quality of the harvest and the available stock, one or the other of these factors prevailed. Low supplies and therefore high grain prices encouraged merchants to import, whereas in good years, when the profits were lower, less effort was made to import grain from abroad.

4.2.2 Meat

Likewise, meat consumption increased in Antwerp in the sixteenth century. Already in 1500, the increasing demand for meat led to the building of a new meat hall with 62 stands.[31] The demand peaked in the 1540s and 50s.[32] Meat prices were at a relatively high level between 1500 and 1525 and continued to rise throughout the sixteenth century, although to a lesser degree than bread grain.[33] As was the case with grain, a significant part of the provisions of meat had to come from abroad. Oxen were increasingly imported from Denmark and the northern Low Countries, i.e. Friesland, Holland, Drente, and Zeeland, while at the same time, imports from Brittany and Normandy diminished. The towns of Dordrecht and 's Hertogenbosch played an important role in the transit of this commodity.

The town of Lier, only some kilometres away from Antwerp, became a major cattle market in the sixteenth century. In the 1540s, the number of oxen sold there per year reached a maximum of ca. 20,000.[34] Lier could not impose its staple right on Antwerp, however. The St.Elisabeth Hospital in Antwerp did not buy its oxen or cows exclusively in Lier, for example, but also at the market at Hoogstraten or at other places in the Kempen.[35]

Buying lean oxen and fattening them in the meadows around Antwerp became a profitable activity for butchers and cattle merchants. Profits from fattening could exceed 70%.[36] Imported oxen were not the only source of meat, however. Antwerp institutions also bought cows, lambs, sheep, wethers, pigs and poultry.[37] The latter were of local and regional origin, rather than imported. The increased demand for meat therefore formed a stimulus not only for cattle merchants and butchers, but also for local producers. These could be large-scale cattle farmers, but also peasants selling a bit of poultry or merely a calf or pig each year.

30 *Ibidem*.
31 Baetens, *Lokale markten*, p. 183.
32 Van der Wee, *Growth*, II, p. 210.
33 Scholliers, *Loonarbeid*, pp. 36–38.
34 H. Van der Wee, E., Aerts, "The Lier livestock trade".
35 Antwerp, OCMW S.E. Reg. 4, account 1504/1505.
36 Scholliers, *Loonarbeid*, p. 38.
37 E. Scholliers, "Prijzen en lonen te Antwerpen (15e en 16e eeuw) – Prix et salaires à Anvers (15e–16e siècles)" in C. Verlinden et al., *Dokumenten voor de geschiedenis van prijzen en lonen in Vlaanderen en Brabant (Xve–XVIIIe eeuw),* vol. I, Gent 1959, pp. 291–308.

4.2.3 Dairy Products

Dairy products, consisting mainly of butter and cheese, were the third category of agrarian products sold on a large scale at the Antwerp market. The demand for butter increased during the first half of the sixteenth century. While the St. –Elisabeth Hospital bought 600-650 kg every year in the late fifteenth century, that quantity increased to 1000 kg a year by the middle of the sixteenth century.[38] Butter was imported in great quantities from Flanders and Holland. Even great landowners, such as the abbey of Villers, had to buy Flemish and Dutch butter at the Antwerp fairs.[39] From about 1500, Dutch butter, especially from Delft, seems to have replaced Flemish butter at the St. Bavo fair in Antwerp.[40] It was only during the Revolt that imports from the North decreased and both Flemish and Kempen butter (from Wuustwezel and Zundert) once again became more important in the Antwerp market.[41]

Holland was also the main supplier of cheese for the Antwerp market. At the beginning of the sixteenth century, cheese from Flanders, England and from the land of Herve was sold at the Antwerp fairs.[42] By the end of the sixteenth century, Italian cheese, especially from Parma, also appeared on the Antwerp market. Among the Brabant cheeses, *Tiense kaas* (named after the town of Tienen/Tirlemont) was especially popular. This type of cheese did not necessarily come from Tienen, however: the name was also applied to cheese produced in the immediate surroundings of Antwerp.[43] Other sources mention sweet cheese among the local types of cheese.[44] Dutch cheese became the most popular type during the revolt against Maximilian of Habsburg, when prices for Flemish cheese increased sharply. From Antwerp, Flemish and Dutch cheese was further distributed to the Brabantine hinterland and throughout Northwestern Europe. The Rupelmonde toll register from 1541/42 refers to whole shiploads of Dutch cheese being shipped to the Brabantine interior as well as to Flanders.[45] In the Antwerp *certificates*, many German merchants also figure as buyers of Flemish and Dutch cheese.[46]

Peasants probably had a greater share in the supply of other agrarian products, such as eggs, poultry, vegetables or fruit, than they had for grain. Poultry was present in almost any rural household. Moreover, most farms had an orchard and a vegetable garden. Although the production of each household was probably very limited, the mass of furnishers meant that their collective contribution was quite considerable. Some of these products were also

38 P. De Commer and H. Soly, "De zestiende eeuw. Harde Tijden voor zusters en zieken (1490–1585)" in *Het St.-Elisabethziekenhuis te Antwerpen. 750 jaar Gasthuis op't Elzenveld 1238–1988*, Brussel, 1988, p. 82. Similar increases can also be observed for institutions in Brussels during the fifteenth and especially the sixteenth century. Van der Wee, *Growth*, I, p. 210.

39 G. Ploegaerts, "L'abbaye cistercienne de Villers pendant les cinq derniers siècles de son existence" in *Annales de la société archéologique de l'arrondissement de Nivelles XI (1913–26)*, p. 360.

40 Van der Wee, *Growth*, I, p. 210, Scholliers, *Prijzen en lonen*, p. 315–318.

41 Van der Wee, *Growth*, I, p. 210.

42 Ploegaerts, "L'abbaye" p. 360.

43 The lease contract for the Salincrode farm in Mortsel from 1521 stipulates the payment of "*10 thiensche kazen' soe zij daer gewoonlijk zijn te maken*"; SAA, Coll 4, fo. 215 r. (1 mei 1521).

44 SAA, Coll. 4 fo. 203r. According to a lease contract for a farm in Wuustwezel (1529) (owned by the St. Elisabeth hospital): "*twaalf soete casen gelijk men daer gewoenlijc is te maken*".

45 ARA, Rk. Reg. 22739 and 22740. In 1541/42 more than 12,000 pieces of cheese were shipped up the Rupel.

46 R. Doehaerd, *Etudes anversoises. Documents sur le commerce international à Anvers, 1488–1514*, 3 vols., Paris, 1963, passim.

produced within the town itself. Although the consumption of fruit was of secondary importance in comparison to that of grain, meat and dairy products, it is striking how lively the traffic of fruit was from the Brabantine hinterland toward Antwerp. Great quantities of fruit were shipped down the Rupel and Scheldt from southern Brabant and eastern Flanders.[47]

4.2.4 Industrial Crops

Besides food, industrial crops were also in high demand in Antwerp. The term *industrial crops* refers to a variety of plants including flax, hops, dyeing plants (such as woad or madder), and oily plants (such as colza and rapeseed). The cultivation of industrial plants had already been widespread in the Low Countries since the late Middle Ages. The cultivation of flax had increased considerably in the fourteenth century and was particularly important in the area around Aalst and Gent.[48] The main sorts of dyeing plants that were grown in the Low Countries were madder and woad. While madder and teasels were typical for the coastal areas, and especially for Zeeland, woad (for pastel colours) was more common in the clay soils of southwestern Brabant and eastern Flanders. Woad was also grown in the South of Brabant, but the demand for it decreased from the late fifteenth century, because of the declining local drapery production and the increasing imports from the area of Toulouse.[49] Hops were grown in different areas of the southern Low Countries, including the area around Aalst and the Land of Heusden. For the Antwerp market, the area of Aalst was of major importance.[50] Within Brabant, the area of Asse was also specialised in the cultivation of hops.[51]

Another type of industrial crop were those plants that whose seeds provided oil for lighting. These oil-producing plants were typically sown in fallow. The seeds of the turnip or rape plant were commonly cultivated in the late Middle Ages, but this crop was replaced in the clay areas of Brabant and Flanders during the sixteenth century by *colza*, which was more rich in oil and gave a higher output.[52]

In the surroundings of Antwerp, two types of industrial crops prevailed. Flax was grown in the Kempen as well as on various farms between Lier and the Scheldt that belonged to the St. Bernard Abbey at Hemixem.[53] The only dyeing plant that was produced in the immediate surroundings of Antwerp was madder, which was planted in great quantities in the polders of Lillo and further north toward the town of Bergen op Zoom.[54]

47 ARA, Rk. Reg. 22739 and 22740.

48 G. Dejongh and E. Thoen, "Arable Productivity in Flanders and the Former Territory of Belgium in a Long-Term Perspective (from the Middle Ages to the End of the Ançien Regime)" in B.J.P. van Bavel and E. Thoen, eds. *Land Productivity and Agro-Systems in the North Sea Area. Middle Ages – 20th Century. Elements for Comparison*, Turnhout 1999 (CORN Publication Series, 2), pp. 30–46; Thoen, *Landbouweconomie*, vol. II, p. 980–1020.

49 Van Uytven, "In de Schaduwen".

50 In the 1540s, there was a lively trade of hops from the Aalst area to Antwerp, ARA, Rk. Reg. 22740.

51 H. Soly, "De economische betekenis van Zuidnederlandse brouwindustrie in de zestiende eeuw. Problematiek" in *Economische geschiedenis van België: behandeling van de bronnen en problematiek: handelingen van het Colloquium te Brussel, 17–19 nov. 1971*, Brussel 1972, 97–117.

52 Lindemans, *Landbouw*, vol. II, p. 269f.

53 The farms of Vlaesten, Lachene, Allier, Vremde and Bogarde had to pay between 10–12 ells of linen as part of their lease. RAA KA St. Bernards, no. 10. See also: Lindemans, *Landbouw*, II, 219 note 15.

54 G. Asaert, "Handel in kleurstoffen op de Antwerpse markt tijdens de XVe eeuw" in *Bijdragen en mededelingen betreffende de geschiedenis der Nederlanden*, 88 (1973), pp. 377–402; Lindemans, *Landbouw*, II, pp. 255–257.

To summarise, local supplies and regional trade could only provide part of the food Antwerp needed in the sixteenth century. Especially grain, meat and dairy products had to be imported. Nevertheless, local and regional supplies still formed the basis of the town's food supply. Especially in the case of grain, the proportion differed considerably between years of good harvest and bad years. Without any doubt, the high demand and thus high food prices in Antwerp will have stimulated the local producers to produce for the urban market, rather than to withdraw from it and to turn toward subsistence farming.

4.3 The Response to the Rising Urban Demand

The rising demand for agrarian produce formed a challenge for town and countryside alike. For the town and its inhabitants, it was crucial to safeguard the supply of sufficient provisions and to avoid price manipulation by merchants that could lead to unrest among the population. Religious and charitable institutions, merchants, butchers and bakers, but also the urban consumers, each had their own strategy to get a hold of their supplies, or to make profits by provisioning the town. In the following section, we will not be analysing these different strategies as such, but rather the consequences they had on the agrarian structures of the surrounding countryside. The town magistrates and merchants, whose influence on agriculture was rather indirect, will be treated rather briefly. More attention will be paid to the effects of the strategies of landowners and farmers.

4.3.1 The Town Authorities

The town magistracy was not directly involved in agrarian production. As in the Middle Ages, they controlled the marketing of victuals, so as to avoid hoarding and to prevent abuses by intermediaries. Only in periods of extreme shortages, such as in 1556-57 and 1565, did they purchase grain to provide to the population.[55] In normal circumstances, inventories of stocked grain were made, not only to monitor the quantities available but also to avoid hoarding and speculation.[56] One of the main concerns of the urban provisioning policy was to avoid food riots and to maintain the public order.[57] The general principle behind this policy was to provide enough grain for the population at a just price. In order to achieve this goal, they applied a staple policy, which in effectively forced the transit trade to sell parts of the load in town. In times of famine, sales outside the town limits were forbidden. To guarantee a just price for consumers, the market was regulated by numerous measures, mainly in order to avoid price speculation or *voorkoop*, i.e. the practice of intermediaries of buying food and then reselling it at a higher price.

Another group whose interests had to be defended were the guilds. Hence, competition from outsiders was limited as much as possible. A third point of interest,

55 The town generally had some grain stocks, which were regularly renewed. The sale of these stocks could also serve as a means of regulating prices. See: T. Masure, *De stadsfinanciën van Antwerpen 1531–1571. Een poging tot reconstructie*, 2 vols., MA. thesis, Univ. Ghent, 1986, p. 144.

56 Ordinances from 18 November 1556 and 4 June 1557 in F. Génard, "Index der gebodboeken 1489–1620" in *Antwerpsch Archievenblad* 1 (1864), p. 260 and 261.

57 F. Janssens and E. Van Cauwenberghe, "Stedelijke bevoorradingspolitiek en graanwetgeving in crisistijd te Antwerpen ond het midden van de zeventiende eeuw" in *Bijdragen tot de Geschiedenis*, 62 (1979), p. 231.

and probably not the least important, was taxation. As urban taxes were based largely on the indirect taxation of the consumption and distribution of food, the town magistrate controlled the traffic of grain, beer and other products outside the city in order to avoid that a considerable part of these escaped urban taxation.[58] It was especially through this concern that the town interfered with the economic life of the surroundings. To avoid the loss of income through excises missed as a result of brewers situated in the rural areas, for example, the town pledged or bought the seigniorial rights of surrounding villages or made arrangements with the local lords concerning the urban excises. This intervention mainly affected village businesses such as breweries, taverns, bakeries, and butchers, but not so much agriculture.[59]

Urban policy could nevertheless affect agrarian productivity indirectly, namely by improving the transport infrastructure to and from the town. Fast and easy transport provided an incentive for farmers to bring their produce to the urban market and favoured the transport of urban waste to the countryside, which in turn could be a major factor for increased agrarian productivity. P. Hoffman discovered that the improvement of transport around big urban centres such as Paris was one of the major factors that explained the high agrarian productivity in their surroundings.[60] Antwerp, of course, had a marvellous waterway system, consisting of the Scheldt on the one hand, which connected the town with the North Sea and with Flanders and the granaries of northern France, and the Brabantine river network on the other hand, which made a wide hinterland accessible by boat. In the 1540s, the capacity of the Antwerp port was increased by the construction of a new port in Nieuwstad, in the northern part of the town. Furthermore, Antwerp was connected with its hinterland by numerous roads, which nevertheless were only paved for a few kilometres outside of town.[61] The town authorities took the initiative to increase the quality of the roads around the town at several occasions, partly after complaints from merchants.[62]

4.3.2 Merchants

Merchants were responsible for the provision of goods from outside the direct market area. They bought grain and other merchandise in remote markets and had them transported to Antwerp. In normal years, they were likely to search for their merchandise in areas less distant, which made transport cheaper and reduced risks. In years of grain shortages, in contrast, they imported from areas farther away, especially from the Baltic. Periods of shortage promised high profits for such grain merchants, who could provide large quantities when prices were highest. Hence many Antwerp merchants speculated with Baltic grain at the Amsterdam market in the 1560s, a period of bad harvests in Western Europe. In 1565 a group of rich, Antwerp-based merchants was accused of monopolistic practices. In a period when Antwerp was suffering a severe grain shortage, they were holding great stocks in their

58 Baetens, "Lokale markten", pp. 185–89.

59 See also Chapter 7, which deals with the non-agrarian sector.

60 Hoffman, *Growth in a Traditional Society*, pp. 178–84.

61 A.K.L. Thijs, "Een ongeziene commerciële bloei" in K. van Isacker and R. van Uytven (eds.), *Antwerpen. Twaalf eeuwen geschiedenis en cultuur*, Antwerpen, 1986, p. 95; B. Ballaux, "Molenstenen voor de Kempen: landvervoer en transportkosten in de vijftiende en zestiende eeuw" in *Het transport en het stedelijke netwerk in de Zuidelijke Nederlanden*, *Bijdragen tot de Geschiedenis* 82 (1999) p. 271f.

62 Masure, *Stadsfinanciën*, p. 197f.

storehouses in Amsterdam and Antwerp without selling them.[63] One grain merchant, Paul van Dale, was discovered to have engaged in similar practices when his granary collapsed and huge quantities of rye streamed out on the street.[64] The public opinion considered the speculative practices and monopolies of grain merchants to be the main reason for the extreme price explosions in some years. More likely, however, those things were merely rather exceptional abuses of a system that was meant to soften price peaks.

4.3.3 Landowners and Land Users

Merchants and other townsmen were nevertheless also more directly involved in agrarian production, i.e. through purchasing real estate in the countryside. Besides the advantages of a secure investment, landed property offered a regular income in the form of rents that were payable both in money and in kind. Especially in a period of rising land rents, farmland property promised high profits. At the same time, land rents paid in kind served as supplies for the landowner and made him independent of the urban market for a number of basic goods, such as grain, meat, fruit or timber. If the holding was sufficiently large, rents paid in kind could also be sold at the market and thus produce profits.

In fact, there was a veritable real estate boom in the surroundings of Antwerp during the sixteenth century, with townsmen purchasing property within an ever-larger area. While a large part of the land owned by Antwerpers during the fifteenth century was situated within ca. 13 km of the town,[65] in the sixteenth century, the area concerned was greater, extending especially towards the north. Some townsmen acquired considerable holdings in the polders north of Antwerp. There are indications that heavy investments were made in the polder area along the Scheldt, in order to reclaim land that had been flooded in the previous decades. In 1515, for example, Jean Wyts received permission to dike about 105 ha of polder land in the villages of Oosterweel and Wilmarsdonk.[66] Antwerp merchants were also involved in land-reclamation projects in Zeeland, which thus to some degree became part of the immediate provisioning area of the metropolis.[67] Also within this area, the proportion of urban landed property strongly increased.

Antwerp citizens were not the only ones to profit from agrarian incomes resulting from growing demand in the city, however. For landowners from outside the city, too, purchasing land in the agrarian hinterland of Antwerp was promising. At the same time, the demand for leases was also very high. The high population density in the closer surroundings of Antwerp points to a very intensive use of land in the second half of the sixteenth century. A declaration concerning the state of the villages of Boom and Rumst around that period confirms this assumption. According to the village aldermen, not a single *bunder* of land was empty on the eve of the Revolt.[68] A comparison of the cultivated area of Rumst as described in the aldermen's declarations with the total village area in 1686, although hazardous,

63 Van Tielhof, *Hollandse graanhandel*, p. 223.

64 G. Van Havre, ed., *Chronijck der stadt Antwerpen* [attributed to G. Bertrijn], Antwerp, 1879 (Uitgave der Antwerpsche Bibliophilen, 5).

65 See Chapter 2.

66 L. Galesloot, *Inventaire des archives de la Cour Feodale de Brabant*, Brussel, 1870–1884, vol. I, p. 20.

67 See Chapter 10.

68 *'Voor de troebelen waren de voors. dorpen vol volks en in vol labeur van hun goederen, niet een bunder ledig. – ja het was moeilijk de huring te krijgen'.* SAA, VG 5, Declaration concerning Rumst and Boom 1593.

nevertheless shows that the 450 *bunders* of arable land or pasture in Rumst would have comprised ca. 64% of the area of that village, while in Boom, that was only 24%. In the neighbourhood of Antwerp, the percentage of cultivated land was considerably higher: in Deurne it was 76% of the village area, and in Mortsel, the amount of cultivated land was almost identical with the total village area.[69] In other places, the percentage of farmland lay between 30 and 40%.[70] In general, land use seems to have been particularly intense in the more immediate surroundings and to the south of Antwerp, whereas in the Kempen, as well as in the proto-industrial place of Boom, it was rather low. The result of this high demand for land was a continuing increase in both real estate prices and lease prices. In fact, the tax value of land near Antwerp, based on the lease value, was among the highest in the whole duchy of Brabant.[71] We will concentrate on the effects this real estate boom had on the rural property relations in chapter 10. In the following sections, we will be focusing on the agrarian implications strictly speaking.

The alternative to an expansion of the cultivated area was to introduce qualitative changes. From a technical point of view, there was a whole range of possibilities for increasing the agrarian output without increasing the total amount of land. One was by changing the composition of the land-use. M. Overton distinguishes six forms of such change: land reclamation or improvement, a changing ratio between grassland and arable, a reduction in fallow, the introduction of fodder crops, a changing balance among different crops, and regional specialisation.[72] Switching between arable and pasture allowed the farmers to adopt to changes in the demand patterns for animal products and arable crops. Furthermore, the energetic output of arable farming per unit was much higher than that of livestock farming. A reduction in fallow, for example by growing legumes or fodder crops in the third year of the crop rotation, provided an additional harvest. Fodder crops, in turn, formed a way to increase the output of livestock without having to extend the pasture and hence diminish the land available for arable. At the same time, fodder crops such as turnips had fertilising effects for the land and helped to control weeds.[73] Regional specialisation, finally, was a way to increase overall output by concentrating the productive forces on the agrarian product that was most fit for the area. While this did not necessarily signify an increase in local productivity for the product in question, it avoided investment in less productive sectors and thus increased overall output. By specialising in livestock farming, for example, Holland and Friesland essentially left le grain production to other areas.

---

69 OCMW, EG 172, Cohier van de zeven kwartieren van Antwerpen 1686, see also: F. Prims, "Het 'denombrement' van de zeven kwartieren van Antwerpen van 1686" in *Bijdragen tot de Geschiedenis* 37 (1954), pp. 108–122. The strong deviations among the different villages show the difficulty of this comparison. The community areas which the figures of 1570 refer to may have differed from those of 1686. Hence, the low percentage of cultivated land in some places may partly be the result of a different calculation of the community area, and not only be due to structural differences between the villages. The comparison with the percentage of cultivated land in 1686 helps to distinguish between structural factors and methodological imprecision. So, for example, Aartselaar and Wommelgem had a similar degree of cultivated land as Mortsel or Deurne in 1686. The low figures in 1570 are therefore more likely to methodological factors than in Boom or Schoten where the degree of cultivated land was low in 1570 and in 1686.

70 SAA VG 4–5, Toestand der dorpen in 1593, see also A. Cosemans, "Het uitzicht van Brabant".

71 Blondé, B. and Limberger, M., "De gebroken welvaart" in R. van Uytven, et al., eds., *De geschiedenis van Brabant van het hertogdom tot heden*, Zwolle 2004, p. 317–319.

72 M. Overton, *Agricultural Revolution in England: the Transformation of the Agrarian Economy, 1500–1850*, Cambridge, 1996 (Cambridge Studies in Historical Geography, 23), p. 88.

73 Overton, *Agricultural Revolution* p. 99.

Besides these ways of increasing output by extending or changing the use of land, there were also possibilities for increasing the productivity of either the land or the labour. Agrarian historians have paid special attention to the productivity of land, i.e. the increase of the output – particularly of grain – per hectare.[74] Not only is the increase of output per hectare one of the most visible aspects of agrarian productivity, it is also one of the most effective means of increasing agrarian production. According to Tits-Dieuaide, the yield of wheat per hectare in the area of Brussels increased by ca. 25% between the fifteenth and nineteenth century, for example.[75] An increase in the productivity of land could be achieved through a higher input of seed-corn, manure or labour. While an increase in the amount of seed had only a limited effect, the factors of manure and labour were crucial. Finally, the productivity of labour could also be increased, either through technological innovations or through economies of scale, i.e. through larger farm sizes and therefore through an optimal use of tools, horses and the labour force.

Landowners who did not farm their holdings themselves could, in theory, influence the farming process through the stipulations in the lease contract, although their freedom of choice was not unlimited. There was only a limited range of products and combinations that made sense economically and that were technically possible. They also had to find a farmer who was willing to lease the farm under their conditions. Given the fact that leasing a farm was an enterprise with a considerable risk, farmers would not venture to take a farm under too-uncertain conditions. It was rather the farmer who tried to increase his profits by changing the crop rotation, the combination of the crops or the farming techniques. On the other hand, landowners were careful to prevent the farmer from ruining the farm in the long term by running it in an abusive way. The exhaustion of the soil as a result of inappropriate farming practices and the poor state of the farm buildings, ditches and fences were major concerns that the owner tried to avert through the lease contract. Lease contracts are therefore good for gaining insight into the farming practice of those days from the perspective of the landowner's active intervention and standard passages aimed at simple protection of his property. In what follows, we will therefore be using lease contracts, among other sources, to help fill in the details of the farming system applied in the rural surroundings of Antwerp during both the fifteenth century – thus before it's commercial boom began – and the sixteenth century, in order to detect any changes in that system.

74 Dejongh and Thoen, "Arable Productivity"; see also H. Van der Wee, and E. Van Cauwenberghe, eds., *Productivity of Land and Agricultural Innovations in the Low Countries (1250–1800)*, Leuven, 1978.
75 Tits-Dieuaide, *Formation*, p. 93.

CHAPTER 5

Agrarian Production and Productivity in the Fifteenth Century

5.1 The Trend Towards Intensive Husbandry in Medieval Flanders and Brabant

One of the secrets of the Low Countries that helped the area to resist the late medieval depression relatively well was their particular economic organisation in general and their advanced agrarian system in particular.[1] The fact that the area did not suffer a more severe positive check of mortality despite its relative overpopulation at that moment, led E. Thoen to call the southern Low Countries "the problem child of Malthus".[2] This progressive agrarian system had been developing since the late thirteenth century and helped Flemish and Brabantine peasants obtain higher and more diversified yields than those in other parts of Europe. In this regard, the southern Low Countries differed sharply from the northern provinces, where according to de Vries the rural economy around 1500 was hardly specialised and not very productive.[3]

By the late fifteenth-century, Brabant – along with Flanders and northern France – had reached a high degree of agricultural productivity. Cereal yields there were among the highest in Western Europe, comparable with those in the Lille area in northern France and the most productive areas of England.[4] The origins of this intensification extended back to the middle of the thirteenth century. Authors such as Verhulst and van Uytven, and more recently Thoen, found indications of alternative crops being planted during the fallow period, a first attempt to increase the number of harvests per year.[5] Another way the farmers broke with the classical three-field system was by sowing seeds other than barley or oats, the traditional summer –grains, but rather beans, peas, flax, weld and vetch – a practice called *verantzaden* or *hoervruchten* in contemporary documents. Sometimes these plants were also sown together with the traditional summer grains as so-called *dubbelfruchten* (double-crops) in order to increase the output per hectare while, at the same time, spreading the risk of crop failure. *Verantzaden, dubbelfruchten* and cultivating the fallow fields seem to have been very common practices in late medieval Flanders and Brabant. The owners of lease farms tried

1 E. Aerts, E. Van Cauwenberghe, "Die Grafschaft Flandern und die sogenannte spätmittelalterliche Depression" in F. Seibt ed., *Europa 1400. Die Krise des Spätmittelalters*,, Stuttgart, 1984, pp. 221–232.

2 Thoen, "A Commercial Survival Economy", p. 103.

3 De Vries, *Dutch rural economy*, p. 32f.

4 M.-J. Tits-Dieuaide, "L' évolution des techniques agricoles en Flandre et en Brabant du XIVe au XVe siècle" in *Annales E.S.C* 36 (1981), p. 363f. For Lille: A. Derville, "Le rendement du blé dans la région lilloise (1285–1541)" in *Bulletin de la Commission historique du Département du Nord* XL (1975–1976), pp. 23–39.

5 R. van Uytven, "Vroege inbreuken op de braak in Brabant en de intensieve landbouw in de Zuidelijke Nederlanden tijdens der 13de eeuw" in *Tijdschrift van de Belgische Vereniging voor aardrijkskundige studies* LIII 1984/1 (Bruxelles, 1984), pp. 63–72. A. Verhulst, "The 'Agricultural Revolution' of the Middle Ages Reconsidered" in *Law, Custom and the SocialFabric in Medieval Europe,* Essays in Honor of Bryce Lyon, B.S. Bachrach, D. Nicholas, eds., Kalamazoo 1990, pp. 17–28.

to restrict these techniques as much as possible in order to guarantee the fertility of the soil in the long run. These practices were originally forbidden in the contracts of lease farms in order to avoid exhausting the soil. The farmers were obliged to stick to the traditional three-course rotation system. By the late Middle Ages, however, many a landowner reduced this restriction to the last three years of the lease. On small holdings owned by the peasant himself, these restrictions were absent. It is therefore likely that the tendency to abandon the classical three-course system was stronger in the small peasant holdings than in the large lease farms. According to P. Lindemans, the lesser peasantry generally applied a free system of crop rotation aimed at production for the market.[6] There is evidence, therefore, that Flanders and Brabant agriculture had already gone through their first "agrarian revolution" by the fifteenth century, and already had a very advanced and intensive agriculture. This is also the conclusion of A. Verhulst in a recent article on the medieval agricultural revolution: *"If the use of the term "agricultural revolution" is justified anywhere, it is certainly here, in densely urbanized north-western Europe during the thirteenth century."*[7]

The major aces of Flemish and Brabantine intensive husbandry in its early stage were, according to the same authors: the intensive use of fertiliser, a varied production and the intensive input of labour on small holdings. The availability of manure was a crucial problem of pre-industrial agriculture. It was linked directly with the amount of livestock, and therefore with the size of the available pasture. Expanding the latter, however, was only possible at the expense of the fields. Medieval farming was therefore caught in a tug-of-war between the need for fertiliser and the need for farmland.[8] A high degree of intensification, on the other hand, was also dependent on a low land-labour ratio. From this point of view, the high population density of the Low Countries along with the related subdivision of holdings, helped the development towards intensive farming.

To what degree does this general picture match the situation in the surroundings of Antwerp? By means of a sample of lease contracts for about 60 farms and plots of land in the Antwerp area, together with a number of available studies, we will be analysing the degree to which the preconditions were favourable for intensive husbandry, and the extent to which this was applied on western Brabantine farms in the middle of the fifteenth century. The purpose of this section is to sketch a general picture of the agrarian system in the surroundings of Antwerp in the fifteenth century in order to detect, in the following part of our study, to what extent the changes of the urban demand patterns during the sixteenth century led to changes in the agrarian structure.

5.2 Lease Contracts As Sources of Agrarian Techniques

We find two major types of farms in late medieval Brabant: peasant farms that were generally smaller than five hectares, and lease farms, which could range from two to about 100 hectares. Small peasant holdings were often exploited by the owners themselves. Their obligations consisted of paying a yearly rent in money or in kind to the landlord, plus the tithe, and any seigniorial usage duties. They were not bound to any restrictions concerning

6 Lindemans, *Landbouw*, I, p. 101, although he fails to provide evidence for his assumption.
7 Verhulst, "Agricultural revolution", p. 24.
8 Tits-Dieuaide, "L' évolution", p. 363.

their agrarian activity, however. Their payments in kind, as registered in seigniorial accounts, give us some idea of the main products of these holdings. Large parts of the accounts of the estates of lay landlords as well as of those of the ducal domains consist of the registration of rents in kind payable in each village. These rents constituted a fixed amount, however, and did not change over the centuries. The payments therefore form a rather static indicator and are not very representative of the fifteenth century. More useful for reconstructing the agrarian techniques and practices of the late Middle Ages are the contracts of farms on land leased out by their owners for a certain period. Direct exploitation by great landowners, such as ecclesiastical institutions, had already been abandoned in the High Middle Ages. Leasehold provided a regular income, which could be adapted to price movements. In the contracts, the owner fixed the conditions of the lease, the terms and amount of the payments, as well as the duties of the farmer. These contracts therefore serve as valuable sources for analysing the agrarian practice – although only within these particular lease farms. Lease contracts have their limitations, of course. They are an agreement between the landowner and the farmer that protects the interests of both parties and are meant to prevent abuses by either or both parties. Hence, they form only a general framework of the farming process and stress only particular aspects that were important for either of the two parties, but especially for the owner.

Similar considerations have to be made with regard to the lease payments in kind mentioned in the contracts. An analysis of the composition of these leases makes it possible to draw some conclusions concerning the major crops on the farms. Of course, leases paid in kind only partially reflect the crops that were cultivated; to a large extent, they also reflect the demand of the landowner. This is a disadvantage of leases that were payable in kind as a source for the study of agrarian production. In the context of possible responses to the urban demand, however, they are particularly useful, because the demand factor is strongly present in the lease contracts. Most of the owners of the farms we have analysed can be identified as urban citizens or urban institutions. Although we have to distinguish between the demand of specific landowners and the urban demand in general, they are very likely to coincide to a large extent. Moreover, the degree to which the leases in kind are representative is not to be underestimated. Not only would it be unrealistic for a landowner to demand the production of goods that were not at all common in the area, but lease payments could reach proportions of 30 to 50% of the total harvest, and therefore do represent a considerable part of the total production. Leases in kind therefore are an indicator of the needs of townsmen for particular agrarian products, while at the same time an indication for the presence – and to a certain extent the relative importance – of the different crops. Finally, the fact that landowners stipulated the payment by means of particular crops will have formed an impulse to produce these goods on the farm in question, which forms another aspect of the influence the urban demand had on the countryside.

For our analysis we have compiled a sample of fifteenth-century lease contracts from the area around Antwerp. There is a very useful source for retrieving a more or less representative sample of contracts, i.e. the registers of the Antwerp aldermen.[9] They have

9 These registers, kept in the Antwerp City Archives, cover the period from the 15th century on. See discussion in chapter 10.

the advantage of containing properties held by different owners (individuals as well as institutions) and at different locations in the area surrounding the town.[10] To compensate for the limitations of these samples, information from other contracts cited in local studies and other primary sources has been added to obtain a more varied spectrum. This was for example the case with several contracts pertaining to farms to the south of Antwerp (Edegem, Wilrijk, Kontich), to the Anderstad farm near Lier[11] and to the Bremdonk farm in Ekeren.[12] All in all, we obtained a collection of 64 contracts – a sample that, while not representative of the whole area, is sufficiently indicative of the general situation (see appendix 1).

The contracts contain wide-ranging information concerning the farmer, the crops and the livestock, as well as all kinds of specifications about the use of the land. Our primary goal is not so much a global analysis of the lease contracts, however, but rather to get an idea of the agrarian techniques and organisation. In my analysis, I have therefore concentrated on the following points:

- the major products
- the composition and size of the farms
- the field rotation
- the use of fertiliser
- the maintenance of fields and buildings

5.3 An Example: The Share-Cropping Contract of the Manor Farm "Ter Anderstad" from 1464

On 2 June 1464, Willem Smet, called Rademakere, signed a lease for the manor farm of Anderstad, outside the town of Lier, as a sharecropper from Jan van Wezemaal, Lord of Mortsel, Phaleys and the Land van Mechelen.[13] The term of the contract was nine years, and the farmer had to accept the following conditions, which had already been valid for his predecessor, Wouter Gielis:

- He had to fertilise and seed nine *bunders* (9.5 or 11.12 hectares[14]) with rye every year, and he had to give half of all the "summer fruits" he cultivated to the owner.
- He had the right to seed three *muddeken* (64.875 litres) of linseed to his own profit; half everything above these three *muddeken* belonged to the owner.
- He had to cultivate a plot of *wijngart land* for the owner, who had to provide the necessary seeds.
- Apart from these fields, the lease included a meadow in front of the farm towards the

10 SAA, SR 43 (see Appendix1). 34 of these contracts, concerning goods situated in Deurne, have been analysed in Nooyens, *Deurne,* vol. I, pp. 417–457.

11 Van Passen, *Edegem*, Idem, *Kontich*, Idem, *Geschiedenis van Wilrijk,* Wilrijk, 1982. Lindemans, *Landbouw*, passim. The contract of the Anderstad farm is discussed at length in the following section.

12 E. Geudens, *Le "Peerdsbosch" ou le domaine rural du Bremdonck*, Antwerp, 1908 (Annales de l'Académie royale d'archéologie de Belgique), p. 26–32.

13 The contract is copied in the account of the ducal demesne the Land van Mechelen of 1467/8. RK reg. 11897, fo. 18v°–19v°. The castle of Anderstad was already built in 1247 on the banks of the river Nete, near the town of Lier, and belonged then already to the Land van Mechelen, at that time a possession of the powerful family of Berthout. See A. Bergmann, *Geschiedenis der stad Lier*, Lier, 1973², p. 56.

14 Based on the *bunder* of either Duffel (1.054 ha) or Mechelen (1.2364 ha), respectively, both of which were valid within the Land van Arkel. Van de Walle, *Oude maten*, p. 53.

river Nete, for which the farmer had to pay 50 guilders (1 *gulden rhijnsch* = 0.25 pound Brabantine groten).

- He was allowed to let 20 pieces of cattle, old or young, graze in the forest of the owner, where the cattle of the surrounding farms are driven every year.
- He was also allowed to let his sheep graze in the same forest during the winter, as long as they caused no damage.
- He had a small orchard at his disposal, which was situated in front of the farm.
- He was allowed to cut undergrowth for firewood, but he had to bring half of it to the barn of the landlord – according to the principle of *helftwinning*, whereby half of the production went to the landowner.
- He was also allowed to cut as much peat as he needed to fuel his own fires, but could not sell or give it to anyone else. He was not allowed to cut any peat in places where there were trees or where roots of trees were growing.
- He had to maintain the farm and the fields. He had to dig trenches and build dikes at his own expense for the "benefit of the farm", and he was supposed to keep the walls and the roof of the farm in good condition.
- At the end of his lease period, Willem had to leave eight *bunders* of well-fertilised land seeded with rye for the new leaseholder, and, because there were no animals on the farm during the last year and therefore no manure was available, he was given a discount of 12 guilders.

So much for the conditions of the lease contract, which form a good example of the regulations governing fifteenth-century lease farms. In the following analysis, we will be looking at the features of this example in comparison with the other sample contracts in or collection. We will then consider the western Brabantine patterns within the context of the southern Netherlands as presented in the literature.

5.4 An Analysis of Lease Contracts from the Antwerp Area

5.4.1 Major Crops and Livestock

Lease contracts contain some qualitative information about the kind of products that were cultivated on the property in question, for example in the *lating*, which stipulates the way the property has to be left at the end of the lease. Quantitative figures are relatively scarce and can be found essentially in the stipulation of the lease payments in kind. In the case of the Anderstad farm, we are told that the farmer was supposed to sow nine *bunders* of his fields with rye. The summer crops, on the other hand, are not further specified. The contract mentions a certain quantity of linseed (65 l) that the farmer was allowed to grow for his own benefit. In the event that he grew more than this (modest) quantity, he had to pay half of the harvest to the landowner. With regard to livestock, the contract mentions twenty pieces of cattle and an undefined number of sheep. Finally, the usage rights of firewood and peat are specified. From this limited information, we only obtain a limited picture of the production of this important manor farm of the Land van Mechelen. Unlike that of many other farms of the period, the lease for this farm is not specified in the contract, due to fact that it was leased under the condition of *helftwinning*, a form of sharecropping in which, at least in theory, half of the harvest had to be paid to the owner.[15]

A preliminary overview of the major crops and farming products of the Antwerp area can be obtained by looking at how frequently different products are mentioned in our sample of contracts. The qualitative information in the contract can be quantified to some degree by looking at the composition of the leases in kind (Table 5).

Table 5: Mentions of Farm Products in Lease Contracts

Product	Frequency	Total lease	Avg. lease	Comment
Rye	31	352 zister	12.6 z.	Lease, lating
Wheat	3	25.6 z.	8.5 z.	Lease: Mortsel, Hove, Deurne
Winter rye	2			Lating
Corn	2			Reduction of lease, lating
Winter corn	1			Lating
Rough oats (evene)	14	130.6 z.	10.8 z.	Lease (normally 3/4 or equal to rye), lating
Summer crops	4			Lating
Buckwheat	2	4.5 z.	4.5 z.	lease: Schoten, Ekeren
Oats (haver)	1	15 z.	15 z.	lease in Mortsel: in combination with wheat, rye and evene
Barley	1			Lating
Peas	1			Lating
Rapeseed	1	0.5 z.	0.5 z.	Ekeren
Linseed	2			For benefit of owner
Flax	3	9 stones	3 stones	Lease
Vegetable garden	3			
Turnips	1			
Orchard	8			
Apples	3			1 zister, "the apples"
Pears	2			
Cherries	1			
Fruit				Lease: 1/2 the fruit
Vineyard	1			

15 The actual lease revenue is cited in the accounts of the demesne the Land van Mechelen and forms a good source for reconstructing the global production of the farm, see further.

Product	Frequency	Total lease	Avg. lease	Comment
Animals (beesten)	6			
Cattle	2			
Sheep	2			
Pigs	3			
Capons	18	157	8.8	
Chickens	6	35	5.8	
Geese	6	38	6.33	
Pigeons	5	12	12	
Eggs	10	950	94.444	9 x 100 + 1 x 50
Butter	6	33 lb + 27 l		
Cheese	1	6	6	Ekeren: thiensche kazen
Wethers (hamel)	5	10	2	Ekeren, Deurne, Zundert
Lambs	3	4	1.33	Ekeren, Deurne, Merksem
Fishpond	1			
Wax	6	35 lb	6.2 lb	

Grain was without any doubt the basic crop in the Antwerp area. Many passages refer to grain, *koren* or rye, as the major product. The farmer of a farm situated in Berchem and Wilrijk would be granted a reduction of his lease in case of damage to the corn through tempest or thunderstorm, for example.[16] The stipulations concerning the *lating* of the farms are also very explicit in terms of the predominance of grain among the crops. Leases for fields were mostly payable in grain. The dominating winter crop in the Antwerp area was rye. It made up more than 90% of the lease payments in winter crops and two-thirds of the total grain rents due. Wheat was part of the lease payments in only three farms, all of them situated in the fertile area south of Antwerp, and the quantity of wheat was substantial in only one of those: the Zadelroede farm in Mortsel. The farmer had to pay 22.5 *zisters* of rye, 22.5 *zisters* of wheat and 40 *zisters* of rough oats.[17] In the other two cases, the quantity of wheat was much smaller than that of rye.[18] Among the summer crops, rough oats (*evene*) were the most frequent, followed by buckwheat, light oats (*haver*), barley and peas. Rough oats made up 87% of the payments due in summer crops. In most cases, the amounts were between 75 and 100% of the quantity payable in rye. Leases were due in buckwheat at

16 *'Bij schade aant coren bij tempeste ende weerlicht'*, SAA, SR 43, fo. 260. (Appendix 1, contract no. 4).
17 SAA SR 43, fo. 403–404 (contract no. 7).
18 At the *'hof ter Bist'* farm in Hove: 3 *zisters* of wheat, 14 *zisters* of rye and 12 *zisters* of oats (SAA SR 43, fo. 433–434)(contract no. 9); at the *'hoeve ter Biest'* at Deurne: 1/8 *zister* of wheat, 4 1/2 *zisters* of rye and 3 1/2 plus 1/16 *zisters* of oats (SAA SR 70, fo. 331 r.], cited in Nooyens, Deurne, I, p. 437. Lindemans, *Landbouw* II, p. 13, calculated that in the fifteenth century 10–30% of the leases in winter grain the Brussels area were due in wheat, whereas during the fourteenth century, farm leases payable in grain consisted exclusively of rye.

farms situated in the sandy area northeast of Antwerp, in combination with rye,[19] or rye and oats.[20]

There is some mention of alternative crops in the contracts, such as peas, turnips, rapeseed and linseed, but considering the minor interest these crops would have had for the landowners, the references are relatively seldom. Only flax was mentioned in several contracts as part of the lease payment. On the other hand, none of the contracts forbids the use of alternative crops or techniques such as *verantzaden* or *dubbelvruchten*. Furthermore, the contracts also mention vegetable gardens (*waarmoeshof*), orchards with apple, pear and cherry trees, and even a vineyard. The latter, however, was reserved for the personal use of the landowner.[21]

Cattle and sheep were without any doubt the major types of livestock on Brabantine farms, although the contracts contain few if any quantitative figures. The contract of the Anderstad farm refers to 20 pieces of cattle that the farmer was allowed to graze, together with his sheep, in the owner's forest. Another contract concerning a farm in Zandvliet, in the polders, speaks of 112 sheep that could graze on the stubble.[22]

The income of the grazing rights in the Land van Mechelen in 1464 sheds some more light on the amount of livestock that farmers had in the surroundings of Antwerp. Among 63 tenants who paid for grazing their cattle in the ducal woods, 13 paid for one piece, 21 for two, 9 for three, 10 for four, and only one for five. Furthermore, ten tenants had one or more horses or foals.[23]

Cattle were thus grazed on plots of pasture (*weide, eusel, beemd*) on the stubble of grain fields or on common meadows after haying, or in woods, as we saw in the example above. Meadows along the rivers, in particular, were better fit for pasture or haying than for growing grain. On the other hand, cattle were also held in stables, where they were fed with hay. Stable feeding was important for the preservation of the dung, which, mixed with straw, served as major source of fertiliser. Hay and straw were therefore important farm products and as such were regularly mentioned in the contracts. In Edegem, for example, peasants had to pay a hay tithe.[24] In 1449, the lord of Ekeren turned his former feudal rights into the payment of a wagon-load of hay or two *gouden pieters*.[25] Straw, for its part, was highly valued for producing fertiliser as well as for roofing. As horses were the major hauling animal, larger farms almost inevitably had at least a couple of them. Considering that heavier wagons were drawn by four or even six horses, larger numbers of horses were not exceptional.[26] Besides cattle, sheep and horses, the contracts refer to pigs, chickens, geese, pigeons, and in one case even a fishpond, but they do not contain any details.

19 *'T oud steden* farm at Schoten, SAA SR 43, fo. 84 (1450) (contract no. 5).

20 *Bremdonk* farm at Ekeren, in 1423 and 1455, Geudens, *Peerdsbosch, p. 26–27.*

21 At the farm of Gillis Sanders, a local nobleman, in Hemixem (1450), SAA, SR 43, fo. 87 r (contract no. 2).

22 SAA, SR 43, fo. 576 vo. (contract no. 14). The sheep were held in share by the owner and the farmer. After three years, the increase in the livestock was divided. See also Lindemans, *Landbouw*, vol. I, p. 223.

23 ARA, Rk. 11897, Account, ducal desmesne the Land van Mechelen 1464/65, fo. 12r.–14r.

24 Contract of the farm Crockenrode (1452), SAA, SR 45, fo. 460r. cited in Van Passen, *Edegem* (contract no. 62).

25 E. Geudens, *Peerdsbosch*, p. 31–32; (1 *gouden pieter* = 4.5 s. Brab. gr. ARA, MW 113 (1465)).

26 Van Uytven, "Landtransport", p. 471–499.

5.4.2 The Size and Composition of Holdings

The contract of the Anderstad farm is not exactly explicit about the dimensions of the farm; it only tells us that it was composed of farmland and meadows, situated on both sides of the river Nete. What it does tell us is that the farmer was supposed to sow 9.5–11 hectares of land with rye. In the medieval three-course system, the proportion of land used for winter crops was, in principle, a third of the total farmland.[27] The total amount of farmland of the Anderstad farm would therefore have been 28.5 to 33 hectares. Moreover, although the contract does not indicate the size of the meadows, we can roughly estimate their size via the lease price of 50 guilders. Lease prices for meadows in western Brabant in that period ranged from 4 to 6 guilders per hectare.[28] This would make an approximate size of 8.3–12.5 hectares. The total farm size must therefore have been between 30 and 45 hectares. This means that the Anderstad farm will have been among the larger farms in the Antwerp area. Of the 19 farms for which we have information, only two were larger than 45 ha, 11 were smaller than 20 ha, and two were between 20 and 30 ha.

The fragmentary information we have in terms of the size also makes it difficult to estimate the proportion of farmland to meadows at the Anderstad farm. Roughly speaking, it must have been somewhere between 19 and 26%. Very few contracts indicate the proportion of land to pasture, and the figures we do have differ considerably from case to case:

Table 6: The Proportion of Arable to Pasture, ca. 1450

Farm	Fields (ha)	Meadow (ha.)	Meadows as % of total
Campdonk (Deurne):	24.4	10.98	31%
Crockenroede (Edegem)	18.9	3.66	16.2%
Hoeve in het dorp (Edegem)	18.3	3.66	16.6%

In most cases the proportion was ca. 15–30%. This corresponds with the so-called *eusel*-farm, the term that P. Lindemans uses for the predominant type of farm in West Brabant. Together with the Flemish *dries*-farm, the Brabantine *eusel*-farm was the most productive among the four major exploitation systems that he discerns within the area of modern Belgium.[29] While *dries* refers to a plot of land that was used as pasture for several years and then as farmland during another period,[30] the *eusel*-farms were divided into fixed

27 In reality, this proportion could differ, as Thoen has shown for neighbouring East Flanders. He calculated that the percentage of land sown with winter seeds comprised 45–60% of the total area in the sixteenth century. Thoen, *Landbouweconomie*, vol. II, 713.

28 A sample of leases of pastures in the Grimbergen area north of Brussels had an average price of 4.1–5.7 guilders per ha. ARA MW I 796, I 797, M 113.

29 Lindemans, *Landbouw*, vol. I p. 19–43.

30 E. Thoen, "Driesch" in *Lexikon des Mittelalters*, vol. III, München, Zürich, 1984–1986, kol. 1399–1400; and Idem, „Technique agricole, cultures nouvelles et économie rurale en Flandre au bas moyen age" in *Plantes et cultures nouvelles en Europe occidentale au Moyen Age et à l'époque moderne* (Centre culturel de l'abbaye de Flaran. Douzièmes Journées internationales d'histoire, 11,12,13 septembre 1990), Auch, 1992. p. 63.

plots of farmland and meadows (*eusels*) in a relation of 1:5 (in some parts of eastern Flanders even 1:3). Farmers had considerable livestock, which provided great quantities of manure in addition to milk and meat. The *eusel*-farm therefore had a disadvantage in comparison with the Flemish *dries*-farms, which was that the additional fertilising effect of ploughing the meadows was not used. This was compensated by the natural fertility of the southern Brabantine clay –area.[31] In the south of the Low Countries as well as in the north of France, the classical three-field rotation system was applied and led not only to an increasing demand for grain, but also to a system of extensive cultivation. The low degree of fertilisation nevertheless formed a great disadvantage of this technique.[32]

The fourth type of farm, found in the areas with less fertile soil in the north of Brabant, is generally referred to as the *Kempen type* farm. Here, sheep were kept on the vast heaths that made up a large part of the farm area, and their dung was collected for fertilising the fields. Cattle were also raised in stables, thus providing a very large amount of manure. Here, the large amount of manure gained from stable feeding compensated for the low fertility of the soil.[33]

Of course, the western Brabantine farms did not exclusively consist of fields and meadows. Most of them also had orchards and vegetable –gardens, and some even had a few wooded areas connected to th farm. Generally they also had fishponds and or dovecotes, which were mostly reserved for the owner. In that case, the farmer only had some usage –rights, as in the case of the Anderstad farm, where the farmer was allowed to graze sheep and 20 pieces of cattle in the seigniorial forest for free and where he was also allowed to cut small wood and dig for peat.

5.4.3 The Field Rotation

Among other specifications, the farmer of the Anderstad farm was obliged to leave eight *bunders* of his land sown with rye. This passage of the contract, indicating the state in which the farmer had to leave the farm at the end of his contract, is called the *lating* and contains valuable information on the type of field rotation. As mentioned earlier, we do not know the proportion of these eight *bunders* to the total farm area in this case. In most of the Brabantine contracts, about a third of the area was reserved for winter grains. So, for example in a farm in Wommelgem, near Antwerp, one-third had to be left sown with winter rye, another part with spring seed and the third part had to be left fallow.[34] Another contract from the Antwerp area specified that a third had to be left sown with rye, a third with peas and the final third left fallow.[35] Generally, the contracts specify that one third had to be sown with winter grains (rye or winter rye), another third with spring or summer seeds (generally oats, but also peas or others), and that the final third had to be left fallow, which is to say according to the traditional three-course rotation system.[36] That

31 Lindemans, *Landbouw*, vol. I, pp. 27–39.

32 *Ibidem*, vol. I, pp. 39–43.

33 *Ibidem*, vol. I, p. 54f. and 74–77.

34 Contract concerning the Immerseel-farm in Wommelgem (1477), Nooyens, *Deurne, vol.* I, p. 433.

35 Goed te Pulle (Deurne-Wijnegem) 1448, SR 39, fo. 316r., *Ibidem*, vol. I, p. 440.

36 Goed te Pulle (Deurne-Wijnegem): 1/3 rye, 1/3 peas, 1/3 fallow; Immerseel farm (Deurne): 1/3 winter rye, 1/3 spring seed, 1/3 fallow; see Nooyens, I p. 432–433; Moensgoed (Kontich, contract no. 57): 2.5 b. winter rye, 2.5 oats or summer seed, 2.5 fallow, ploughed once; Crockenroede (Edegem) (contract no. 62): 5b. winter grain, 5b. summer seed, 5 b. fallow, ploughed

this three-course system was still at the basis of the farming system in the Antwerp area can be deduced from the fact that, like other conditions of the contract, the *lating* was in many cases fixed by customary law and does not specify any particular system. In the sources we find passages such as: "as a good farmer is supposed to do", "in the good farmers' way" or "following the customs and habits of the land".[37] Several contracts contain the expression *hofrecht* (farm law). This so-called farm law is explained in the customary laws of Deurne as follows: "Item, at the end of the lease, the lessee has to leave all the manure that lies on the land or on the dung heap and which has been made by the cattle. He has to leave a third of the land fallow upon his leaving, without removing any straw or manure, unless otherwise agreed in the lease contract."[38] In other words, not a strict application of the three-course rotation is imposed here, but rather the leaving of a third of the land fallow at the end of the lease. The term *verantzaden*, which appears quite frequently in lease contracts of the Brussels area, is totally absent in the Antwerp documents.[39] This can be explained by the fact that the Antwerp contracts generally referred to whole farms and were less restrictive than contracts concerning individual plots. In one particular contract, the practice was explicitly accepted, albeit only for one *bunder*: at Gillis Sanders' farm in Hemixem, the farmer was allowed to sow one *bunder* of land with turnips, but he had to sow rye or barley on the same plot the same year.[40]

5.4.4 Fertilising

One of the main secrets of the high productivity already achieved in the fourteenth and fifteenth centuries in the suthern Low Countries was the intensive use of fertiliser. The Flemish had no monopoly on the use of manure in the late Middle Ages, but whereas other, less densely settled areas took the path of extensive grain farming, the high proportion of pasture in the form of a *dries* or *eusel* in Flanders and Brabant provided great quantities of manure and therefore formed a good basis for intensive husbandry.

The question of fertilisation was also heavily stressed in the late mediaeval lease contracts. Willem Smet, the farmer of the Anderstad farm, was required to "sow nine *bunders* of land every year with rye and to fertilise them well and laudably".[41] In the Antwerp area, almost all the contracts contain passages specifying that straw and manure had to be kept on the farm[42] or that it was not allowed to put it to any use outside the leased property or to sell it.[43] In a number of cases, the farmer was supposed to leave the manure on the farm at the end

---

for summer grain.

37 See contract nos. 2, 4, 7, 9, 13, 17, 56, D4, D26, D28, D29, D33.

38 See for example the Bremdonk farm in Ekeren (owner: St. Elisabeth hospital) SAA, Coll. 4 fo. 214 r. 1 mei 1521 'During the last year leave two-thirds sown and a third fallow'; also the farm 'inde Waesdonck', Deurne 1542 (owner: Jan van Kruiningen), SAA, SR 208, f° 201r°: 'leave the two-thirds of the land sown and the final third fallow or empty' (cited in Nooyens, *Deurne,vol. I,* p. 433).

39 Compare the lease registers of the abbeys of Grimbergen and Groot Bijgaarden near Brussels; ARA, KA, 8264bis (Grimbergen) and 8108 (Groot Bijgaarden). For example: '*en binnen zijne leste dryen jaere niet veransayen*'. Heembeek, 1426, 1 *dagwand* of land owned by the abbey of Grimbergen.

40 SAA SR 43, fo. 87 r. (contract no. 2).

41 "Te weten dat hij Jaerlijcs besaeyen ende mesten moet wel ende loffelijk IX buender lants in rogge". ARA, RK reg. 11897, account 1467/8, fo. 18v°.

42 Appendix 1, contract nos. 4, 5, 8, 10, D5, D11, D19.

43 Contract nos. 3, 5, 7, 9, 11, 14, D13.

of his term, as part of the *lating*.[44] A considerable number of owners are even more specific about the kind and source of fertiliser to be used. The farmer of Anderstad was granted a reduction of 12 guilders on his lease during the first year, because there was no manure left on the farm. For that sum, he would be able to buy the necessary manure outside the farm. A similar purchase to be made at the beginning of a lease was also referred to in the contract concerning a farm between Berchem and Wilrijk, near Antwerp: the farmer was allowed to keep as much straw (which was also necessary for making fertiliser)at the end of his contract as he had *bought for money* during the first year in the tithe-barn of Wilrijk. He had to leave the rest of the remaining straw and manure according to the *hofrecht*.[45]

In some cases, the straw and the manure gained from the livestock were not sufficient to provide a good fertilising effect. Farmers therefore used any number of alternative fertilisers available to them, such as pigeon dung, urban waste, or fecal matter. Some of the available sources were reserved for privileged groups of farmers, i.e. the holders of large seigniorial demesnes. As was the case at the "s'Bocx goed" farm in Deurne[46] and at a farm in Mortsel,[47] such famers had the right to hold dovecotes or to keep the dung. Another considerable source of fertiliser was the straw from tithe payments. The beneficiaries were the farmers of the tithe-rights, often the farmers of manor farms. These privileged farmers had a tenth of the straw produced in the surrounding farms at their disposal in addition to their own.[48]

Sources of fertiliser were also available to larger groups of the peasantry. In the clayich soils of southwestern Brabant and eastern Flanders, there was marl, for example, which was spread on the fields to make the soil lighter.[49] A similar technique can be seen in the term *karren*, as found in the contract of Gillis Sanders' farm in Hemixem, south of Antwerp. According to Lindemans, *karren* meant to put earth from drains on the fields in order to fertilise them.[50] This may also have been the aim of the obligation to "dig two *voeder* of clay every year and bring it to the farm" at the ter Biest farm in Deurne.[51]

A source of fertiliser typical of the highly urbanised areas of Flanders and Brabant was the use of urban waste, which already appears in documents from the early fifteenth century. Around 1450, street waste from Antwerp was sold and shipped to the surrounding country.[52] In later centuries, this practice of using urban waste developed into what was called *l'engrais Flamand* (street waste, industrial waste). A striking example of this habit is the use of *weemoes*, i.e. the remains of the dyeing plant woad, as fertiliser.[53] This early example of the use of "industrial" waste as fertiliser is documented for several farms to the south of Antwerp: each year the farmer of Gillis Sanders' farm in Hemixem had to put 12 guilders

44 Contract nos. 4, 5, 8, 10, D5, D11, D19.

45 "Peter mag behouden zoveel stroe als hij dit jaer gecocht heeft om geld uit de thiendeschueren te Wilrijk. laet moet stroo en mes laten naar hofrecht" (contract no. 4).

46 ,s Bockx goed (Deurne, 1430) (Contract no. D8).

47 Letter of the Antwerp aldermen, 24 may 1451, see G. Beterams, *Antwerpse schepenbrieven bewaard op het Rijksarchief te Antwerpen 1300–1794*, Brussel, 1959.p. 20 no. 123; the farmer had to pay 1 halster of oats per year.

48 Lindemans, *Landbouw*, vol. I, p.56.

49 Marl is a combination of light sedimentary soils. Lindemans, *Landbouw*, vol. I, 43–48, 55f.

50 SAA, SR 43 (contract no. 2), *Ibidem*, vol. I, 204–206.

51 Hoeve ter Biest (Deurne, 1467) (Contract D28).

52 SAA, SR 50, f°.99r., 25.10.1455.

53 A.K.L. Thijs, "Weemoes, weemoesputten en weemoesvelden: kanttekeningen betreffende de invloed der stedelijke lakenververij op de ontwikkeling van de landbouw in het Antwerpse", in: *Bijdragen tot de Geschiedenis* 57 (1974), 189–202.

worth of *weemoes* on the fields; several farmers in Kontich had similar obligations.[54] *Weemoes* seems to have been used in great quantities: in 1473, a shipman from Ghent owed Jan Pluym from Boom seven shiploads of nine *vierendeel* each.[55] Another type of industrial waste that was used as fertiliser in the area around of Antwerp was soap ashes, a waste product from soap production.[56]

5.5 The Physical Productivity

For a reconstruction of the physical productivity of the soil, lease contracts form an insufficient source. They mainly contain qualitative data, referring to the productive process. The amounts of the lease payments in kind give only very vague indications, because the relation between the total production and the lease price is not specified in the contracts. More useful types of sources are the accountability concerning goods that were exploited directly by their owners. On the other hand, tithe records can also provide useful information. Both of these kinds of sources were the object of detailed research carried out in the late 1970s in the framework of two major research projects on the physical productivity of land in the Low Countries.[57]

In the late Middle Ages, many farms were exploited on a sharecrop basis. During the fifteenth century, however, the contracts were changed into leases for a fixed amount of money or grain. For some of these farms, we possess accounts concerning the payments in kind. These accounts are very scarce for Brabant and Flanders, however, and almost non-existent for longer periods.[58] Among the few surviving examples of such accounts is the one of the Anderstad farm. Unfortunately, it is only available for a period of four subsequent years: from 1465 to 1468.[59] The lease revenue for those years is as follows:

TABLE 7: Payments in Kind, Anderstad Farm, 1465-1468 (in litres)

Year	Rye	Buckwheat	Barley	Oats	Peas	Turnips
1465	5,968.5	197.2	135.6		346	15 roeden
1466	5,709	64.9	194.6			1384
1467	6,271			346	302.75	
1468	6,314				324.4	5s 6p

54 Contract nos. 2, 58, 60, 61.

55 SAA, SR 83 fo. 46 r. see C. VERSTREPEN, *Stadsarchief Antwerpen Schepengriffie. Antwerpse schepenbrieven betreffende de dorpen van de Rupelstreek. Aartselaar, Boom, Boechout, Hemiksem, Kontich, Niel, Reet, Rumst, Schelle, 1384–1565*, vol. III (1461 – 1479), Brussel, 1993.

56 According to a document from 1472, Aart Wraghe from Wilrijk bought soap ashes for not less than 15 *viertel* of rye. VAN PASSEN, *Wilrijk*, p. 441.

57 VAN DER WEE and VAN CAUWENBERGHE, eds., *Productivity of Land*; and A. VERHULST, and C. VANDENBROEKE, eds., *Landbouwproductiviteit in Vlaanderen en Brabant, XIVe–XIXe eeuw*, Gent 1979.

58 TITS-DIEUAIDE, *Formation*, p.52f., see also VAN DER WEE, *Growth*, vol. I, p.52.

59 ARA RK, reg. 11897 accounts 1464/65–1467/68.

If we take for granted that the *helftwinning* of the farm was consistently applied during these years, we can partly reconstruct the production of the farm by means of the accounts. As far as the production of rye is concerned, we can even make an approximation of the physical productivity of its fields. For the summer crops, on the other hand, the surface reserved for each of the crops can hardly be estimated, which also means that the yield per hectare cannot be calculated. The revenue in rye remained relatively stable during the whole period at between 5,700 and 6,300 litres. On the basis of the information from the lease contract (see above) we can make a rough estimate of the yield per hectare (yield = lease x 2/ size): the gross yield for rye at the Anderstad farm (9.5 ha sown with rye) ranged, according to this information, from 1,201.89 litres (1466) to 1,329.26 litres (1468) per hectare (average 1,276.9 litres).[60] This is considerably higher than the only productivity figures of the Antwerp area known thus far, which concerned the village of Deurne at the beginning of the fifteenth century. According to calculations by F. Nooyens, the average yield per hectare in Deurne was as low as 500 litres between 1406 and 1413; it only rose to a level of 1,200 litres in 1418.[61]

In comparison with the data that M. J. Tits-Dieuaide calculated for the fields in the surroundings of Brussels that were directly exploited by the town's Grand-Beguinage, these figures are relatively low. The productivity in the area around Brussels ranged from 600 to 2,959 litres per hectare between 1449 and 1471, with a mean value of 1,793 litres. This was a top level by European standards, equalled at that moment only by a few other regions such as the Oudenaarde area in eastern Flanders, just 50 to 60 kilometres west of Brussels, and the Valenciennes area in northern France.[62] It is also higher than the figures calculated for England in the thirteenth to fifteenth centuries by J.Z. Titow[63] and for the Bruges area by J. Mertens.[64] The productivity of the Anderstad farm, which is more or less comparable with the results for the Leuven area (407 to 1,988 litres), are nevertheless not far below the most productive areas of Europe.[65] The difference in comparison with the neighbouring Brussels area can be explained on the one hand by the different quality of the soil (clay to the north of Brussels versus sand and clay near Lier), and on the other hand by other variables, such as the density of sowing, fertilisation and the intensity with which the soil was worked.[66]

Because we have no precise information concerning the areas sown with each of the different crops, we are not able to make further estimates about the productivity at the Anderstad farm. The only indication our source gives is about the distribution of summer crops. Between 1465 and 1468 the lease was composed of peas, barley, buckwheat, and oats. The small percentage of oats in the lease is striking and does not match the general practice,

---

60 The result would be between 1,038 and 1,148, if we calculate on the basis of the "*bunder*" of Mechelen (9 b. measure of Mechelen = 11 hectares) instead of the *bunder* of Duffel. Vandewalle, *Oude maten, gewichten en muntstelsels in Vlaanderen, Brabant en Limburg*, s.l.,1984 : (Centrum voor landelijke geschiedenis, Publikatie 82), p.53.

61 Nooyens, *Deurne*, vol. I, p. 350 f.

62 For Oudenaarde, see Thoen, *Landbouweconomie, vol.* II, pp. 817–820.

63 Tits-Dieuaide, *Formation*, p. 98f.

64 J. Mertens, *De laatmiddeleeuwse landbouweconomie in enkele gemeenten van het Brugse platteland, (Historische uitgaven: reeks in –8°), Pro Civitate, Brussel, 1970,* 78–81, cited in E.Thoen, *Landbouweconomie, vol.* II, p. 818.

65 Tits-Dieuaide, *Formation*, p. 94 and 98.

66 The figures of Tits-Dieuaide have been characterised as being very optimistic. They derive from an atypical form of exploitation, i.e. the direct exploitation by an ecclesiastical institution. The relatively large Anderstad farm, on the other hand, was probably closer to the average farm. Derville, *Le rendement* p. 804–811, cited in Thoen, *Landbouweconomie, vol.* II, p. 819.

according to which oats would have been the most frequent summer crop. The low quantities for all summer crops taken together suggests, on the other hand, that the lease for summer crops must have been lower than 50% of the total production.

5.6 Conclusion

The analysis of lease contracts shows that the farms in the Antwerp area can be considered progressive for their period: they applied a mix of grain farming and some livestock, with about 15 to 30% of the land being meadows, and they were completed with various secondary products such as fruit, vegetables, poultry or fish. The surroundings of Antwerp did not achieve the same level of productivity as the Brussels area, however. The three-course system was still the basic form of crop rotation, although it was not strictly applied. *Verantzaden*, the practice of sowing fodder or industrial crops during the fallow period, was hardly ever mentioned in the contracts, although some indications show that it did exist. The fertility of the soil and the use of fertiliser was a major concern for the landowners. The intensive use of fertiliser was obligatory, and the contract stimulated the farmers to use external sources of manure for fertilising their land. In various cases, this was done through buying urban street or industrial waste and bringing it to the fields. The result of these efforts was a high physical productivity of the soil. The surroundings of Antwerp lagged somewhat behind the exceptional figures observed for the Brussels area, certainly because of their sandy soil. The owners and farmers made up for this by using enormous quantities of manure. Their farms were perhaps less productive than those near Brussels, but they were still more productive than farms in most of the rest of Europe.

CHAPTER 6

Changes in the Agrarian System during the Sixteenth Century

In the previous chapter, we have seen that, by the late Middle Ages, the southern Low Countries were already very advanced in terms of agrarian techniques. We can now return to the issue of how the agrarian structures of the area surrounding Antwerp responded to the changes that took place in the urban market during the sixteenth century. Was there a fundamental change in the kind of agriculture, the degree of specialisation or the size of farms as a reaction to the increasing demand for agrarian products? And, was there a measurable difference between the Antwerp area and other areas nearby? According to the commercialisation models put forward by Wrigley, Hoffman or de Vries, the agricultural sector of the surrounding areas will have responded to the commercial impulse by both specialising and increasing its production and in many cases by increasing its productivity. According to the specialisation model of de Vries, large market-oriented farms would prevail, while peasants without sufficient land would move to the town.

Several studies have shown that the sixteenth century brought about a further diffusion of the innovating agrarian techniques that had been introduced during the late Middle Ages, increasing the specialisation and intensification of agriculture in the southern Low Countries. The major advances consisted of the spread of alternative rotation systems, which helped reduce the fallow periods considerably, and the cultivation of alternative crops. The latter were mainly fodder crops – which allowed an increase in livestock – and industrial crops.[1] The urban influence is considered to be one of the major factors behind these improvements, together with the rising population density.[2] According to Verhulst and Vandenbroeke, however, a productivity-ceiling had already been reached early in the sixteenth century that could hardly be pushed further within the limits of the traditional agrarian system. This happened some decades later in Brabant than in Flanders, however.[3] Admittedly, the sources we have at our disposal for proving whether any of these ways of increasing agrarian output were actually applied in the surroundings of Antwerp are very deficient. Some of the main types of sources generally used to analyse changes in agrarian productivity are absent for sixteenth-century Antwerp and its surroundings.[4] We were unable to find any usable probate inventories, for example. Probate inventories have been used by several authors recently and prove to be a very adequate source for the study of agrarian productivity. Tithe documents – which can serve in making a long term-analysis

1 Dejongh and Thoen, "Arable", pp. 37–45.

2 H. Van der Wee, "The Agricultural Development of the Low Countries as Revealed by the Tithe and Rent Statistics. 1250–1800" in Idem and E. Van Cauwenberghe, eds., *Productivity of Land*, pp. 9–12.

3 A. Verhulst & C. Vandenbroeke, "Inleiding" in Idem, eds., *Landbouwproductiviteit in Vlaanderen en Brabant, XIVe-XIXe eeuw*, Gent 1979, pp. VI–VII.

4 Van der Wee, *Growth*, vol. I, pp. 51–53; had to take similar conclusions.

of the productivity of land – do exist, but provided unsatisfactory results. The tithes were either leased out, which meant they did not directly reflect the quantity of grain that was harvested, or the revenues they provided were booked in the accounts as an invariable value, as was the case for the tithes of Antwerp's St. Elisabeth hospital. Likewise, farmers' accounts, a source that has been used by British agrarian historians as well as Dutch specialists, are also lacking for our research area.[5] We have therefore had to restrict ourselves to a number of sources that either provide very general and qualitative information, such as the declarations of the state of the Brabantine villages in 1570 and in 1593, or refer only indirectly to agrarian productivity, such as lease contracts and series of lease prices, documents concerning land transactions, and the 100th-penny tax lists of 1569/70. These documents are complemented by normative sources such as texts concerning customary law.

6.1 A General Balance of the Antwerp Countryside around 1570

The record in the Antwerp town archives entitled "the situation of the villages in 1593" contains descriptions of the villages located throughout the entire district of Antwerp. Twelve of them are situated within our research area.[6] The descriptions of the villages of Brabant from 1593[7] are generally considered to be rather unreliable and should be treated with some caution. The representatives of the villages, i.e. the aldermen or other inhabitants who had been living in the village over a long period, were asked to describe the situation in their respective villages both before and after the religious troubles. Their statements contained answers to the following questions: a) how many houses, couples, communicants or inhabitants were there before and after the troubles, b) how many farms (*hoeven*) and ploughs were there, c) how much livestock was there in the village, d) how many brewers, innkeepers, and artisans were there, and finally e) which crops were cultivated.[8] The declarants had an interest in exaggerated statements pertaining both to the damage of the war and to the welfare of the village prior to the revolt.

Bearing in mind these precautions about the accuracy of the data they contain, however, we can still find very valuable qualitative information about the economy of the Brabantine countryside in these declarations. The descriptions of the "good times" before the troubles are especially useful. While we can expect these to be somewhat idealised, they are by no means pure fantasy. First, ducal officials were normally aware of the general conditions such as the number of houses, farms and *bunders* of arable land in a village from previous taxations. The declarants therefore had to stick to a plausible description, although some details may have been invented. Furthermore, even if idealised, the village aldermen gave a representation of their own economic condition and generally did not invent a fictional social and economic structure. The description of the Brabantine villages therefore

5 About the sources concerning agrarian productivity in the southern Low Countries, see Dejongh & Thoen, "Arable", pp. 32–34.

6 Aartselaar, Berlaar, Broechem, Deurne & Borgerhout, Boom, Ekeren, Mortsel, Oelegem, Onze-Lieve-Vrouw Waver, Rumst, Schoten, Wommelgem.

7 An overview of these descriptions is given in A. Cosemans, "Uitzicht", For the surroundings of Antwerp, these documents are conserved in the Antwerp city archives in the Vreemde Gemeenten collection (SAA, VG. nos. 4, 5 and 14).

8 The structure of the questionnaire can best be seen from the declaration concerning Berlaar, where the answers to these questions were numbered; SAA VG. 5, fols. 7–14.

presents a very lively, if somewhat overstated and idealised picture of the rural economy of the Antwerp surroundings – a picture that essentially reflects their socio-economic reality. Unfortunately, these sources are far from complete. Not only have no more than a handful of such documents survived, but there is also considerable variation in terms of the detail in which each of the declarants answered the questions.

The description of Rumst is one of the most explicit of these documents and can therefore serve as an example. According to the declaration of the village aldermen, the village had 450 *bunders* of arable and pasture, 400 of which were worked with summer and winter crops, while the rest lay fallow. Furthermore there were 100 *bunders* of wood. Most of the farmland belonged to 14 or 15 "beautiful lease farms with house, barns and stables, each with two or three ploughs and many young horses, cows, oxen, cattle and sheep". Besides these lease farms, there were also sixteen to eighteen cottars (*cossaten*), who had "small farms, with some bad horses to pull wood for a wage, and two or three cows". Rumst was not predominantly agrarian, however.[9] The 14-15 *hoeven*, which were normally farms of more than 5 *bunders,* only made up ca. 6% of the total number of households. Counting the small farms, or *steden*, the percentage of farms was not higher than 13%. The rest of the population was defined as labourers who had one or two cows for their subsistence.[10] In Boom, the brick-makers village on the river Rupel, the agrarian sector was even less significant. There were only three large farms and 12 small ones inhabited by cottars, while the village is estimated to have had a population of ca. 400-500 inhabitants.[11] In other places, the proportion of farms was considerably higher: in Wommelgem, east of Antwerp, there were 43 farms compared to 80 labourers, which corresponds to a proportion of 34% of farms. The village contained 365 *bunders* of arable land, and its livestock consisted of 73 teams of horses, 323 pieces of cattle and more than 1000 sheep.[12] For several other villages, even more precise figures concerning the distribution in terms of farm size can be calculated by means of the 100th-penny tax lists of 1569/70. In Boechout, 29% of the holdings were *hoeven* of more than 5 *bunders*, while in Schoten that was 25%, and in Edegem 17%.[13]

In the villages of Aartselaar, Mortsel and Deurne, in the closer surroundings of Antwerp, the percentage of farms was somewhat lower, i.e. between 10 and 15% of the total number of households. A considerable share of the inhabitants of these villages did not live from agriculture. Mortsel, for example, had 126 households, including 19 large farms, a mill, a number of innkeepers, brewers, bakers, smiths, carters, grocers, harness makers and other craftsmen. The rest of the heads of households were cottars and labourers. Deurne and Borgerhout were listed together but had already developed a dualistic structure by the sixteenth century: while Borgerhout became increasingly commercialised, becoming one of the first suburbs of Antwerp, Deurne remained mainly agrarian.[14] Hence, we can probably situate a large share of the 20 breweries, 150 taverns, and 50 butchers of the village

9 See Chapter 5.
10 SAA VG. 4, fos. 84–88: Rumst.
11 *Ibidem*: Rumst, Boom.
12 SAA VG 5, fo. 121: Wommelgem.
13 RAA, Oud Gemeentearchief Boechout, no. 93 (Boechout); ARA, Audientie, no. 618 /1 (Schoten); SAA, VG 14 (Edegem). See Chapter 10 for a detailed discussion.
14 Nooyens, *Deurne*, p. 557ff.

in Borgerhout. Deurne, on the other hand, will have assumed most of the 800 *bunders* of land that were under cultivation (56%), including pasture and meadows (*beemden*), the 60 large farms with their 64 teams of horses, ca. 20 pieces of livestock each, and 4000 sheep.[15] We can therefore distinguish between villages with a predominantly agrarian structure and those with a more varied structure that were either situated in the surroundings of the city or were themselves commercial or industrial centres, such as Rumst and Boom.

The area under cultivation in each village appears to have been very high in the late sixteenth century. The document concerning the villages of Rumst and Boom explicitly states that they "were full of people and their land was fully cultivated. Not one *bunder* was empty. It was therefore difficult to obtain a lease".[16] If we compare the figures given in the statements with the community size, we obtain percentages of between 20 and 30% of the total village territory. In those cases where meadows and pastures were included in the calculation, the percentage even reached between 50 and 60%.[17]

The description of the crops that were cultivated in each village is only precise in some places. Aartselaar is the only place in the closer surroundings for which an explicit list of crops is given: rye, wheat, oats, buckwheat, peas and beans. For the surrounding villages, the crops were defined in very general terms as "hardy and weak crops" (Deurne) or "summer and winter crops" (Rumst). Farther south, the descriptions were more precise: in Berlaar these were rye, wheat and barley, while in Onze-Lieve-Vrouwe-Waver, the summer crops were specified as oats, buckwheat, barley, peas and vetches. The reference to wheat in Aartselaar and Berlaar is remarkable, since this had been a rather marginal crop in the Antwerp area until the fifteenth century, only becoming more widespread in some places there over the course of the sixteenth century.[18] The livestock of the Antwerp countryside consisted, according to the descriptions, of hauling-horses, cattle and sheep. In Aartselaar, the average farmer had 3.2 pieces of cattle, and 17 farms had a flock of sheep. In Wommelgem, the average amount of livestock per farm was 2.5 pieces of cattle and eight sheep. There were only 73 teams of horses for the 43 *hoeven* and 80 cottars. If the larger farms had two or three teams of horses, as stated in the descriptions of Berlaar and Rumst, many smaller farmers and cottars will have had to do without their own horses. In Deurne, the number of cattle was exceptionally high: for only 60 large farms, there were 1200 pieces of cattle, an average of 20 pieces per farm. This fits with the reference to 50 butchers in the same village. Furthermore, there were 4000 sheep and 64 teams of horses.

The authors of the declarations thus distinguished clearly between full farms (*hoeven*), smaller cottages (*steden*) and simple houses without any significant plot of farmland. It is nevertheless not entirely clear if the social distinction between farmers and cottars coincides exactly with the distinction between *hoeven* and *steden*, which has to do with the size of the farm. *Hoeven* were normally larger than 5 *bunders*, or 6 hectares, while *steden* held about 2.5 to 6 hectares.[19] The large farms made up ca. 15-30% of the households

15 SAA VG 5, fos. 20–21.
16 *"Voor de troebelen waren de voors. dorpen vol volks en in vol labeur van hun goederen, niet een bunder ledig. – ja het was moeilijk de huring te krijgen".* SAA, VG 5, Declaration concerning Rumst and Boom, 1593.
17 SAA VG 4-5, Toestand der dorpen in 1593. See also: A. Cosemans, *Het uitzicht van Brabant*, passim.
18 See Chapter 5.
19 Compare the analysis of the 100th-penny tax lists later in this chapter.

in the villages near Antwerp and small farms for another 30-35%. Farmers were, according to the declarations, mainly involved in grain farming, combined with the raising of cattle and sheep. They used up to 60% of the total village area for farming activities. While we see signs of commercial and (proto-) industrial activities, the declarations only rarely refer to agrarian specialisation in industrial crops. The farmers of the Antwerp area responded to the demand for foodstuffs, primarily rye, rather than to industrial demands. This sketch is of course based only on subjective, qualitative data, so far. Therefore, we will try to confirm these impressions with other kinds of sources, i.e. with lease contracts and, to some extent, with the 100th-penny tax lists of 1569/70.

6.2 Qualitative Changes According to Lease Contracts

Lease contracts and lease registers, in spite of their methodological limitations, provide information concerning qualitative aspects of farming. By analysing a series of these documents, we can detect changes in the ratio between grassland and arable, in the reduction of the fallow, in the introduction of fodder crops, or in the balance between different crops, and in regional specialisation.[20] The lease contracts concerning farms and separate plots of land in the surroundings of Antwerp do not, at first sight, reveal any revolutionary changes in agrarian techniques. These contracts are generally less explicit than those from the fifteenth century, but rather merely refer to "farm law" (*hofrecht*) or "to the way a good farmer is supposed to keep his farm". Some contracts do contain explicit passages stipulating the way the land should be left (i.e. the *lating*) instead of just referring to the farm law. This limitation is not very restrictive but forms rather a minimum guarantee for the owner against the exhaustion of his land. During the rest of the lease, the lessee was free to use whatever rotation system he liked.[21] In fact, the practice of sowing rye in the first and second years became common around 1500. In the beginning, landowners restricted this form of rotation: the contract concerning the farm of Salincrode, in Mortsel, from 1501, for example, not only obliged the farmer to leave the land in the appropriate rotation (*in tijdigen lagen*), but also told him "to keep for summer crops what was for summer crops". The same passage is found in a contract from Deurne, from 1505.[22] The contract from 1529 for a farm in Wuustwezel, in the Kempen, is also very explicit. It says: "the lessee is not to sow winter grain out of season, but must keep to the right schedule."[23] In 1518, the owner of the Altena farm in Kontich specified the state the fields should be in at the end of the lease: 6 *bunders* had to be sown with fallow-rye (*braakrogge*), to prevent them from being in the second course of the rotation.[24] As early as 1537, the cultivation of winter crops in two subsequent years is explicitly allowed in a contract, with a reference to customary law: "Leave the land according to the law of the land for Deurne, i.e. two-thirds planted with winter corn and the third part fallow".[25] On the other hand, evidence that the fallow was omitted is rare. Only

20 M. Overton, *Agricultural Revolution*, p. 88.

21 G. de Longé, *Coutumes du Kiel, de Deurne et de Lierre*, Bruxelles, 1875 (Coutumes du Pays et Duché de Brabant: Quartier d'Anvers, 5).

22 OCMW, SE d.30 lease contracts for the farms of Salincrode, Mortsel, 1501 and Deurne, 1505.

23 Wuustwezel, 1529.

24 SAA Coll.4, fo. 21r.

25 Middelmolen farm in Deurne, 1537 (owner: Jf. Philippote van Schoonhoven); SAA Pk. 1176, 26r, cited " in Nooyens,

the estimates of the yield of two farms in Deurne, from 1587, confirm the application of this practice, together with the increased cultivation of rye: on the Kattenberg farm, 63% of the land was sown with rye, 3% with barley, and ca. 33% were left fallow. On the Stertingen farm, there was no land left fallow at all. 57% was sown with rye, 29% with barley and 14% with buckwheat.[26]

A precondition for such an increase in rye production was the availability of a sufficient quantity of manure through keeping the cattle in stables or by using fertilising products from outside the farm.[27] The lease contracts do not refer to either of these practices, however. The low proportion of meadows – as shown in the few contracts that mention the ratio of fields to meadows, nevertheless implies that the cattle were indeed kept in stables.[28] Stable feeding, in combination with the cultivation of fodder crops, was the most effective way of accumulating manure for fertilising.[29] Fertilising the land was a major concern for the lessors. The farm law, as well as most contracts, obliged the lessee to keep the dung heap in a good state and strictly forbade him to take any straw or dung away from the farm. Any initiative to purchase other types of fertiliser, such as urban waste or industrial waste,[30] would have been taken by the lessee. Only in exceptional conditions, for example if the farm had already been vacant for some time, did the owners buy extra fertiliser. This was the case in 1503, when Antwerp's St. Elisabeth hospital bought a new farm in Merxem. To fertilise the fields, the hospital bought manure in Antwerp for 15 Brabantine shillings.[31] One way of obtaining additional highly fertile farmland that is mentioned in sixteenth-century lease contracts is that of ploughing plots of pasture at regular intervals and using them as arable land. This form of up-and-down husbandry, or *Koppelwirtschaft*, was known in different parts of the southern Low Countries. In Flanders it was called "*dries*".[32] In the area around Antwerp, too, this technique can be found in lease contracts dating from around 1500. The lessee was not free to break up grassland whenever he wanted, however. He was only allowed to plough plots that had been ploughed before. Furthermore, he had to leave it as grassland at the end of his term.[33]

Deurne, vol. I, p. 433.

26 Nooyens, *Deurne*, vol. I, p. 552. It is remarkable that most of the references to this change in crop rotation pertain to Deurne.

27 See Chapter 5.

28 Bovendonk farm in Hove, 1566: 19 *bunders* of arable, 1.5 b. of meadows; Hof ter Loo in Broechem 1567, 22 b. of land, 4.5 b. of meadows. RAA, KA, St. Bernards no. 10 fo. 1 and fo. 43.

29 Verhulst, "Agricultural", p. 24.

30 In Deurne, a village close to Antwerp, for example, a brewer sold his brewing-mash as fodder. Nooyens, *Deurne*, vol. I, p. 575.

31 Antwerp OCMW, EG reg. 4. Account 1502-1503.

32 Lindemans, *Landbouw*, vol. I, p. 76. See also: Van Bavel, *Transitie*, passim. E. Kerridge, *The Agricultural Revolution*, London, 1967, saw the introduction of up-and-down husbandry in England at the end of the sixteenth century as a major agrarian innovation.

33 See the contracts for the farms Salincrode (Mortsel) and Illicrode (Hove) (owner St. Elisabeth hospital) from 1501, OCMW, SE box 30.

6.3 The Composition of the Crops: Evidence from Leases Payable in Kind

The contracts contained only very few obligations concerning the kinds of crops to be sown. A sharecropping contract from Wommelgem, dating from 1522, is the only one that stipulates that the lessee was to sow 2 *bunders* of turnips in the fallow and 2 *viertel* of linseed. On the other hand, the lessee was allowed to cultivate 1 *bunder* of buckwheat for his own personal use, without having to pay rent for it.[34] Some farm owners also wanted their farmers to plant fruit trees.[35] For more detailed information about both the introduction of new crops and the relative importance of the various crops planted, we will have to consider the lease payments made in kind.

Leases paid in kind were still quite frequent in the sixteenth century, not only for lands belonging to charitable institutions, but also for property belonging to individuals. In general, some 30% of leases were either mixed or wholly due in kind.[36] The farm leases of individual landowners differed from case to case but tended towards a simple combination of cash and rye. Larger farms in particular paid a considerable share of their lease in kind. In comparison with the fifteenth century, the payments became increasingly standardised in the sixteenth century and generally consisted largely of rye (ca. 80-90%). The rest of the payments consisted of oats (10-20%) and wheat (7.3% in Edegem and 16% in Duffel ter-Elst) and sometimes of small quantities of other agrarian products, like barley, buckwheat, peas, butter, hens and capons. Leases in kind did not necessarily have to be paid in kind: lease prices might be expressed as a certain quantity of grain – in order to avoid losses due to shifts in the grain price – but could actually be paid in cash. This practice, called "*verdingen*" in contemporary sources, was regularly applied by institutions and the receivers of the ducal desmesne. Lease contracts were nevertheless very explicit about the place and conditions of delivery of the rent payments in kind. In most cases, rents in kind still were actually paid in kind, especially when the contract distinguished between several sorts of agrarian products. Thus in 1525, the abbey of St. Michael in Antwerp allowed the farmer of the Middelheim farm in Wilrijk to pay cash for one-fourth of his lease that supposed to be paid in rye; the rest had to be paid in kind.[37]

A group of landowners that relied particularly on income provided in kind were charitable institutions, whose agrarian income made up a considerable share of their provisions.[38] These institutions therefore demanded a broad range of goods in their lease contracts. Hence, the lease for the Salincrode farm at Mortsel, payable to St. Elisabeth hospital in 1521, consisted of 20 pounds, 22 shillings of Brabantine *grooten* in money, 2 *viertel* of wheat, 22 *zister* and 2 *viertel* of rye, 2 *viertel* of rough oats (*ruwe evene*), 15 *zister* of oats, 20 capons, 20 hens, 4 fat lambs, 200 eggs, 70 lbs of butter and 10 pieces of cheese.[39]

34 SAA Coll. 3, fo. 63r.

35 For example in the contract for the Bremdonk farm in Ekeren in 1521: "the lessee has to plant 7-8 fruit trees" SAA, Coll. 4 fo. 214 r.

36 Calculations made on the basis of the 100th-penny registers of Schoten, Edegem, Boechout and Duffel ter-Elst.

37 SAA, Coll. 5, fo. 75v.

38 This is why the accounts of these institutions form very useful sources for the study of food consumption during the *ancien régime*. See the studies by both H. van der Wee and Tits-Dieuaide, for Antwerp, also E. Scholliers.

39 SAA, Coll 4, fo. 215r.

The predominance of rye in the lease payments, 80% on average, is due in part to the fact that rye was the major crop in the Antwerp area. The high demand for rye was another important factor, however. The same held for wheat, which was generally uncommon in the area around Antwerp. In a number of places south of Antwerp, however, i.e. in the villages of Mortsel, Edegem, Hove, Boechout, and Kontich and in the southern part of Deurne, wheat formed a considerable share of lease payments during the sixteenth century.[40] Although we do not know the actual spread of wheat growing, its increasing share in lease payments is a sign that the urban demand had stimulated its cultivation in the more fertile areas of the Antwerp hinterland.

Among the summer crops, oats and – in the Kempen – buckwheat prevailed in most contracts. In the farms of Antwerp's St. Elisabeth hospital, however, a change seems to have occurred towards the middle of the century. The leases that were listed in the hospital's rent registers of 1557 very often contain payments of barley, which had been nearly absent before. At the same time, light oats replaced rough oats (*evene*) that had been predominant at the beginning of the century. The lease of a 10-*bunder plot* in Deurne was changed in 1574, for example: instead of 33 *viertel* of *evene*, the farmer now had to pay 16.5 *viertel* of light oats. The relatively low percentage of oats in the leases – compared to rye and wheat – can be explained by the increasing cultivation of rye, but also by the relatively low urban demand for the typical forage-crop oats.[41] Legumes, i.e. peas and beans, figure among the lease payments after the 1540s, particularly to the south of Antwerp. Industrial crops were seldom among the products given in payment. An exception was rapeseed, which figured among the lease payments of the farms belonging to St. Elisabeth hospital after 1557.[42] Flax appeared in small quantities in contracts from Kontich, Edegem and Wommelgem. The abbey of St. Bernard in Hemixem demanded linen sheets and napkins from their farmers in Broechem and Boechout, which implies that a certain amount of flax was indeed grown and woven at those farms.[43]

In contrast to farmland, meadows and pastures were paid for in most cases with cash. The reasons are obvious: while it was possible to pay a specified proportion of the grain harvest, payments in cows would have been rather impractical for both the lessor and the lessee. This makes it difficult to estimate the relative importance of livestock farming by means of lease contracts. The amount of livestock was never included in the contracts. The distribution of farmland and pasture was seldom indicated, nor could that resolve the problem, as long as we do not know the quantity of animals that were held per hectare. Nevertheless, some contracts pertaining to larger farms, especially those belonging to St. Elisabeth hospital, mention payments to be made in diary products and even in lambs and wethers, and these enable us to draw certain conclusions about the importance of livestock at the farms near Antwerp. In the Salincrode farm in Mortsel in 1501 and 1521, for example, the amounts specified were 70 lbs of butter and 10 soft cheeses, while in other cases, the quantities varied between 12 and 60 lbs of butter. Payments made in cheese were

40 Nooyens, *Deurne*, vol. I, p. 439.

41 We have to bear in mind, however, that a) rich urban landowners also had horses to be fed, and b) that oats were also used for other purposes, such as brewing. There was therefore also a certain demand for oats in the town.

42 OCMW, SE 178. fos. 65-89.

43 RAA, KA, St. Bernards no. 10, pp. 43 and 112. See also: Lindemans, *Landbouw*, vol. II, p. 242, fn. 15.

less frequent and varied between 8 and 12 pieces., On the one hand, these payments imply that there was a significant amount of livestock on the farms in question, though dairying was apparently only of secondary importance in comparison with arable farming. The lease contract for the abbey of St. Bernard's Boeverij farm in Hemixem, situated on the banks of the Scheldt, has much more in common with that of a dairy farm.[44] The farmer had to pay 20 lbs of butter each week during the 22 weeks after Easter; this is an exceptionally high payment that was typical for areas with rich pastures along river valleys.[45] Evidence for an abundance of livestock on the Boeverij farm can also seen in the fact that the farmer also had to pay two calves per year, which was rather uncommon in the farms near Antwerp. In addition to cattle, most farmers in the area near Brabant had sheep. The payments in lambs and sometimes also wethers made in connection with numerous farms form a clear indication of their presence there. The number of such animals cannot be deduced on the basis of these payments, however.

The analysis of lease prices paid in kind can also be applied to a few entire villages in order to verify the results of the study of individual farms. The registers of the 100th-penny tax of 1569/70 for four villages within our research area provide data that will enable such an analysis. Edegem, south of Antwerp, had the greatest variety of crops among the lease payments made in kind: the proportion of wheat there was higher than in the other villages, and besides oats, *evene* and barley, there is also mention of peas, flax and beans. Two farms paid with considerable quantities of butter, and one paid with a calf. In Boechout, situated only few kilometres east of Edegem, the variety of crops was much smaller. There, lease payments in grain consisted entirely of rye and rough oats. While Duffel ter-Elst lay much farther to the south, the profile of that village nevertheless had more in common with that of Edegem: the proportion of wheat was only little smaller, but oats were more important. Here, the more rural character of the lease farms in Duffel may have played a role: rural landowners tended to demand more oats for their horses than townsmen would have. Also, just like in Edegem, there were two farms in Duffel ter-Elst that paid a larger amount of butter,. In contrast, the village of Schoten, situated northeast of the town, is more representative of the farming system of the Kempen. Rye made up 99.3% of the lease payments made in grain. Wheat, buckwheat and barley figured only in very small quantities. Likewise, the amounts of payments made in butter were much lower than in the villages south of Antwerp.

6.4 Traces of Specialised Farming in the Surroundings of Antwerp

The evidence from lease contracts for whole farms shows that farmers in the surroundings of Antwerp generally concentrated on grain production, albeit combined with other crops and some livestock farming for dairy production and fertilising purposes. For indications of other forms of specialised agriculture, we have to refer to other types of holdings, i.e. individual plots of land. It was on those plots, rather than on farms, that

44 RAA, KA, St. Bernards no. 10, pp. 81–82.

45 See Lindemans, *Landbouw,* vol. II, p. 388, fn. 2. Another example of such farms situated along the banks of a river was the farm *in den Bermorter* in Duffel. In 1527/28, it paid a lease of 122 guilders and 100 lbs butter (ARA, MW, O 910: Account of the Land van Duffel 8-6-1527–8-6-1528).

"poulterers made loans to warreners and themselves bred poultry. Fruiterers helped to establish orchards and leased them when established [and] butchers became graziers," as E. A. Wrigley put it so colourfully in his article on the importance of London.[46] In the polders north of Antwerp, beginning immediately outside the city walls, there were extensive pastures that the sources refer to as "waterlands". St. Elisabeth hospital in Antwerp owned 74 hectares of polders in Oosterweel and near the town gates that were apparently used primarily as pastures for cattle, but also for haying and growing oats.[47] That the latter use was less common can be seen from a lease contract from 1550, in which the lessee was explicitly told to use the polderland exclusively as pasture.[48] Among the lessees of these pastures were numerous Antwerp butchers who used them for fattening cattle and oxen for slaughtering (Table 8). The polders north of Antwerp had already been used by butchers and cattle merchants in the fifteenth century.[49] In the sixteenth century, fattening imported oxen in the meadows near Antwerp became increasingly important became a profitable business, especially after the 1540s.[50] Even at the end of the seventeenth century, the Steenborgerweert area north of the town walls was still described as being meadows primarily used for fattening cattle.[51]

Table 8: Butchers Leasing Plots of Waterland from St. Elisabeth Hospital

Name	Size (years)
Willem Scoyt, "vleeshouwer" Cornelis de Molenare, "vleeshouwer"	1 gemet (1502-1513) 4.5 gemeten (1507-1525), 2 gemeten + 9 vierendeel, (1520-1526), 4.5 gemeten (1544-1550)
Gijsbrecht de Volder "slager in 't vleeshuis"	1 stuk waterland (1527-1533)
Jan de Molenare, "vleeshouwer"	7 gemeten (1527-1533)
Jan de Leeuwe, "vleeshouwersknaap"	1 gemet (1527-1533)
Jan Kermans, "vleeshouwer"	3 gemeten (1542-1548)
Steven Vernuyen, "vleeshouwer"	3 gemeten (1539-1551)
Joost de Smedt, al. "de slager"	5.3 gemeten (1540-1555), 7 gemeten (1550-1556), 7.5 gemeten (1556-1561), 1 stuk waterlands (1551-1557), 13 gemeten (1557)

46 E. A. Wrigley, "Model", pp. 226–227.

47 OCMW EG reg. 4, account 1501-1502 "*waterland int Steenborgerweerdt gehoyt, met haver besaeit ende geweydt voort gasthuis*". See also: Soly & De Commer, "Harde tijden", p. 79.

48 OCMW, EG,no. 170 fo. 49v.

49 See Chapter 6.

50 See the section concerning the meat supply in the present chapter.

51 F. Prims and H. Dierckx· *Atlas der Antwerpsche stadsbuitenijen van 1698. Fac-simile van de kadastrale plattegronden van C.J. Van Lyere vergeleken met den tegenwoordigen toestand*, Antwerpen, 1933, p. 9 "*wezende meest weyen voor vetbeesten*" cited in F. de Nave· "De vrijheid van Antwerpen (vanaf de middeleeuwen tot de tijd van Rubens)" in L. Voet, et al., *De stad Antwerpen van de Romeinse tijd tot de 17de eeuw: topografische studie rond het plan van Virgilius Bononiensis, 1565*, Brussels, 1978, p. 91, fn. 45.

The hospital also held plots of land further to the southeast, in the so-called St. Willibrordus field, situated just outside the city gate called Rodepoort. It is there that we can observe another form of specialised agriculture that expanded during the sixteenth century. While butchers held their cattle in the polders, the plots in St. Willibrordus' field were rented by commercial gardeners (*hoveniers*).[52] In fact, St. Willibrodus' field was one of the two major concentrations of market-gardening near the city gates of Antwerp. Besides this area outside Rodepoort northeast of the town, there was another in the south, outside St. George's gate.[53] Aldermen's registers contain various references to large gardens in those areas.[54]

Besides vegetables, *hoveniers* also cultivated fruit. A very detailed lease contract between the Antwerp patrician Aart Schoyt and *hovenier* Dierick Claes from 1539 concerns a house with a garden and an orchard. The orchard contained numerous cherry trees (200 early, 80 late, 14 black, four Spanish and three wild cherry trees), two pear trees, three apple trees and two nut trees. The lessee had the right to the cherries only, but not to the apples, pears or nuts, nor to the wood of the trees.[55]

Gardening was also an important agrarian activity for small farmers and cottars whose grain surplus was insufficient for selling it at the market. Gardening was highly labour intensive and therefore particularly fitted for smallholdings. There were also specialised gardeners in some of the villages surrounding Antwerp, such as Mortsel or Borgerhout.[56] Market gardening was, however, not exclusively restricted to specialised gardeners. Most farms and even small houses in the countryside around Antwerp had a vegetable garden, the yields of which could be sold partly in town. The actual expansion of this form of "peasant gardening" can hardly be established on the basis of the documents we have at our disposal. We do have indirect indications, however. The gardeners who had immigrated to Antwerp during the sixteenth century came from places that were concentrated within an area of 10 to 15 km east and southeast of the town.[57] Most of them will have already been familiar with gardening before moving to Antwerp. It is therefore very likely that gardening was a common occupation in this relatively fertile area.

---

52 Adriaan Mus, *hovenier* 1539-1557, Jan Mus al. de Vleminck, *hovenier*, Peter van Leemputte *hovenier* 1552-1557, OCMW EG no. 170, fos. 30, 40, 42, 45, 55 and EG no. 178, fos. 41, 98.

53 In the South: Markgravelei, St. George's gate (St. Jorispoort), Lozanne and Haringrode; in the East: Kipdorp, Carnotstaat, Stuivenberg. See: Baetens, "Lokale markten", p. 178.

54 *"Gielis van Kerkhove hovenier gaf hofstad met land t'erve buiten de Rodepoort"*; SAA Coll 3, fo. 36v. (1525); 1547: 7/8 of a garden (*hoveniershof*) with two houses in Beerschot (Beterams no. 464), 1550: Hof ter Beke outside Antwerp, (St. George's parish) with gardens (*hoveniershoven*) and brewery of Jan Alleman (Betermans p. 83, no. 481) "*hof in St. Joris buiten de muren*" (1550, Beterams, no. 484) "*hoveniershof buiten de buitenste Kipdorppoort*" (Beterams 487, 1550); "*Jan Mertens koopt hoveniershof opt Kiel bij Beerschot*", SAA, SR 241, fo. 36r.(1551); "*een hoeveniers hof gelegen in de losaen buyten dezer stadt*"; SAA, SR 258 fo. 243r. (29-4-1556) (Verstrepen no. 38); "*een hoveniershove groot 1 1/2 bunder buiten dezer stad*". SAA, SR 259, fo. 255v. (9-10-1556) (Verstrepen no. 61); "*een stuc van een hoeveniers hoeve groot 5 1/2 roeden op 't Kiel*" SAA, SR 262, fo. 230v (30-10-1556), (Verstrepen no.149); "*de helft van een hoeveniershoeve groot 1 1/2 bunder gelegen buiten dezer stad op de nonnen velt*" SAA, SR 273, fo. 316v (6-7-1559), (Verstrepen no. 377); "*zeker boerenhof buyten de kipdorpoorten welcke hoeveniers hoff met pertienen in de scheidinge ende deilinge op 22-9-1538 tusschen de erfg. van wijlen Augustyn Vermylen ten deel bevallen is tegen huer broeders en susters*" (19-1-1561) SAA no.° 283, fo. 31r (Verstrepen, no. 551). Jan Mondekens, *buitenpoorter* (*extraneus*), *hovenier* in Berchem SAA, Vierschaar 148 (6 June 1561), (Stadsarchief Antwerpen, ed., *Antwerpse Poortersboeken*, 1533–1561, Antwerp, 1977, vol. 1, p. 36).

55 SAA, Coll. 3, fo. 294r. Unfortunately, the place is not specified.

56 Mortsel: '*een stede met een hove te Mortsele die Wouter De Winter hoevenier nu ter tyt in laetscape bezetene*" (20-11-1562) SAA no.° 281, fo. 147v. (Verstrepen no. 526).

57 Kontich 6, Broechem 4, Ranst 3, Schoten 2, Aartselaar, Berchem, Borsbeek, Bouchout, Deurne, Ekeren, Kalloo, Kruibeke, Mortsel, Schilde, Zandhoven (one each); *Antwerpse Poortersboeken*, passim.

The fattening of cattle north of Antwerp and market gardening in a limited area near the Antwerp city gates seem to have been the major forms of specialised agriculture in the closer surroundings of that city. In comparison with other areas, industrial plants were relatively uncommon. The cultivation in the polders of plants used for dyeing and of flax in the Kempen and some places south of Antwerp, as mentioned above, do not seem to have formed the main activity of the farmers in question and cannot be considered as forms of specialised agriculture.

6.5 The Evolution of Lease Prices

Having investigated the qualitative changes in the agrarian system of the surroundings of Antwerp, we shall now consider their effects by means of the development of the land rent. According to A. van der Woude, the movement of land rent forms an indication of the rate of profitability in agriculture.[58] To a certain degree it reflects the value of the land in the area in question. The term "value" has to be understood in a broad sense, however, because various factors were involved in the formation of lease prices. F. Daelemans lists four major items that influenced lease prices of farmland: the availability of land, the quality of the plot, the degree of population pressure, and the negotiating power of the lessee and the lessor.[59]

These factors are closely related with each other. The availability of land depended on the population pressure, and also the negotiation power of the lessee and the lessor depended on the ratio between land and population. Finally, the quality of the land itself depended on different factors: its physical fertility, its location (near the town, a river, a road or the farm of the lessee), the size of the plot, etc. Although most of these factors were essentially relatively static, lease prices were subject to short-term movements as a result of shifting price levels and incidental circumstances such as political unrest or plagues. In the longer term, lease prices could be affected by structural changes, such as an increase in the physical productivity or an improvement of the location, as we saw in the case of the plots near Antwerp. Another factor that could become more significant in a relatively short period, and hence cause an increasing demand for leases, was population pressure.

The leases of farms were payable in many cases partially in money and partially in kind. This makes quantification very complicated. For composing lease-price series, institutional or manorial accounts are the most useful sources. The accounts of the ducal desmesne contain useful price data for different types of holdings, including mills, farms, and farmland. Using the accounts of the domain of Antwerp, for example, H. van der Wee was able to establish a rent index for plots of polder land in Lillo and Zandvliet and for farmland near Lier[60] The ducal desmesne Land van Mechelen provided, among various other lease data, the lease prices of the Anderstad farm for the period between 1464 and 1555.[61] For the immediate surroundings of Antwerp, though, useful accounts are relatively scarce.

58 A. M. van der Woude, "Large Estates and Small Holdings. Lords and Peasants in the Netherlands during the Late Middle Ages and Early Modern Times" in P. Guns and T. Hoffmann (eds.), *Large Estates and Small Holdings in Europe in the Middle Ages and Modern Times.* National Reports Budapest, 1982, p. 204, cited in F. Daelemans, Pachten en welvaart op het platteland van Belgisch Brabant (15e–18e eeuw)" in *AAG Bijdragen*, 28 (1986), p. 166, fn. 8.

59 Daelemans, "Pachten", p. 166.

60 Van der Wee, *Growth*, vol. I, p. 33 and Appendix 40, pp. 477–482.

61 ARA, Rk. Reg. Nos. 11897-11909.

The accounts of St. Elisabeth hospital contain some farm leases, but neither the name nor the size of the farms is specified.[62] This makes the calculation of lease prices a daunting and hardly worthwhile enterprise. The lease registers of the St. Elisabeth hospital nevertheless do contain information concerning 72 different plots of land situated in the closer surroundings of Antwerp, with a total size of 228 ha.(see appendix 2)[63] On the basis of these documents, a sample of some 600 lease prices payable in money could be established for the period between 1501 and 1560. (see Graph 1).

GRAPH 1: Lease Prices of Farmland and Meadows near Antwerp, 1501-1560

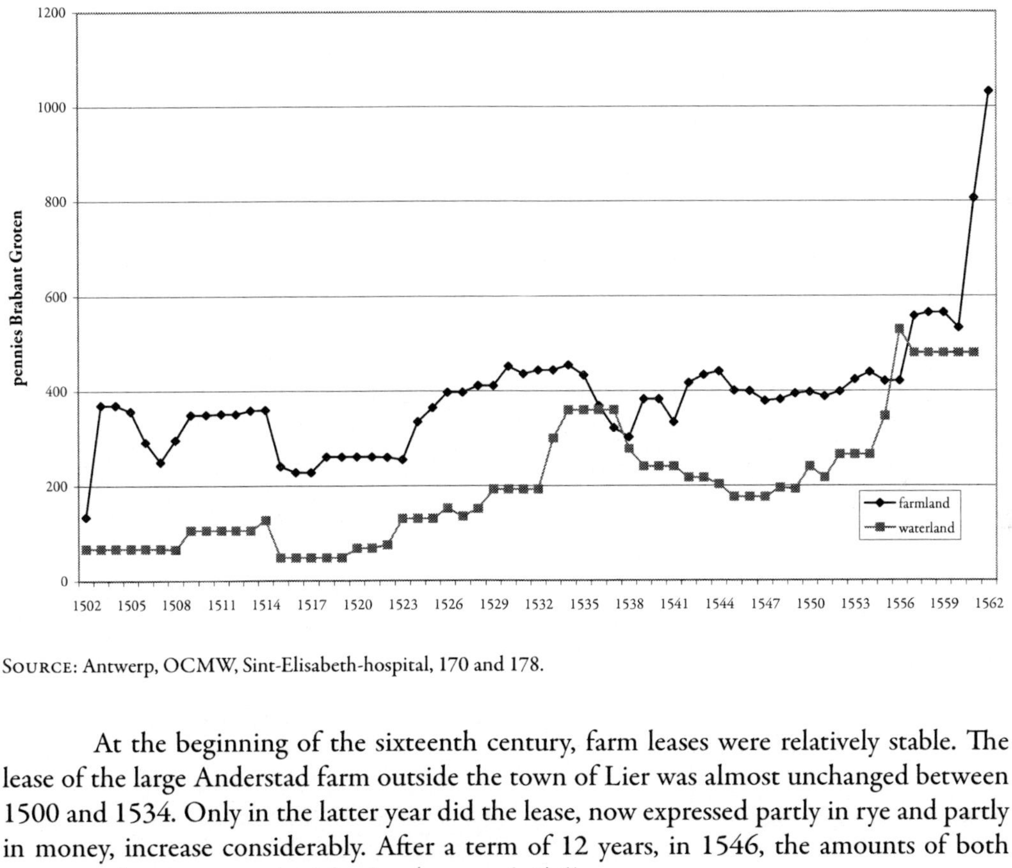

SOURCE: Antwerp, OCMW, Sint-Elisabeth-hospital, 170 and 178.

At the beginning of the sixteenth century, farm leases were relatively stable. The lease of the large Anderstad farm outside the town of Lier was almost unchanged between 1500 and 1534. Only in the latter year did the lease, now expressed partly in rye and partly in money, increase considerably. After a term of 12 years, in 1546, the amounts of both money and grain were raised further (see graph 2).[64]

62 So for example the lease of the Salincrode farm in Mortsel consisted of 20 lbs of Brabantine grooten and a whole range of agrarian products: wheat, rye, rough oats, light oats, capons, hens, lambs, eggs, cheese and butter. In the account of that year, only the revenues received in money and those received in wheat, rye and oats were registered, in disparate chapters and under the name of the lessee, Michiel Vandermijlen, rather than under the name of the farm. OCMWA, EG, d.30. EG reg. 4, account 1501-1502.

63 OCMW EG 170 and EG 178.

64 Unfortunately, the series ends in 1555, when the prince mortgaged the farm, together with many other parts of the domain. M. Baelde, *De domeingoederen van de vorst in de Nederlanden omstreeks het midden van de zestiende eeuw (1551-1559)*, Brussel, 1971, p. 48. In this context, see also: "Financiële politiek en domaniale evolutie in de Nederlanden onder Karel V en Filips II (1530–1560)" in *Tijdschrift voor Geschiedenis* 76/1963, pp. 14–33.

Graph 2: Lease Price of the Anderstad Farm near Lier, 1500–1555

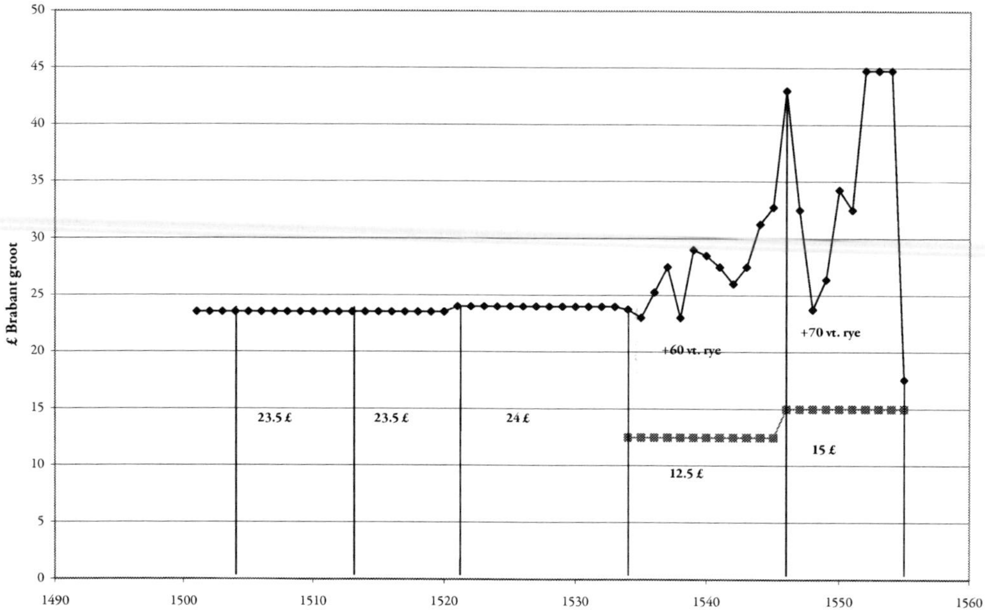

Source: ARA, Rk. Reg. Nos. 11897-11909.

The leases of several farms near Antwerp cited in the lease contracts confirm this tendency. The lease of the Salincrode farm in Mortsel, for example, was in most points identical in 1501 and in 1521. Only the amount of rough oats due had decreased sharply during that period. The leases of the hospital's farms in Merxem and 's Gravenwezel were not significantly increased during the first decades of the sixteenth century either. Any changes concerned the composition of the lease rather than the total amount due.[65] The rents of separate plots of farmland near Lier and leases in other parts of the southern Low Countries followed a similar trend.[66] In contrast, the figures concerning polderland in Zandvliet increased quite sharply during the same period.[67] The leases of farmland and waterland belonging to Antwerp's St. Elisabeth hospital followed the general trend during the first decades of the sixteenth century. Lease prices were relatively stable from the beginning of the century until about 1520. From 1523, there was a sharp increase in the leases, followed by a sudden decline starting in 1535, at which point farm leases and leases of waterland diverged: while the farm leases would soon return to the level before the fall and remain stable until the 1550s, the leases of waterland kept declining until 1548 but then recovered very quickly, even closing the gap with farm leases. The leases of arable correlated strongly with the price

65 Salincrode farm in Mortsel (St. Elisabeth) 1501: OCMWA, EG d.30, 1521: SAA, Coll 4, fo. 215r.

66 For leases of farmland near Lier, see: Van der Wee, *Growth*, vol. I, p. 477-482. F.G. Scheelings, "Pachtprijzen in midden- en zuidwest -Brabant in de zestiende eeuw. Enkele methodologische beschouwingen bij het schetsen van een landbouwconjunctuur" in *Bijdragen tot de Geschiedenis*, 65 (1982), pp. 41–64; Daelemans, "Pachten", pp.165–184.

67 Van der Wee, *Growth*, vol. I, pp. 477–482.

of rye.[68] However, they did not increase to the same degree as grain prices. While grain prices increased by 183% from the decade 1501-1510 to 1551-1560, lease prices only increased by 53% during the same period.

In comparison with leases in other parts of Brabant, the lease prices for farmland near Antwerp grew faster during the period 1525-1535, but later on lagged behind those in the area of Lier where leases continued to increase until after 1570. The plots of waterland in the polders north of Antwerp were relatively cheap in comparison with arable (an average of 85 *grooten* per ha. during the period 1502-1510, which was about half the price of arable). While the prices for arable nevertheless increased sharply after 1520, prices for pasture remained low and only rose around 1550.

The period around 1550 seems to have been a turning point. While prices for arable stagnated after that point, leases for pasture increased sharply and almost reached the values of arable. This rise was remarkable with the lease prices even exceeding those for pasture in nearby areas. While the trend of lease prices for pasture near Antwerp was generally comparable with that for polder land in Zandvliet and Lillo and for pastures along the river Nete near Lier, the pasture lease prices in the Antwerp area increased more quickly than in the latter areas from 1535 on. After 1555, this rise became significantly sharper. The impact of Antwerp butchers such as Joost de Smedt may have been responsible for this exceptional rise.

Another register of the revenues from leases and land rents paid to St-Elisabeth hospital provides information concerning the evolution of farm leases near Antwerp for the years 1557-1581.[69] It contains the revenues from 14 farms paid in money and grain; income paid in other sorts of agrarian products was omitted, as in the accounts. During the 25 years that the document was used, the leases were changed at different moments.[70] The nominal lease price in money increased on average by 43%, while leases in kind increased by 19%. Lease prices continued to increase between 1557 and 1581, although to a lesser degree than the price of rye. This rising trend coincides with the general tendency of the southern Low Countries, although the rise in the area of Antwerp in the latter period was sharper than elsewhere.[71]

The analysis of lease prices of farmland and pasture in the surroundings of Antwerp indicates that agriculture responded effectively to the urban market. Rises in market prices were followed immediately by adaptations of the leases, although the latter could not keep pace with the rise of grain prices. The increase of lease prices payable in kind after 1560 suggests that the productivity of the land increased during the first half of the century. At the same time, rising lease prices constituted a pressure for the farmers of the surroundings of Antwerp and were in themselves a stimulus for raising the productivity of agriculture.

68 The correlation between the lease price and the seven-year gliding average of rye prices is as high as 0.68, and therefore statistically significant (a = 0.1).

69 OCMW EG no. 178, fos. 65-90.

70 In the document these changes were registered by overwriting the previous amount or putting the new amount next to the old lease price together with the indication *modo*. Determining the exact date of a change is often only possible by comparing the handwriting with that used in a certain year.

71 VAN DER WEE, "Agricultural Development", p. 9.

6.6 Land Values near Antwerp and in the Rest of Brabant

The available lease-price series do not enable us to make exact statements concerning the relative advance of the Antwerp area in comparison with other areas. The individual price series are too heterogeneous for measuring the quantitative differences between the price levels. There is nevertheless a source that provides a comparison of the average land values in almost every village of Brabant. The 100th-penny tax of 1569-72 was a taxation of the inhabitants' personal property. While both movable goods and immovable goods were taxed in the towns and in some larger villages, the taxation of the countryside occurred almost entirely on the basis of the lease value or the estimated value of each holding. The tax value of leased goods was calculated by multiplying the lease value by a factor of 16 for entire farms including farm buildings and by a factor of 22 for land without any buildings. Therefore, by dividing a village's income by its area, it is possible to calculate the average tax value per hectare for every village. The tax value was to a large degree determined by the local lease prices, which formed the basic reference for the estimate of the value of the land.[72]

Around 1570, the tax values of leased goods near Antwerp were among the highest in the whole duchy of Brabant. Deurne-Borgerhout and Berchem, situated in the immediate surroundings of Antwerp, stood out in particular, with values exceeding 300 guilders (fl) per hectare. The average value in Hemixem and Oosterweel was still higher than 200 fl/ha and in an additional 17 villages near Antwerp it was higher than 100 fl/ha (see Table 9).

Table 9: Tax Value per Hectare in the Villages near Antwerp, 1569–71

Village	Total	Ha	Fl/ha
Berchem	2384.2	653	365.1
Deurne	4619.3	1427	323.7
Hemiksem	1188.5	545	218.1
Oosterweel	3011.9	1462	206
Mortsel	1239.3	780	158.9
Kontich	2992.2	1896	157.8
Schelle	1191.9	781	152.6
Borsbeek	586.2	392	149.5
Ekeren	3467.25	2345	147.9
Rumst	1210.15	832	145.5
Niel	752.6	526	143.1

72 The 100th-penny tax accounts for the duchy of Brabant and the county of Flanders are edited " in P. Stabel and F. Vermeylen, *Het fiscale vermogen in Brabant, Vlaanderen en in de heerlijkheid Mechelen: de Honderdste Penning van de hertog van Alva (1569-1572)* (Commission Royale d'Histoire/Koninklijke Commissie voor Geschiedenis), Brussel, 1997; for a discussion of the modalities of the taxation, see the Introduction.

Village	Total	Ha	Fl/ha
Aartselaar	1530.65	1092	140.2
Edegem	1200.75	866	138.7
Wilrijk	1989.25	1489	133.6
Hove	762.55	600	127.1
Ranst	1255.55	1023	122.7
Boechout	1601.35	1392	115
Wommelgem	1464.05	1300	112.6
Onze-Lieve-Vrouw Waver	1672	1530	109.3
Reet	1017.9	946	107.6
Wijnegem	828.55	783	105.8
Broechem	1247.5	1179	105.8
Waarloos	498.35	472	105.6

There was nevertheless a clear difference between the lease prices to the north Antwerp and those to the south. While the villages south and southeast of Antwerp generally had average tax values of more than 100 fl/ha. the average values were much lower to the north. The area ca. 20 km from Antwerp, for example, including the polder villages of Wilmarsdonk, Lillo and Berendrecht, as well as places such as Merxem-Schoten and Brecht, had average values of between 50 and 100 fl/ha. The only places in that area that had higher values were Ekeren and Oosterweel.

These high values near Antwerp stood in sharp contrast with the Kempen, where the average land value was beyond 50 fl/ha. South of Antwerp, a ribbon of high land values extended until Brussels and the south-western edge of the duchy. The area between the three major Brabantine towns, i.e. Antwerp, Mechelen and Brussels, can hence be considered to have formed the economic core area of Brabant during the sixteenth century. Further east, towards Leuven, land values were considerably lower[73]. This confirms Van Uytven's findings concerning the economic problems of that area during the fifteenth and sixteenth century.[74] Southeast of Brussels, the forest of Soignes stands out with its very low values. But in southernmost Brabant, too, the values were again extremely low, in spite of the natural fertility of the Walloon part of Brabant.[75]

Along with natural features such as soil type and topographical conditions, the urban impact seems to have been a decisive factor for the land values. A high demand for land, together with easy access to the town but also the productivity of the land were factors

73 Blondé and Limberger, "De gebroken welvaart", p. 319-320.

74 Van Uytven, "In de schaduwen", passim and Idem, "Sociale krisis", passim.

75 These low values are in sharp contrast with the figures of the nineteenth century, such as for example according to the general agricultural census of 1846, see Klep, *Bevolking*, p. 30.

that determined the (lease-) prices of the land.[76] The most expensive land was concentrated in the immediate surroundings of the larger cities: Antwerp and Brussels, and to a lesser extent Mechelen.

6.7 Conclusion

On the face of it, the agrarian system in the surroundings of Antwerp appears not to have undergone any fundamental changes during the sixteenth century. The declarations of the village aldermen give a rather conventional image of agriculture in the Antwerp area around 1570. They characterise the villages there as having a considerable number of relatively large farms that grew rye, some wheat, oats, barley, and – in the parts with poorer soil – buckwheat, just like in the fifteenth century. Secondary crops, such as beans, peas and oil plants were also common. On the other hand, they made no references to specialised farming. Although most large farms had 10 to 20 pieces of cattle, large flocks of sheep and workhorses, livestock farming was subordinate to arable farming. The Antwerp countryside therefore does not reflect the Dutch success story as told by Jan de Vries.

Nevertheless, while the agrarian economy looks rather traditional at first glance, there are clear signs of positive responses to the urban demand: farmers were able to increase their output of bread grain by growing rye during two subsequent years or by eliminating the fallow; the production of wheat increased in the most fertile places of the area. The rising lease prices form an indication that agrarian productivity, at least in the short term, increased during the sixteenth century. By 1570, lease prices were higher in the surroundings of Antwerp than in most other parts of Brabant aside from the Brussels area. In turn, high lease prices exercised a strong pressure on agriculture, forcing the producers to increase the productivity of the land. Farmers had to augment their production in order to be able to pay the rent. This led moreover to a certain selection among the farmers: only the most productive could afford to lease farms or plots of land. Less productive farmers had to find other sources of income, like wage labour on larger farms, or transporting wood and other products to the urban market. Market gardening and the fattening of cattle were the major types of specialisation with an eye to the urban market. References to industrial crops were found in different places, but such crops appear not to have attained predominance in the surroundings of Antwerp. We are less well informed about the smaller producers, who are said to have played an important role for the development of intensive husbandry. According to the descriptions of the village aldermen, cottars were not so much specialised in intensive agriculture but rather poor labourers trying to make a living off their small plots of land, with a cow and various other additional sources of income. While this does not preclude the possibility that many small peasants did some market gardening or grew cash crops on their plots, the local declarants did not consider these activities worth mentioning. For them, agriculture was the domain of the large farmers and not so much of the cottars.

76 Compare the classical theory of economic rent; the economic rent of a specific plot of land is determined by factors of demand and the relative productivity costs. See: J. Hatcher and M. Bailey, *Modelling the Middle Ages: The History and Theory of England's Economic Development*, Oxford, 2001, pp. 24–25.

CHAPTER 7

The Non-agrarian Sector Faces the Urban Challenge

7.1 Introduction

Agriculture in the surroundings of Antwerp was stimulated by the rising urban demand during the sixteenth century. Nevertheless, almost half of the rural population of the Antwerp countryside had insufficient land to produce an agrarian surplus or even to guarantee their subsistence. Rather than being able to profit from the impulse the increasing urban demand gave to local agriculture, the tenants of these smallholdings therefore had to take recourse to alternative sources of income.[1] For many, this meant labouring for a wage on one of the larger farms or in the woods belonging to large landowners. Furthermore, there was a series of non-agrarian activities in the Antwerp countryside serving either the village community or the urban economy. Although the economy of rural western Brabant, as elsewhere in late medieval Europe, was in large part agrarian, most villages in Brabant had a small range of basic services for the surroundings, such as a blacksmith, a cart-maker or a miller. Or, as M. Postan put it: "Some opportunities for trade were therefore to be found in all places and, above all, at all times".[2] Local masons, roofers and carpenters were employed to build or repair manorial castles, farms, or mills. Carters were hired to transport wood, grain or building materials.[3] Furthermore, many villages had brewers and tavern keepers.[4] Non-agrarian labour was therefore a normal feature in the Brabantine countryside. Some of these local crafts achieved importance beyond the local level, however, also working for a larger market. Some provided products or services for the Antwerp market, and some even produced for export. The sector that comes to mind first of all in this context is the rural textile industry. Some of the rural textile centres that flourished during the fifteenth and sixteenth centuries in the southern Low Countries were in fact situated in the surroundings of Antwerp.[5] The variety of non-agrarian labour linked with the urban economy was much larger, however. H. Van der Wee mentioned commercial forestry (in the surroundings of Lier) and the intensive land reclamation (along the coastline and in the estuary of the Scheldt in particular) as two sectors that provided an increasing demand for wage labour from the late

1 For the role of non-agrarian labour, see: Hatcher and Bailey, *Modelling the Middle Ages*, pp. 21–65.

2 M. Postan, *The Medieval Economy and Society: An Economic History of Britain, 1100-1500*, London, 1972, p. 183.

3 For example: Jan Wilemans *herbergier en barbier*, and Jan de Bast called *de brouwer*, both in Kontich. In the accounts of the ducal demesne Land van Mechelen, for example, the wages of masons, carpenters, smiths, roofers, diggers, street workers, woodcutters, wagoners, etc., many of whom came from the surrounding villages, were registered every year.; ARA, Rk. reg. 11 895-11916, 1464-1591.

4 See below, Section 2.2.

5 On the importance of rural textile industries in Flanders see, for example: E. Coornaert, *Draperies rurales, draperies urbaines. L'évolution de l'industrie flamande au moyen âge et au XVIe siècle*; and Van der Wee, "Industrial Dynamics", passim.

fifteenth century on.[6] However, some sectors were directly linked with the urban economy, which means that the growth of the town in demographic (and therefore physical) as well as in commercial terms will have formed an enormous stimulus for these activities.

In general terms, we can distinguish at least three categories of non-agrarian labour that increased in importance around Antwerp during the sixteenth century. First, there were the rural crafts (including weaving), the economic scale of which extended beyond the local level. Second, there was the retrieval or elaboration of local raw materials. Finally there were transport and related services.

The development of these non-agrarian activities under the influence of Antwerp's growth is the main subject of this chapter. The central question is whether the rise of rural crafts and services in the town's surroundings provided relief for the landless peasants in those surroundings. Although the kinds of activities listed above do not correspond to either the strict definition or the chronological framework of proto-industrialisation, they did have one of the major functions of proto-industrial labour: they provided an additional source of income to the rural population, who could profit from the opportunities offered by the interregional market.[7] Putting the question like this assumes that it was in fact the poor peasants who benefited from these activities, however, and not the specialised craftsmen or rural entrepreneurs. Depending on the particular form of organisation of each individual activity, this differed from one type of occupation to the other. For that reason, I will be paying particular attention to the social background of the rural merchants, craftsmen and labourers involved in these occupations.

Yet, the non-agrarian sector formed an essential part of the rural economy itself, which went beyond the specific function of a labour supply for the small-scale peasants and cottars. Although agriculture was the most important single element in the pre-modern rural economy, it was by no means the only element.[8] Non-agrarian occupations marked the occupational and social profile of the community of the villages in question; the latter became rural craft centres, shipping and fishing villages, etc. instead of being predominantly agrarian communities, with their own specific elites and their own type of social relations. In the following sections we will see how some of these sectors prospered in particular places, due to specific factors, while in other places they remained relatively unimportant. These factors could be of local origin, such as physical preconditions, the situation along transport routes or the availability of a labour force. But they also could be related to Antwerp, either through the importance of a particular product for the provisioning of the town, through the commercial functions of Antwerp for the marketing of a product, or simply through a village's short distance from the town.

The analysis of non-agrarian labour in rural Brabant is hampered by the lack of adequate sources to an even stronger extent than was the case for agriculture. There are no statistics concerning the occupational structure of the villages in question, nor are there contracts or figures of production. All that has survived in different sorts of documents are

6 VAN DER WEE, *Growth*, vol. II, p. 303.

7 This definition was used by J.L. van Zanden for similar economic activities in sixteenth-century Holland. See J.-L. VAN ZANDEN, "A Third Road to Capitalism? Proto-Industriaization and the Moderate Nature of the Later Medieval Crisis in Flanders and Holland, 1350-1550" in HOPPENBROUWERS and VAN ZANDEN, (eds.), *Peasants into Farmers?*, pp. 85–101; and J.-L. VAN ZANDEN, *The Rise and Decline of Holland's Economy*, Manchester, 1993.

8 P. MUSGRAVE, *Land and Economy in Baroque Italy. Valpolicella, 1630-1797*, Leicester, 1992, p. 33.

some individual statements concerning the importance of a particular sector in a village and references to individuals with a specific occupation. Cloth weaving in the village of Duffel forms an exception here. A number of ordinances, some documents deriving from lawsuits and even a few concerning the exportation of Duffel cloth help us to construct at least the outline of this rural textile industry.[9] For the production of bricks along the rivers Scheldt and Rupel, too, there are some data from the literature.[10]

For other sectors, the material is limited to a number of isolated references. The registers of the Antwerp aldermen form the richest source on this topic.[11] Besides references to real-estate transactions, they also contain contracts, wills, gifts and similar documents, some of which reveal the concentration of non-agrarian occupations in some places near Antwerp. A systematic study of the registers is impossible due to their volume. Nor does the study of samples form a satisfying alternative, because of the small number of relevant documents per year.[12] The summaries that the genealogist Ch. Verstrepen made of deeds in the aldermen's registry pertaining the some of the villages south of Antwerp were therefore an extremely helpful tool for gathering information on countrymen who were active in the non-agrarian sector.[13] These lists nevertheless have the disadvantage that they focus only on part of the Antwerp surroundings: the villages between Antwerp, Mechelen and Lier. As a result, we have hardly any documentation on the polder area north of Antwerp and the Kempen. I have therefore limited my analysis to the south of Antwerp and have tried to fill the gaps by referring to the – very limited – available literature concerning the rest of the surroundings of Antwerp. Another handicap of the records of the aldermen as a source for information on non-agrarian labour is the very nature of these sources. They refer in the first place to transactions concerning real estate, annuities and debts, and only very sporadically to questions of employment proper. These documents generally either mention the occupation of one of the parties involved in a transaction or they refer to the infrastructure (the brewery, lime kiln, boat, etc.) that is necessary for certain occupations. In some cases, the documents concern debts incurred for the payment of rural products, such as wood, bricks or beer. They say nothing of the number of labourers employed in a sector, their social background, and the size of their wages, however. Some of these questions can be answered by means of alternative sources, such as published wage-series or statements made by contemporaries, by extrapolating from what is known about similar occupations or, failing all else, by approximation.

Instead of trying to cover all sorts of non-agrarian labour in our research area, I had to restrict myself to the scant material this specific type of source offers. Therefore, only a number of occupations can be looked at, the relevance of which is reflected by a certain

9 These documents are published in *Dufflaea, Bijdragen tot de geschiedenis van Duffel*. See the following section for further details.

10 J. Hollestelle, *De steenbakkerij in de Nederlanden tot omstreeks 1560*, Arnhem 1976^2; R. Baetens, "Omvang en produktie van de baksteennijverheid in de Rupelstreek (16e - 20e eeuw)" in *Bijdragen tot de Geschiedenis*, 62 (1979), pp. 103–183. De Schepper, *Hemiksem*, and more recently H. Rombaut and P. De Niel, "De kleinijverheid in de Rupelstreek (13de - 20ste eeuw): een kort overzicht van het steenmaken, dak-pannen en plaveien" in *Ons Heem*, 53, 1999, pp. 135–165.

11 On the registers of the Antwerp aldermen as a quantitative source, see for example: H. Soly, *Urbanisme*, pp. 75–76 and R. Doehaerd, *Etudes anversoises*, vol. I, pp. 9–15.

12 Generally speaking, only about ten or twenty records out of 2400 to 4000 per year refer to non-agrarian activities in the countryside. This would mean the analysis would have to be limited to very few years.

13 Verstrepen, *Antwerpse schepenbrieven*.

frequency of mentions in the records of the aldermen. I will be analysing especially the geographical spread, or rather the concentrations of each of these activities, their economic importance and their potential for generating extra income for the local peasants. Finally, the link with the growth of Antwerp is made by relating this to the products or services provided by the rural economy with the urban demand, the market facilities for rural products and other potential factors.

7.2 Village Crafts Beyond Local Importance

7.2.1 Cloth-Weaving in Duffel, Walem, Kontich and Rumst

7.2.1.1 The Origins of Weaving North of Mechelen

The origins of wool weaving in the area north of Mechelen can be traced back to the high Middle Ages. In the surroundings of Lier and the Kempen, sheep farming was already widespread in the twelfth and thirteenth centuries. Hence, weaving for local demand may have begun at that time. In any case, cloth making on a larger scale had become established in Duffel, Walem, Kontich and Rumst at the end of the fourteenth century. These places were situated along the river Rupel, which formed the major transport route between Mechelen and Antwerp and lay on the trade route between Cologne and Bruges. Before long, the light woollens from the Rupel area were being exported to Germany and other parts of the Hanseatic trading area.[14] During the fifteenth century, the exportation essentially took place via the Brabant fairs of Antwerp and Bergen op Zoom as well as via the Frankfurt fairs. By that time, the production of cloth from Duffel was already the most important; it was exported to Danzig, Riga, Reval, Lübeck and Hamburg. But also cloth from Walem, Rumst and Kontich was mentioned among the exported textiles.[15] The cloth-makers' villages along the Rupel and Nete were already settlements of considerable size by the fifteenth century. Duffel, for example, was referred to as a "*villa notabilis et populosa*" in a document from 1488.[16] Walem was not only a large village, but also had a dyeing workshop, a seal house and a so-called weavers' street (*weversstraat*), which are indications for a relatively high degree of organisation.[17] Both places, with their numerous inhabitants, their impressive houses, etc. give the impression of having been almost-towns rather than rural settlements. This is also reflected by the privileged status of Duffel, Walem and Rumst, all of which were so-called liberties (*vrijheden*). The same type of large village with special liberties and a specialised economy as Walem, Rumst or Duffel had also existed in the greater surroundings of Brussels. They seem to have been a favourable place for the rise of a textile industry.[18]

14 R. van Uytven, "La draperie Brabançonne et Malinoise du XIIe au XVIIe siècle: grandeur éphémère et décadence" in *Produzione, commercio e consumo dei panni di lana (nei secoli XII-XVIII) Firenze*, 1976, pp. 85–97, 93f.

15 *Ibidem*, p. 94; C. Slootmans cites various merchants selling cloth from Duffel at the Fairs of Bergen op Zoom, around 1500: C.J.F. Slootmans, *Paas- en koudenmarkten te Bergen op Zoom*, (BtGZN LXIV-VI) Tilburg, 1985, vol. III p. 1502. See also: W.S. Unger, *De tol van Iersekeroord. Documenten en rekeningen 1321-1572*, (Rijks geschiedkundige publicatiën, kleine serie, 29) p. 91 and Index, p. 611.

16 *Dufflaea*, 99, p. 185.

17 See the description of Walem in Chapter 9.

18 R.Van Uytven, "Die ländliche Industrie während des Spätmittelalters in den südlichen Niederlanden" in H. Kellenbenz (ed.), *Agrarisches Nebengewerbe und Formen der Reagrarisierung im Spätmittelalter und 19./20. Jahrhundert* (Bericht über die 5. Arbeitstagung der Gesellschaft für Sozial- und Wirtschaftsgeschichte, (Stuttgart 1975), p. 70.

Merchtem, some 15 km west of Brussels, also had its own cloth production for which it even received the ducal privilege of establishing a drapers guild in 1409, for example. After troubles with Brussels, however, the guild was already abolished in 1411.[19] No such interferences from Mechelen or Antwerp are recorded for Duffel or Walem. This may be due to the fact that they were situated outside the immediate sphere of influence of both these cities. Mechelen had its own territory, which formed an enclave within Brabant, but which did not include either of the two places in question. Antwerp, on the other hand, was situated almost 20 km away and did not have a particularly protectionistic policy with regard to its cloth industry. Furthermore, the villages in question were in the hands of powerful noble families like the Rotselaars, the Hoornes and the Wezemaals, and not in those of Brussels patricians, as was the case in Merchtem. Thus, the village draperies of Duffel, Walem, Rumst and Kontich developed in a way similar to that of the urban cloth centres, but on a smaller scale. In comparison with the Brabantine cloth-makers' centres, they also had a delay of about one century in their development. As a result, the wage level there was lower than in larger centres with a further developed guild organisation, which made textiles from such "younger" centres cheaper than those of ancient drapers' towns.

7.2.1.2 Duffel as a Rural Centre of Cloth Export

During the sixteenth century, Walem, Kontich and Rumst seem to have lost importance in comparison with Duffel. The Antwerp certificates and sixteenth-century export registers only mention cloth from Duffel as an export product, but no woollen products from Walem, Rumst or Kontich, the other cloth-producing villages of the area. Evidence concerning the real quantitative importance of the cloth industry of Duffel is very scarce, however. From the beginning of the century, only isolated references confirm cloth exports from Duffel. Certificates from Bergen op Zoom mention several inhabitants of Duffel as sellers of (Duffel) cloth: in 1500, Joos Debie sold cloth for 28 Brabantine shillings and 3 pennies, and in 1519, Hendrik and Matheus van den Steene sold cloth for ca. 15 pounds Brabantine grooten.[20] A certificate from Antwerp, dating from 1512, refers to 27 pieces of Duffel cloth being transported from Duffel to Cologne by a certain Peter Lemmens of Pere.[21] Another, from 1509, mentions a certain Peter Smit of Duffel who bought three sacks of wool from Marburg.[22]

It is only for the period around the mid-century that registers of export taxes enable a rough quantification of the importance of Duffel cloth. Among the products listed as having been exported from the Low Countries to the Iberian Peninsula between April 1552 and August 1553, for example, were 42 pieces of Duffel cloth, worth 255 Flemish pounds, but none from any of the surrounding villages.[23] In comparison with other rural

19 A. Wauters, *Histoire des environs de Bruxelles ou description historique des localités qui formaient autrefois l'ammanie de cette ville,* (Brussels, 1855) (reprint, Brussels, 1975), vol. IV, p. 158.

20 Slootmans, *Paas- en koudenmarkten,* vol. III p. 1502.

21 Probably Peer in the province of Limburg.

22 Doehaerd, vol. III p. 5, no. 2143; and Idem, vol. II, p. 291 no. 2007.

23 L. Bril, *De handel tussen de Nederlanden en het Iberisch Schiereiland (midden XVIe E.). Een kwantitatieve peiling,* Ghent, unpublished Master's thesis, 1962, p. 149 and 165 (thanks to Filipp Vermeylen for communicating these figures). J. A. Goris, *Etude sur les colonies marchandes méridionales (portugais, espagnols, italiens) à Anvers de 1488 à 1567,* Louvain, 1925, p. 298 refers to 60 pieces and one pack.

textile centres, such as Hondschoote, this is nevertheless a very modest quantity. This raises the question of whether the fame of the drapery of Duffel was in fact as great as local historians have made us believe.

The few surviving documents and testimonies also support another hypothesis, however: that the big boom in the local cloth production dates from the period after 1553. The testimonies of contemporaries speaking of the great fame of Duffel as a weaving centre all date from the seventeenth century and refer to the period before the Revolt but not to the first half of the sixteenth century. Even Guicciardini was not very explicit in his description. According to him, Duffel was "a barony of great income and jurisdiction", while he mentions Walem as rural centre of cloth export.[24] Only in the revised edition of 1612 is Duffel described as a great centre of cloth and serge export.[25] Likewise, the archival evidence concerning the production process and marketing of woollens from Duffel only dates from the second half of the sixteenth century. As the privilege for of producing serge was only given in 1553, according to representatives of the Duffel weavers, Duffel serge could therefore only have become famous after that date.

7.2.1.3 The Organisation of Cloth Production and Marketing

The above-mentioned certificates contain important indications concerning the organisation of the Duffel cloth trade. First, the trade via Bergen op Zoom at the beginning of the sixteenth century was in the hands of Duffel merchants, and not in those of intermediaries from Antwerp. Second, in the case of the freight of Peter Lemmens, the transport went directly from Duffel to Cologne, and not via Antwerp or Bergen op Zoom. Finally, wool was imported by drapers or wool merchants from Duffel itself. These indications point toward a relatively independent drapers sector in Duffel in the first half of the century, rather than to a classical case of a putting-out system in the hands of Antwerp merchants,. In regard to the second half of the century, a series of regulations have survived that shows that the quality of the production was controlled by six officers who were appointed by the aldermen of the three local manorial courts, for the "welfare of the community".[26] Duffel produced a broad variety of woollens, including so-called Spanish *"serges"* but also traditional cloth and so-called *"friezen"* and *"baaien"*, which were marked with the seal of the three seigneurs of Duffel. Not only the size and weight of the fabric and the wool to be used in the process but also the wages of the weavers and fullers were all clearly stipulated. The same regulations also prescribed that the weavers had to make a cloth or a baai after every six *serges*, in order to maintain a balance between the very cheap *serge* and more expensive sorts of cloth. The Duffel drapery's general ordinance from 1574 contains the name of some local drapers. Frans, Gerhard and Pauwel van Tolhuisen, Antoon van den Branden and Hieronimus Keulemans alias Handelijns belonged to the most respected and probably the wealthiest families of Duffel, as reflected by the fact that they were relatives of the officials of the local manorial courts.[27] Some of them were aldermen themselves, such as Hendrik Keulemans, draper

24 Cited in W. Brulez, "De handelsbalans der Nederlanden", p. 301.

25 Cited in *Dufflaea*, p. 454.

26 RAA, OGA Duffel No. 402: Ordinance concerning the weaving of wool in Duffel, 18 Nov. 1574. Edited in *Dufflaea, Bijdragen tot de geschiedenis van Duffel*, pp. 467–482.

27 This ordinance is published in *Dufflaea* nos. 75-78, pp. 467–482. In the same ordinance, Karel and Jan van

and dyer in 1573.[28] Besides these local drapers, Antwerp merchants were also involved in marketing the products. In 1568, the manorial courts of Duffel sign an agreement with the Antwerp cloth merchant Jan Andries concerning the sale of a new sort of cloth, the so-called *"frisaden" or "vriezen"*. Andries obtained the monopoly of selling the *frisaden* from Duffel for a period of nine years. The fact that the ordinance concerning the production of *frisaden* dates from the same day as the contract with the Antwerp cloth merchant makes it very likely that the introduction of this fabric was an initiative of the latter.[29]

The information we have about the simple weavers is insufficient to consider them a-priori as peasants. We do not know to what degree the weavers from Walem and Duffel were also cottars with some farmland or full-time weavers. Only for the second half of the sixteenth century do some documents allow us to deduce that there were specialised weavers in Duffel who were to some degree not active in agriculture.[30] The 1569-70 register of the 100th-penny tax for Duffel ter-Elst reflects the social stratification of a part of Duffel, and can therefore help answer this question. Although situated outside the centre of the village, the Ter Elst manor was nevertheless affected by the cloth-weaving trade. The manor was involved – at least formally – in the organisation of the cloth production, since the aldermen of Ter Elst signed the ordinances together with those of Duffel - Land van Mechelen and Duffel under the lord of Merode. The few inhabitants of Duffel ter-Elst who can be identified as drapers, or their relatives, were among the richest of the village: the heirs of Matheus vanden Steene, who was mentioned in 1519 as a cloth exporter, were the largest local landowners of Ter Elst with more than 21 *bunders* of land.[31] Charles van Tolhuisen, who owned a house and half of a large farm, and who was perhaps identical with Karel van Tolhuisen, the bailiff (*schout*) of Duffel - Land van Mechelen, was without any doubt family of the above-mentioned drapers by the name of Van Tolhuisen. The names of the weavers, on the other hand, are unknown. Nevertheless, the fact that Duffel ter-Elst had an extremely high percentage of landless or almost-landless inhabitants makes it very likely that the weavers were in many cases identical with the inhabitants of these smallholdings.[32] If this was the case, agriculture can only have played a very secondary role for them.

Hence, Duffel was the only weavers' village in the area between Mechelen and Antwerp to have attained a significant status as such during the sixteenth century. This may be due to the relative advantage that it had over Walem, Rumst or Kontich already during the fifteenth century. The Brabantine fairs, and later Antwerp, formed a major factor in the success of the cloth industry of Duffel. These markets opened a wide market for the village drapers. In the second half of the sixteenth century, a remarkable diversification of the cloth production took place. Here, too, the influence of Antwerp was decisive. The drapers from Duffel seem to have reacted quickly to the changing demand, either at their own initiative, or via Antwerp merchants like Jan Andries. As a result of the high standards required in the

Tolhuisen figured as representatives for Duffel under the Land van Mechelen, and Laureis van den Brande as a representative for Duffel ter-Elst.

28 Record of the Duffel aldermen, cited in *Dufflaea* 73, p. 459.

29 *Dufflaea* 32-33, pp. 196–198.

30 De inwoners die eensdeels de landwinning niet oefenen generen hen met laken, sargiën en anderen wollenwerk welk in verscheidenen landen en steden met grote menigte vercocht wordt" L. Guicciardini, *Beschrijvinghe* cited in Dom, *Dufflaea*, p. 454.

31 See Appendix 9.2.

32 See Chapter 10.

local ordinances, the woollens from Duffel were of relatively high quality for having been produced in a village drapery. Duffel was therefore a particular case corresponding with the model of a small centre of cloth production, rather than with that of a proto-industrial area. The other rural drapery centres in the area north of Mechelen started off similarly, but did not attain the same degree of specialisation and professionalisation as Duffel. Walem continued being a weavers' village until the sixteenth century, although its importance lagged behind that of Duffel. Rumst, on the other hand, became a commercial centre of regional importance, with lively brewing and shipbuilding activities (as we will see in the following sections). Finally, although a large village with some local commerce, Kontich remained predominantly agrarian.

7.2.2 Brewers and Tavern Keepers

7.2.2.1 The Breweries of Rumst

Brewing was another local craft that would increase significantly in some villages during the sixteenth century. One of the largest brewing centres in the larger surroundings of Antwerp was Rumst, a large village situated at the confluence of the rivers Rupel and Nete, ca. 10 km north of Mechelen. It was a ducal toll station and the major market place of the Rupel area. The existence of some breweries was quite normal for a village of its size, yet the favourable transport facilities via the rivers Rupel and Scheldt meant that beer from Rumst could be sold far beyond the limits of the village and its closer surroundings. Certificates from Bergen op Zoom dating from the years 1523-36 refer to brewers from Rumst as exporters of beer and as buyers of barley via the fairs of Bergen.[33] In Antwerp, brewers from Rumst and Walem were listed together with those from the towns of Mechelen and Lier as providers of beer in 1526.[34]

Around 1570, Rumst was said to have nine highly profitable breweries that sold numerous shiploads of beer to places in Brabant, Flanders, Holland and Zealand. Most of these brewers had their own beer ship for this purpose. According to the authors of the description of Rumst before the Revolt, the brewers and the owners of the breweries made great profits and employed many servants. Each of these breweries was taxed like a large farm, although according to the village authorities, a brewery was three times as profitable as a farm. Some of the brewers were said to be farmers as well, keeping a great number of horses, cattle, oxen and pigs. The residues from the brewing process thus served as fodder for fattening livestock.[35]

33 Slootmans, *Paas- en koudenmarkten,* vol. 3, p. 1422.

34 Ordinance from 4 August 1526, Index der gebodboeken 1489-1620" in *Antwerpsch Archievenblad* 1 1864, p. 184.

35 SAA,VG 5, fo. 84: Rumst-Boom. See also Cosemans, "Uitzicht", *passim* on brewers fattening pigs; See also Chapter 6.

TABLE 10: Breweries in Rumst in the Sixteenth Century

Name	Owner	Place	Year(s)	Description
Den Wildeman[1]	J.van Cauwenberg Jan Thijs	Markt	1520- 1530	After 1535 only "house", but no brewery
Den Wijngaart[2]	G. van Ossendrecht		1530	3 vierendeel
	Jan Nonne[3] (Mechelen)	's Herenstraat	1539	
	G. Colaes	Binnen vrijheid	1539	With a stone house, a stable, 1 bunder of land
	W.Bouwens	Onderwijkt	1539	4 bunders, later 2 bunders of land
	Mr. R. van Haarlem (Antwerp)[4]	Markt	1540	Seized after delay of payment
Den Engel[5]	P. van Erdenborg	Walemsveer	1540- 1544	Including a farm and a meadow: 4 bunders.
De Rode Leeuw[6]	W. van Haecht	Aant veer	1545	1547 bought by ship-builder
	G. Broer	Markt	1561	
Hollandse tuin[7]	A. Saerens	Markt	1563	

1 SAA, SR 157, fo. 176v; SR 178 fo. 39; RAA, OA Rumst 26.
2 SAA, SR 178, fo. 39.
3 RAA, OA Rumst 26, fo. 43v.
4 RAA, OA Rumst 26, fo. 21r.
5 SAA, SR 198, fo. 272.
6 RAA, OA Rumst 26, fo. 149r.
7 See fn. 46.

By means of the registers of the aldermen of Antwerp and those of Rumst itself, some of the features of this description can be verified. Five breweries could be identified by name and five others by their owner or location (Table 10). Some of the brief descriptions in the registers confirm their notable size and partly agrarian character, as claimed in the description of Rumst mentioned above. The brewery "den Hollandsen tuin" of Adriaan Saerens, situated at the market square next to the house of Melchior Schets and the former brewery "den Wilden man", contained a stable, a barn and a courtyard.[36] Also, the brewery that Jan Nonne sold to Willem van Haecht in 1541 had a pigsty as well as a meadow.[37] Some of the breweries had up to 4 *bunders* of land.

36 "*Adriaen Sarens x Maria Baey te Rumpst vercocht, (rente),op een huys genaempt de hollandsche thuyn dwelck en brouwery is met stallinge schuere metten hove gelegen te Rumpst aen de merckt tussen Heer Melchior Schetz N en O, Z 's Herenstraete W het huys de wildeman*' (SAA, SR 295, fo. 138r, 1-10-1563 = Verstrepen 779).
37 RAA, OA Rumst 26, fo. 68v.

Some of the brewery owners were townsmen from Mechelen or Antwerp, like the Mechelen silk merchant Jan Nonne and the Master van Haarlem who seized the brewery of Jan Cloot in 1538. Others were members of the local elite, such as Adriaan Saerens, the son of the former alderman Willem Saerens. Aside from his brewery at the market square, he also owned an additional three houses in Rumst.[38] These wealthy owners probably leased their breweries out, possibly with a hereditary lease. Other, less wealthy, breweries keepers were explicitly called brewers in the documents, such as Godevaart de Rouwe, G. van Ossendrecht, Jacob van Haecht, or Gielis van Gottengies. Some were the owners of their breweries; others leased them.

7.2.2.2 The Later Suburbs of Antwerp

Brewing was also one of the major non-agrarian activities in the villages immediately adjoining Antwerp.[39] Profiting from the town's low beer production as a result of its poor water quality, they became the major providers for Antwerp. Already in 1508, the town magistrate responded to their competition by purchasing the manorial rights of several neighbouring villages and by forbidding the inhabitants of Antwerp to go drinking outside the town. In 1516, Berchem and Borgerhout, the greatest producers, finally agreed to pay half the excise that Antwerp brewers had to pay.[40] Despite these regulations and the radical reorganisation of Antwerp's own brewing industry in the 1550s, the breweries of the Antwerp suburbs survived. According to a document from 1578, there were 13 breweries in Borgerhout, and 25 more in Berchem, Deurne, Dambrugge, Merksem, the ferry station of "Bakkersveer", Kiel, and Wilrijk.[41]

As in Rumst, some of the breweries in Borgerhout and Deurne also included considerable quantities of farmland. Most of the breweries were not exploited by their owners but leased out to professional brewers. Since their lease value was generally comparable to that of a larger farm, as mentioned in the declaration of the aldermen of Rumst, they will have formed a good source of income for both the owners and the brewers who operated them.[42] Furthermore, the larger breweries offered employment to helpers and servants and – indirectly – to boatmen, carters and coopers.

The later suburbs of Antwerp, Berchem and Borgerhout, cannot be considered typical of the development of the rural surroundings of the metropolis, however. As a result of the rapid rise of the city, these villages underwent a quite exceptional expansion with rapid demographic growth during the sixteenth century. J.B. Stockmans maintains that "within

38 "*Adriaen Sarens (fs Willem) x Maria Boen te Rumpst verc,. (rente),op een huys mette hove "de volgelensanck" metten stal lande gestaen tot Rumpst achter de kerke, als medepand twee woningen met fundo tot Rumpst in de veerstraete tegenover t'huys "de geldenland"*" (SAA, SR 301, fo. 156v, 5-5-1565 = Verstrepen 902). Willem Saerens was alderman at least from 1537 to 1545, RAA, OA Rumst no. 26, Records in the register of the aldermen of the "liberty" of Rumst 1536-1547. Summaries of the contracts are published in Ch. Verstrepen, *Schepengriffie, Vrijheid van Rumst 1536-1547,* Brussel, 1989.

39 See also M. Limberger, "Periferie urbane e processi di sub-urbanizzazione ad Anversa nel XVI secolo. "Forze di mercato" e "mano visibile"" in: *Società e Storia*, 112 (2006), p. 267- 284 (special issue: P. Lanaro and G.M. Varanini, eds., Perieferie e spazi periferici nella città europea del medioevo e dell' età moderna (secoli XIV-XIX) : le trasformazioni indotte dall'economia).

40 Nooyens, *Deurne*, vol. I, pp. 558–562, Soly, "Brouwerijonderneming", pp. 339–340.

41 Ibidem, p. 1202.

42 Nooyens, *Deurne*, vol. I, pp. 568–575. In 1544, the lease values of the breweries mentioned in a taxation list concerning Deurne and Borgerhout varied between 40 and 70 guilders.

several hours' journey, there was no place that displayed as much liveliness and activity as Berchem". In the case of Borgerhout, the example that is best documented, a large village with a highly diversified professional structure grew up beside the road from Antwerp to Cologne. The intensive traffic along this road and other traffic axes provided a living for innkeepers, brewers, blacksmiths, carpenters and others alike.

The strong impact of these roads on the local economy of the villages situated alongside them is also confirmed by documents concerning the villages of Oelegem and Broechem, situated some kilometres further away from Antwerp. In the descriptions of these villages we find: "there is a great road passing through the village, hence there are six relay stations (*uitspannen*) and several breweries and inns" and also "...along these streets and on the square near the church many crafts were practiced...." There are similar testimonies pertaining to the villages of Ekeren and Kapellen, situated along the road leading north to Breda and Bergen op Zoom. The latter descriptions mention "...many and great crafts in the village for travellers to Breda..." and "great relay stations on the road towards Bergen."[43]

Around 1580, Borgerhout had some 150 tavern keepers, 50 butchers, 16 hat makers, 13 brewers and seven bakers, as well as a great variety of local crafts. The large number of butchers, brewers, and bakers can only be understood in the context of the demand from the nearby city. Of these, the butchers seem to have been the first to settle in the village, already by the beginning of the sixteenth century. Hat makers, on the other hand were anything but common in sixteenth-century villages. Based on declarations from 1580, F. Nooyens thinks the industry of making hats in "the Spanish fashion" only developed in the 1560s and that most of the hat makers of Borgerhout were immigrants.[44]

In contrast to these future suburbs of Antwerp, Rumst does not appear to have been directly impacted by the rise of Antwerp. While the urban demand for beer was high, this did not benefit Rumst in particular. It must have been the combination of local factors such as the existence of breweries for the local and regional markets and the good transport facilities on the one hand and the increasing demand on the other hand that helped to raise the brewing activity in Rumst to such a high level.

7.3 Building Materials and Fuel for the Metropolis

7.3.1 General Remarks

A second category of non-agrarian occupations practiced in the countryside were those related to the extraction or processing of raw materials that could serve as building materials or fuel. Raw materials serving industrial purposes could be included here too, although the presence of these was hardly significant in the surroundings of Antwerp. Such activities generally did not take place in villages, but rather close to the resources they exploited. The raw materials referred to, such as wood, peat, stone, lime or clay, belonged to the landowners on whose property they were found. Nevertheless, their exploitation was in the hands of specialised "entrepreneurs" who either leased the necessary land or bought the exploitation rights.

43 Antwerp City Archives, VG 5.
44 Nooyens, *Deurne*, vol. I, pp. 599–600.

In the surroundings of Antwerp, two sectors within this category of non-agrarian occupations attained exceptional dimensions: brick making and woodcutting. While the exploitation of peat would also make a very interesting topic in this context, we have decided against including it in our analysis for two reasons. To begin with, there were no significant sources of peat in the area under consideration. Peat cutting was only a marginal activity to the south of Antwerp. There were some small peat-cutting operations in the valley of the Nete, near Lier. Tenants who wanted to cut peat for their own use in the woods of the duke had to pay a fee of 6 pennies for each *roede* (32.9 m^2) they dug. The number of tenants who benefited from this cheap source of fuel was considerable, and the duke's income reached relatively high values as well. Even so, the total area of peat that was cut was limited, never exceeding 8 hectares.[45] There were two major peat-cutting areas in the southern Low Countries that were actually situated very close to Antwerp: the north of Flanders and the northern Kempen. As these areas were important suppliers for Antwerp, that town's rise formed an impulse for the exploitation of peat there. A detailed consideration of this sector would nevertheless go beyond the geographical limits of our study.[46]

7.3.2 Brick Production along the Rivers Scheldt and Rupel

7.3.2.1 The Origins of the "Rupel Area" as a Centre of Brick Production

Bricks were produced on a large scale in the villages along the Scheldt and the Rupel. In fact, brick burning was a widespread activity in the southern Low Countries during the Late Middle Ages. Many towns – and even some local seigneurs – had a brick oven in the immediate vicinity, wherever some amount of clay was available. While in most places these ovens were only used temporarily and remained important only on a local scale, the production in the Scheldt-Rupel area had already risen to a very high level in the fifteenth century. The basis for this rise was the presence of a thick layer of clay that was well suited for brick production.

Hemiksem, Schelle, Niel and Boom all had numerous brick ovens and limekilns that produced primarily for Antwerp, but also for Mechelen and Lier. By around 1400, they already formed one of the greatest concentrations of brick production in the Low Countries.[47] While clay was a local resource, lime had to be shipped in from the surroundings of Brussels via the river Zenne. Peat from northern Flanders was used for firing the ovens.[48] The number of ovens is estimated to have been ca. 50 around the year 1500. While exact outputs for the period before the sixteenth century are not known, the Antwerp aldermen's

45 The income was highest in 1558/9, when it made up for 61 pounds of Brabantine *grooten*.

46 On the economic importance of peat in general terms: J.W. de Zeeuw, *Peat and the Dutch Golden Age; the Historical Meaning of Energy Attainability*, A.A.G. Bijdragen, 21, pp. 3–31. On northern Flanders, see: A. Verhulst, *Landschap en landbouw,* Brussel 1995, pp. 81–83. B. Augustyn, "Traces of a Protoindustrial Organization of the Medieval North Flemish Peat Region. Test Case Kieldrecht, a Peat Diggers Village ca. 1400" in H.J. Nitz (ed.), *The Medieval and Early Modern Rural Landscape of Europe under the Impact of the Commercial Economy,* Göttingen, 1987, pp. 61–73. On the Kempen: K.A.H.W. Leenders, *Verdwenen venen, Een onderzoek naar de ligging en exploitatie van thans verdwenen venen in het gebied tussen Antwerpen, Turnhout, Geertruidenberg en Willemstad 1250-1750*, s.l. 1989.

47 J. Hollestelle, *De steenbakkerij in de Nederlanden tot omstreeks 1560,* Arnhem 1976², p. 124, See also: H. Rombaut & P. De Niel, "De kleinijverheid in de Rupelstreek (13de - 20ste eeuw): een kort overzicht van het steenmaken, dak-pannen en plaveien", in *Ons Heem*, 53, 1999, pp. 135–165.

48 G. Asaert, *Scheepvaart*, p. 331.

registers from the first half of the fifteenth century refer to deliveries of up to 190,000 bricks by one individual brick maker.[49] Bricks and tiles from Hemiksem, Boom and Rumst were sent in ships to building sites in the area and particularly to nearby Antwerp. In fact, the bricks had to conform to the Antwerp standards.[50] But there was also a considerable export trade. Bricks from the Boom and Hemiksem area already appear in building accounts from various places throughout the Low Countries from before 1400.[51]

7.3.2.2 Owners and Operators of the Brick Ovens

Originally, the loam pits and brick ovens were located on land belonging to landlords and great landowners such as St. Bernard's Abbey in Hemiksem, but given out in copyhold to masons or specialised brick makers.[52] As various examples show, those who held brick ovens were in most cases members of the wealthier local families.[53] The Pluym family of Boom, for example, had considerable landed property. On 2 March 1475, Hendrik Pluym sold 7 *bunders* of land; the same day, the sale of an annuity on a brick oven with 1 *bunder* of wood and land by Jan Pluym was registered.[54] Together with his two brick ovens, Laureis Schellekens of Boom held a farm of 20 *bunders*.[55] Antwerp citizens already owned some ovens by around 1400, but their role in brick production was not a major one at that time.[56]

It is no coincidence that the people who held the brick ovens belonged to the wealthier class. Brick making was highly capital intensive. They had to have access to quite large clay grounds for their primary material, they needed a plot of land situated nearby the river to transport the bricks by ship, and they had to buy wood or peat to heat the ovens.[57] Hence the value of the brick ovens was very high. The tax value of a brick oven in Boom was estimated to be like that of a farm of 6–8 *bunders* in 1575.[58]

Furthermore, the labour factor was also considerable. The production of bricks required at least one qualified brick maker and some five workers. Indeed, a document from 1443 refers to a certain Adriaan Vleminck not as the owner of a brick oven, as usual, but explicitly as a brick maker (*steenmaker*).[59] There were quite some brick makers that either owned their own ovens or held them in copyhold, such as Adriaan Pinten and Peter van Boom of Hemiksem or Jan Robbijns of Hoboken.[60] Others leased their ovens like Gilis de Hage of Hoboken did in 1496.[61]

---

49 Hendrik de Cammere had to deliver 190,000 bricks to Gillis de Gramme of Boom. SAA, SR 31, fo. 408v; in 1429, Jan Zegers of Hemiksem obliged himself to deliver 100,000 bricks per ship to a certain Gilis de Grave, De Schepper, *Hemiksem*, p. 24.

50 SAA, SR 120, "Gillis van der Heyden, steenbakker te Callebeke onder Hemiksem debet 300,000 careelstenen en 1200 cleyn steen naer de kuer van Antwerpen," 1501.

51 Hollestelle, *Steenbakkerij*, p. 130.

52 For example in 1520: "Peter Wijchmans te Hemiksem geeft in erf aan Martin van Wijnegem metser een steengeleg met hove en huizinge gelegen te Hemiksem" ARA SR 156 fo. 173r. (Verstrepen).

53 Families like the Wielancs were among the most important landowners in the area.

54 SAA, SR 87, fo. 221v.

55 SAA, SR 34, fo. 275r.

56 De Nave, *Antwerpen*, pp. 422–426, Hollestelle, *Steenbakkerij*, pp. 126, 129.

57 Asaert, *Antwerpse scheepvaart*, p. 331 mentions various records referring to the purchase of peat from Flemish boatmen.

58 SAA, VG 5, fo. 85.

59 ARA, SR 32, fo. 645r.

60 They were called *steenbakkers* and at the same time figured as owners of a brick oven in the documents (see appendix 3).

61 SAA, SR 110, fo. 131r.

The number of brick ovens in the early sixteenth century is difficult to quantify. Hollestelle estimates there were about 50 ovens along the banks of the rivers Scheldt and Rupel between Hemiksem and Rumst around 1500. On the other hand, for the period around 1550, there are thought to have been no more than about 35 brick ovens in Hemiksem, Hoboken and Boom taken together. This means that between 200 and 300 workers, both men and women, could be temporarily employed in brick production. Considering that the total population of the brick-makers' villages taken together was ca. 2850 in 1496, this would have made up for ca. 7 – 10% of the population.[62] According to the Antwerp real-estate speculator and building entrepreneur Gilbert van Schoonbeke, the number of workers employed in the production of bricks along Scheldt and Rupel around 1550 lay between 400 and 500. Considering the demographic growth of the area during that period, the degree of employment therefore remained about the same.[63]

7.3.2.3 The Consequences of the Antwerp Building Boom

The growth of Antwerp during the sixteenth century brought about a veritable building boom in the town. The number of houses there increased by 5700 between 1496 and 1568, a new fortification was built between 1542 and 1552, and a number of impressive public buildings, such as a new meat hall (1501-1504), the *Beurs* (1531-1533), the town hall (1561-1565), and the Hessenhuis (1563-1565). This boom created employment for thousands of workers from Antwerp and its surroundings. It also resulted in a huge demand for building materials.[64] The high demand made prices for bricks rise sharply from 1540s on. In 1548, during the building of the new fortification, the Antwerp magistrate complained about the excessive prices for bricks, which they attributed to monopolistic practices among the brick makers.[65] Although there is no proof for these accusations, the brick production was at that moment in fact concentrated in the hands of some local brick-maker clans that had a *de facto* monopoly on the brick ovens. The Pluym family, for example, had been the leading brick makers in Boom since 1438, the Van der Eyckens of Hoboken had been active since 1496, the Wyckmans of Hemiksem since 1497, and the Pintes, also of Hemiksem, since 1518. They not only passed on their ovens within their own families, but they were also in close contact with each other, so that price-fixing agreements cannot be excluded (see Appendix 3).[66]

The Antwerp building entrepreneurs Jacob van Hencxthoven and Gilbert van Schoonebeke had a very effective response to this problem: they bought their own loam pits in Hemiksem and established their own brick ovens there. This helped them to reduce the

62 Hoboken, Hemiksem, Niel, Schelle, Rumst (incl. Boom) together had 568 households in 1496, Cuvelier, *Dénombrements* pp. 462–474.

63 H. Soly, *Urbanisme*, p. 249; in 1526 the population of the brick-makers' villages had increased to 3500. Considering further that the population kept growing by ca. 36% between 1526 and 1570, it can be estimated at ca. 4800 in 1550 (see also Chapter 3).

64 Soly, *Urbanisme*, p. 54.

65 Soly, *Urbanisme*, p. 246. Compare also the brick prices in Lier "in Van der Wee, *Growth*, vol. I, Appendix 18, pp. 257–261.

66 This shows from numerous transactions between brick makers, concerning the purchase or mortgage of brick ovens, and other real estate; For example, in 1504, Gielis van der Eycken of Hemiksem sold a brick oven to Jan Robbijns of Hoboken that he had bought from Merten van Standonk. SAA, SR 125, fo. 152r.

price of bricks by 25 %. They also seem to have attracted additional workers by providing housing for 60 families and offering compensation (in the form of a *godspenning*) for the winter period, when the brick ovens were not in operation.[67] This "capitalistic" form of organisation was very exceptional and rather short lived, however. The Van Schoonbeke and Van Hencxthoven company only lasted from 1549 to 1551. Van Schoonbeke sold his 11 brick ovens in 1553 to the local brick makers Jan and Peter van Boom, who appear as brick makers in records up until the seventeenth century.[68] Van Hencxthoven's engagement in Hemiksem lasted longer and went even further than Van Schoonbeke's. He kept his ovens, and in 1559 he bought the jurisdiction, thus becoming the local seigneur.[69] His ovens were operated by Jan Adriaensen and his son, Jan Adriaensen the Younger, who had an additional five ovens of his own besides the four belonging to Van Hencxthoven in 1553.

Aside from the building entrepreneurs Van Schoonbeke and Van Hencxthoven, there were few other Antwerp citizens who bought brick ovens, perhaps because of the strong grip the local brick makers had on the brick production.[70] One of the few Antwerp citizens who owned a brick oven in Hoboken was the mason Aart Wils. He had inherited the property from his father, who in turn had family ties with the local brick-maker' s family Colaes.[71] The local masters, on the other hand, were themselves increasingly attracted to the town. They either became citizens, bought real estate in town or established marriage ties with townsman. Jan and Peter van Boom owned some parcels in the Antwerp Nieuwstad in 1565 for example,[72] and Katelijne Robbrechts, daughter of Martine van der Eycken of Hemiksem, got married to the Antwerp merchant Jan Olis in 1556.[73] The most striking example of this urbanisation of the rural brick makers was Jan Pluym, the scion of the main brick-maker clan from Boom. From 1562 on, he appeared in documents as a mason and brick merchant in Antwerp, where he owned several houses.[74] The massive intervention of the two Antwerp building entrepreneurs in the brick industry of Hemiksem therefore resulted in a strong increase in the number of brick ovens and in a – temporary – reorganisation of the production process. The local brick makers continued with their activities during and after the 1550s, although they increasingly urbanised, as the above-mentioned examples suggest.

Although the number of brick ovens in Hemiksem had increased by 15 to a total of 32 in 1549, the core of the brick-making area moved toward Boom during the second half of the sixteenth century. According to De Schepper, there were only three brick ovens there in 1550 – a number that seems too low, considering the frequent mentions of brick makers from Boom in the registers of the Antwerp aldermen and the importance that Boom apparently already had at the beginning of the sixteenth century.[75] In 1562 there were 13

67 SOLY, *Urbanisme*, p. 266.
68 DE SCHEPPER, *Hemiksem*, p. 26f.
69 See Chapter 9, Section 1.
70 There is for example a reference to a certain Jan Hellemans the Younger, of Antwerp, who sold his brick oven in Niel to Claus Staeck (SAA, SR 113 = Verstrepen no. 722).
71 SAA, 286, fo. 441v.
72 SAA, SR 302, fo. 6v.
73 SAA, SR 258, fo. 4r.
74 SAA, SR 291, fo. 124r, SR 294, fo. 313. Upon his death in 1565, he left his property in Boom to his son Gillis, SR 304, fo. 5v.
75 See for example the agreement from 1513 between brick makers from Boom and representatives of Vilvoorde, Antwerp and Mechelen concerning regulations on brick making and lime-burning, see J. NAUWELAERS, *Histoire de la ville de Vilvorde*,

brick ovens and even 17 in 1568.[76] In 1575, according to the description of the villages before the Revolt, the number had risen to 18 brick ovens and limekilns and eight tile ovens. The level of employment in brick production also rose accordingly. The representatives of Boom declared in 1593 that the majority of the village inhabitants had been employed in the brick industry in 1575. The master brick makers therefore not only paid the wages for their workers but also their contributions in the ducal taxes. Sixty brick workers who lived in workers-houses were characterised as poor folk who had no work during the winter and therefore had to live from the poor relief.[77]

The rising urban demand for bricks and lime during the sixteenth century thus led to a major expansion of brick production in the Scheldt and Rupel area. As a result, a considerable share of the local population was employed in this sector. Except for a temporary investment by Antwerp building entrepreneurs, the production and trade of bricks remained in the hands of the long-established local brick-maker families, who were the major employers and the greater landowners in their villages. Their ties with Antwerp increased as a result of their professional contacts, so that some of them finally became townsmen or at least owners of urban real estate.

7.3.3 Woodcutting south of Antwerp

7.3.3.1 The major forms of marketing wood: selling woodcuts and direct exploitation

In addition to their dependency on bricks and stones, the towns were also dependent on fuel. In the late Middle Ages, the major source of fuel was wood. The Low Countries were not particularly rich in forests. Guicciardini mentions the forests of Zoniën, Groothout, Meerdaal, and Zaventerlo as the largest of Brabant. Aside from these larger forests, there were low woods of alders, oaks, beeches and poplars in various places of Brabant that served as a fuel supply for the towns. For Antwerp, the woods along the Scheldt, south of the city, seem to have been a particularly important source of fuel. Firewood from Niel and Schelle was even shipped down the Scheldt to Bergen op Zoom.[78] The owners of these woods were primarily great landowners like the sovereign, noblemen or religious institutions. In the sixteenth century, rich townsmen also increasingly began purchasing woods.[79] The wood that was cut was mainly used as firewood, which was sold in bundles, and only to a much lesser extent as lumber for light construction. Lumber of greater dimensions to be used for example as beams for larger buildings had to be imported.[80] For the landowners, wood formed a major source of income. The receiver of the ducal demesne Land van Mechelen sold between 65 and 112 hectares of cuts per year, which made up between 30 and 40% of the total receipts, in the beginning, and up to 80% in the third quarter of the sixteenth

Parijs, Brussel, Kortrijk, 1941, p. 345.

76 An overview of the quantitative evolution of the brick industry in the Rupel area is given in R. Baetens, "Omvang en produktie van de baksteennijverheid in de Rupelstreek (16e - 20e eeuw)" in *Bijdragen tot de Geschiedenis*, 62 (1979) 130.

77 "*60 keine huiskens arbeiders op de geleyen werkende., schamel lieden gedurende de winter egeen werk en hadden. En bijde heilige geest moesten leven*," SAA, VG 5, fo. 89.

78 Slootmans, *Paas- en koudenmarkten*, vol. III p. 1273.

79 See Chapter 10, Section 2 b.

80 Sosson, *Travaux publics*, pp. 102–112. See also Chapter 6.

century.[81] The sale of wood generated income not only for the landowners, however, but also for dozens of wood merchants and hundreds of rural workers. The common practice was to sell a plot of wood to a wood merchant for cutting. Many such cuts were registered with the Antwerp court of aldermen. The merchants who bought woodcuts in the area along the Scheldt and south of Antwerp (i.e. in the villages of Schelle, Hemiksem, Kontich, Aartselaar, etc.) came in most cases from the closer surroundings of the woods in question, and not so much from Antwerp itself (see Appendix 4). The background of these wood merchants was similar to that of the brick makers. They formed a relatively well-off group who bought the cut and organised the trade and the transport of the wood to the market. One of these wood merchants was Lucas Bal of Aartselaar, who figures in the Antwerp town accounts of 1549-1550 as a provider of firewood. The Bal family was among the leading local families during the fifteenth and sixteenth centuries.[82] For the actual cutting, the wood merchants employed workers whom we may presume also lived nearby. Considering that woodcutting was a seasonal activity that took place mainly during the winter, this offered wage labour to numerous peasants during the dead season of agriculture.

An alternative to selling merchants sections of woods for cutting was the direct exploitation of those sections by the landowners. Charitable institutions in Lier, for example, exploited their woods around that town by means of "whole armies" of woodcutters.[83] Also the Antwerp St. Michael's Abbey sold wood from direct exploitation. In 1500, for example, it delivered wood, bark, bundles of firewood and laths to a certain Joos van der Tommen in Reet for 33 pounds and 6 shillings.[84] The Villers Abbey sold between 8000 and 14000 faggots every year from its woods in Schoten.[85] Other institutions, such as St. Elisabeth hospital in Antwerp, sold their wood both in whole cuts and via direct exploitation.[86]

7.3.3.2 Woodcutting as a source of extra income

As far as the number of workers who found work in woodcutting is concerned, there was no fundamental difference between whether the cuts were organised by wood merchants or by the landowners themselves. In practice, there may have been differences in the types of workers who were employed and in the types of contracts made. One might argue, for example, that specialised merchants, who tended to buy various cuts every year, offered more continuity of employment than landowners, who cut their wood at irregular intervals. On the other hand, the merchants may have preferred to work with experienced workers whom they employed for a whole season, while landowners with only little wood to cut may have employed workers only occasionally and for shorter periods. St. Elisabeth hospital, for instance, employed woodcutters only every second year during the first half of the sixteenth century. The average number of daily wages the hospital paid to woodcutters

81 ARA, Rk. reg. 11898- 11915 (1474/75-1589/90); see also Martens, *L'administration du domaine ducal*, p. 142f.

82 P. Génard, "De rekening der stad Antwerpen van het jaar 1549-1550" in *Antwerpsch Archievenblad*, 1(1864), p. 77; Limberger, "Credit, land market", passim.

83 Van der Wee, *Growth*, vol. I, p. 238 (Appendix 13).

84 SAA, SR 118, fo. 110v.

85 G, Ploegaerts, L'abbaye cistercienne de Villers pendant les cinq derniers siècles de son existence" in *Annales de la société archéologique de l'arrondissement de Nivelles XI (1913-26)*, p. 347 refers to the accounts of the abbey for the period between 1504 and 1517.

86 De Commer & Soly, "Harde tijden", p. 84.

per year was not higher than 25. In the second half of the century, in contrast, the number of workers increased significantly.[87] Especially in the periods 1548–1552, 1559–1561, 1565 and 1570–1571, the number was very high.[88] Likewise, the sales of firewood of the demesne Land van Mechelen increased considerably during the second half of the century (graph 3).[89] It is striking, however, that the purchases of cuts mentioned in the registers of the Antwerp aldermen decreased sharply at the same time. The number of cuts in the middle of the fifteenth century was much higher than in the middle of the sixteenth century. Between 1536 and 1546, 24 cuts were registered, against only nine between 1536 and 1546. Finally, in the decade between 1556 and 1565, not a single cut was registered. This is even more surprising if one considers that at the same time the institutions in Lier switched to selling their wood *en bloc*.[90] The disappearance of registered woodcuts during the sixteenth century may therefore be a result of changing administrative habits rather than of any actual change in the exploitation.

Graph 3: Sales of Wood of the Demesne Land van Mechelen 1476-1590

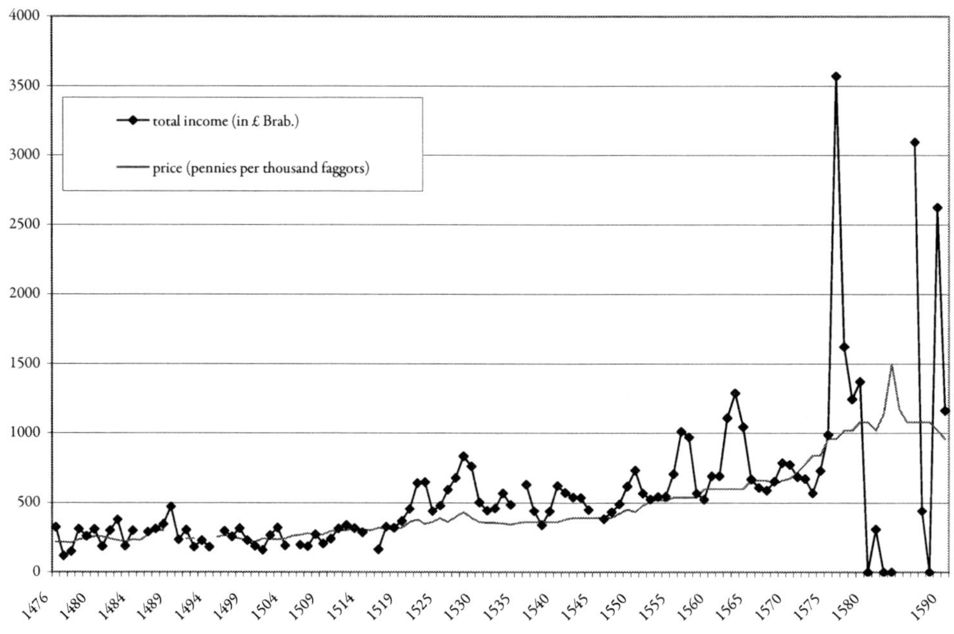

Source: ARA, Rk. Registers 11897-11915.

87 Scholliers, *Prijzen en Lonen*, pp. 348–351.

88 The sudden increase after 1548 and the following seven years without employing any woodcutters can be explained by the fact that after the intensive cutting the woods may have needed a period of growth before they could be cut again. The subsequent years show similar intervals between cuts.

89 Here, too, there was an interval of about six years between the years of high sales.

90 Van der Wee, *Growth*, vol. I, p. 238.

Prices for firewood increased sharply in the second half of the sixteenth century.[91] This meant that the landowners could make high profits by selling great quantities in years of high prices, inasmuch as the yields of their woods permitted this. This in turn meant that many peasants found work as woodcutters during the winter as a result of the increasing urban demand for fuel. Wage data from St. Elisabeth hospital show furthermore that the wages for woodcutting were comparable to and even slightly higher than those of mason's labourers in Antwerp during the winter. Although the wages for this kind of work were among the lowest a worker could earn in the city and therefore often insufficient for survival if one had no other work, they would have formed a considerable extra income for small peasants and cottars (Graph 4).

Graph 4: Wages of Woodcutters near Antwerp 1502-1570

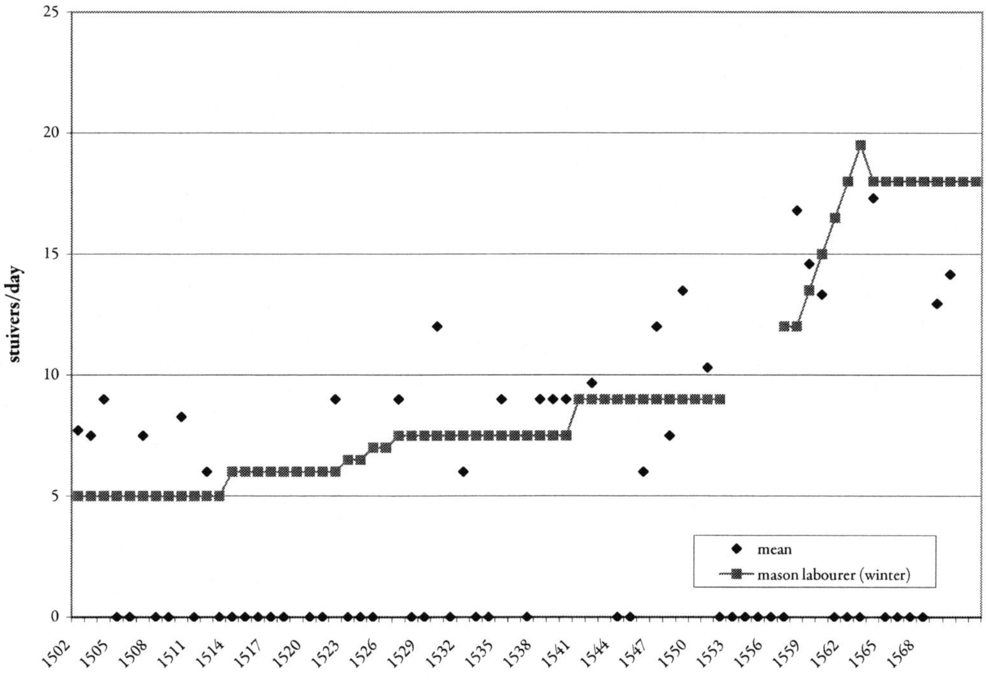

SOURCE: SCHOLLIERS, *Prijzen en lonen, pp. 348–351.*

91 *Ibidem*, p. 238 (Appendix 13) and E. SCHOLLIERS, *Prijzen en lonen*, pp. 348–351.

7.4 Labour in the Transport Sector

7.4.1 Carters and Wagoners

A third type of rural labour that was immediately connected with the urban economy consisted of occupations in the transport sector. Boatmen, carters and carriers formed a necessary connection between the rural economy and the town. They brought rural products such as grain, bricks and wood to the town and urban goods to the countryside.[92] Many farmers had a team of horses that they used not only for ploughing but also for pulling a cart or wagon. The frequency with which farmers had to provide transport services to Antwerp and other places shows that they were capable of transporting freight over longer distances. In general, the farmers used their wagons not so much for corvees, but rather to carry agrarian produce or wood for their own purposes or for payment.[93]

Any farmer could transport freights with his wagons during the low seasons, and even cottars sometimes had one or two horses with which they could haul a cart. The latter is explicitly confirmed for the village of Rumst. Around 1570, there were said to be sixteen to eighteen cottars with smallholdings who had a team of humble horses for hauling wood against payment.[94] However, the transport services performed by peasants were limited by the seasonal requirements of the agricultural activities. The Antwerp fairs, for example, coincided with agrarian peak periods and were therefore not the ideal moments for peasants to earn extra income as carters.[95] Country people could also specialise in transporting, however, and thus work independently of the farming year.

Especially for the transport of heavy or very bulky goods, the services of specialists were needed.[96] Some inhabitants of villages of the Kempen, including Tongerlo, Mol and Geel, were active as carriers between Antwerp and Cologne, although they were less numerous than those from the Limburg area.[97] For the closer surroundings of Antwerp, no such a specialisation in long-distance transport can be detected. Along the rivers Scheldt and Rupel, however, inland navigation was an important non-agrarian occupation. The villages of Rumst, Schelle, Niel and Boom, for example, were home to dozens of boatmen who went to Antwerp and beyond to transport wood, bricks, beer and local agrarian products. In the following section we will concentrate on these boatmen and their links with the other non-agrarian sectors of the area on the one hand and with Antwerp on the other.

92 "The purpose of village carriers was to unite a market town with villages of its hinterland, with the local area dependent on it." A. Everitt, "Country Carriers in the Nineteenth Century" in D. Gerhold *Road Transport in the Horse-Drawn Era*, Aldershot, 1996, pp. 1–3.

93 J. Masschaele, *Peasants, Merchants and Markets. Inland Trade in Medieval England, 1150-1350*, New York, 1997, pp. 204–207. Masschaele used the stipulations concerning transport corvees in order to analyse the capacity of medieval carting in England.

94 "*16-18 kossaten op kleine landsteden,hadden een paar slechte paardekens om tegen loon hout te rijden.*" SAA, VG 5, fo. 84.

95 van Uytven, "Landtransport", p. 486.

96 Ballaux, "Molenstenen", p. 275.

97 R. Doehaerd, *Études Anversoises*, vol. I, pp. 51–52.

7.4.2 Inland Navigation and Shipbuilding along the Rivers Scheldt and Rupel

Shipping activity had been bustling along the navigable rivers of the Antwerp area since the Middle Ages.[98] The Scheldt formed the major axis, connecting the town with the North Sea on one end and, via a dense network of navigable rivers, with a large part of the southern Low Countries on the other. The first of these tributaries – seen from the perspective of Antwerp – was the Rupel, which joined the Scheldt at Rupelmonde. Via its headwaters the Zenne, the Nete, and the Dijle, the Rupel connected Antwerp to southern Brabant by water.[99]

Although Antwerp and Mechelen both had their respective shipping corporations with strong monopolies in interurban transport, boatmen were also active in some smaller places along the rivers, especially in terms of the transport of local products like stones, bricks and wood, as well as agrarian products.[100] Along the Scheldt, there were boatmen in Hemiksem, Schelle, Niel and Hingene; along the Rupel, the major shipping villages were Rumst and Boom. In the description of Boom before the religious troubles, the village is said to have been a very busy shipping centre. "Many boats came to load and unload wood, peat, coals, stone, lime and tiles. There used to be seven or eight boatmen living there who did their business with their boats and *pleiten*."[101]

The registers of the Antwerp aldermen contain a considerable number of records concerning boatmen from these villages. Although these references are hardly representative, they do indicate a concentration of boatmen in the places Rumst, Boom and Schelle.[102] The spread of boatmen within the surroundings of Antwerp can also to a certain extent be analysed via the lists of new Antwerp citizens. Such lists are naturally only indirect indicators of the occupational structure of a place since they mention a new citizen's occupation in Antwerp rather than in his place of origin. An example of this is the fact that some of the boatmen originally came from places such as Brecht, Broechem or Kontich, which were not situated along a river. Both the specific requirements inherent to shipping and the strong concentration of boatmen in some places along the Scheldt do however allow the conclusion that most of the new citizens came from a background where shipping was common. The lists of new Antwerp citizens also reflect a concentration of boatmen in Rumst, Boom and Schelle. The number of skippers seems to have been considerably higher in the polder villages north of Antwerp, however. Thirty-five boatmen came from the villages of Stabroek, Berendrecht, Zandvliet, Lillo and Oorderen to become Antwerp citizens between 1534 and 1561, while only 10 came from the above-mentioned villages south of Antwerp.[103]

In addition to the names and residences of boatmen, the registers of the Antwerp aldermen provide some more specific information concerning inland navigation near Antwerp. One of the most frequent reasons for boatmen to appear in front of the Antwerp

98 See Chapter 1.

99 Y. Urbain, "La formation du réseau des voies navigables en Belgique. Développements du système des voies d'eau et politique des transports sous l'Ancien Régime" in *Bulletin de l'iinstitut de recherches économiques et sociales,* 10 (1938-1939), pp. 274–276.

100 On the shippers' guild in Antwerp, see: G. Asaert, *Scheepvaart*, passim.

101 Source: SAA, VG 5, fo. 89. For more on *pleiten*, see below.

102 On the limitations of the registers of alderman, see above.

103 *Antwerpse Poortersboeken, 1533–1608*, Antwerpen, 1977, vols. I-II.

aldermen was for the purchase of a boat. They would declare from whom they bought their boat, the type of the boat, and either the full price paid or the amount still due to the seller. From these declarations, we can deduce the value, and thus the approximate size, of the riverboats. The great majority of the boats were so-called *"pleitschippen"* or *"pleiten"*, a relatively large type of riverboat that was generally used for the transport of wood, salt, peat and other merchandise.[104] The price of these boats was considerable. Around 1560, such a boat was worth up to 50 pounds Flemish *grooten* (75 pounds Brabantine *grooten*), i.e. more than twice the yearly lease of a large farm. The boats bought by rural boatmen were slightly cheaper but still cost between 30 and 40 pounds Flemish *grooten*. To afford such enormous sums, the boatmen had to have a strong financial potential. This practically excluded river shipping as an alternative source of income for impoverished peasants. At most, the latter could only work as helper on a boat or lease the boat of a wealthier colleague.[105] Another interesting fact that can be deduced from the records concerning the purchases of boats is the existence of a number of ship-carpenter workshops in several places along the Scheldt and the Rupel. The major centre of shipbuilding between Antwerp and Mechelen was Rumst, followed by Schelle and Hemiksem. The shipbuilders of these villages regularly constructed boats – not only for local customers, but also for boatmen from Antwerp, Brussels and Lier – as well as ferryboats. The major shipbuilders in Rumst were Gillis Bertels and Cornelis Wouters, and later Adriaan Saerle. Wouters was active between 1520 and 1559. The accounts of the ducal demesne show that Wouters employed two assistants (Appendix 5).[106]

7.5 General Patterns

This overview of different non-agrarian types of labour in the countryside near Antwerp shows that non-agrarian labour had already formed a considerable share of the rural economy of western Brabant since the late Middle Ages. In some places, like Duffel, Rumst or Borgerhout, rural industries achieved considerable dimensions during the sixteenth century. The exploitation and processing of primary materials outside the villages formed a source of income for a large share of the population in places such as Boom and Hemiksem.

The main protagonists in all these sectors were merchants or craftsmen from the higher ranks of village society and, contrary to what is commonly held, only in the second place townsmen.[107] They had both the necessary skills and the financial potential. Most of the non-agrarian activities required considerable investments, which only the richer villagers could pay. Ownership of land or social ties with the local community may have played a role too.[108] Brick makers, wood merchants, and ship carpenters formed a relatively

104 J. Van Beylen, *Schepen van de Nederlanden. Van de late middeleeuwen tot het einde van de 17de eeuw*. Antwerpen, 1970, p. 167.

105 We have no evidence for either of these options for rural boatmen. They were common in the urban context, however. See: F. Prims, "De schippers en hun ambachtskamer in het oude Antwerpen" in *De binnenscheepvaart* vol. I, 1945-1948, pp. 10–13, 10 and F. Corryn, "Het schippersambacht te Gent (1302-1492)" in *Handelingen van de Maatschappij voor Geschiedenis en Oudheidskunde te Gent*, 1 (1944), pp. 165–204, 193.

106 ARA, Rk. 11909, account of Land van Mechelen, Oct. 1556–Sept.1557. "Cornelis Wouters, shipbuilder, with two assistants".

107 Hollestelle, *Steenbakkerij*, p. 126, De Nave, *Antwerpen*, pp. 422–426. Asaert, *Scheepvaart*, p. 331.

108 Good relations with the local community formed an advantage in the negotiations with fellow villagers and helped in

small group whose members often passed their business on to their heirs, so that many of the family enterprises lasted several generations. This may be one of the reasons that townsmen had such difficulty gaining access to these trades.

As far as the employment potential was concerned, woodcutting was the sector with the widest geographical range.[109] There were some woods to be cut throughout the surroundings of Antwerp, although the area near Niel, Schelle and Reet formed a focus, being situated near banks of the Scheldt and therefore having good transport facilities. Woodcutting was moreover well suited for combination with agriculture because it was an activity that took mainly place during the winter and did not require any particular skills or equipment.

The other types of non-agrarian labour mentioned above were heavily clustered in small areas or in some particular villages, where they offered work for a relatively large share of the inhabitants. Brick making played an important role for the villages of Hemiksem, Boom and Hoboken, for example, while weaving was clustered in Duffel and Walem. The percentage of weavers in the population of Duffel during the sixteenth century is unfortunately unknown. We can only make estimates of the social impact of the cloth industry there using the tax roll from 1569/70: About 36% of the villagers had only a house with a garden and were therefore potential full-time weavers. Furthermore, 27% of the peasants had less than 2 *bunders* of land and can therefore be regarded as cottars. For them, weaving may have played an important role in providing additional income besides their farming activity. For those who held larger agrarian holdings, there will have been less of a need for weaving. Even so, some spinning and weaving may also have been done on the larger farms.[110]

If we may believe the village authorities of Boom, most of the population of that village was engaged in brick making and lime-burning around 1570. Sixty workers' families lived in small houses and received assistance from the poor relief during the winter. Including the owners of the brick ovens, whom we can classify as brick makers or brick merchants, they may have made up 60-62% of the households. The description of Boom from 1593 also mentions a number of other non-agrarian sectors. Seven or eight of the inhabitants were boatmen, and there were three brewers, one baker and no less than eighteen tavern keepers. In comparison, there were only three large farms and twelve small cottages (Table 11).

obtaining credit. See: J. Dewald and L. Vardi, "The Peasantries of France, 1400-1789" in T. Scott, ed., *The Peasantries of Europe from the Fourteenth to the Eighteenth Centuries*, London and New York, 1998", p. 33.

109 Sosson, *Travaux publiques*, p. 80.

110 See Chapter 9, Section 4.3. For weaving on larger farms, see: Chapter 8, Section 3.4.

Table 11: Occupational Structure of Boom and Rumst, 1570

Occupation	Boom	%	Rumst	%
Farmers	3	2.8	14–15	4.7–5
Cottars	12	11.4	16–18	5.3–6
Brewers	3	2.8	9–10	3
Tavern keepers	18	17.1	25	8.3
Bakers	1	1	3	1
Boatmen	7–8	6.7–7.6	?	
(SHIPBUILDERS)			(4)	1.3
Grocers			3	1
Millers			1	0.3
Fishermen			Some	
Brick merchants Brick workers	10–15			
Labourers	60	57	Rest	69
Total (est.)	**115–120**	**100**	**ca. 300**	**100**

Source: SAA, VG 5, fos. 84-89.

In Rumst, too, a great proportion of the inhabitants worked in the non-agrarian sector. Farms made up only about 10-11% of the estimated households, while some 70% consisted of workers' houses, 3% of breweries, 8% of taverns and a variety of other craftsmen's houses. In the villages around Antwerp, which grew into real suburbs during the sixteenth century, the commercial and artisanal occupations were even more dominant: There were 10 farmers compared with 160 people holding a variety of non-agrarian occupations.[111] Of all these activities, only very few offered alternatives to agriculture for poor peasants and can therefore be considered as proto-industrial occupations in the most general sense.[112] These occupations were woodcutting, brick making and to some extent weaving. Most of the other crafts required either a high capital input or skills and only a relatively small number of workers. Shipping, brewing and shipbuilding were capital-intensive activities that offered only little employment, for example. The same was the case for bakers, millers, grocers and tavern keepers.

111 See the example of Borgerhout referred to above (Section 2.2.2).

112 That is, providing an additional source of income to the rural population, by profiting from the opportunities of the interregional market. See the introduction to this chapter.

"Proto-industrial" labour in the sense of non-agrarian occupations for cottars was therefore a phenomenon that was limited to a very few villages and very few sectors. It is remarkable that these centres of "proto-industrial" labour were clustered in a small strip along the Scheldt and its tributary, the Rupel. The reason for this clustering was presumably its strategic location along the area's major traffic axis, in combination with local factors such as the availability of clay, wood, and wool, and people. A third factor was the proximity of the large towns of Antwerp, Mechelen and Lier.

The impact that the growth of Antwerp had on these non-agrarian activities was in the first place a strong increase in demand, which made the town an outlet for their production. This demand was the strongest for wood and bricks, especially from the middle of the century on. The increasing trade in bricks and wood formed, in turn, an impulse for the shipping activity to and from Antwerp. In the case of Duffel, the major stimulating factor was not the local demand, but the export facilities at the Antwerp market, which meant that the rural drapers' centre could profit from the increasing international demand for cheap textiles.

Around the middle of the sixteenth century, we notice a tendency whereby townsmen began to exert a direct influence in the rural sector. The most apparent intervention was by Gilbert van Schoonbeke and Jacob van Hencxthoven in the brick-maker's village of Hemiksem. Another example is the involvement of the Antwerp merchant Jan Andries in the exportation of woollens from Duffel in 1568, where local merchants had still handled the sales at the beginning of the century. Finally, there was also the case of someone from Antwerp holding a brewery in Rumst in 1540. These interventions by Antwerp citizens were relatively limited and rather occasional, however. In any case, they did not replace the prevailing structure, which was based on local merchants or entrepreneurs. The local entrepreneurs had close contacts with Antwerp, however, and gradually began to urbanise in turn. To illustrate this process I mentioned some masons and brick merchants who bought real estate in Antwerp and ultimately became Antwerp citizens. Rural wood mongers also became townsmen in that way. One of the leading building entrepreneurs of Antwerp, Jacob van Hencxthoven, had such a background. His father, Willem, was a wood merchant from Duffel who had moved to Antwerp.[113] Most of the village merchants remained where they were, however.

113 The Van Hencxthovens had immigrated to Brabant in the fifteenth century from Germany and lived in Duffel. Jacob's father, Willem, was a wood merchant active in the surroundings of Duffel and Kontich (SAA, SR 131, fo. 135, 3 Oct. 1507); a Van Hencxthoven widow was active in the wood trade in Duffel and Putte in 1542 (ARA, Rk. 11907, Account of Land van Mechelen, Oct. 1541–Sept. 1542). Jacob himself was born in Antwerp but had properties in Duffel (SAA, SR 207, f. 52 v, 19 July 1542). See also: H. Soly, *Urbanisme*, p. 365.

CHAPTER 8

Landlords and Great Landowners in the Fifteenth Century

8.1 Introduction

Having analysed the impact of the growth of the Antwerp market in demographic terms both from the perspective of the rising demand for rural goods and from the point of view of the labour supply – an analysis which might be labelled a commercialisation approach – we will now turn to the question of property relations. This part is dedicated to the second major focus of this book, i.e. the question of the potential of merchant capital to transform rural property structures and hence contribute to the development of agrarian capitalism.

In his influential article from 1976, Robert Brenner identified class structures and property relations as the decisive factors that led to different long-term developments in the transition from a feudal economy to a capitalist economy in different parts of Europe. Class relations, moreover, he sees as being highly resilient in relation to the impact of economic forces; as a rule, they are neither shaped by nor alterable in terms of changes in demographic or commercial trends. In Brenner's view, economic development can only be fully understood as the outcome of the emergence of new class relations that are more favourable to both new and technical organisations of production, technical innovations, and increasing levels of productive investments, while these new class relations were themselves the result of previous, relatively autonomous processes of class conflict.[1] For Brenner, merchant capitalism was therefore incapable of separating the peasantry from their direct access to the land and hence unable to make them dependent on market access, which he considered to be a major precondition for the development of agrarian capitalism. This statement probably holds true for most of Europe.

B. van Bavel also came to the conclusion that commercial factors generally failed to cause major transformations in the distribution of landed property between the fourteenth and sixteenth centuries. He nevertheless found one major exception whereby market factors could lead to important changes in the property relations: highly urbanised areas with a high degree of peasant-owned property. He states that, "if some wealthy townsmen turned to the accumulation of landed property and to a patient assembly of larger holdings, a transformation of the property relations became possible". He was thinking primarily of the west of Holland and, to a lesser extent, late-medieval Flanders. Other examples he mentions are the environs of Paris and parts of Northern Italy.[2]

Although van Bavel does not discuss it, Antwerp forms the ideal test case for this hypothesis. It was probably the place with the highest concentration of merchant capital

1 R. Brenner, "Agrarian Class Structure and Economic Development in Pre-industrial Europe", in *Past & Present*, 70 (1976), p. 30-75, 31, 37.
2 Van Bavel, *Transitie*, p. 645.

in Europe during the sixteenth century, and its immediate hinterland was therefore the area with the highest probability of being impacted by the investments of the Antwerp merchants. In this chapter, we will be discussing both the potential and the limitations of merchant-capitalist developments for bringing about structural change in property relations. The question is therefore, was merchant capitalism capable of influencing property relations in the immediate hinterland of the major commercial centre of the period, and if so, to what extent and by which mechanisms? The failure to observe any fundamental change would confirm Brenner's hypothesis that such a structural break was impossible without what he called class conflict.

A substantial part of our analysis will focus on late medieval, feudal property relations in the Brabantine countryside. Due to the complexity of the problem, we will describe these in two separate chapters. The first deals with the different groups of landlords and their landed property, while the second considers the tenants and their access to land. We then go on to analyse the impact of urban investments on landed property in the countryside during the sixteenth century. The various types and dimensions of investment will be presented here. The changes in rural property relations during the sixteenth century will be the focus of chapter 10.

As was the case in most of the rest of medieval Europe, the prince, the nobility and the Church owned a great deal of the land in the surroundings of Antwerp. In practice, however, they were not the actual holders. Rather, they gave it out in fief or in tenure, receiving a land rent in turn from the tenants. The tenants, on the other hand, had a number of property rights and could essentially dispose of the farms or plots of land they held as they saw fit. They could sell it, leave it to their heirs, mortgage it or lease it out, without interference from the landlord.[3] Landlords and tenants were not strictly defined social groups, but rather relative terms. They coincided in a very general sense with the social categories of nobility, clergy, and rich citizens on the one hand, and peasants on the other hand, but this was not necessarily the case.

The concept of property was not as clearly defined in the late medieval period as it is today. Different persons could have property rights concerning the same goods, in different forms, which makes the situation very complex, if not confusing, at first sight. Furthermore, it is impossible to deal with landed property in the Middle Ages outside the framework of manorial and feudal relations. The seigneurie was "omnipresent"; it formed "the fundamental framework of society" in the late Middle Ages.[4] Landed property was necessarily linked with manorial or feudal factors, which determined the type of property and the status of the owner. The discussion of property relations is therefore split into two parts. In this first part, we will deal with those at the top of the hierarchy of landowners: the sovereign, the nobility and the urban patriciate on the one hand, and the numerous ecclesiastical institutions on the other. These were not only the owners of the largest landed properties, as we will see, but they also formed the group of landlords who received either rent for their tenures or an income from their seigniorial status, either in form of tithes, seigniorial (socage-) rights or fines. The second part will deal with those who actually held the land: the tenants.

3 See also: P. Musgrave, *The Early Modern European Economy*, Basingstoke, London, New York, 1999 (European History in Perspective), p. 41.

4 Cf. G. Bois, *Crise du féodalisme*, Paris, 1981, p. 195.

8.1.1 The Different Types of Landed Property

When dealing with late medieval property relations, we have to take into account that our contemporary legal concepts of property are not applicable. The Middle Ages had a totally different concept of (landed) property. According to L. Génicot, there is nothing more foreign to medieval mentality than the concept of property.[5] According to our modern concept, property is absolute and belongs to no more than one person. Any limitations of this principle are exceptional and in principle temporary. In the Middle Ages, however, different persons or institutions could have rights on one estate.[6] In most of Western Europe, medieval law distinguished between a whole range of different types of property status: free "allodial" property, fief (*leen*), copyhold (*cijns*) and hereditary lease (*erfpacht*). Each of these types implied for the holder a different degree and kind of dependency on the prince, a landlord or owner.[7] According to the status of his property, the holder had to pay succession rights or an annual rent, or simply have any succession or transaction registered. All of them can nevertheless be considered as property in contemporary terms.[8]

Allodial property, fief and tenure were relative terms: they stood in a hierarchical relation with each other. Allodial or free property (*vrij eigen*) was the highest degree of property. It was not subject to any payment or succession rights, nor was any registration with a feudal court necessary. The owner of an "allod" was free and the sovereign owner of his property. (The law of succession formed the only restriction: the owner could not pass on his property to anyone he pleased). The holder of fiefs, on the contrary, was subject to the feudal lord, either the sovereign or any of his vassals. He paid no rent and he could sell or mortgage his property, but he had to register each transaction with the feudal court. Service fiefs were also linked to their feudal lord by means of military service. This service also decreased towards the end of the Middle Ages. The great majority of holdings consisted of tenures based on rent or "*cijns*", a form of holding comparable to the English copyhold.[9] These tenures were subject to yearly payments of a fixed amount of money or payments in kind. Although not absolutely free of manorial dues, these tenures had a quasi-ownership status in the fifteenth century. Already in the sixteenth century, tenants were being referred to as proprietors in official texts.[10] Tenants could pass on their goods to their heirs, sell them or mortgage them. In theory, then, most land belonged to feudal lords, but the real possession belonged to the tenure holders.[11] Especially in towns, the value of the rents paid in money dropped radically as a consequence of devaluation, as we can see in the case of fifteenth-century Brussels.[12] Regardless of its status as property (allodial good, fief, tenure), each property could be

---

5 L. Génicot, *L'économie rurale namuroise au bas Moyen Age (1199-1429)*, vol. I, Leuven-la Neuve, 1943, p. 123.

6 Godding, *Droit privé*, p. 151.

7 P.C.M. Hoppenbrouwers, *Een middeleeuwse samenleving. Het Land van Heusden (ca.1360 - ca. 1515)*, (Historia Agriculturae 25), Groningen, 1992, vol. I, p. 287.

8 See the discussion in Hoppenbrouwers, *Middeleeuwse samenleving*, p. 291f.

9 On copyhold, see: R.W. Hoyle, "Tenure and the Land Market in Early Modern England: or a Late Contribution to the Brenner Debate" in *Economic History Review*, XLIII, pp. 1–20, and Idem, Redefining Copyhold in the Sixteenth Century: The Case of Timber Rights, " in P. Hoppenbrouwers & B. van Bavel, eds., *Landholding and Land Transfer in the North Sea Area (late Middle Ages - 19th Century)*, (CORN-Publication Series, 5), Turnhout, 2004, 250-264.

10 See: Godding, *Droit privé*, pp. 151–153, and Hoppenbrouwers, *Middeleeuwse samenleving*, p. 291.

11 Dewald and Vardi, "Peasantries of France", p. 27.

12 Godding, *Le droit foncier à Bruxelles au moyen age*, Bruxelles, 1960.

subject to charges: a tithe, an annual rent, corvees or charges towards the collective, such as pasture rights, and usage rights.[13]

Although differing from each other in legal terms, each of these forms of holding implied a practical ownership status for the holder, whether he was the owner of an allod, a fief holder or tenure holder. Thus, if we were to consider only the top of the hierarchy of owners of each property as being the "actual owner", we would obtain an unrealistic picture, in which a huge percentage of the land would be in the hands of the duke, the nobility and the clergy. On the other hand, by looking only at the bottom of the pyramid – at the tenants and lease farmers who actually worked the fields – we would get a different picture, but it, too, would be incomplete and false. We will therefore be looking at the different levels of landed property to be able to reconstruct the various interferences and interrelations between them. We will be doing so from the top downwards, rather than from the bottom upwards, in order to cope with the chronological evolution that underlay the divisions and subdivisions of land, as we generally find them at the middle of the fifteenth century.

8.1.2 Seigniorial Rights

The manorial dependencies and the rights of their owners were closely related to the different types of property. We will not be going into the principles and origins of the manorial system of Western Europe here, as these have already been widely studied and dealt with in historical literature.[14] What we are interested in within this chapter is the distribution of different forms of seigniorial rights among the different groups of landlords. In particular, we will be focusing on the economic aspect of the seigniorial relations: the income connected with different rights as well as the burden that seigniorial rights form for the tenants.

Our sources confront us with different forms of lordship. The term "lordship" (Du.: *heerlijkheid*, Fr.: *seigneurie banale*) was used for the juridical domination of the inhabitants of a particular village, part of one village, or even a group of several villages, which was not immediately linked to their tenure.[15] Customary law distinguished between high jurisdiction – which in most of the Brabantine villages was in the hands of the duke – medium jurisdiction and low (i.e. civil) jurisdiction, with the latter two being in the hands of the local lord. The seigneurie was generally administered by a mayor (*meier*) and seven aldermen (*schepenen*). Normally, the juridical lordship in a village went hand in hand with various socage rights (*banrechten*). These could include the monopoly on milling, fishing and hunting, as well as the use of forests and woods, further tolls and passage rights. Other lordly dues were

---

13 Godding, Droit privé, p. 151.

14 See for example: R. Boutruche, *Seigneurie et féodalité, vol. II, l'apogée (Xie - XIIIe siècles)* Paris, 1970; L. Génicot, *Economie*, vol. I; M.L. Bush, Tenant Right and the Peasantries of Europe under the Old Regime" in Idem, ed, *Social Orders and Social Classes in Europe since 1500: Studies in Social Stratification*, London, 1992, pp. 136–157. For a general discussion of feudal and seigniorial relations in Brabant: E. Van Ermen, *Feodaal-heerlijke verhoudingen en territoriale patronen in het middeleeuwse hertogdom Brabant (12de - 14de eeuw) met bijzondere aandacht voor de regio Leuven*, 6 vols., (PhD dissertation, KUL) Leuven, 1989; F. Daelemans and F.G. Scheelings, "De economisch impact van de heerlijkheid op het platteland" in *Les structures du pouvoir dans les communautés rurales en Belgique et dans les Pays limitrophes (XIIe - XIXe siècle)* (13e colloque international, Actes. Spa, 3 -5 Sept. 1986 (Bruxelles 1986), pp. 451–468.

15 Boutruche, *Seigneurie*, p. 125.

the conveyance fees (*pontgeld*, *pontpenning* or *coopgeld*), generally amounting to 5%, that were levied on purchases of immovable property. Corvees existed in several cases, but were eventually reduced to single days of transport, haying or mowing.

Besides juridical lordship, which was linked with the territory of a seigneurie, the most frequent form of lordship was manorial lordship (*grondheerlijkheid*) over particular plots of land that were held in tenure and for which the lord received rent, payable either in money or in kind. A different sort of seigniorial right, this time of ecclesiastical origin, was the tithe. Although tithes were in principle a prerogative of the parochial clergy, some were usurped by the duke or some other nobleman. In the fifteenth century, many tithes were held by abbeys. Besides the ancient or great tithe, which was levied on bread grains like rye and wheat, other tithes were introduced on different or new crops. These new tithes can therefore serve as indicators for changes in agriculture.

8.1.3 The Sources

The distinct forms of property titles and manorial rights compel us to use different kinds of sources for our analysis, as there are no general overviews of the landed property in Brabant, or for that matter on a more local level, for the fifteenth century. Such an overview is only possible for the second half of the sixteenth century, thanks to some tax registers that have survived. This lack of a homogenous body of sources makes our analysis very much like piecing together a jigsaw puzzle consisting of very different types of documents.

In terms of the sovereign's properties, a very useful body of sources is available. First, the accounts of the ducal demesne provide very detailed information on the different property titles held by the duke. Second, as far as feudal property is concerned, we can get an impression of the size and composition of the fiefs that came under the direct authority of the duke, by means of the so-called *dénombrements* of fiefs of the feudal court. Although a very rich source covering many hundreds of fiefs within the duchy, these are not complete, as we will discuss later in this chapter. The third kind of source we have at our disposal are feudal rent registers, which are of help in analysing the lowest category of property rights: the tenures. These are especially difficult sources to work with, due to the limited information they contain in many cases. Very often the registers contain no more than a list of names with the indication of the amount of money that was due to the landlord. Furthermore, the number of tenants subject to a particular landlord varied strongly from case to case.

By restricting ourselves to these sources, however, a whole category of property escapes our attention, namely the free allodial property. While allodial property is mentioned in individual charters or deeds in the aldermen's registry, hardly any source gives a broad overview of the allodial property per village, seigneurie or any similar such unit. On the other hand, for an understanding of the landed property of individuals, the allods can be disregarded, since allodial property held by individuals lost much of its former importance during the fifteenth century. In comparison with feudal tenure and copyhold, freehold seems to have been quantitatively less significant. Allodial property held by ecclesiastical institutions such as monasteries, church chapters or parish churches nevertheless remained important. To cover this major segment among the Brabantine landowners, we took recourse to a number of specific sources dealing with the property of ecclesiastical institutions: there are countless accounts, statements of property and other documents in the archives of monasteries, cathedrals and other institutions. A large share of the information nevertheless stems from the rich literature about the individual institutions.[16]

8.2 The Different Groups of Landlords and Great Landowners

8.2.1 The Duke of Brabant

At the top of the political and social hierarchy of Brabant stood the sovereign, the duke of Brabant. The house of Burgundy had held the title of duke of Brabant since 1405, after having become counts of Flanders in 1384. Philip the Good, who reigned after 1430, was therefore one of the most powerful and richest princes in Western Europe. In the duchy of Brabant, he could base himself on the heritage of the Brabant dukes from the house of Leuven, who had acquired dominion over almost the entire Brabant territory by the fourteenth century. The rule of Philip the Good brought about an integration of the different territories, but also a tendency towards homogenisation within Brabant.[17]

As territorial prince, Philip the Good had a number of sovereign rights, such as the contributions (*beden*) of the territorial estates. Moreover, the duke held the highest jurisdiction in a large share of the duchy.[18] In the districts of Brussels and Antwerp, there were only 14 villages where the high jurisdiction belonged to another lord than the duke. For the medium jurisdiction, this was the case for another 32 villages.[19] Aside from his princely and juridical power, the duke also had a large demesne of his own, and he was the feudal overlord of much of the Brabantine territory. In practice, however, his direct property rights were limited to the so-called ducal demesne. The possessions to which the duke had direct property rights – and which made up an important share of the princely income in the late Middle Ages – were administered separately from the fiefs in the ducal demesne.[20] This demesne was a collection of very different property titles belonging to the duke and consisted of tenures, land, farms, tolls, income from fishing and hunting rights, income from juridical and administrative rights, tithes and many other types of ducal rights. It was divided in local units so called "receipts" – also called demesnes – which incorporated almost every village of the duchy. Two out of these fourteen domanial units of Brabant[21] were situated in the Antwerp area: the demesne of Antwerp and the demesne of Lier and Herentals, east of Antwerp.

16 See especially the volumes on Brabant and Antwerp in *Monasticon Belge*, published in 1964-1971 and 1992-1993, respectively, which deals with each abbey in a very detailed way.

17 Van Uytven, "Centrale plaatsen", p. 37.

18 According to Van Ermen, *Feodaal-heerlijke verhoudingen*, vol. II, pp. 342–388, this was the case for 84% of the villages within the duchy; in the Flemish-speaking part, the percentage was even higher: 91.4%.

19 *Ibidem*, pp. 349–358 and 376-381.

20 The organisation of the ducal demesne has been analysed for the late medieval period in a very detailed study by M. Martens, *L'administration du domaine ducal en Brabant au moyen âge, 1250-1406*, (*Mémories: collection in-8°*, 2e série), Brussels, 1954. For the sixteenth century, E. Van Cauwenberghe, *Het vorstelijk domein en de overheidsfinanciën in de Nederlanden (15de en 16de eeuw). Een quantitative analyse van Vlaamse en Brabantse domeinrekeningen* (Gemeentekrediet van België, Historische Uitgaven Pro Civitate r. 8°, 61) Brussels, 1982, gives a quantitative analysis of the financial aspects of the domanial administration.

21 Jodoigne, Tienen, Nivelles, Brussels, Tervuren-Vilvoorde, Leuven, Antwerp, Lier-Herentals, 's Hertogenbosch, Yssche, Asse, Hoeilaart, Turnhout; Martens, *Administration*, p. 267.

The demesne of the duke was more important in the south of Brabant than in the northern districts. While he had tenures in nearly all villages in the areas of Brussels and Leuven, the number of ducal villages was relatively limited north of the rivers Rupel and Dijle. In 1470, the large seigneurie known as the Land van Mechelen, covering part of the fertile area south of Antwerp, became part of the ducal demesne.[22] Until then, this demesne had belonged to the powerful lords of Wezemaal, who had to sell it to Charles of Charolais (i.e. Charles the Bold) shortly before 1465.[23]

The composition of the sources of income differed considerably among the various demesnes of the duke. In the demesne of Antwerp, they were more urban in character. In addition to land rents and the sales of agrarian products, there was a large variety of tolls and taxes. Indeed, the greatest source of income was the great Brabantine water toll, which yielded ca. 50,000 pounds Brabantine *grooten* or 80% of the total income.[24] Land rents made up only 3% of the classical domanial income, while land leases were only good for 1.7%. Other major sources of income were the taxes on grain consumption (*lepelgeld*), the urban excises, the fish market, the fees new citizens had to pay, etc.[25] In the demesne of Lier, land rents made up 56% of the income. Tolls, including the Lier cattle toll, made up another 42%, while income from leasing out offices made up the rest.[26]

A more detailed look at the composition of the sources of income mentioned in the annual accounts of the demesne the Land van Mechelen[27] shows that the largest share of the income came from the sales of wood from the domanial forests situated in Duffel and Waver (44%). The income from land rents paid in money in 1475 totalled 316 pounds Brabantine *grooten* or 41% of the total income.[28] These land rents, in the form of feudal rents and hereditary leases, came from 16 villages situated between Antwerp, Mechelen and Lier, where ca. 750 tenants paid their rent directly to the duke.[29] The second category of sources of income came from seigniorial rights such as tolls and passage rights, mills, and the leases of offices. In the Land van Mechelen, these made up only 7.7% of the total income. This low percentage can be explained by the fact that the demesne was originally a seigneurie and had only just become part of the ducal demesne. Also, the leases of landed property belonging directly to the duke formed only a relatively small share of the domanial income. Farms, land and pasture, breweries, ponds and mills were generally leased or rented out from the second half of the fourteenth century on.[30] Within the demesne of the Land van Mechelen, these were limited to one manor farm, called the Anderstad farm, some meadows

22 See further, Section 2.2.2.

23 E. Van Ermen, *De landelijke bezittingen van de heren van Wezemaal in de middeleeuwen,* 2 vols, Leuven, 1982 (Belgisch Centrum voor landelijke Geschiedenis, 68).

24 33,300 pounds Flemish *grooten*, see: M. Baelde, *De domeingoederen van de vorst in de Nederlanden omstreeks het midden van de zestiende eeuw* (1551-1559) Brussel 1971 (Verzameling van onuitgegeven Belgische kronieken en van onuitgegeven documenten betreffende de geschiedenis van België: reeks in-8°, 85), p. 84.

25 *Ibidem*, pp. 83–85.

26 *Ibidem*, pp. 87–88.

27 Brussels ARA, RK, reg. 11895-11916 (1434/35; 1464/65-1595/6).

28 These could either be feudal rents (*cijns*) in the proper sense of speaking, but also hereditary rents (*erfelijke renten*). Although there were differences in origin, the accounts do not distinguish between the different types of rents. Each particular entry of feudal and hereditary rents was listed separately, but they were all summed up in one category.

29 Aartselaar, Duffel, Waarloos, Kontich, Niel, Schelle, Rumst, Reet, Zellaar, Putte, Rijmenam, Sint-Katelijne Waver, Beersel, Bonheiden, Schriek, Grootlo. For the number of tenants, see the rent registers of the demesne from 1516-1519 ARAB, RK, nos. 45597, 45599, 45601.

30 Martens, *Administration*, p. 299.

along the river Nete and a windmill situated in the village of Kontich. Together, the leases from these holdings made up 52 pounds Brabantine *grooten* or 6.8% of the domanial income.

A considerable share of the duke's holdings was not part of the demesne, however. These were fiefs that he received, together with his ducal authority, from the emperor and which he in turn passed on to his vassals, originally in exchange for military service. These fiefs, which constituted a significant share of the Brabantine territory, contained the most diversified goods: "land and villages, castles and manors, farms and little farmsteads, mills, breweries, forests, meadows, vineyards, ponds, rivers, tithes, land-rents, hereditary rents, tolls, fishing and pasture rights, and the rights on the wind (for milling), but also on grain, poultry, bread, eggs and wax."[31] The duke's proprietary rights on these goods were mainly juridical and in practice rather limited.[32] As the feudal lord, he of course received any transfer rights, but the major benefit he had from the fiefs were the service and the loyalty of his vassals, who were bound to the prince mainly by means of these feudal links. From an economic point of view, we consider the owners of these feudal goods to have been not the prince, but rather his vassals, the noblemen and their sub-vassals, who actually worked on them. We will therefore treat with this heterogeneous group, which includes nobles, urban patricians and others, in more detail in the following paragraphs.

8.2.2 The Fief-Holders of the Feudal Court of Brabant

For the analysis of the landed property that was in the hands of individuals during the Middle Ages, we have very few sources at our disposal. Although charters or declarations concerning individual holdings may in some cases help us to reconstruct the property of individual noblemen or members of the urban patriciate,[33] there are no sources that offer an overview of the distribution of landed property among the different social groups. As a consequence of the segmentation of landed property into allodial property, fiefs and tenures, we have no sources that deal with all three of these kinds of property together.

There is nevertheless one source that does cover a wide range of properties of different size and composition: the ducal fief registers. While these registers cover only part of the total landed property, namely the ducal fiefs, they do contain indirect information on the number of tenures, as well as on the sub-vassals of the vassals who were dependent on them. Only one type of property is not even indirectly included: allodial property. Even so, we believe the fief registers contain enough information to enable us to reconstruct the distribution of land and manorial rights among the population. With information on almost all categories of landed property (seigneuries, manorial rights, large and mid-sized farms, as well as small plots of land), they form a good sampling of landed property held by individuals, whether noblemen, urban citizens or peasants. This being only a sample and not a complete overview of the total situation in terms of landed property, however, we will not attempt to quantify our results. Rather, we will try to discern the different types of property compositions that were typical for a particular social group.

31 L. Galesloot, *Inventaire des archives de la Cour Feodale de Brabant,* 2 vols., Brussel, 1870-1884, p. XXXV f.

32 L. Voet, "De Vorsten: de middeleeuwse vorst" in De Clercq C., e.a., eds., *Flandria Nostra: ons land en ons volk, zijn standen en beroepen door de tijden heen*, vol. V, *Flandria Nostra,* Antwerp, 1960, p. 70.

33 See for example: Van Ermen, *Landelijke bezittingen*, passim.

For the administration of the direct fiefs (i.e. the lands that were not given out as sub-fiefs by their holders), the duke had a powerful institution at his disposal: the feudal court (*leenhof*).[34] A survey of the ducal fiefs can be made by analysing the *dénombrements* of fiefs that were established by the feudal court in order to gain an overview of the military dues to be paid by the duke's vassals.[35] The first detailed *dénombrement*, based on the declarations of each of the vassals, concerns the year 1440.

Register no. 8 of the archives of the feudal court of Brabant contains the descriptions for the district of Antwerp.[36] The declarations in this *dénombrement* were made up by each vassal and consisted of a description of the fief, including its type and size, the accompanying seigniorial rights, as well as the number of sub-fiefs and tenants. For example, Aart van Immerseel, lord of Wommelgem, near Antwerp, declared that his fief consisted of the jurisdiction of the village, two farms of 59 *bunders* and 24 *bunders*, respectively, the great tithe of the village and 81 tenants. Among his seven sub-fiefs was a tithe in nearby Schoten, held by the abbey of St. Bernard, and a farm of 26 *bunders* held by Peter Pot, the renowned Antwerp merchant.[37]

The accuracy of these declarations was checked by the ducal officers by means of a comparison with the official feudal records (*leenboeken*), and in case of deviation, any missing items were added.[38] Although highly accurate, the source has its imperfections. Several owners, especially noblemen, did not mention the size, but only the number and kind of their fiefs. This is especially the case for a few illustrious noblemen such as Jan van Luxemburg, seigneur of Rumst, or Jan van Wezemaal, seigneur of the Land van Mechelen and owner of fiefs in Lier, Kessel, Itegem, Emblem, Bevel, and Berlaar. In such cases, we can determine the category of the fiefs by means of qualitative data, but we cannot include them in a quantitative analysis. As a result, the nobility is underrepresented in the quantitative figures of our analysis. The great landlords only figure with part of their possessions, whereas the information pertaining to the more modest holdings was precisely checked by the ducal administration. The smaller holdings therefore tend to figure in their entirety.

Another disadvantage of the *dénombrement* of fiefs is its incompleteness. The owners of fiefs were obliged to declare their holdings. But did they actually do so? Or are the registers complete in terms of the copies of the declarations they contain? These questions can only be answered by checking the *dénombrement* of fiefs against the registers of the feudal court (*leenboeken*).[39] Some holdings indeed seem to have escaped registration, but this lack of completeness is compensated largely by the systematic compilation of the *dénombrements* and the detailed types of information they contain.

---

34 M. MARTENS, *Administration*, p. 23.

35 This source has been used by H.G. KOENIGSBERGER, "Property and the price revolution (Hainault, 1474 - 1573)" in *The Economic History Review*, Second Series, vol. IX, no. 1 (1956), pp. 1–15. Many local historians also use the detailed descriptions for their studies.

36 ARA, LB no. 8. For the compilation of our data we made a selection on a geographical basis. Fiefs situated outside our research area were neglected. Hence, only fiefs situated within ca. 20 km of the town were selected. For a list of the declarations see Appendix 6.

37 ARA, LB no. 8, fos. 159-160.

38 So, for example, the declaration of Jan van Hoenderbeke from Steenhuffel, near Brussels; was corrected from 1.75 *bunders* into 2 *bunders* and one sub-fief, according to the information of the official records, ARA LB no. 7, fo. 31r.

39 GALESLOOT, *Inventaire*, vol. I, p. L, mentions that, according to his own investigations, about a third of the declarations are missing.

In any case, we have to be aware not only that the *dénombrement* does not include all fiefs, but also that the information concerning the size of the fief is not always very precise, especially in case of the nobility, who the administration seem to have trusted more than they did the average fief holder. We can therefore only partly quantify our analysis of the *dénombrements*. We will have to complete the results with qualitative information and, in some cases, with material from alternative sources.

8.2.2.1 The General Distribution of Landed Property

Our sample of fiefs contains a total of 62 persons from different social categories. For 32 of these fiefs, the size is given. This ranges from less than 1 hectare to over 100 hectares. Only four of the holdings were larger than 100 hectares, while all the rest were under 40 hectares, and 19 were even less than 20 hectares (Graph 5). Aside from the size of the landed property, however, there were other attributes that were at least as important. For instance, 12 of the fiefs, among which almost all the very big holdings with more than about 60 hectares, included both the low and medium jurisdictions of a village, along with other seigniorial rights.[40] Almost all seigneuries, but also other fiefs (in total 18), contained tenures with between five and 83 tenants. Four fiefs had secondary fiefs, which in turn could vary enormously in size and importance. For instance, Jan Van Ranst, a nobleman who had fiefs in Mortsel, Wijnegem, Wommelgem, had 22 sub-fiefs. Jan van Wezemaal, lord of the Land van Mechelen, even had 116.

Graph 5: Size of Fiefs in the Surroundings of Antwerp, 1440

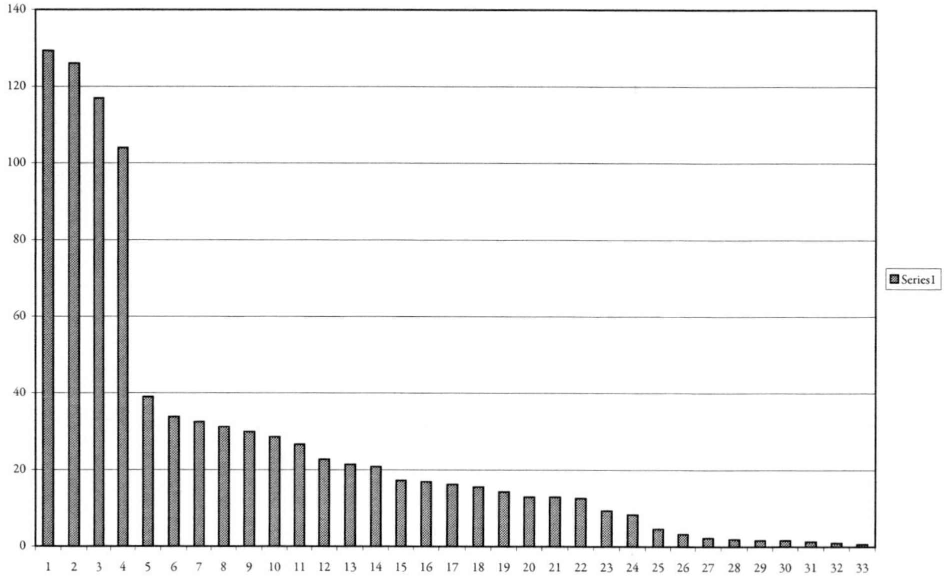

Source: Brussels, ARA, LB no. 8.

40 These could be rights with respect to milling, fishing, tolls and passage (*weggeld*), passage rights for tenures and, in some cases, corvees.

The *dénombrement* of fiefs for 1440 contains members of the high nobility as well as unknown owners of little plots of land. Koenigsberger speaks of feudal property, as reflected in the *dénombrements*, as being a socially widespread form of property.[41] In the case of the Brabant *dénombrement* of 1440, the higher social ranks, including nobles, local landlords and urban upper class, are very strongly represented. They comprised nearly half of fief holders and held approximately 63% of the land.[42] It is about these higher ranks of society that the *dénombrement* offers the most detailed information.

8.2.2.2 The Nobility

The Brabantine nobility hardly formed a cohesive group, and not only in terms of property. The term "noble" could be used to refer to a variety of people, ranging from a small number of prestigious families within the Burgundian court nobility, via a group of secondary importance, down to what we might call the lower knighthood or local gentry. The latter were low noblemen, who often had just one fief: manorial rights in a village, with some tenants, and a house or castle. In our analysis, we are restricting our use of the term "noble" to the highest ranks of the Brabantine nobility and members of the Burgundian court, in other words: persons who could be clearly identified by means of secondary literature.[43]

The largest fiefs of the area were in the hands of the nobility. Together, 28 noblemen possessed 37% of the land declared in the *dénombrement*, 58% of the seigneuries and 60% of the tenures. The typical fief of a nobleman consisted of the seigniorial rights in a village or part of it; a large farm with a considerable amount of arable land, meadows and forests, which was in most cases leased out; the land rents from a number of tenants; some sub-fiefs; and in some cases a tithe, a mill or a toll. The greatest vassal in the area under consideration was Aart van Immerseel, lord of Wommelgem, whose fief of Wommelgem included two farms of 59 *bunders* and 24 *bunders*, respectively, 81 tenants, some great sub-fiefs, the great tithe of the village, and another fief, in nearby Deurne, containing 16.5 *bunders* of land and 12 tenants. But not all noblemen could claim such large holdings: Whereas only two nobles had fiefs larger than 50 *bunders*, there were ten who had smaller holdings or who did not declare any landed property but merely a seigneurie or a fief, without any further specifications. Some of them, however, can certainly be accused of understating their property, as for example Jean de Luxembourg, lord of Rumst (Appendix 6).

Within the first group, the higher nobility, we find a number of old Brabantine houses that had dominated the duchy throughout several centuries. Some members of these old noble families are cited as members of the ducal council in the late fourteenth and early fifteenth centuries. Over the course of the fifteenth century, this group began losing ground to the new group of nobles, at least as far as important political positions were

41 H.G. Koenigsberger, "Property", passim.

42 The calculations were only made for the fiefs whose size is indicated in the source.

43 J. Bartier, "De Bourgondische adel" in Broeckx J.L., e.a., eds., *Flandria Nostra: ons land en ons volk, zijn standen en beroepen door de tijden heen*, vol. IV (1959), pp. 319–344; P. de Win, "De lagere adel in de Bourgondische Nederlanden" in *Bijdragen tot de Geschiedenis*, 69 (1986), pp. 171–207. R. Van Uytven, "De Brabantse adel als politieke en sociale groep tijdens de late middeleeuwen" in *De adel van het hertogdom Brabant*, Brussel, 1985, pp. 75–88. Van Ermen, *Feodaal-heerlijke verhoudingen,*, passim. Other sources that proved to be very useful for the identification of all kinds of individuals is A. Wauters, *Histoire des environs de Bruxelles ou description historique des localités qui formaient autrefois l'ammanie de cette ville*, 10 vols, Bruxelles, 1855 (reprint, Brussels, 1975) and Galesloot, *Inventaire*, passim.

concerned. Even so, we still find this group of old Brabantine nobility as wealthy seigneurs with numerous fiefs and seigneuries. A good example of someone from this group is Jan van Wezemaal, lord of Wezemaal, Faleis and the Land van Mechelen, one of the most ambitious and powerful noblemen of Brabant during his period.[44] In the *dénombrement*, he figures as the owner of several fiefs in the surroundings of Lier, with 116 "*mannen*" (feudal tenants). The seigneurie the Land van Mechelen, north of Mechelen, was among the largest of the seigneuries in our research area. Its revenue in 1464/65, when it was sold to Charles of Charolais, the later Charles the Bold, was ca. 700 pounds Brabantine *grooten*.[45]

The new "Burgundian" nobility is a new group of noblemen who set foot in Brabant with the arrival of the house of Burgundy. Already in the first decades of the fifteenth century, we find the seigneurs of Glymes and Nassau in the ranks of the high Brabantine nobility.[46] In 1440, the presence of this group was already considerable in the area of Brussels and Antwerp: Jan van Wittham, related to the powerful seigneurs of Beersel, held the seigneurie of Boutersem near Leuven and ten fiefs in the surroundings of Antwerp and Lier.[47] Jean of Luxemburg was lord of Rumst and the surroundings, an area that was economically interesting because of its toll on the river Rupel and its brick-ovens.[48] Rickald van Merode, seigneur of the "*voogdij*" of Duffel, also had other seigneuries outside of Brabant.[49] On the other hand, some seigneuries seem not to include any landed property. This can be explained in part by the incompleteness of the description, but not entirely. The analysis of the accounts of different lay demesnes shows that the landed property of lay Brabant landlords was rather modest. Even some of the greatest seigneuries, such as the Land van Mechelen, included a relatively small reserve, which was land immediately in the hands of the duke or lay landlord for personal use.[50]

8.2.2.3 The Lower Nobility: Knights and Local Seigneurs

Hardly distinguishable from the high nobility in late medieval Brabant, the lower nobility or gentry consisted of a group of seigneurs who were simply referred to as lord (*heer*) or knight (*ridder*). A distinction between these two groups can be made on the basis of an individual's (or his ancestors') political functions or position at the ducal court. Another point of distinction is certainly the size of a nobleman's demesne or wealth. Using these two criteria, the lower nobility was a bit more numerous among the vassals of the duke than the high nobility (36 compared to just 28 high nobles). Inequality and social mobility

44 Van Ermen, *De landelijke bezittingen*, vol. II,

45 ARA, Rk. Reg. 11897 Account Land van Mechelen, 1-10-1464–30-9-1465, and Rk. 45597, 45599, 45601. Rent registers, 1516-1519.

46 E. van Ermen, "Een Brabantse adellijke familie in de Middeleeuwen. De heren van Wezemaal en hun verhouding tot de vorst, de geestelijkheid, de steden en andere adellijke families" in *Lopend rechtshistorisch onderzoek*, handelingen van het achtste Belgisch-Nederlands rechtshistorisch colloquium; (1984), pp. 119–142 (reprint " in *Historica Lovaniensia* 169, Leuven, 1984), p. 126.

47 ARA, LHB no. 8, fo. 19-328.

48 ARA, LHB no. 8, fo.?.

49 H.J. Domsta, *Geschichte der Fürsten von Merode im Mittelalter*, Düren, 1981, (Beiträge zur Geschichte des Dürener Landes, 15-16).

50 See for example the accounts of the manor of Grimbergen (de Glymes), barony Grimbergen (Nassau), Duffel-Walem (de Merode), [Brussels, ARA, *Merode-Westerloo Family Archives*]; Land van Mechelen (until 1464: van Wesemaal, after 1464: dukes of Brabant), Tervuren-Vilvoorde (dukes of Brabant); [ARA, *Rekenkamer*, registers No. 4751-4793 and 11895-11916].

among nobles was great in the fifteenth century. The leading families were easily replaced by members of the lower nobility or the urban bourgeoisie,[51] and renowned families could lose status after several generations. As a result, there are several vassals mentioned in the *dénombrement* who can be counted either among the high nobility or among the gentry.

The fiefs of the lower nobility did not differ very much from the holdings of the high nobility. They could include the seigniorial rights of a village or part of it, a residence, and a farm with its land. The individual holdings were usually smaller than those of the high nobility, however. In fact, none of the fiefs of the lower nobility was larger than 50 hectares. Nevertheless, the major difference, was not the size of the fiefs, but the number. The lower nobles generally held only one or two fiefs, whereas the great seigneurs such as Jan Van Wesemaal, Frank Van Borssele or Jan Wittham had fiefs spread throughout the duchy and sometimes even beyond it. In contrast, the local seigneurs never left their place of origin. Their property was relatively limited in geographical terms. In some cases, the local origins of these families are revealed in their names: Margerite van Lille was the seigneur of a village of the same name in the Antwerp Kempen, and Liesbeth van Wezele held the seigneurie of 's Gravenwezel, also east of Antwerp.

8.2.2.4 Urban Patricians

The next group of fief owners was the urban patriciate of Antwerp, Brussels or Mechelen.[52] Among our sample of vassals of the duke of Brabant in 1440, we identified eight members of the Antwerp patriciate, which amounts to 13% of the total. While the difference between the urban elite and the (predominantly rural) nobility is very clear in theory, it is still hard to make a clear distinction in some cases. As observed in other areas, such as Flanders, the lifestyle of urban patriciate of the late Middle Ages hardly differed from that of the nobility.[53] In fact, many leading figures of the Brussels or Leuven patriciate were ennobled for their services, and both groups intermarried. Some noble families, for example the Van Lieres and Van de Werves, who held the seigniorial rights on the villages surrounding the town, as well as landed property, played an important part in the political life of the town. Different members of the Van Ranst, Van Liere and Van de Werve families served as aldermen or even mayor of Antwerp. Despite their being nobles, we can count them therefore among the Antwerp patriciate.

Other important families who frequently held functions in the city magistrate were the Van Sompekes, the Pots and the Van Mechelens. Their properties were situated within some kilometres of Antwerp and were only slightly smaller than those of the high nobility. For example, the fief of Gillis Sanders, who was lord of Vaelaereik in Aartselaar near Antwerp and from an Antwerp family, still contained 97 *bunders*. Jan van Mechelen, an Antwerp alderman from 1447-1449, owned 90 *bunders* in Kontich, and Peter Pot, a well-known

51 J. Dewald, *The European Nobility 1400-1800,* Cambridge, 1996, p. 19.

52 Although the appropriateness of the term "patriciate" is a subject of debate, it is generally used in the Flemish and Brabantine contexts. For Flanders see: F. Blockmans, *Het Gentsche stadspatriciaat tot omstreeks 1302*, Bruges, 1938, cited in M. Boone, "Terre", p. 159; P. De Win, Adel en Stadspatriciaat in het Hertogdom Brabant in de 15de eeuw" in Spiegel Historiael 16 (1981), pp. 407–411; J. Bartier, "Un document sur les prévarications et les rivalités du patriciat bruxellois au Xve siècle" in *Bulletin de la Commission Royale d'histoire CVII* (1942), pp. 337–365.

53 Blockmans, *Gentse stadpatriciaat*, cited in Boone, "Terre", p. 159.

Antwerp merchant, owned 26 *bunders* in Wommelgem. The fiefs of the urban patriciate, just like those of the nobility, could be of considerable size, consisting of a farm with up to 90 *bunders* of land, tenures and sub-fiefs. Nevertheless, their holdings normally did not include seigniorial rights. Besides the owners of large fiefs, the majority of whom were members of the social elite, we find many more Antwerp citizens among the owners of tenures.[54]

One group that was practically absent among the ducal vassals in the surroundings of Antwerp were the high officers of the ducal administration or holders of court functions who were so prominent in the Brussels area.[55]

8.2.2.5 Small-Scale Local Landlords

Nobility, urban patricians and ducal officers formed the top of the social hierarchy of feudal Brabant. Together, they held over half the ducal fiefs, including a great share of the larger ones. Beneath this top was a middle-class or lower upper class of medium landowners whose fiefs could reach considerable proportions and included tenures or sub-fiefs. That is why we can still count these medium landowners among the group of landlords. While they did not hold the jurisdiction of a village, they did have a number of tenants who owed them rent. In others cases, they had some feudal tenants (*leenmannen*).

In some cases, the holdings of these local landlords could be quite substantial, including a large farm of 10 to 25 *bunders*. The number of tenants these local landlords had is unknown in many cases. The register only mentions that the fief included tenures.[56] Nonetheless, from the examples for which we do know the number, we can deduce that it generally was less than those of the nobility.[57] On this secondary level, too, sub-infeudation took place. Many of the holders of larger fiefs, in turn, had feudal tenants. This phenomenon, which we already noticed among the noble vassals of the duke, also existed within the lower ranks of the feudal hierarchy. There was less of a tendency towards sub-infeudation in the Antwerp area than near Brussels, probably as a consequence of the older tradition of ducal fiefs in the latter area.

These medium landowners are more difficult to identify than the social top. Aside from the description of their property, we hardly have any information about these people. Even so, we can distinguish between two types. On the one hand, there were the townsmen, less renowned than the Pots or Van Sompekes, but still of a respectable fortune. On the other hand, there were those of local origin. Among Antwerp citizens, the possession of fiefs in the countryside was generally limited to the small elite of patricians, however. Townsmen held tenures more frequently than fiefs.[58]

---

54 See Chapter 6.

55 In the *dénombrement* of the vassals of the Brussels area, we find numerous such officers, such as Hendrik Magnus, a member of the Council of Brabant and lieutenant of the feudal court, or Jan Hinckaert, viscount of the ducal castle of Tervuren. In exchange for their services, the dukes gave them fiefs or special privileges such as regular gifts or pasture rights. ARA, LB no. 29, fo. 325 and LB no. 7; L. Galesloot, *Inventaire*, passim and J. Bartier, Un document sur les prévarications et les rivalités du patriciat bruxellois au XV e siècle" in *Bulletin de la commission royale d' histoire/Handelingen van de koninklijke commissie voor Geschiedenis*, CVII (1942), p. 339, fn. 3.

56 In most cases, the register mentions "*den cijns*", without stating the precise number of tenants.

57 The mean number of tenants per manor was 23.3, with values ranging between 5 and 62.

58 De Nave, *Antwerpen, stad en land*, p. 442.

The owners of these medium-sized fiefs were more typically members of a group that can be defined as a local elite: the owners of large farms, who often figured as local officers and aldermen. It seems that some of these local elites, together with their kinsmen, quite dominated the landed property of their village, as some examples from the Land van Mechelen show. In the register of fiefs, drawn up in 1473, several such dominant families appear among the vassals. In the village of Reet, for example, three families seemed to have occupied a predominant position among the local fief holders. Claus Wielanckx held the farm Hof van Hijselaar with 31 *bunders* of land, tenures and 17 sub-fiefs. Five of these sub-fiefs were held by Katelijne and Peter Wielanckx – most probably a relative of Claus Wielanckx, as their common name suggests. Members of two other families, the Bals and the Van Loockes, each had four holdings in fief from Claus Wielanckx. One of them, Arnout van Loocke, had a farm with the respectable size of 11 *bunders.*[59]

8.2.3 Ecclesiastical Institutions

Although they were not among the major vassals mentioned in the feudal registers, the truly great landowners of late medieval Brabant were the numerous abbeys, collegiate churches and other ecclesiastical institutions.[60] The great abbeys' role of importance was typical for the whole of the southern Low Countries, if not most of Western Europe. In Brabant, however, their predominance seems to have been especially great. The fact that there were seven Premonstratensian abbots among the twelve representatives of the clergy in the estates of Brabant is a good indicator for this predominance. In 1477, the estates themselves acknowledged that the abbots of the great Brabantine abbeys formed the backbone of the council.[61] While there are no precise figures concerning their share in the landed property for the late Middle Ages, by the end of the ancien regime, their share of the total landed property was 30 to 50% in some parts of Brabant, a higher percentage than in the neighbouring provinces of Flanders and Hainaut.[62] Considering the fact that the patrimonies of many abbeys were formed in large part during the medieval period, these numbers also have an indicative value for the situation in the fifteenth century.

Beginning with a relatively modest demesne donated by the duke or local seigneur during the eleventh and twelfth centuries, the Brabantine abbeys and collegiate churches accumulated further land and other properties during the twelfth and especially the thirteenth centuries. These acquisitions were either donations from generous noblemen or bequests or endowments from individual members upon their entry into the institution.[63] While lay demesnes were split up through inheritance, the ecclesiastical patrimonies absorbed ever-

59 O.H. Thys, "Lenen van het leenhof van Mechelen te Aartselaar en Reet, 1473" in *Vlaamse stam* VIII (1972), pp. 444f.

60 The infeudation of ecclesiastical institutions was generally avoided because of the negative effects for the duke. See: R. van Uytven, "Wereldelijke overheid en reguliere geestelijkheid in Brabant tijdens de Late Middeleeuwen" in *Bronnen voor de religieuze geschiedenis van België / Middleeuwen en Moderne Tijden*, Leuven, 1968, p. 107.

61 R. van Uytven, "De premonstratenzerabdijen en de politiek in de Nederlanden" in *De glans van Prémontré. Oude kunst uit Witherenabdijen der Lage Landen*, Heverlee, 1973, p. 47.

62 F. Daelemans, "Sociale en economische betekenis van de abdij van Grimbergen in de ontwikkeling van de lokale samenleving (17de-18de eeuw)", in: *Analecta Praemonstratensia LXVIII*/1992, 1-2, p. 111.

63 This was the case, for example, for a farm of 20 *bunders*, situated in Edegem, near Antwerp, which was given to the "Falcontinnes" convent in 1438. Van Passen, *Edegem*, p. 158.

new possessions.[64] By the fifteenth century, some ecclesiastical institutions had acquired demesnes that were equalled only by the sovereign and some members of the high nobility.

One of the few of such institutions for which we have a rough estimate of the size of its holdings was the abbey of Villers, in the very south of the duchy.[65] According to De Moreau, who dedicated a major study to the abbey's early history, its demesne covered around 10,000 hectares of land, meadows and forests along with seigniorial rights, in different parts of Brabant, as well as in the county of Namur. Among its possessions were considerable holdings in Schoten near Antwerp, more than 80 km away from the abbey.[66] The demesne of Schoten consisted mainly of gifts that the abbey had received during the second half of the thirteenth century. Since 1251, Villers held the jurisdiction in half of the village.[67] In 1272, it had 63 tenants and 24 vassals in Merksem and Schoten. The abbey also bought land, especially forests that still had to be cultivated. During the fourteenth century, the abbey had thus increased its property in Schoten by more than 150 ha.[68] After 1500, it therefore possessed more than 700 ha of land including six farms, a house, forests, meadows and farmland.[69]

8.2.3.1 The Institutions in Comparison

The detailed material we have on the abbey of Villers is an exception, however. Our knowledge of the late medieval landed property of most of the Brabantine abbeys is rather vague and does not allow us to quantify it. There are individual studies on the history of nearly all of them, but the focus of these studies differs from case to case; the landed property was not always the question that the various authors were most interested in. This makes it impossible to establish the relative hierarchy among the Brabantine abbeys and convents on the basis of their property ownership. Nevertheless, such a hierarchy can be reconstructed by means of a list of the contributions each institution made in taxes *(beden)* consented to the duke of Brabant in 1436 and in 1451.[70]

Of the thirteen greatest abbeys in Brabant, three were situated in the district of Antwerp. These three – the abbeys of Tongerlo, St. Michael and St. Bernard – were the main contributors in 1436. This concentration of large abbeys in the Antwerp area is striking. The large number of farms that ecclesiastical institutions held in the town's surroundings also reflects this.[71] The abbey of Villers, ranking eighth, was situated somewhat further in the south, in the Walloon part of Brabant. Even so, it had considerable properties in the surroundings of Antwerp.

64 Van Uytven, "Premonstratenzerabdijen", and Idem, "De Premonstratenzers in het sociaal-economisch leven der Nederlanden", in *De glans van Prémontré*, pp. 63–74.

65 Villers-la-ville (comm. Tilly, arr. Nivelles).

66 The major properties were situated in the surroundings of the abbey, near Nivelles, further west in the area of Perwez, in Velp, Bierbeek and Roosbeek near Leuven, in Chassart and Ostin in the county of Namur, and in Merxem and Schoten, northeast of Antwerp. E. Brouette, "Abbeye de Villers, à Tilly" in *Monasticon Belge IV, Province de Brabant*, deuxième fascicule, Liege, 1968, p. 385.

67 R. Baetens, *Schoten, De geschiedenis van een tweeluik*, Schoten, 1982, p. 4.

68 Ploegaerts, "L'abbaye Cistercienne de Villers pendant le cinq derniers siècles de son existence, Histoire religieuse et économique du monastère" in *Annales de société archéologique de l'arrondissement de Nivelles XI*, 1926, pp. 188–9 and 198-9.

69 Baetens, *Schoten*, pp. 37–38.

70 ARA, Rk. reg. 15722 and 15724, edited in Cuvelier, *Dénombrements*, p. 32.

71 See below.

Table 12: Contributions of Brabant abbeys in the Ducal Aids of1436 and 145 (in Philips Guilders)

Abbey	1436	Rank	1451	Rank
Tongerlo	380	1	190	2
St. Michael's, Antwerp	378	2	188	3
St. Bernard's, Hemiksem	372	3	156.5	6
Heilissem	360	4	187.75	4
Affligem	310	5	198	1
Averbode	310	7	124.875	7
Park (Heverlee)	310	6	99.75	13
Villers	305	8	176.75	5
Vorst	285	9	120	9
La Cambre (ter Kameren)	285	10	100.875	12
Grimbergen	260	11	124.875	8
Kortenberg	190	12	68.25	17
Groot Bijgaarden	185	13	72	15

The amount an abbey contributed did not directly reflect the size of its property holdings. It also included an aspect of the traditional, political importance of that institution. A comparison of these fifteenth-century rankings with the landed property of the Brabantine abbeys in the second half of the eighteenth century nevertheless reveals a very similar hierarchy in both periods.[72] On the other hand, a comparison of the contributions the abbeys paid in 1436 and 1451, respectively, shows that the contributions were not based on a fixed rate. The hierarchy among the abbeys changed considerably within the two *beden*. Affligem, which had ranked only fifth in 1436, was in 1451 the greatest contributor, before Tongerlo and St Michael's. The abbey of St. Bernard lost some ground and was surpassed by Heilissem and Villers. These changes in the hierarchy show that the contributions were linked to some extent to the economic situation of the abbeys. For instance, the relatively low ranking of Affligem in 1436 could have been the result of a malaise that this traditional leader among the Brabantine abbeys had suffered during the first half of the fifteenth century.[73]

There is yet another source that can serve as an indicator for the immovable property of ecclesiastical institutions: a list of payments for the amortisation of ecclesiastical properties. In 1474, Charles the Bold gave orders that the religious institutions were to pay an amount of money for the *mainmorte* rights of the acquisitions they had made during the last sixty years.[74] This offers us an insight into the recent purchases made by the various institutions,

72 J. M. Goris, "Het abdijgoed" in *Een kaartboek van de abdij Tongerlo. 1655-1794*, Brussels, 2001, p. 25; data based on R. van Uytven and J. De Puydt, "De toestand der abdijen in de Oostenrijkse Nederlanden, inzonderheid der Statenabdijen, in de tweede helft de 18de eeuw. Het verslag De Kulberg en de proceverbalen der abtskeuzen", in *Bijdragen tot de Geschiedenis*, 48 (1965), pp. 5–80.

73 A. Despy-Meyer and C. Gérard, Abbaye de Affligem, à Hekelgem, in *Monasticon,*, vol. IV, fasc. 1, pp. 48–50.

74 ARA Rk, reg. 24660 Rekening van ammortisatie kerkelijke goederen (nieuwe aanwinsten) 1474-1476, with many thanks to Prof. R. van Uytven who pointed out this source to me.

although not into the size of their total patrimony. The list of amortisations of 1474 (Table 13) therefore shows us the most dynamic institutions of the fifteenth century on top:

Table 13: Amortisation in 1474 (Contributions in pounds Flemish grooten)

Name	Amount
Collegiate Church of Our Lady, Antwerp	2750.15
Collegiate Church of St. Gudule's, Brussels	2149.6
St. Michael's, Antwerp	850
Dielegem	250
Vorst	202
Carthusians – Our Lady of Grace	186.5
Tongerlo	180
Dominicans, Antwerp	150
Grimbergen	120
St. Bernard's – Hemiksem	120
Kortenberg	110
Hertoginnendaal	110
Carmelites, Brussels	100
Villers	100
St. Clare's, Brussels	91,9
Affligem	90
Beguines, Antwerp	85
Minorites Brussels	80
Nazareth, Lier	80
Klein Bijgaarden	70

Source: ARA Rk, reg. 24660.

8.2.3.2 The Major Collegiate Churches

The most remarkable feature of this list is the outstanding position occupied by the collegiate churches of the later cathedrals, Our Lady of Antwerp and St. Gudule's and St. Michael's in Brussels. They had to pay twice or three times as much as the greatest abbey (i.e. St. Michael's in Antwerp), and more than ten times as much as any other Brabantine abbey. The collegiate churches were complex organisations that consisted of a number of different foundations and chantries, each of which had its own patrimony and incomes. Together with the "*praebendae*" of the canons, they included the "church factory": the demesne that had to provide the income and furnishings for the church buildings. As the motherchurch of nearly all Antwerp parishes, the church of Our Lady in Antwerp represented most of the secular clergy of the area. As a result, the landed property of the collegiate church did not form a homogenous demesne, but rather a heterogeneous agglomeration of the land and farms that its subordinate churches or foundations had received as a gift.

The chapter of Antwerp's Cathedral of Our Lady imposed its role as mother church on the Antwerp parishes. Although their income was not directly part of the administration of the collegiate church, the chapter repeatedly tried to control them. A survey of properties from the mid-fourteenth century contains 60 farms, and 129 *bunders* of land, spread over 15 villages in the immediate surroundings of Antwerp and to the east of the city.[75] The fact that the Antwerp chapter was much more active buying land during the fifteenth century than its larger counterpart in Brussels could be a reflection of the increasing dynamic of Antwerp as an urban centre.

As a landlord, the chapter collected tithes primarily, but also feudal rents. In contrast, it had only a few seigniorial rights and fiefs, and there were few villages where it had jurisdiction. Nevertheless, the chapter received various kinds of income linked with the religious services, such as collections and fees for masses, funerals, etc.[76] Its landed property comprised numerous but scattered plots of land, some of which could attain a remarkable size, although they did not form a homogeneous demesne.

8.2.3.3 The Abbeys

The holdings of the large Brabantine abbeys offer a very different picture. Originally made up of gifts from pious donors among the nobility, the abbeys increasingly tried to complete and round off their property by trading plots and buying land in particular areas. Such a strategy can be observed for the properties that Ghent's St. Bavo's Abbey had in the surroundings of Antwerp during the fifteenth century.[77]

A characteristic feature of the great abbeys in the district of Antwerp was the great number of large farms they possessed, both in the polders and in the Kempen, that served as centres of exploitation in newly cultivated land. The abbey of Tongerlo was the most striking example in terms of this strategy. The abbey possessed 88 farms, spread over the Kempen and the surroundings of Antwerp.[78] A list of "free farms" (*vrijhoeven*) in the district of Antwerp confirms the primacy of Tongerlo. The Norbertine canons possessed 43 of these free farms in seven places in the Kempen, of which 18 were in Essen-Kalmthout and ten in Tongerlo itself. Second in this ranking was the abbey of St. Michael in Antwerp with 34 farms. These were concentrated in Zandvliet, Stabroek, Berendrecht and Oorderen in the Antwerp polders, while others were located in various places in the Kempen.[79] The Abbey of

75 Hove (7 lots), Mortsel (7), Deurne (5), Hoboken (4), Wommelgem (4), Ranst (2), Antwerp *extra muros*, Borsbeek, Edegem, Merksem, Oelegem, Oorderen, Viersel, Zoersel; see J. VAN DEN NIEUWENHUIZEN, "Een status bonorum van het O.L. Vrouwe-Kapittel van Antwerpen (1346-1362)", in *Bijdragen tot de Geschiedenis*, 42, 1959), pp. 123–143.

76 DE RIDDER, *Inventaris,*, p. 13.

77 See below. Another example of an institution with such a rational management of its patrimony was the abbey of Vorst, situated just outside Brussels: C. BILLEN, "La gestion domaniale d'une grande abbaye périurbaine: Forest à la fin du Moyen Âge" in *Peasants and Townsmen in Medieval Europe.* Studia in honorem Adriaan Verhulst, Gent, 1995, pp. 493–515.

78 VAN DER WEE, *Growth*, vol. III, p. 36f, Graph 12.

79 CUVELIER, *Dénombrements*, pp. 161–214.

St. Michael was one of the greatest landowners in the Antwerp area. Its patrimony included numerous farms, fields and various kinds of property in the immediate surroundings of the town, in the polder area north of it and in the western part of the Kempen.[80] The list of this abbey's purchases during the fifteenth century gives a good impression of the dimensions of its landed property.[81]

In Deurne, only a few kilometres east of the city, St. Michael's was the greatest individual landholder, followed by some of the most renowned Antwerp patricians and local noblemen. Furthermore, a number of other ecclesiastical institutions owned land there, such as the collegiate church of Our Lady in Antwerp, the old and the new Antwerp hospitals, the church of neighbouring village of Wijnegem, and the church of Deurne itself. Each of these had more or less important possessions, ranging from a small plot of land to several large farms. Although none of them had very large holdings, they jointly formed the greatest group of landowners.

The primary difference between the great ecclesiastical patrimonies such as those of abbeys like Villers or St. Michael's and the holdings of smaller institutions was their size. Like those of the major institutions, the holdings of the smaller institutions also consisted of a number of farms and farmsteads, land and other properties. In contrast to the larger institutions, however, the smaller ones only seldom dominated a whole village through juridical lordship. On the lowest level of the hierarchy of ecclesiastical landowners we find parish churches, small monasteries and local hospitals, each of which held some tenures, farms or plots of land and thus contributed to the predominance of ecclesiastical landownership, but none of which was itself a great land owner.

The predominance of the major abbeys and other ecclesiastical houses as landowners can also be seen in other examples. In Kontich, one of the larger villages between Antwerp and Mechelen, numerous ecclesiastical institutions held tithes and landed property. Indeed, no less than ten institutions held tithes within the limits of the community.[82] There are traces of twenty ecclesiastical institutions owning a total of at least 432 ha of land in Kontich during the fifteenth century, or 22% of the total village area.[83] These 432 ha must be seen an absolute minimum value, considering the fact that the size of several properties was not specified, although they will presumably have covered numerous hectares.[84] The greatest ecclesiastically owned property in Kontich, the Moederhove farm, comprising 54 *bunders* with another 26 *bunders* of land and meadows, was only bought between 1448 and 1450 by the Abbey of St. Bavo in Ghent. This Flemish abbey then already owned great properties, including 14 farms in the neighbouring village of Boechout and various other villages in the surroundings. The purchase of this farm in Kontich can therefore be understood as means of completing their holdings in this area.[85]

---

80 At the end of the eighteenth century, St. Michael's had 82 farms, especially in the polder area along the Scheldt, north of the town, and in the Kempen; van Uytven, "Premonstratenzers", p. 67.

81 J. Van den Nieuwenhuizen, "Abbaye de St. Michel à Anvers", in *Monasticon Belge* vol. VIII, 1, pp. 195–262.

82 Van Passen, *Kontich*, pp. 69–84.

83 *Ibidem*, pp. 85–99.

84 Such as the Quaethove farm of the abbey of St. Bernard or the Lillaer farm of the abbey of Nazareth, *Ibidem*, pp. 86 and 92.

85 *Ibidem*, p. 98; A. E. Verhulst, *De Sint-Baafsabdij te Gent en haar grondbezit, 7de-14de eeuw: Bijdrage tot de kennis van de structuur en de uitbating van het grootgrondbezit in Vlaanderen tijdens de middeleeuwen*, Brussel, 1958, pp. 536 (note 134) and 539.

Most of the other landowners in Kontich were institutions situated in the surroundings of Antwerp, Mechelen or Lier, thus within 15 km. The only institutions owning land there that were situated further away were two abbeys from the Brussels area (Rooklooster and Groenendaal), the Abbey of Tongerlo in the Kempen, and the hospital of St. Nicholas in Aarschot. Properties consisting of farms, land and woods were distributed between large and small institutions. The greatest among them did not always hold the largest properties in one particular village. St. Michael's abbey, the greatest landowner in the Antwerp area, had only relatively small possessions in Kontich, for example, whereas abbeys of secondary importance, such as that of Rosendaal or St. Salvator's in Antwerp, had considerable properties there.

8.3 Conclusion

Having analysed the different groups of Brabantine landlords, their manorial rights and landed property, we can now turn to the question of whether we should see these landlords as strong or weak. This question is of major importance in connection with the concept of social property relations. According to R. Brenner, the feudal relations were based on extra-economic power, which meant that the lords could reinforce surplus extraction through non-economic coercion.[86] On the other hand, de Vries referred to the "weak landlords" of Holland and Friesland as one of the explanations for the fundamental transformation of the Dutch rural economy during the early Modern Period.[87]

As the Brabatine landlords were divided into different groups, the answer will have to be specified per group. The duke of Brabant was both powerful and wealthy. Besides having political power in the whole of the Burgundian Low Countries, he was the greatest landlord of the duchy. He held the high jurisdiction in most Brabantine villages, as well as a range of manorial rights, tenures and immovable goods in hundreds of places. In the Antwerp area, however, the ducal demesne was relatively weak in comparison to its standing in the south of Brabant. The high nobility also had considerable demesnes. The greatest of these were comparable in type and dimension with the individual ducal demesnes. For both the duke and the nobility, however, the dimensions of their personal reserve were relatively limited in comparison with their tenures and fiefs. In that sense, Brabant is comparable with the Dutch situation, where "only few noblemen owned more than several hundreds of hectares, land given out in customary tenure included."[88] For Flanders, too, the same tendency has been observed.[89]

The third great group of landlords, the ecclesiastical and charitable institutions, were in fact the largest of the great landowners of Brabant. While customary tenure and manorial rights prevailed in the demesnes of the duke and the nobility, the abbeys and collegiate churches had large demesnes with numerous farms and much land, in addition to high incomes from tithes. Brabant was an area with great and wealthy abbeys, and the area near Antwerp was no exception.

86 Brenner, "Agrarian Roots", section II: Class structure, class organization and feudal development in medieval Europe.
87 De Vries, *Dutch rural economy*, p. 25.
88 *Ibidem*, p. 36.
89 Thoen, *Landbouweconomie*, vol. I, pp. 492–500.

Besides these the duke, the nobility and the greater ecclesiastical institutions, we have distinguished a number of lesser landlords. The lessor lay landlords included members of the gentry, patricians and ducal officials. Their demesnes differed from those of the high nobility primarily in scale rather than in quality. Above all, the number of manors was smaller. Furthermore, the size of the reserve and the number of tenure-holders was lower, and the range of manorial rights more limited. At the low end of this hierarchy were the owners of a limited range of manorial rights who can hardly even be considered landlords. They held either some tenures (*cijnsen*) or feudal tenures (*lenen*) but had hardly any rights of jurisdiction. There was also a large group of small institutional landlords. These were convents of modest dimensions, hospitals, parish churches, or poor (relief) tables with some landed property and some lordly rights or a tithe. Although none of these smaller institutions played a dominant role as local landlord or great landowner, their great number made this group significant.

Although it would be exaggerated to maintain that the landlords were insignificant in Brabant, the picture that emerges from this overview is similar to that for the rest of the Low Countries. Lay lords were primarily holders of local jurisdictions and manorial rights, while the ecclesiastical houses were mainly great land landowners and holders of tithes. The major change in this pattern during the sixteenth century was the strong increase of the amount of landed property held by townsmen. In fact, there was a real rush on real estate by merchants and other wealthy Antwerp inhabitants. This phenomenon will serve as the point of departure for Chapter 10, in which we will discuss the changes in property relations and the economic structure.

CHAPTER 9

The Peasants and their Access to Land

9.1 Introduction

In the previous chapter, we saw that a large proportion of the land in Brabant belonged in one form or another to the privileged groups of population: the duke, the nobility or the Church. In most cases, however, they were not the immediate holders or users of the properties.[1] If the land had been given out in tenure, their property title guaranteed them some form of land rent, together with any manorial rights linked to it. For fiefs that were sub-infeuded, the fief holder did not receive any land rent from his sub-vassal. He could only count on an entry fee at the moment of infeudation.[2] The property rights of the copyholders and the holders of sub-fiefs, on the other hand, were very similar to property rights as we would understand them today.[3] Finally, even the landed property held immediately by the great landowners was generally not directly exploited by those owners in the fifteenth century. They usually gave it out in short-term leases, either in a form of sharecropping or, in most cases, as a fixed lease. The land was therefore generally given out to some kind of tenant who held one or several plots in copyhold, sub-fief (or feudal tenure) or as a temporary lease.

Despite its attractive simplicity as a dualistic model, the division between lords and tenants was not that neat in reality. Lords and tenants did not exist as two distinct, socially or legally defined groups; the same individual could be lord and tenant at the same time. Hence, in many rent registers, we find noblemen, urban patricians and ecclesiastical institutions listed as tenants in legal terms. In most cases, however, they leased their tenures out, rather than exploiting them themselves. On the other hand, there are also examples of small but sub-infeuded fiefs, the holders of which can be considered as feudal lords, even though they may have only possessed a few plots of land and had only two or three sub-vassals. Throughout this chapter, "tenant" will be defined more from an economic perspective than from a legal one: it refers to the final holder in any property chain. In economic terms, tenants are the ones who use the land, as opposed to those who receive any form of land rent for it. We will therefore be dealing with the peasants or farmers who actually worked the land, whether it was their own plot of allodial property, a small sub-fief given to them by a local landlord, or, as in most cases, a piece of land they held in copyhold.

1 In a few exceptional cases, ecclesiastical institutions still exploited some small reserves on their own, but these were not considerable in size.

2 The holder of such a sub-fief (*achterleen*, also: rear fief or feudal tenure) was nevertheless not excepted from the payment of other manorial dues to some manorial lord.

3 F. L. Ganshof and A. Verhulst, "Medieval Agrarian Society in its Prime: France, The Low Countries, and Western Germany" in *The Cambridge Economic History of Europe*, Vol. I: The Agrarian Life of the Middle Ages, Cambridge, 1971², pp. 291–339, 299.

The leaseholders, finally, were a group of land users who had no actual property rights, but rather only temporary usage rights on their holdings. The property status of leaseholders differed from that of the feudal tenants or copyholders, but their economic role was particularly important. Already in the late Middle Ages, most of the large farms were held in leasehold, and certainly in the sixteenth century, temporary lease was the predominant form of landholding in the Antwerp area. Therefore we will be paying particular attention to this form of landholding and to the economic profile of the late medieval leaseholder.

9.2 The Copyholders (*Cijnshouders, laten*)

Considering the low percentage of the *reserve* (i.e. the landed property that was *immediately* in the hands of the duke or the lay landlords) as discussed in the previous chapter, the great majority of land belonging to individual lords was held in tenure. Almost every landlord set up his own seigniorial court, where the tenures he had given out in copyhold were administered.[4] Ecclesiastical institutions also gave out a considerable part of their land in tenure, but in comparison to the lay lords, they retained immediate ownership of a greater part of their holding, leasing out many farms and individual plots of land and meadows.

For the study of tenures in copyhold, we have had to rely on manorial sources that refer to single manors rather than to whole village communities.[5] Indeed, registers referring to entire villages hardly even exist for the fifteenth century. In contrast, countless manorial rent registers have survived, with sometimes very detailed information about the tenure holders and what they paid. Even so, these manorial rent registers are very inhomogeneous as sources. Their quality varies strongly from case to case. Some describe each tenure in detail, including the size, while others are rather vague. Another problem inherent to these sources is the limited extent to which they are both representative and complete. Any village had tenures belonging to various manors, which means that the holdings within one particular manor will have formed only a fraction of the total landed property in that place. Moreover, what is even worse is that we can hardly begin to guess the exact proportions of the tenures of one individual manor in the total village area, because the limits of the manors were not identical with the modern boundaries of the villages in question. The rent registers of individual manors therefore have to be considered as samples, and not as reconstructions of whole villages. As such, they have to be selected according to clear criteria. They must contain some basic information in order to allow a systematic analysis: the name of the tenants, a classification of the tenures (land, farm, etc.) and the size of the holding, or at least some indirect indication of it.[6]

In the following section, two rent registers from different landlords and concerning two different villages situated in the surroundings Antwerp are analysed in detail. The first concerns the manor of Walem, a large marketplace near Mechelen with a considerable

4 Godding, *Droit privé*, p. 171.

5 Most authors stress the difference between the boundaries of the village and those of the manor. For England, see for example: R.H. Hilton, "Social Structures in Warwickshire" in *The English Peasantry in the later Middle Ages*, Oxford, 1975, p. 124.

6 On the methodological problems involved in working with rent registers, see: C.Billen, "Problèmes de méthodologie autour de l'utilisation des censiers du bas moyen age" in *Histoire économique de la Belgique. traitement des sources de état des questions.* Actes du colloque de Bruxelles, 17-19 novembre 1971, pp. 439–471.

village centre, where signs of a lively industrial and commercial activity can be noted. It is a particularly detailed and complete document that contains information on a considerable part of the village community and is therefore particularly well suited as an example. Our second example concerns the manor of Helmont, in Kontich. This was not situated in the village itself, but rather somewhat outside, and had a mainly agrarian character.[7] The selected registers display different constellations of property and different ways of organising copyhold tenures. We will therefore be checking any general trends we observe against information from other documents pertaining to our area. For this purpose, we have systematically studied the ducal rent register of Aartselaar, situated ca. 10 km south of Antwerp and the rent register of the manor of Bisschoppenhof in Deurne, only a few kilometres east of the town.[8]

9.2.1 Walem, ca. 1480[9]

The village of Walem, situated on the river Nete five kilometres north of Mechelen, already had 366 households, or ca. 1800 inhabitants, in 1437, and was therefore among the most populated villages in the area.[10] The manor of Walem was held in those days by the van Rotselaar family, which also owned part of the neighbouring village of Duffel.[11] The 582 holdings in the manor of Walem were distributed among 307 tenants, which almost corresponded with the number of households in the village.[12]

The land rent was levied in different types of coins, although the prevailing type was the Brabantine *grooten*. Other currencies used include "*oude groten*", and Leuven pounds. Along with these payments in money, the tenants also had to pay with chickens, capons and geese, oats and some rye.[13]

The extensive rent register for the manor of Walem, which dates from ca. 1480,[14] offers us insight into the topology and the socio-economic structures of the village, thus reaching beyond mere property structures. The list of tenures begins with 206 items situated in the village centre, around the church, near the well and near the ferry over the river Nete.[15] References to a Lombard house, a weavers' street, a dyeing workshop and a seal house indicate

7 R. Van Passen, "Het cijnsboek van Helmont (Kontich) van 1431" in *Bijdragen tot de Geschiedenis*, 49 (1966), pp. 139–156.

8 Aartselaar: ARA, Rk. no. 45583, fos.1r–13v, ca. 1440-1460, Deurne Bischoppenhof: ARA, Rk. 44976 fos. 31r–51v, analysed in Nooyens, *Deurne*, vol. I, pp. 257–261.

9 Brussels, ARA, MW 327, Rent register of Walem for 1480 and 1500.

10 J. Cuvelier, *Dénombrements*, p. 450 In the dénombrement of 1480, the year when the rent book was made up, the number of taxed households was only 131. Such a low figure seems rather unlikely and if not impossible, if we compare it with the number of tenants mentioned in the rent register:, 307. Presumably some of the households of Walem were counted together with a neighbouring village.

11 A. Wauters, *Walem*. See also: MW, G 674 about the gift of the seigneuries to Jean de Merode in 1525.

12 This high degree of correspondence can be misleading, however, as the tenures holders were not necessarily identical with the inhabitants of the village. They may also have lived in surrounding villages or towns.

13 The calculation was made on the basis of exchange values mentioned in the source itself (*lovense*), and from alternative sources. Poultry and grain were calculated on the basis of prices mentioned in the domanial accounts of the Land van Mechelen for the year 1480.

14 The documented is not dated. We can nevertheless situate the date of edition via the first – dated – changes that were registered. This was the case in 1480 and again in 1484, when a new holder was inserted for a *keurgoed*. The document was therefore most probably drafted before 1480, but surely before 1484.

15 "*Achter/voor de kerke*": nos.: 25, 31, 69, 86, 87, 88, 143 and 198; "*bij de borrenputte*": no. 118; "*bij het veer*": no. 108; "*bij de Nete*": no. 147.

that Walem not only had a textile production of some importance, but also lodged, or had once lodged, a Lombard, or moneychanger.[16] There was also an archer's guild, which had its shooting-stand in the *Zand*.[17] The names of various houses in the village, for example the Eagle, the Red Shield, the Rose, or the Horseshoe, indicate that they were of a considerable size and quality as village houses.[18]

Although the register fails to mention the size of most of these items, we can infer it roughly from the amount of the land rent that was to be paid.[19] The holdings within the village limits were relatively small in comparison with the goods situated outside. The former were primarily houses with small plots of land. Only a few religious institutions such as the abbey of St. Bavo in Ghent or those of Rozendaal and Hanswijk held larger holdings.[20] The holdings of individuals, in contrast, were generally limited to some houses without any considerable landed property. Where the size of a parcel was mentioned, this ranged from 0.25 *bunder* (a *vierendeel*) to 1.25 *bunders*; only one holding was 2 *bunders* in size. Various tenants held more than one parcel. In most cases this was two or three small houses with some plots of land; any more than this was exceptional. The major exception in this context was Augustijn van den Eynde – the general forester of Brabant – whom we will meet again as the owner of a fief in Kontich given by the feudal court of the Land van Mechelen.[21] He held five houses in the village – among which "the Little Swan" and "the Mint" – and five plots of land. Furthermore, he also had a farm and some land and meadow, in total 3.5 *bunders*, outside the village. Like Augustijn van den Eynde, some other tenants with houses in the village also held tenures outside. Joos Raes, for example, had two houses in the village and 8 *bunders* of land outside, and Jan Vernauen had a house and a little field (*veldeke*) in the village along with four plots outside, one of which was 2 *bunders* in size. But this group remained limited to a few individuals.

The larger holdings were situated almost entirely outside the village centre. The toponymical descriptions of these tenures (items 208 to 598) refer not to things like fields and marshland (*broek*). The size of almost all these tenures is specified in the rent register. The greater tenants were to be found among the holders of "*keurgoeden*", i.e. tenures that were subject to a transfer fee the moment the holder of the *keur* died.[22] Remarkably, many of these larger tenures, among which the three greatest holdings, did not include a farm or a house. This means that their holders will have resided either on a feudal or allodial property or outside the manor of Walem. This could also have been the case for those tenants whose holding did include a farm or a house, as this did not necessarily have to be where they lived. Indeed, there is no direct proof that the tenants listed in the rent register actually lived in Walem. Some of them can nevertheless be identified as residents of Walem via indicators from the source. For example, there are individuals whose names are identical with a local

16 "*In de weverstrate*": nos. 2, 3, 6, 110, 134; "*het lombaerdenhuis*": no. 81; "*verwerijen*": no. 107; "*het zegelhuis*": no. 85.

17 "*Op het zand bij het schuttershof*": no. 37.

18 *De Aar: no. 176, De Rode Schilt: 175, De Zwaan: 56, De Roos: 56, De Drie Koningen: 59, De Schere: 91, Het Hoefijzer: 11, 131, De Maan: 139, De Munte: 163.*

19 See below.

20 St. Bavo's held 19 *bunders* of meadow, Rosendaal 1 *bunder* of land and Hanswijk 3 *bunders*.

21 O.H. Thys, "Lenen van het leenhof van Mechelen te Kontich, 1473" in *Vlaamse stam* IX (1973), p. 633.

22 The holders of the tenures found a way to postpone this moment as long as possible by registering one of their children as holder of the *keur*. The *keur* holders registered in the document were in most cases minors and not identical with the tenant.

toponym, such as Willem van Papenbroek, Gielis and Jan van Eekele (Eekelbroek), or Geert, Lijsbeth and Jan van Binnebeke. Their origins will presumably have been near the toponym in question. Another indicator is the frequent occurrence of the same family name: There were nine tenants called van Else, five called Frans and four called Muyl. Furthermore, there were three Inden Manes, Binnebekes, Raeses, Boelses and De Neves. Of course this could also have been mere coincidence, especially if the name is rather common, such as Gielis, Raes or Frans. For more specific names, however, this is less likely. In many cases, moreover, the holdings of individuals with identical names were listed next to each other, which makes it almost certain that they will have been members of the same family.

In terms of the size of the larger holdings outside the village, we can observe a great differentiation (Graph 6).[23]

GRAPH 6: Size of Tenures at Walem, 1480

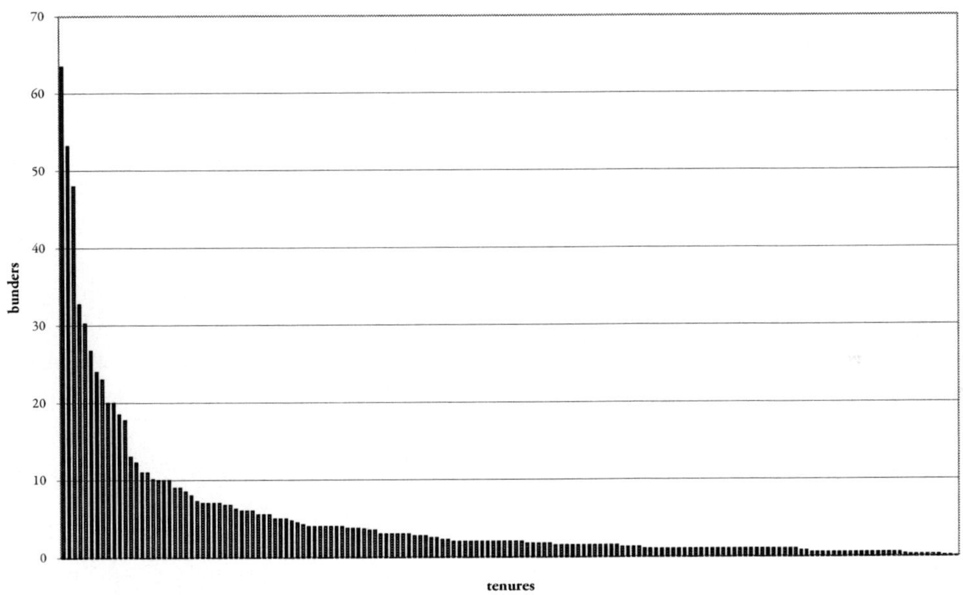

SOURCE: ARA, MW 327.

The greatest holdings had between 48 and 63 *bunders*, while the smallest (of those for which the size was indicated) consisted of no more than 5 *roeden* (164.5m^2). The three largest holdings consisted to a considerable extent of woods and land. The tenants were a certain Jan van Oyenbruggen, the abbey of St. Bavo in Ghent and a man called Jan van Boxelaar. As one of the greatest landlords and landowners in the whole area, St. Bavo's hardly needs any introduction. Jan van Oyenbruggen was probably a citizen from Mechelen. He is also known as the owner the large Buizegem farm in Edegem, south of Antwerp, a fief of the seigneur of Mortsel and Cantecroy.[24] The identity of Van Boxelaar

23 For 298 tenures, the size is known.

24 A document from Antwerp, dating from 1471, mentions a certain Jan van Oyenbruggen as being a citizen from Mechelen:

is not clear. He was either a member of the local elite, or a citizen of nearby Mechelen or another town.

Besides these three largest holdings, there were another 35 that exceeded 5 *bunders* in size. They consisted either of one or several farms along with their fields and meadows or only of parcels of land or meadow without any farm buildings. Willem van Papenbroek, for example, held three farms, with a total of 32.75 *bunders* of land and meadows.[25] Among the holders of these larger properties, we can also recognise representatives of a few local families: Peter van Else, for example, with a holding of 24 *bunders*, Jan and Lijsbeth van Binnebeke with their farms of 23 and 20 *bunders*, respectively, and Jan Muyl, whose farm was 11 *bunders* in size. The holders of medium-sized holdings, consisting of only a few plots of land or small farms, were a bit more numerous (45 or 15%). Local families predominate among the tenants of these holdings, but also social and religious institutions in Walem itself, as well as from Mechelen and Antwerp, had holdings of an intermediate size. For example, there were tenures held by the Holy Spirit poor relief table of St. Rombout and St. Catherine's hospital in Mechelen, the Holy Spirit poor relief table of Walem, and the abbey of St. Bernard in Hemixem. Finally, there were even two noblemen among the tenants: "*heer*" Lodewijk van Cotthem and Jan Vilain, lord of Zemst.

A final category consisted of smallholdings of less than 2 *bunders*. There were 78 such holdings, making up 48.5% of the total. This number understates the part of very small tenures, however. Smallholdings, consisting of a cottage with a small plot of land, were generally listed without any indication of their size. This was especially the case for the tenures situated in the village, which generally were listed merely as "house", "house with garden" or as "property". The actual percentage of these very small holdings has to be estimated as much greater.

As far as the land rent is concerned we have to distinguish the tenures situated in the village from the larger holdings situated outside. The most frequently recorded amount due for a tenure in the village was 9 pennies Brabantine *grooten* + 1 capon. This was the basic amount for a tenure when it was given out. Tenure holders whose tenure had a higher value had to pay twice or even several times this amount. 29% of the tenants paid up to twice as much and 11% paid three times as much or more. The land rent for the tenures outside the village varied but seems to have been in function of the size of the holding. While there was no fixed amount per *bunder*, the rents generally ranged between 5 and 20 pennies per *bunder*, with an average value of 15.83 pennies. There were nevertheless strong deviations.[26]

With its large village centre and thus almost urban character, the village of Walem had a dual property structure. The inhabitants of the village had only smallholdings that could hardly produce an agrarian surplus, whereas outside the village, holdings of more than 10 *bunders* were not exceptional, and a great majority held between 1 and 5 *bunders*. It is remarkable that only very few tenants who had holdings in the village also had land outside. The village community and the tenants outside the village seem to have formed two separate groups.

Boek van dagvaarden, in *AAB*, p. 213. For his landed property, see: Van Passen, *Edegem*, pp. 60–61.

25 It is interesting that some of these large holdings consisted only of two or three items, whereas others literally collected parcels: Willem van Papenbroek's holding consisted of 16 items; the Sels children held 13 items and Peter van Else 19. This accumulation of parcels indicates that certain tenants had enhanced their property holdings since the establishment of the manor, whether through the purchase or the inheritance of other tenures.

26 The standard deviation is 29.12.

9.2.2 The Tenants of the Manor of Helmont (Kontich) 1431

The second rent register we will consider, from 1431, comes from the manor of *Helmont*, a fief of the Land van Mechelen situated in *Kontich*. The tenures it mentions are spread over the villages of Aartselaar, Kontich, Reet and Waarlos; one holding was situated in Duffel.[27] The landlord, Henrik van Helmont, received 16 pounds, 1 shilling and 3 pennies *lovens* (= 9 pounds, 9 shillings Brabantine *grooten)* plus several rents in other coins,[28] 17.3 *viertel* (1756.8 litres) of oats (20 tenants), 57 chickens and 11 capons (48 tenants) and 13 days of mowing and harvesting corvees (*maai en snijdagen*) from a total of 78 tenants.[29] The size of the individual parcels is known in 52 cases and varies between 0.25 and 7 *bunders*. A great number of these (42) include a farm building with an average of 2.6 *bunders* of land, although this figure only reflects the size of the holdings for which the size was mentioned. For many houses, most of which were probably rather small, this was not the case. We therefore have to estimate the average actual farm size to have been considerably lower than 2.6 *bunders*. Thirty-eight parcels were plots of land without any buildings; their average size was 1.74 *bunders*. The high percentage of woods (18 parcels), with a total size of 24.7 *bunders*, is also remarkable.

Unlike the case in Walem, there was a very low degree of accumulation of parcels. Only one holding consisted of five plots: the tenure of a certain Rombout Embrechts consisted of four pieces of land and a parcel of wood, comprising not more than 3.5 *bunders* in total. Two other tenants held four plots, while three others held three items. This means that the great majority of the tenants (72 holdings or 92.3%) held only one or two plots. The average size of the holdings in the manor of Helmont was relatively small (2.2 *bunders*). Only a third of the holdings consisted of more than 2 *bunders*, and the holdings of more than 5 *bunders* made up only 12% of the total.

Ecclesiastical and charitable institutions were foremost among the holders of these large tenures. Three of the four largest holdings belonged to abbeys and poor relief tables. The abbey of St. Bavo in Ghent held the largest of these three. Its holding, consisting of four plots (i.e. the Ten Bossche farm, two pieces of land and a piece of woods called De Teyshage) comprised 9.5 *bunders*. The second largest tenant, the priory of Groenendaal in Hoeilaart, south of Brussels had 7 *bunders* of land, while the Holy Spirit poor relief table of St. Rombout in Mechelen held 5.5 *bunders*.

Among the greatest individual tenants we find several citizens from Antwerp and Mechelen. Although we do not know the origins of Augustijn Voesel, who held a farm and some woods with a total size of 6.5 *bunders*, we do know that his son, Pauwel, who inherited the tenure, was a tanner in Antwerp. Peter van den Dijke, the tenant of the "Ter Clocken" farm with 4 *bunders*, is identified as coming from Mechelen.[30] 68.3% of the holdings contained between 0.25 and 2 *bunders*. Most of them consisted either of land, forests or pastures without a house or farm buildings. We can identify many of the tenants of these

27 VAN PASSEN, "Helmont", p. 139.

28 34 shillings *payement*, 20 shillings *tournois*, 2 old *grooten*, and 2 Flemish *grooten* (= ca. 4 shillings, 5 pennies)

29 The persistence of corvees in the fifteenth century is not exceptional. They still existed in various manors of Brabant. In the south of the duchy, they were generally more numerous than in the northern part, where they had been abandoned or transformed into money rents; PH. GODDING, *Droit privé*, p. 164.

30 VAN PASSEN, "Helmont", p. 141, item 2.

holdings as belonging to the local population via their names, which occur frequently in documents pertaining to the area (e.g. Nulaet, Van Regenmortel, Van den Wouwer and Vanden Loecke).

The holdings mentioned in the register without any indication of their size are not as easy to classify as was the case in Walem. Whereas in the latter village, the low value and systematic composition of their land rent allowed us to classify them generally as very small holdings, the situation in the manor of Helmont was more complex. The land rents mentioned vary significantly from case to case, and there is no basic amount per unit as in the village of Walem that would help to categorise the holdings. The lack of a strict correlation between the size and the amount of land rent also means that we cannot make any precise statements concerning the dimensions of a large share of the unspecified holdings.

9.2.3 General Features

The two examples of manorial rent registers discussed in the previous sections reflect quite different situations. Not only did they pertain to different types of villages and landlords, but each of them referred to a different kind and number of parcels held by a different number of tenants. Whereas the manor of Walem was divided in two parts – the village centre, with only very small holdings, and the part outside the village, consisting of holdings of a considerable size – such very large holdings were absent in the manor of Helmont, although the latter place did have a similar differentiation between large, medium-sized and small holdings. Nevertheless, we can deduce some general patterns. The distribution of the holdings among the tenants was anything but even in both cases. The rent registers of both manors contain tenures that comprised numerous parcels, as well as holdings consisting of a single plot. Moreover, the individual parcels varied significantly in terms of their size.

The holdings in both cases can be divided into three major categories according to their size: ahe large holdings with more than 5 *bunders*, which are comparable to the English yeoman holdings,[31] the medium-sized holdings with between 2 and 5 *bunders*, and the small holdings with less than 2 *bunders*, which were in large part held by cottagers, although some of them formed part of larger holdings that were situated partly outside the manor in question. Although the percentages of holdings in each of these categories differ from manor to manor, there are some striking parallels between the cases for which we could calculate the size of the holdings (Graph 7):

31 See for example: R. Duplessis, *Transitions to Capitalism in Early Modern Europe*, Cambridge, 1997 (New Approaches to European History, 10), p. 21.

GRAPH 7: Size of Tenures (in Bunders) in Walem, Helmont (Kontich) and Aartselaar

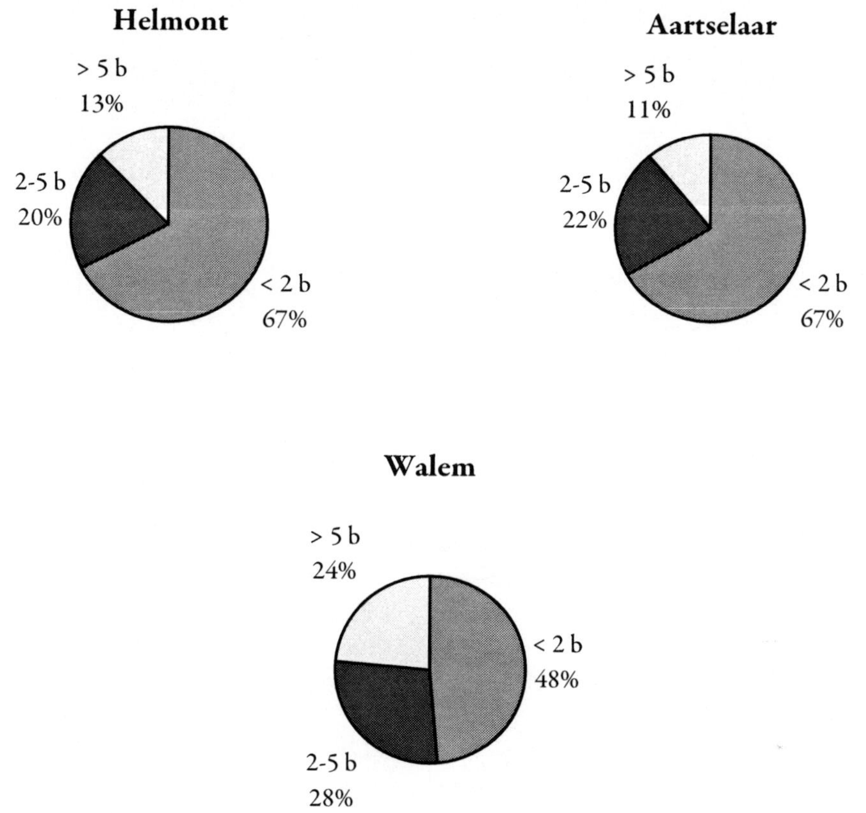

The holders of large tenures were a small minority, belonging in large part to the same social groups as the landlords: ecclesiastical institutions, urban citizens and, to a lesser extent, noblemen. The number of tenures held by townsmen was not particularly high in either of the two cases discussed above. Their presence in Walem was somewhat more pronounced than in Kontich. In the villages nearby Antwerp, in contrast, a high concentration of urban tenure holders can be observed already in the fifteenth century. A major share of the large tenures of the Bischoppenhof manor in Deurne, for example, was held by Antwerp aldermen and other figures in the urban patriciate in the middle of the fifteenth century.[32] While the area with a strong concentration of landed property held by townsmen was still very limited in the fifteenth century, the share of townsmen in the landed property of the surrounding villages increased sharply in the sixteenth century – also in places situated further away from the town, as we will see in the next chapter.

32 ARA, Rk. 44 976, fos. 31r-51v, cited " in NOOYENS, *Deurne*, vol. I, pp. 257–261.

Table 14: The Ten Largest Tenants of the Bisschoppenhof in Deurne, Mid-fifteenth Century

Tenant	Status	No. of items	Rent in Antwerp pennies
St. Michael's Abbey	Eccl. inst.	14	293 + 13 d. lov. + 1 d. flem. + 3 s. payem.
Bode, Jan, heer	Nobility	11	264
Van der Heyden, Claus	Antwerp citizen	8	198 + 4 d. lov. + 1 zwerte tornoise
Chapter of Antwerp	Eccl. inst.	2	216
De Coninck, Jan	Antwerp citizen	3	121
Megnaerts, Willem	Antwerp citizen	1	84
Van Immerseel, Aard, heer	Nobility	1	72
Soetmond, Jan		1	64
Bollaert, Wouter		1	63
De Herde, Jan, heer	Nobility	1	62

Aside from these outsiders to the village community, the larger and medium-sized holdings were in the hands of a limited number of leading local families. Various members of those families are found as holders of considerable farms, plots of land and other holdings. Some also appear as holders of fiefs of any subordinate feudal court. Some of them were butchers, smiths or bakers. It was the members of these local elites who often held the position of alderman or mayor of a village.

A considerable number of those who held larger properties sublet their holding to leaseholders and therefore becoming landlords or *rentiers* themselves. We can assume that this was the case for most of the ecclesiastic institutions, of course, for the noblemen and for most of the urban citizens.[33] It is likely that local tenants also sublet their holdings, but there is no explicit evidence for this in the documents. It is nevertheless highly probable that holders of two or more distinct farms of substantial size will have leased out at least one of them. From an economic point of view, these large holdings were big enough to produce a significant agrarian surplus that could be sold on the market. On the other hand, the lessors would normally have depended to some extent on wage labour, at least during the mowing periods and harvests.

The mid-sized holdings were much more numerous than the large holdings. Among their owners were some "outsiders", just as was the case for the large holdings, but the share of local tenants was considerably higher than that for the large holdings. The category of mid-sized holdings is generally seen as the typical family holding that produced without or nearly without using wage labour and that kept production costs low, while still being large enough to produce a surplus.[34] Especially considering the intensive agrarian techniques applied in the area, this category seems to have been very prosperous in the late Middle Ages.[35]

33 Antwerp citizens exploited some forests, brick ovens, tithes and tolls directly, however. De Nave, *Antwerpen, stad en land* (see Chapter 7).

34 Thoen, *Landbouwekonomie*, vol. II, pp. 876–77.

35 Bois, *Crise*, p. 138f.

The smallholdings, finally, were the most numerous of all. They made up two-thirds of all the holdings in Kontich and Aarstelaar and at least 50% of those in Walem. Holdings with less than 2 hectares of land are generally considered to have been insufficient for producing a regular surplus for the market. Of course, we have to consider that the data from a few manorial rent registers do not allow us to define the precise percentage of tenants below this crucial limit, since tenants could also have held some land from another landlord. Moreover, they had the possibility of leasing a plot of land in order to increase the size of their holding. Even if we situate the limit somewhat lower than 2 hectares for areas, like Brabant, that had intensive agriculture, we can state in general terms that a large share of the tenants remained beneath the limit for producing a marketable agrarian output.

9.2.4 The Value of the Land Rents

The land rents were made up of different types of money and agrarian products. The prevailing type of payment in kind was grain, in most cases oats. The basic rent for each house in the village centre of Walem was 9 Brabantine pennies and 1 capon. 60% of the houses paid this basic value, 29% paid up to twice as much and 11% three times or more.

For farmsteads outside the villages, the land rents were less systematic but still related to the size and the quality of the holding. Without taking into account the qualitative differences of the holdings, we can establish a rough average land rent per *bunder*. For holdings with rents paid in money, the average value was 20.4 pennies in Walem and 26.2 pennies in the manor of Helmont. Both values can be adjusted, however, by eliminating the maximum values (i.e. 800 pennies in Walem and 338 pennies in Helmont), as these are isolated cases and not representative for the whole of the series.[36] By doing so, we obtain averages of 14.8 pennies per *bunder* in Walem and 17 pennies per *bunder* in the manor of Helmont. For the latter we can also calculate the values of the land rents payable in both grain and money: the values varied between 4.8 litres of oats and 3.4 pennies per *bunder* on one hand and 135.5 litres and 2.4 pennies per *bunder* on the other. Land rents payable exclusively in kind ranged from 17 litres to 121 litres of oats per unit. These values are comparable with those calculated for the rent registers of the ducal domain. The tenants of the manor of Aartselaar paid an average of 14.4 pennies per *bunder* (with a minimum of 0.5 and a maximum of 46.4 pennies).

9.3 The Holders of Small Fiefs

In our analysis of the ducal fiefs in the previous chapter, we concentrated primarily on the large fiefs, which included manorial rights, tenures and sub-fiefs. The ducal fief holders were not exclusively great noblemen, patricians and ducal officers, however. They also included individuals with smallholdings of between 1 and 5 hectares, or even of minute parcels measuring less than 1 hectare. Of the ducal fiefs in our sample, 37.6% were smaller than 5 hectares, while 12.9% were even smaller than one hectare.[37]

36 As both values refer to very small plots with relatively high rents, this results in a very high amount per *bunder*.

37 Out of the 101 ducal fiefs in chief, for which the size was given, 74 (73.3%) were smaller than 20 hectares, 54 (53.5%) smaller than 10 ha, 38 (37.6%) smaller than 5 ha, and 13 (12.9%) smaller than 1 ha.

The registers of 1440 do not give us precise information concerning the size of the holdings. They mention the number of the sub-fiefs of many ducal vassals, but only rarely include information about their size and the name of the holder. As we have seen, the dimensions of some of these sub-fiefs – especially those given by powerful seigneurs – could still be considerable.[38] Others, however, did not exceed the size of a normal tenure. The fief that Jan Wycman held from Aart van Immerseel, seigneur of Wommelgem, was not bigger than 1 *bunder*,[39] for example, and the meadow of Lancelot Gottengijs, sub-vassal of Aart van Zevenbergen in Onze-Lieve-Vrouw-Waver, measured just 1.25 *bunders*.[40]

The lack of information about the size of some of the sub-fiefs mentioned in the ducal registers means that we cannot use them to analyse the distribution of sub-fiefs among its holders. Instead, we have to investigate the registers of a subordinate feudal court. One of the most detailed and most complete of those registers at our disposal for the research area is the feudal register (*leenboek*) of the Land van Mechelen from 1472. The Land van Mechelen – one of the largest and most privileged seigneuries of the whole area – became part of the ducal domain in 1464, when John, lord of Wesemaal, gave it to the Charles, count of Charolais, the later Charles the Bold. Some years later, a detailed register of the fiefs within the Land van Mechelen – now part of the ducal domain – was drawn up. This register gives a good indication of how feudal property was distributed at the lower levels of the feudal hierarchy.[41]

Among the fiefs within the Land van Mechelen there was a considerable number of large holdings, which included a farm and, in some cases, manorial rights and their own sub-fiefs. Although the sub-fiefs were generally clearly smaller than the fiefs in chief, they cannot be equated with tenures in held in copyhold. Sub-fiefs were much less numerous than the tenures of any manorial lord, and they were held by a small group of families. In many cases, the sub-vassals had personal links with the fief holder in chief. Among the 17 sub-fiefs that Claus Wielancx (mentioned earlier as an example of a small feudal lord) had given out in the village of Reet, for example, most were monopolised by three families: the Wielancxs themselves (five holdings), the Bals (four holdings) and the Van Loockes (four holdings).[42] In Kontich, one of the largest communities within the Land van Mechelen, similar patterns can be observed: among the Kontich fiefs there were remarkably many large holdings, including manorial rights and various sub-fiefs. The greater vassals of the lord of the Land van Mechelen belonged either to the nobility or the urban patriciate, or they were ducal officers, such as Augustijn van den Eynde, the chief forester of Brabant, who held the farm of Eindonk and ca. 10 *bunders* of land, 7 sub-fiefs, tithes and meadows in Kontich and its surroundings. It is this group that monopolised the holdings larger than 10 *bunders*. Among the holders of mid-sized holdings, a small number of families was predominant, just as in Reet, where Henrik de Keyzer held two large farms and three other De Keyzers each had some holdings. We have no proof that they all were members of the same family; only Willem de Keyzer is specified as being the son of Henrik. The fact that the holdings in questions were all situated close to each other nevertheless points to close relations.

38 See above, Chapter 3.
39 ARA, LB no. 8, fo. 160v.
40 ARA, LB no. 8, fo. 54v.
41 O.H. Thys, "Lenen van het leenhof van Mechelen te Aartselaar en Reet, 1473" in *Vlaamse stam* VIII (1972), pp. 441–447; and Idem, "Lenen van het leenhof van Mechelen te Kontich, 1473" in *Vlaamse stam* IX (1973), pp. 628–638.
42 Thys, "Aartselaar en Reet", passim.

Another group of kinsmen that we encounter frequently were the Van Regenmorters (or Van Regenmortels), whose members held four fiefs in Kontich.[43]

The holders of small fiefs and sub-fiefs appear to have been a relatively small group made up in large part of several interrelated families. Considering their small number, their close links both with each other and with the feudal lords and their relatively large holdings, they were by no means typical peasants, but rather a local upper class with a high social status. This was probably not the case for all fief holders, however. Some may have acquired a fief via inheritance or purchase, without necessarily having made a social promotion. By the end of the fifteenth century there were no longer any social preconditions for purchasing a fief.

The original free status of a fief holder – in contrast to the unfree status of a tenant – had lost much of its juridical advantage by the fifteenth century. The relation between a fief holder and his feudal lord differed from the relationship between a tenant and his manorial lord inasmuch as the former did not have to pay a land rent, but rather only a one-off entry fee. On the other hand, he did have to pay ducal taxes, some manorial rights and ecclesiastical dues (e.g. tithes). In practice, however, this difference lost part of its significance with the relative decline in the value of the land rents for copyhold.

9.4 The Leaseholders

The third group of tenants we need to consider are the farmers or lessees of farms or individual plots of land. In contrast to the copyholders or the holders of feudal tenures, they had no rights on the leased property. Rather, they had only temporary usage rights on the lease, without any rights to sell, pledge or even sublet. The leases they paid in exchange for a property were much higher than the average land rent for goods held in copyhold. Our survey of landed property showed that a considerable group of both the landlords and the tenants with larger properties did not exploit their holdings themselves. Many landlords not only had land that they had given out in copyhold but they also held parts of their goods in immediate property, which they hardly ever worked themselves by means of wage labour. The countless farms, fields and meadows that noblemen or ecclesiastical institutions held were mostly leased out.

The direct usage of the "demesne" or "reserve" of landlords had been abandoned already in the thirteenth and fourteenth century in favour of a lease system. The most ancient forms of land lease were hereditary lease and sharecropping (French: *métayage*, Dutch: *deelpacht* or *helftwinning*). This system of hereditary lease soon proved inadequate, however. The fixed rents and hereditary character of this system did not allow the owner to adapt the lease price to the fluctuations of grain prices, nor did it give him any possibility of control over the production process. In practice, hereditary lease hardly differed from copyhold, as the lease price was fixed and the duration of the lease was not limited in time.[44]

In order to avoid the loss of value of their land, many landlords introduced the system of temporary lease, starting already in the thirteenth century. This type of contract was more flexible, making it possible to adapt the conditions of the lease at the

43 Thys, "Kontich", passim.

44 Jansen, *Landbouwpacht*, p. 2.

end of each term of either six, nine or twelve years.[45] For sharecropping contracts, the lease price was fixed as a certain proportion of the total production, generally half, which was to be paid in kind. This meant that the lease was not subject to devaluation but remained linked to the total production. It also had a negative effect, however. By fixing the lease price to half of the yield, there was little impetus for the farmer to increase the production. After all, he would have to share the fruit of his efforts with the landlord. In Anderlecht, near Brussels, we see sharecropping contracts being transformed into fixed leases very soon after the introduction of such contracts in the late thirteenth century.[46] This economic disadvantage did not prevent sharecropping from persisting until the end of the fifteenth century. In the Antwerp area, we still encounter numerous examples in the middle of the fifteenth century.

It was the third type of lease, the temporary lease with a fixed lease price, introduced almost simultaneously with sharecropping, that became the most successful. Already in the fifteenth century, it was the most frequently applied system, and by the sixteenth century, it was practically the only lease system applied in the southern Low Countries. The lease price for farms or farmland was either a fixed amount of grain, sometimes along with a few other agrarian products (e.g. poultry, fruit or wax) and/or a certain amount of money. Leases on meadows were generally to be paid only with money.

In many cases, however, a farm lease was paid both in kind and in money. In the first period after their introduction, the duration of leases was very long, but they became increasingly shorter over the course of the fourteenth century, reaching terms of twelve, nine or six years.[47] The leasing of a farm or a plot of land, as well as of any other property, whether a toll, a mill, or even an office, was subject to open competition at the end of every term. In practice, however, the leases were often renewed at the end of a term, offering a certain degree of continuity to the lessee. In other words, farms and farmland could remain in the hands of the same leaseholder for several decades. A contract for a plot of land in Wilrijk, south of Antwerp, dating from 1427, confirms this with the statement that: "Beatrijs Boods has already been leasing this plot for many years, just as her forefathers had done.[48]

In our study of leaseholders, we have to take into account a major distinction between a lease on a whole farm and a lease on individual plots of land. These two types of leased goods were subject to different economic preconditions and had different consequences for the lessees. Whereas the lease of a whole farm with up to 70 hectares of land and meadows was a serious enterprise that demanded a certain amount of capital and know-how and all the energy of the leaseholder, the lease of a parcel of land was also an option for someone who held a mid-sized tenure who wanted to increase the size of his farm. This means that we are dealing with two distinct types of lessees: the holders of large or very large farms that would have outsized most peasant tenures and were generally only manageable by means of wage labour on the one hand, and the holders of one or several plots of land that could serve as a complement to any other holding on the other. Whereas the first group would have

45 Hoppenbrouwers, *Middeleeuwse samenleving*, p. 422.

46 The first documented sharecropping contract from Anderlecht dates from 1296. The contract was already changed into a fixed-lease contract in 1331. M. De Waha, *Recherches sur la vie rurale à Anderlecht au moyen age* (pro civitate serie in 8°, 57,) Brussels, 1979, p. 217.

47 *Ibidem*, p. 217.

48 Van Passen, *Wilrijk*, p. 82.

been wealthy, "professional" leaseholders, the lessees of single plots could have been normal tenants, although probably not the poorest.

9.4.1 The Holders of Large Lease Farms

The largest agrarian holdings in western Brabant were generally lease farms. Their size varied but could attain dimensions of 70 hectares or even more. While there were only very few lease farms that reached such dimensions, it is remarkable that there were not many very small farms either. Lease farms smaller than 5 ha were rather exceptional; a major share of the farms we encountered in area of Antwerp contained between 10 and 20 hectares.[49]

Not just anyone was capable of managing such a big agrarian operation. The lease required a base capital to pay for the lease, the necessary livestock and, in many cases, the wages for farmhands, but it also required experience with operating large farms. These preconditions could only have been met by people with a certain background, even if the landowner helped the lessee – especially during the first year of his lease – by handing over fertilised and sown fields, by furnishing most of the necessary tools and a part of the livestock, or even by reducing the lease price during the first year.[50] As we have seen, the lease price for a farm was normally mixed. Generally speaking, the fields were for the most part paid in grain whereas the lease for the meadows was paid in money. The exact amounts and proportions differed from case to case, which makes it very difficult to calculate an average price.

The leaseholders of large farms therefore have to be sought among the rural upper class, among fief holders or great tenants. According to G. Sivery, for example, the farmers of large-lease farms in Hainaut were richer than any of the tenant farmers and even some of the noblemen.[51] P. Hoppenbrouwers identified the earliest leaseholders in the Land van Heusden, situated on the border between Brabant and Holland, as members of the local elite, who often held local offices such as alderman and "*drossart*".[52] Most historians dealing with Brabant also tend to agree with this opinion. H.P.H. Jansen, who studied the area of 's Hertogenbosch, F. Daelemans in his studies on the Grimbegen area and F. Nooyens in a study of the village of Deurne, near Antwerp, all found that a significant part of local officeholders were among the lessees of large farms in each case.[53] In some cases, there were also family ties between the owner and lessee of a farm. Peter van Loocke, for example, who leased a farm of 48 *bunders* in Hemiksem in 1450, was explicitly referred to as a brother-in-law of the owner, Gielis Sanders.[54] Furthermore, it seems that members of the same families often leased the most important farms in a particular area. In Wilrijk, the leaseholders of large farms belonged to a small number of families. The Van Perke, Bal and Boode families held various large farms over the course of very long periods.[55]

49 For a more detailed analysis of farm sizes, see Chapter 5 on agrarian production and productivity.

50 F. Daelemans, "Peiling naar de evolutie van de landbouw te Grimbergen aan de hand van enkele pachtcontracten (13e-18e eeuw)" in: *Eigen Schoon en de Brabander* 11-12 (1971), p. 421, refers to Slicher van Bath, *Agrarische geschiedenis*, Lindemans, *Belgische Landbouw*, I, pp. 208–238, and Jansen, *Landbouwpacht*, pp. 50 and 71f.

51 G. Sivery, *Structures*, p. 635.

52 P. Hoppenbrouwers, *Middeleeuwse samenleving*, p. 423.

53 Jansen, *Landbouwpacht*, p. 71, Daelemans, "Peiling", pp. 424–426, Nooyens, *Deurne*, p. 457.

54 Antwerp, SAA, SR 43, fo. 87r.

55 Van Passen, *Wilrijk*, pp. 68–82 and 644-672.

9.4.2 The Leaseholders of Individual Parcels

The farms on what once had been the reserves of the large-scale landlords were not the only type of leased goods. Also single parcels of land and meadow were frequently leased out. For the leaseholders of these plots, the lease situation was different from that of a whole farm. As the average size of these plots was much smaller, they came within the reach of a different group of tenants. On the one hand, the lease price was lower, which made the lease of single plot or a number of plots more easily accessible to tenants who could not afford to lease a whole farm. Second, it offered the holders of relatively small and mid-sized farms the chance to integrate the leased plot into their own holding temporarily. In that way, they could adapt the size of their holding to their needs and productive capacities. This helped the owners of mid-sized farms to achieve a high flexibility and productivity. Together with a higher resistance against fluctuations of the market, P. Hoppenbrouwers especially points to the factor of cyclical needs in function of the family life cycle, as Chayanov has suggested. The lease of some extra land helped to compensate for the divergence between the farm size and the family size at a given moment.[56]

The size of the leased-out parcels was considerably smaller than that of lease farms. Normally they ranged from 1 to 5 hectares. They were less subject to *morcellement* than copyhold tenures, however. Leased plots of less than 0.5 hectare – a rather common size for tenant holdings – were exceptional, probably because of the technical problems that could arise from leasing out and collecting the lease for these micro-parcels.[57] The leaseholders of these plots were therefore typically the holders of mid-sized tenures, rather than the minor cottagers who prevailed among the copyhold tenants. For the latter, the lease of a plot more than twice the size of their own holding was in most cases too expensive and too risky.

9.4.3 The Price of Leased Goods

The price for a leased plot of land or farm could vary strongly from case to case. They could be fixed as a certain amount of money, a certain number of goods, or a mixture of both. The most frequent leases in kind were payable in grain: rye, oats, and sometimes also wheat.

In most cases, the leases of farms were payable in kind and in money. In 1450, for example, The lessee of the Ter Biest farm in St. Laureis Hove had to pay the owner, the St. Elisabeth hospital of Antwerp, 14 *zisters* of rye, 3 *zisters* of wheat and 12 *zisters* of rough oats for the fields, along with 24 *Reynaldus* guilders, 14 "precious" capons, 7 hens, 14 pounds of butter, 100 eggs and 4 pounds in Brabantine *grooten*.[58]

The complex composition of lease prices for farms, like that for the Ter Biest farm, makes it difficult to conclude anything about the absolute amounts or the proportions between the different parts kinds of payment. These depended on various factors, such as the size of the plot, the percentage of farmland and grassland, the agrarian potential of the farm in question and the specific needs of the lessor. To obtain a more detailed impression of

56 Hoppenbrouwers, *Middeleeuwse samenleving*, p. 422.

57 A sample of lease contracts from the Antwerp aldermen's registers refers to plots between 0.6 and 9.2 ha; SAA, SR 43 and Nooyens, *Deurne*, vol. I, p. 426. Single plots leased out by the abbey of Groot Bijgaarden ranged from 0.7 ha to 3.54 ha; ARA, KA no. 8108. See also: Thoen, *Landbouweconomie*, p. 869.

58 SAA, SR, 43, fo. 433v.-434r, 18 Dec. 1450.

the leases for entire farms and isolated plots, we made a list of the leases of 23 farms and 35 single plots situated in different villages near Antwerp (Table 15). Where the size of a farm is indicated in the contract, we can roughly calculate the lease per *bunder* or hectare, although the complicated composition of the leases, including different types of money and various sorts of grains, makes this a rather daunting endeavour.[59]

As in the case of the Ter Biest farm, the leases of fields were paid in most cases in grain, while those for meadows were paid in money and sometimes some other products. The leases of all but one of the farms in the list were payable with a combination of a certain amount of money and a certain amount of grain and other agrarian products. Despite the great differences in terms of the amounts specified in the contracts, we can still discern a general pattern. The payments in money varied in most cases from 0.15 to 0.5 pounds Brabantine *grooten* per hectare.[60] Considering that lease payments in money generally only pertained to the meadows, they will have only corresponded with part of the total farm size. The actual proportion between land and meadows is indicated only in one example: the Kampdonk farm in Deurne, which held 20 *bunders* of farmland and 9 *bunders* of meadows. Generally speaking, we can calculate the meadows as making up one-third to one-fourth of the total farm size.[61] We can therefore estimate the average lease price to have been 0.77 pound (factor 3) or 1 pound (factor 4) per hectare of meadow.

While leases on meadows that were part of an entire farm were paid in money, the farmland of a lease farm was generally paid for in grain: either rye (10 out of 22 cases) or oats, or else a combination of rye and oats or rye, oats and wheat. In the surroundings of Antwerp, the average lease price of arable farmland was ca. 0.7 *zisters* (ca. 230 litres[62]) of grain per hectare. For leases payable in rye, the amount ranged from 0.35 to 0.8 *zisters* (i.e. 107.8–264.4 litres) per hectare, whereas leases payments consisting of rye and oats were higher, ranging from 1 to 2 *zisters*, mostly composed of equal parts of rye and oats (i.e. 334–668 litres). Payments in other products, like capons, butter or flax, were very frequent but insignificant in comparison with the payments in grain and money.[63]

In contrast to the situation for entire farms, the leases of single plots of land were composed only of one or two types of payment: mostly money for meadows and rye for land. This makes them easier to calculate than the farm leases. For the Antwerp area, we have only few such cases within our sample: The leases expressed in money ranged from 0.25 to 0.5 pounds. Only one plot, situated near the city gates of Antwerp, was more expensive. The lessee of this parcel, a certain Wouter de Vos, had to pay 6 pounds 12 shillings Brabantine *grooten* for 0.84 hectares of land, a house and an orchard

59 We decided to calculate the amounts in the original measures, because this helps to find out about an eventual systematic. Figures calculated in litres per hectare are highly theoretic and far from the reality as perceived by the people involved. In order to allow comparison, however we also added the figures in litres per hectare.

60 Only one lease was considerably lower. Two values could not be calculated because of their uncommon currency (old *Reynaldus* guilders and Arnhem guilders, both of which were issued in Guelders and had variable values). See: H. ENNO VAN GELDER, "Eastern Netherlands" in MAYHEW, *et al.*, Coinage in the Low Countries (880-1500). Oxford Symposium on Coinage and Monetary History; 3, Oxford, 1979 (BAR international series, 54), pp. 203-215.

61 On the proportion of arable land to meadows, see Chapter 5.

62 An exact calculation is difficult here, because rye and oats were measured in different units: one Antwerp *zister* of rye = 308 litres, while one Antwerp *zister* of oats = 360 litres. See: VAN DER WEE, *Growth*, vol. I, p. 98, VANDEWALLE, *Oude maten*, p. 53.

63 A closer analysis of the different products with which leases had to be paid can be found in Chapter 5.

outside St. George's gate, which amounts to 7.8 pounds per hectare.[64] Payments in grain were made exclusively in rye: The holder of the two plots in Deurne paid 0.7 and 1.14 *zisters* (215.6 and 351.1 litres) per hectare, respectively.

Table 15: Average Leases per Hectare in the Area of Antwerp

	Min.–Max.
1. Farms	
Meadows	0.77–1 pounds Brab. Gr.
Fields	308–348 litres of grain
2. Individual plots of land	
	0.25–0.5 pounds Brab. Gr.

These lease prices were significantly higher than those for comparable plots held in copyhold (i.e. 14 to 21 pennies Brabantine *grooten* or 0.06–0.08 pounds, or 50–150 litres per *bunder*,[65] although the land rent of some isolated plots nearly reached the level of the price of leased goods. The price in grain was between four and six times higher than the land rent for plots in copyhold, while leases in money were up to 16 times higher than the average land rent. The strong difference between the land rents payable in kind and those payable in money may have been due to the long-term devaluation of land rents paid in money, which did not affect the rents payable in kind.

The holdings of the Brabantine tenants differed considerably. Some tenures were as large as 15 *bunders*, while others consisted only of a small house. Among the holders of large tenures, we find some of the same individuals and institutions we encountered earlier as landlords. Similarly, in the category of the mid-sized holdings, we find the same group of townsmen and noblemen as among the landlords, but also some richer local peasants. Only in the categories of the small and very small tenures did the local peasants predominate. The feudal tenures were held by the same members of the local upper class who held the mid-sized tenures. The fact that there were many non-peasants among the tenure holders suggests that the overall proportion of leasehold must have been considerable. This is already the case if we simply exclude members of the gentry, patricians and institutions (who are identifiable) as direct users of their tenures. If we also consider that many holders of several tenures or fiefs sublet one of their holdings, we can estimate the proportion to have been even higher. Nevertheless, most of the tenants held very small holdings with less

64 SAA, SR 43, fo. 84.

65 ARA, Rk. no. 45583, fos. 1r-13v, Aartselaar, ca. 1440-1460, no. 44914, fo. 17ff. Merchtem and Zemst, and 44830, fos. 73r- 76r.

than two hectares and can therefore be considered cottars with little potential to produce a significant agrarian surplus.

CHAPTER 10

ANTWERP AND THE PROPERTY RELATIONS IN ITS SURROUNDINGS DURING THE SIXTEENTH CENTURY

10.1 Introduction

During the period between 1450 and ca. 1570, the property relations in the surroundings of Antwerp underwent considerable modifications. Not only did the demographic changes during that period lead to important internal changes within the local communities, but the rise of the metropolis also had a strong impact on rural property relations. The presence of a numerous bourgeoisie eager to invest in land was a specific feature of metropolitan hinterlands such as our research area. As one of the major commercial centres of Europe, sixteenth-century Antwerp was home to thousands of merchants. Together with other wealthy inhabitants, they formed the basis for an exceptional concentration of capital within the town. They invested not only in trade and financial transactions, but also to a remarkable degree in real estate. Indeed, according to the lists of the 100th-penny tax of 1569, 76.5% of all the taxed wealth of the city derived from real estate.[1] Besides investing in houses, warehouses, and other buildings in the town, merchants also bought landed property in the countryside. In so doing, they would influence the rural land market as well as the property relations in the surroundings of Antwerp.

The first section of this chapter is dedicated to an analysis of the composition and dimensions of the landed property of the Antwerp merchants. The second section will focus on the role of Antwerp citizens in the rural land market, concentrating especially on the real estate transactions pertaining to the surroundings of the town as recorded in the registers of the Antwerp aldermen. Finally, to discover how the urban-owned landed property affected the rural property relations, the tax lists of a sample of villages situated nearby Antwerp will be subjected to closer investigation.

10.2 The Landed Property of Antwerp Merchants in the Countryside

The composition of landed property in the hands of townsmen had changed considerably between the early fifteenth century and the sixteenth century. While landed property of Antwerpers had been characterised by smallholdings and a high degree of self-exploitation around 1400, holdings were larger and were generally leased in the sixteenth century.[2] As H. Soly has shown, the richest merchants of Antwerp had holdings of more than hundred hectares. Some outstanding figures even held considerably more. Vincent de Smit,

---

1 M. A. ARNOULD, "L'impot sur le capital en Belgique au XVIe siècle" in *Le Hainaut économique* 1(1946), pp. 17–45, cited in SOLY, *Betrayal*, p. 33.

2 Cf. Chapter 2. See also: DE NAVE, *Antwerpen*, passim. In more general terms, see for example: VAN BAVEL, *Transitie*, p. 400.

the richest merchant of Antwerp in 1574 had no less than 298 ha of landed property at his death, for example. Jacob de la Faille and the Spaniard Fernando de Bernuy the Elder, each even held 360 ha.[3] The list of Antwerp merchants with large amounts of landed property contains many more examples. In 1574, for instance, François van der Cruyce, the second richest merchant after Vincent de Smit, was the owner of a considerable estate south of Antwerp, including five farms with a total estimated size of 200–250 hectares[4] in Boechout, a farm of 14 *bunders* (18.2 ha) in Lint[5] and a farm of 28 *bunders* (36.5 ha) in Hove.[6] The renowned Italian banker and merchant Giancarlo dell'Affaitadi can also be counted among the large landowners. In 1535 he bought the *Hof van Zelzate* farm in Wommelgem, comprising no less than 60 *bunders* (78 ha), from the noble Van Berchem family[7] and later a farm of 38 *bunders* (50 ha) in Kontich.[8] Finally, one of his kinsmen, Gianbattista dell'Affaitadi, bought the *Buysegem* farm in Edegem for 2800 guilders in 1556.[9]

10.2.1 The Motives for Buying Land

The motives for Antwerp merchants to buy landed property have been discussed in depth by H. Soly.[10] He underlines the practical character of the purchases in particular, such as security, a regular source of income, and especially the credit function, or as R. Gascon succinctly puts it: "security, consideration, pleasure, and profits".[11] It is especially the credit function that Soly stresses, as he is less concerned with those aspects having to do specifically with agrarian property. Nevertheless, he convincingly shows that safety and a regular source income were the prevailing motives here too. In some cases, profits made through speculation on agrarian prices also played a role. Various examples of merchants investing in the reclamation of polders north of Antwerp – in Zeeland and Holland – illustrate this point.[12]

There are no indications that townsmen directly intervened with the production process on their farms, however. On the contrary, the few contracts concerning farms belonging to large-scale merchants seem rather conventional, with minimal attention for controlling the production of the farms. As examples, we can refer to the contracts concerning two farms of Fernando de Bernuy – whom we mentioned as one of the leading landowners among the Antwerp merchants – situated in Wilrijk and Stabroek. These contracts contain no particular passages concerning new crops or specialisation, nor do they specify which crops the farmers had to cultivate. The lease was due in cash and, for one of the farms, partly in rye. The farmers had to respect the farm-law, but were not otherwise limited by any particular regulations. The only thing that might have increased agrarian

3 Soly, *Urbanisme*, pp. 60–64. For Jacob de la Faille, see also: W. Brulez, *Della Faille*, pp. 190–192.
4 RAA, old communal archives of Boechout, no. 93.
5 This farm was purchased in 1578.
6 SAA, SR 262, fo. 195r (Verstrepen no. 147) 16-3-1557 (n. st).
7 SAA, Coll 3, fo. 263r. See also: J. Denucé, *Inventaire des Affaitadi, banquiers italiens a Anvers de l'annee 1568*, Antwerp, 1934, p. 70.
8 SAA, SR 277, fo. 277r.
9 SAA, SR 272, fo. 351r.
10 Soly, "Betrayal", passim. See also: Idem, *Urbanisme*, passim.
11 Gascon, *Grand commerce*, p. 812.
12 Soly, *Urbanisme*, pp. 68–69.

productivity was the fact that Bernuy left the dung of his horses to the lessee as fertiliser. His only particular concern was his orchard: he obliged the lessee to maintain it and to plant cherry, apple and pear trees.[13] It is therefore likely that the popularity of such treatises as Constantin Cesar's *De re Agricultura* and Charles Etienne's *Agriculture et maisons rustiques* among Antwerp merchants who had landed property in the countryside had less to do with any goal of intensifying agriculture than with an interest in nature and the establishment of gardens and orchards.[14] This would imply that the new and innovative techniques, the revolutionary systems of field rotation and the use of clover on the holdings of Antwerp merchants as noticed by travellers such as Richard Weston in the middle of the seventeenth century were thus the result of more recent innovations or, better yet, improvements of existing techniques.[15]

A point that has not yet been discussed in the literature on the landed property of townsmen in the surroundings of Antwerp is the importance of the various incomes in kind and their function within the income policy of the landowners. Although leases and other forms of land rent were increasingly payable in money, an important share of the payments was still due in kind. In a number of villages near Antwerp for which we can calculate the value of the leases in kind using the registers of the 100th-penny tax of 1569-70, the value of leases payable in grain constituted up to 30-40% of the total lease value.[16]

The landlords' motives for demanding part of the lease to be paid in kind could have been of a different nature. On the one hand, leases paid in kind formed a supply of food and hence made the owner of a farm independent of the market for a considerable share of his food provision. This objective can be recognised in contracts specifying the delivery of a broad range of foodstuffs and other farm products. The Antwerp patrician Aart Schoyt, for example, leased out a farm in Wijnegem in 1532 and required the farmer to pay – together with 28 Carolus guilders in money – 12 *zister* of rye, a fat lamb and 12 lb. of butter, and furthermore to deliver a certain amount of firewood to the owner's house in Antwerp. Sharecropping, although becoming outdated in the sixteenth century, was another way of providing food for the owner's household.[17] The Antwerp alderman Hendrik van Berchem was still leasing out his farm in Wommelgem in that way in 1522. The farmer had to keep his landlord's sheep and pigs and deliver one fat lamb for each feast day. He also had to provide peat and firewood for the owner's household.[18]

Most leases in kind were to be paid in rye, however, which was not the typical bread grain for the rich bourgeoisie. This shows that the urban landowners had also other purposes in owning land besides providing themselves with food. In contrast to money, rye was not subject to inflation. Leases payable in rye were therefore safe sources of income that even

13 SAA, Coll. 3 fo. 175r (Elsdonk farm, Wilrijk, 1529), SAA, Coll. 3 fo. 182r (Farm in Stabroek, 1529).

14 Baetens, *Villa rustica*, pp. 184–185.

15 R. Weston, *A discours of Husbandrie used in Brabant and Flanders shewing the wonderfull improvement of Land there, and serving as a pattern for our practice in this commonwhealth*, London, William Du-Gard, 1650.

16 In Boechout, this was 27.3%, in Edegem: 33.4% and in Schoten: 32.1%. In Duffel ter-Elst, on the other hand, the proportion was not less than 47.7%. This result was obtained by multiplying the quantity of grain by the Antwerp rye price of 1569/70, as published in Van der Wee, *Growth*, vol. I, Appendix 1, pp. 176–178. Given the fact that rye made up ca. 90% of the leases payable in grain and that the higher price of wheat would be partially equalised by the lower price of oats, this does not seem to distort the percentage noticeably.

17 Over the disappearance of sharecropping from the fifteenth century on, see Chapter 4.

18 SAA, Coll 3, fo. 63r.

offered possibilities of profits in years of dearth. By combining leases in kind with leases in money, the lessor combined a safe income in kind with the advantages of a payment in ready cash. The extent to which the lease payments consisted of money, rye or other sorts of farm products thus depended on the economic situation or the individual needs of the lessor.

That there were also reasons of prestige and leisure, in addition to the more practical reasons for townsmen to own land, is shown by the large number of country residences that they bought. Merchants, officials, clergymen and even craftsmen retired to their country house during summer or for the weekend and dedicated themselves to hunting, playing or going on excursions through the countryside. At the same time, a sumptuous country house was a symbol of prestige and power.

10.2.2 Types of Holdings

The holdings of these exceptionally rich merchants consisted to a remarkable extent of farms, some of which were quite large. In many cases they held a country residence or a *hof van plaisantie* (i.e. pleasance) together with the farm. R. Baetens has identified not less than 251 of such country residences and villas in the greater surroundings of the town for the second half of the sixteenth century.[19] This also gives an indication of the quantitative dimensions of the holdings of townsmen in the countryside. If one considers that the majority of these country houses made up part of a considerable landed property, it does not seem exaggerated to multiply this number by 10 ha in order to approximate the total size of the holdings, including a country house, which can thus be estimated to exceed 2500 ha.

The farms were generally leased out in temporary lease, as the numerous copies of the lease contracts in the registers of the Antwerp aldermen show. In some cases, however, farms and country houses were given out in hereditary lease instead, that is, for an unlimited period and for a fixed yearly rent.[20]

Besides farms and country houses, polder land was another preferred investment object for Antwerp merchants. Already in 1522, the Florentine Medici family held great properties in Kallo and Kieldrecht on the left bank of the Scheldt that they sold for 1500 pounds Flemish *grooten* to Jan Wyts, the dikegrave of Flanders.[21] Merchants from Antwerp invested in land reclamation projects in the polders along the estuary of the river Scheldt as well as in Zeeland and Holland. Indeed, 62 of the landowners on the island of South Beveland in Zeeland could be identified as inhabitants of Antwerp. Among them were the Antwerp representatives of some of the leading Southern German firms such as the Rehlinger brothers, Meuting and Ehem, Lorenz Tucher and several Portuguese and Italian merchants, as well as renowned entrepreneurs such as Gerard Grammaye, Erasmus Schets and Arnold Pruynen.[22] Woodlands were another characteristic type of property that Antwerp citizens chose. Especially the area

19 R. Baetens, La "Bellezza" et la "Magnificenza". Symboles du pouvoir de la villa rustica dans la region anversoise aux temps modernes, "in R. Baetens and B. Blondé (eds.), *Nouvelles approches concernant la culture de l'habitat / New approaches to living patterns. International Colloquium 24-25 October 1989*, University of Antwerp, Antwerp 1990, pp. 162–166. See also: R. Baetens, La villa rustica" in *Aspetti della vita economica medievale*, pp. 171–191.

20 For example, the merchant Jan de Greve gave a small farm of half a *bunder* to Jeronimus Rombouts in hereditary lease in 1556; SAA, SR 26O 77* 1O2v (Verstrepen).

21 SAA, Coll. 3, fo. 77r (1500 pounds Flemish *grooten* = 2250 pounds Brabantine *grooten*).

22 Soly, *Urbanisme*, pp. 68–69, and R. Baetens, De reacties van Antwerpen op de stormvloeden van 1530 en 1532 in Zeeland" in *Onder de koepel van het Pantheon. Liber Amicorum Jacques Claes*, Kapellen, 1994, p. 252.

around Niel and Schelle on the banks of the Scheldt was a major focus in this regard, but there were also significant plots of woodland in Merksem and Schoten, northeast of the town.[23]

The purchase of manors or seigniorial rights was another common form of investment among the richest Antwerp merchants during the second half of the sixteenth century. There was a small group of prominent individuals among them who manifested their wealth and social position by buying a seigneurie. Around 1500, a large share of the manors in the surroundings of Antwerp was still in the hands of noblemen or members of the gentry. A small group of members of the court nobility had accumulated considerable complexes of manors in Brabant. Among them were the count of Nassau, who held the title of margrave of Antwerp, lord of Breda, Steenbergen, Grimbergen and Rumst; Jan de Glymes, lord of Bergen of Zoom, Grimbergen, Essen, Kalmthout, Merxem and Schoten; and Antoine de Lalaing, count of Hoogstraten, lord of Ekeren, Minderhout and Rijkevorsel.

Only in the 1540s did prominent Antwerp merchants obtain seigniorial rights in the surroundings of the metropolis. The first of these was Erasmus Schets, the entrepreneur and royal councillor, who bought the manor of Grobbendonk, situated ca. 25 km east of Antwerp, in 1545. Another merchant banker with connections at court, Caspar Ducci, followed his example in the same year by purchasing the seigneurie of Hoboken.[24] Another merchant-landlord was Paul van Dale, a grain-importer and owner of sugar plantations in the Canaries, who became lord and dikegrave of Lillo and dikegrave of Berendrecht in 1554.[25] Likewise, Gerard Sterck became lord of Wijnegem and Antonio del Rio became lord of Aartselaar in 1556 and 1557, respectively.

As a result of the financial troubles of Philip II, a whole series of seigneuries and other parts of the ducal domain was given to officials, merchants and noblemen between 1559 and 1561 in return for financial support.[26] During these sales of parts of the ducal domain, many Antwerp merchants became owners of a seigneurie. The above-mentioned Paul van Dale was one of them. He became lord of Berendrecht and Stabroek in 1560, although he was ruined after the second Spanish bankruptcy in 1579.[27] Other merchants who became seigneurs in that period were the cloth merchant François Schot, who became lord of Aartselaar, Kontich, Reet and Waarloos; Gerard Grammaye, who bought the manors of Schoten and 's Gravenwezel; and the building entrepreneur Jacob van Hencxthoven, who bought the manor of Hemiksem, where he owned a number of brickovens.[28] Erasmus Schets' three eldest sons would also become holders of different manors in the 1560s. His eldest son, Caspar, inherited the seigneurie of Grobbendonk; the second, Melchior, accumulated a large number of manors in the Scheldt-Rupel area, among which Rumst, Boom and Willebroeck;[29] and the third, Balthasar, purchased the seigneurie of Hoboken.[30]

23 Gillis Hoofdman owned large forests in Niel and Schelle, while Vincent de Smit had 7.5 ha of woodland in Merksem. Soly, *Urbanisme*, pp. 61 and 66.

24 Soly, *Urbanisme*, p. 70.

25 F. Prims, "Polderstudies: Wilmarsdonk Dalenhof" in *Antwerpiensia 1950 (21e reeks)* Antwerpen, 1951, pp. 65–68; p. 67 and F. Donet, Les Anversois aux Canaries" in *Bulletin de la Société de Géographie d'Anvers*, 20, 1896, p. 235f.

26 Baelde, *Financiële politiek*, passim. Galesloot, *Inventaire*, passim.

27 Galesloot, *Inventaire* vol. I, pp. 72–73.

28 ARA, Rk. Reg. 11912, Account of the ducal domain the Land van Mechelen 1569/70, fo. 4, Soly, *Urbanisme*, pp. 70, 191, 247, 333.

29 H.L.V. de Groote, "De vermogensbalans van Melchior Schets en zij vrouw Anna van Stralen met hun testament van 1 juli 1596" in *Bijdragen tot de Geschiedenis* 55 (1972), p. 233.

30 See Verstrepen no. 654 (1562).

Individual plots of farmland and meadows were less frequent than entire farms, country houses, polders, manors and seigniorial rights among the holdings of the large-scale merchants. This does not mean that they did not buy such plots, but their aim was rather to assemble a coherent demesne around a country house or farm. A very good illustration of this strategy is to be found in a document concerning a holding of Fernando Bernuy the Elder in Oorderen. In 1522, he bought a complex of 37 ha of land in Oorderen, including a country house, from the widow Margriet Sgroten. That same year, he also began to buy numerous single plots from different owners to enhance his holding there. By 1539, he had thus increased his property in Oorderen by 34 plots with a combined size of 58 ha. Together with the 37 ha from the original purchase, this gave him no less than 95 ha.[31] We can observe a similar tactic for enlarging one's demesne in the case of another merchant, François van der Cruyce. In 1563, he bought from Balthasar Schets a small plot of land in Hove and a farm of 5 *bunders* in Boechout, both situated next to his own property, as well as two more *bunders* of land in the latter place. In 1565, he bought two more plots in Hove from the merchant Ambrosio de Sardis and another small parcel in Boechout.[32]

This strategy of assembling large domains by purchasing numerous adjoining plots of land had an impact on the farm size and, as a result, on the productivity of the farms in question. The lessees of these farms could profit from economies of scale, for example in the use of hauling animals and farm-gear. On the other hand, it was especially through these systematic purchases of small plots of farmland that the land-holding peasantry was affected by the real-estate policy of the urban merchants. In contrast to large farms, which were generally the property of the gentry or ecclesiastical institutions, these smaller plots had typically been the holdings of peasants.

10.2.3 The Location of the Holdings

The geographical spread of the landed property of Antwerp citizens expanded dramatically in the sixteenth century. The location of the holdings of the 18 prominent Antwerp merchants that H. Soly analysed differed in a major respect from that of townsmen in the fifteenth century. In addition to sites in the immediate radius of 10 to 15 km from Antwerp, as in the previous century, they were now largely situated in the polders along the Scheldt, up to 50 km from Antwerp, and even beyond, in Zeeland and Holland. The largest holdings in the sixteenth century were situated north of Antwerp: Merxem, Schoten and Ekeren were among the favourite places for merchants to buy land (see Map 10). The geographical distribution of the landed property of 21 Antwerp citizens that was confiscated for religious reasons in 1569 confirms this pattern. Here, too, the largest holdings lay north of the town, especially in Merxem, Lillo and Zandvliet (Map 11).[33]

31 SAA, VG 2, Aldermen's document from 10 Nov. 1563.

32 SAA, SR, fo. 329r Verstrepen, vol. 7 no. 767) (939* 247v) (977* 2O3r)

33 ARA, Raad van Beroerte no. 164. See also M. Limberger, "Merchant Capitalism and the countryside: Antwerp and the west of the duchy of Brabant - (XVth - XVIth centuries)" in Hoppenbrouwers and van Zanden, (eds.), *Peasants into Farmers?* pp. 158–178.

MAP 10: Landed Property of 18 Prominent Merchants during the Sixteenth Century (hectares)

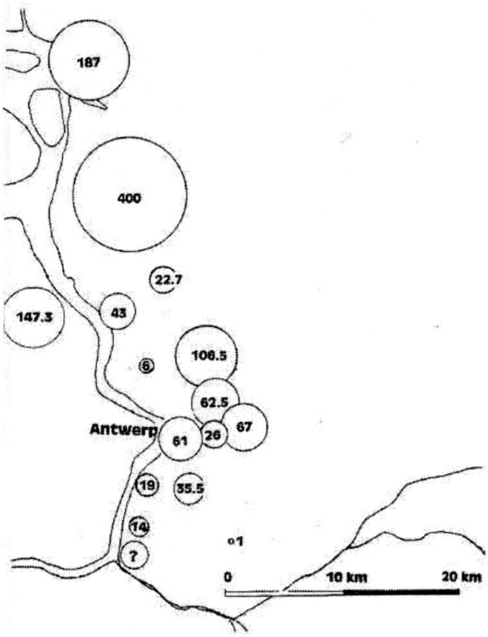

SOURCE: Soly, Urbanisme en kapitalisme.

MAP 11: Confiscated Landed Property of 21 Antwerp Citizens, 1569 (hectares)

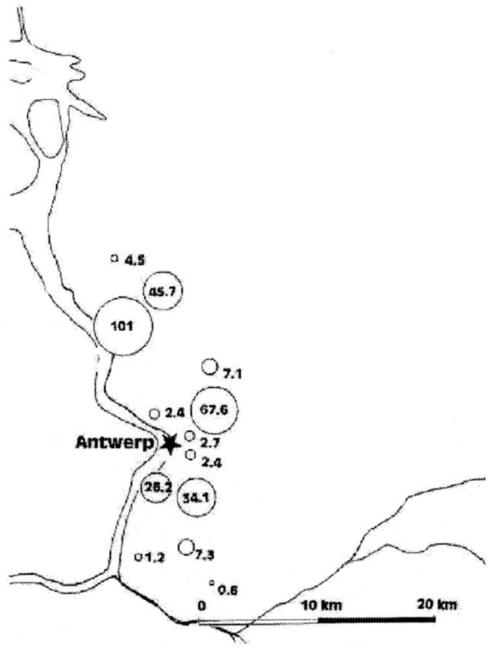

SOURCE: Brussels, ARA, Raad van beroerten nr. 164.

The geographical spread of the country residences of Antwerp townsmen, as mapped by Baetens, also fits with this picture, with the exception of the polder area, where few country houses were built.[34] The relatively weak expansion of landed property south of Antwerp might be explained by the small scale of the holdings that were available and the fierce competition for land in this area. This may have discouraged merchants from buying land there, despite the high productivity of the land. In comparison, large estates were relatively readily available in the polder area and in the less densely populated areas north of Antwerp.[35] Another reason is the close proximity of other significant towns in the south, Lier and Mechelen, which also claimed a share of the land in their surroundings. Indeed, The major purchases of land in the ducal domain the Land van Mechelen, situated between Antwerp and Mechelen, in the first half of the sixteenth century were not made by Antwerp citizens but by a merchant from Mechelen, Cornelis Scadt, who bought two large farms in Putte and Zellaer in 1523 with a total value of 6000 Guilders. No comparable purchases were made by Antwerp merchants in the same area.[36] An analysis of the registers of the Antwerp aldermen concerning real-estate transactions in the area between Antwerp, Lier and Mechelen between 1556 and 1564 actually reveals the presence of townsmen from the latter two towns in the nearby villages. Their number was relatively limited in comparison with that of Antwerp citizens, however. Parties identified as coming from Mechelen were involved in only nine out of over one thousand transactions; in only eight of the transactions was one of the parties unquestionably from Lier. In contrast, Antwerp citizens were involved in at least about 10% of all those transactions.[37]

10.3 Inhabitants of Antwerp on the Rural Land Market

Population density and a high proportion of peasant-owned property, as well as the demand for property among the citizens of other nearby towns may have formed a barrier for Antwerp townsmen that prevented them from acquiring landed property on a large scale, at least while alternatives like the polders and the sparsely populated Campine were available. Nevertheless, the phenomenon of urban participation in the rural land market was by no means limited to the purchase of large domains and country houses by a limited number of wealthy merchants. These prominent figures, well known from the historical literature, merely formed the top of a large group of townsmen who bought landed property in the surroundings of the town. The registers of the Antwerp aldermen contain hundreds of records concerning such transactions. The sheer number of records – the registers contain several thousands of records per year – precludes a systematic analysis. Even so, the collections of individual deeds in the aldermen's registers in the National Archives in Antwerp and in the Antwerp City Archives' "Collectanea" form samples that are relatively easily accessible via analytical inventories. Furthermore, abstracts have been made of the documents of aldermen

34 Baetens, *Bellezza*, pp. 162–166.

35 Limberger, "Merchant Capitalism", p. 172.

36 ARA, Rk. Reg. No. 11904, Account Land van Mechelen 1522/23. Cornelis Schat is mentioned in 1525 as companion of the Antwerp merchants Jan Mertens and Willem de Greve in Strieder, *Notariatsarchive*, p. 12, no. 2.

37 Inhabitants from Lier held property in Boechout (3 items), Kessel, Kontich (2) and Lint (1); inhabitants from Mechelen had holdings in Onze-Lieve-Vrouw-Waver, Putte, Duffel, Reet (2), Rumst, Kontich, in the environs of Lier and even in Wilrijk. Verstrepen, vol. 7, passim. For the proportion of inhabitants of Antwerp in real-estate transactions, see the following sections.

concerning a number of villages south of Antwerp.[38] With these abstracts, we can get a sense of the relative importance of the merchants they mention in terms of the role played on the land market in the surroundings of the town on one hand, while on the other we can sketch a profile of the other townsmen who were investing in land. A major difficulty concerning the second point is that in contrast to the well-known merchants, the middling Antwerp inhabitants can hardly be distinguished from people of the countryside. The documents seldom specify the occupation or place of residence. Indeed, in the large majority of cases, they do not.

A survey of these lists shows that merchants were only one of the groups that bought land. In the first two decades of the sixteenth century, the real estate transactions of townsmen were rather modest. Merchants and artisans mainly bought annuities on rural properties but hardly any large landed property. Most of the substantial transactions concerning farms and larger rural holdings involved Antwerp patricians such as Frank van Halen, Aart de Buekelaar, Gomaer van de Werve and Hendrik van Berchem.[39] Although merchants would become increasingly important in the following decades, the Antwerp patricians continued to play an important role throughout the sixteenth century. Like the wealthiest merchants, they owned large farms and woods, and they were even more likely to own manors in the surrounding countryside.[40]

It is only from the 1520s on that we are more apt to encounter merchants, including many foreigners, being involved in larger real-estate transactions in the surroundings of the town. In 1520, for example, Antonio del Vaille bought the castle of Boechout.[41] It was also in that period that the above-mentioned Fernando de Bernuy began to accumulate landed properties in the Antwerp environs: in 1525, he bought the 26-*bunder* Elsdonk farm in Wilrijk, and in 1529, he was mentioned as the owner of a 36-hectare farm in Stabroek.[42] In the following decades, townsmen frequently bought, exchanged and resold landed property that commonly contained farms of considerable size.

Most of them were merchants, but many artisans were also involved. In contrast to merchants, craftsmen in many cases had specific needs in terms of landed property: butchers needed pasture for their livestock, bakers and brewers may have needed farmland for their own grain supply, etc.[43] A specific example of people with particular economic needs were building entrepreneurs such as Jacob van Henxthoven or Gilbert van Schoonbeke, who owned brick-ovens along the Scheldt for a supply of bricks for their building activities[44].

Besides dell' Affaitadi and Van der Cruyce mentioned above, most of the the townsmen – presumably from Antwerp – mentioned in the registers of the Antwerp aldermen from 1556 and 1557 as landowners in the area south of the town were merchants,

---

38 BETERAMS, *Antwerpse schepenbrieven op het Antwerpse Rijksarchief,* Ch. VERSTREPEN, *Antwerpse schepenbrieven betreffende de dorpen van de Rupelstreek,* 1556 -1565 (SAA, SR nos 258 through 305). Brussels, 1996. The author was so kind as to let me use a disk with the text that facilitated the analysis of this volume.

39 BETERAMS, *Schepenbrieven*, nos. 295, 307, SAA Coll. 3, fos. 35v, 63r.

40 Within the sample of lease contracts of farms that we analysed in Chapter 6, for example, are a considerable number that belonged to members of the Antwerp patriciate.

41 R. BAETENS, La "villa rustica", phénomène italien dans le paysage brabançon au 16ème siècle" in *Aspetti della vita economica medievale: atti del Convegno di studi nel 10 anniversario della morte di Federigo Melis*, Firenze-Pisa-Prato, 10-14 marzo1984, Firenze, 1985, p. 177.

42 SAA, Coll. 3, fo. 182r; Coll. 4, fo. 48v.

43 DE VRIES, *Dutch*, p. 43.

44 See section 7.3.2.

although other professions are also represented. Among the merchants were Matteo de Sardis (ca. 1.25 *bunders* in Hove), Geronimo de la Croix (a farm of 13 *b.* in Aartselaar), Martin Hureau (a farm in Ranst), Jan de Greve (a small farm in Mortsel), Karel Crol (a barn and two houses at "Het Kiel", outside Antwerp), Joos Caluwaert (a house in Schelle with 3 *b.*) and Francois van Wezembeek (4 *b.* land in Hove). In contrast, Jan vanden Broecke, who owned two farms in Aartselaar and Kontich with 24 and 23 *bunders*, respectively, and an inn with land in Aartselaar, was a sugar-boiler. Aart Wils (a farm of 18 *b.* in Niel) was a mason, Claas van Asse (a hayfield in Ekeren) was a "printer", and Geleyn Asseliers (1.5 *b.* of woods in Aartselaar) was a former alderman of the city.[45]

At first sight, the presence of Antwerpers on the rural land market was not overwhelming. The deeds in the registers of the aldermen do not give us the impression that merchants drove the peasants off their holdings by buying the land. After all, only ca. 10% of the transactions concerned townsmen. Even so, this relatively low rate of participation does not mean that the role of townsmen was insignificant in the rural land market. On the one hand, the dimensions of the holdings they bought were large in comparison with those transferred among tenants. On the other hand, there was a major difference between transactions made between local tenants and the purchases made by townsmen. In the first case the land stayed in the hands of the local community and hence remained peasant property, while land that was bought by townsmen was generally lost to the local peasantry, only becoming available to them in the form of a leasehold.

The other parties involved were local tenants, members of the gentry, rural entrepreneurs and some outsiders from more distant places. A group that played a leading role among them was the local elite of fief holders and large tenants. Some of the outstanding families among them were the Bals in Niel, Schelle and Aartselaar, the Van Horcks in Boechout, Hove and Borsbeek, the Van Loocks in Aartselaar and Wilrijk, and the Nulaets in Duffel and Rumst. Members of these families, which were interrelated through marriage, frequently figured as aldermen, members of the local feudal court, etc. They were also the main actors on the local land market. Many transactions apparently took place within kinship groups and professional groups, between neighbours or through other social ties.[46] This is also how many townsmen entered the rural land market. A document from 1561 reflects the complex character of these connections: Geert Wils sold his son Aart, a mason and a citizen of Antwerp, a brick-oven in Hoboken, which he had received as part of an inheritance from his neighbour – and probably kinsman – Gillis Colaes. The holding was charged with two annuities: one payable to Nicolas Felbier and the other to Lijsbeth Pluym, a member of a local brick-makers family.[47] Large farms, the preferred type of property, normally belonged to the traditional great landowners, that is, urban patricians, the gentry, ecclesiastical institutions or the local elites. It was from them that merchants

45 SAA, SR 258-266 (Verstrepen, *Schepenbrieven*, vol. 7, nos. 1-286).

46 It would be interesting to analyse the transfers of landed property within the local population in order to see the role of the local elites on the land market. This would require a thorough prosopographical analysis, however, which would go beyond the scope of this study.

47 "*Gheert Wils heeft vercocht aen Aerd Wils zyn sone een steengeleeghe mette gronde ende toebehoorten gelegen te Herbeke onder de prochie van Hoboken O Adriaen Colaes Z Gillis Colaes erve W aen t'schelt N des voors Antonis Wils ander erve welcke steengeleghe hem comparant op 1-9-1546 tegens Gillis Colaes in scheidinge ende deilinge aengecomen en ten deele bevallen is te warene 4 carolus gulden erf. Nicolaes Felbier en 2 carolus gulden erf. Lysbeth Pluyms*' (SAA, SR 286, fo. 441v, 18 Nov. 1561 = *Verstrepen*, *Schepenbrieven*, vol. 7, no. 631).

bought the greatest share of their landed property. Once established in a place, they often bought smaller plots in the surroundings to complete their holdings. We therefore have to understand the eventual conquest of the countryside by Antwerp merchants as a gradual process rather than the result of a sudden rush.

A phenomenon that helped this transfer of landed property from the local population to urban citizens were annuities, the so-called "*erfelijke renten*" or "*rentes constituées*".[48] Looking through the lists of the Antwerp aldermen, the great number of transactions concerning the sale of annuities is striking. About 50% of all documents concern these hypothecary loans, or mortgages, and the creditor was a townsman in a large share of the cases. This percentage is exceptionally high in comparison with other areas. For rural France, for example, J. Jacquart has estimated that ca. 10% was the average share.[49] While merchants were predominant among the buyers of farms and land in the Antwerp area, the buyers of annuities had all kinds of professions: butchers, weavers, fishmongers, boatmen, goldsmiths, gardeners, etc. Many of them probably did not have the means for large investments but would have had some spare guilders to invest in an annuity. On the other hand, anyone who held a plot of land, regardless of the juridical terms, could use it as a pledge for a loan. Hence, small tenants could borrow some guilders from a grain merchant in exchange for a yearly fee, but large landowners in need of ready cash could do that as well. As a result of this increasing indebtedness of the landowners, many holdings in the surroundings of Antwerp were pledged with a whole number of annuities. Already in the 1520s, half of the goods that figured in the aldermen's documents preserved in the National Archives were mortgaged with one or more annuities: one plot of land even had thirteen, one farm had five, another had four. Others were described as already being heavily mortgaged *("reeds sterk gehypotekeerd")*.[50] Out of 17 holdings in the 1550s, one was pledged once, three with two annuities, three with three, and one with five. One document from 1556 concerning the *Te Broeckhoven* farm in Brecht contains a list of no less than 23 creditors to whom the owner had to pay annuities.[51] In the event of a series of bad harvests, a war or other unfavourable conditions, the debtor could easily have been incapable of paying all these annuities. The high degree of indebtedness therefore often resulted in the owners being forced to sell their holding to one of their creditors, a large share of which were townsmen. Accumulated debts and arrears hence led to alienation, while for the creditors it brought about the capitalisation of their money, the conquest of landed property and social promotion, as has J. Jacquart summarised the mechanism that led to the transfer of landed property from the local peasantry to the urban merchant class.[52] This mechanism was not particular to the area of Antwerp, but its dimensions there during the sixteenth century were exceptional.

48 In general terms, see: B. SCHNAPPER, *Les rentes au XVIe siècle, Histoire d'un instrument de crédit,* Paris, 1957. For the Antwerp context, see: SOLY, *Urbanisme*, pp. 54–59 and LIMBERGER, "Credit".

49 J. JACQUART, *L'endettement paysan et le crédit dans le campagnes*, p. 288.

50 BETERAMS, *Schepenbrieven*, pp. 58–64, nos. 336-370.

51 Ibidem, pp. 83–92, nos. 479-543; for the Te Broeckhoven farm, see p. 89, no. 523.

52 J. JACQUART, *Endettement*, p. 297.

10.4 The Result of the Conquest: The Property Relations in Four Villages in 1569/70

The analysis of the individual purchases of land by townsmen, as well as the comparison with those made by other social groups has helped us to distinguish the sort of properties the townsmen bought, their location and to some extent the way the townsmen acted on the real estate market. Via these sources, however, we could not quantify the absolute and relative dimensions of all the land that townsmen as a group held. Urban landownership could have far-reaching implications for the rural economy of the surroundings of a town. It could lead to new forms of exploitation, changes in the farm size and indirectly also to a stronger market integration of agriculture, commercialisation and specialisation.[53] These changes depended, first of all, on the extent of urban landownership. Only if that attained significant dimensions could it have significant consequences on the property structures and hence the agrarian structures of the surrounding countryside.

10.4.1 The Registers of the 100th-Penny Tax of 1569/70

We can best assess the consequences of the purchases of land that townsmen made in the rural surroundings of Antwerp by means of an overview of the property relations in the second half of the sixteenth century. The most useful source for such an overview are the 100th-penny tax registers from 1569/70, which were drawn up in every village of the Low Countries and which list all immovable goods, together with their owner and leaseholder. To levy this tax, local authorities estimated the value of the properties together with experts.[54] This excellent source therefore enables us to study the distribution of landed property within each village, the farm sizes and the proportion of goods in temporary lease.[55]

The registers also had their its limitations and disadvantages, however. To begin with, they only reflect the situation at one particular moment: the years 1569/70, immediately prior to the Dutch Revolt. The situation at that moment was already being influenced by political unrest, confiscations, etc., which makes this period less than ideal for studying the situation during the economic boom of the sixteenth century, which by then had almost reached its end. Another disadvantage of the registers concerns their reliability. Like all fiscal documents, they were subject to fraud and gaps in the information they contained. Controls were very severe, however, as documents surviving alongside the tax registers prove: owners or lessees who failed to declare a holding or who declared a falsified value were fined four times the original amount.[56] Hence, we can assume that fraud will have only taken place on a limited scale. The fact that the registers were not always complete is also a problem. The exemption of certain groups may have been a relatively insignificant factor in this case:

53 These changes are discussed in De Vries, *Dutch*, pp. 43–46, Van Bavel, *Transitie*, pp. 368–371. Wrigley, *Simple model*, passim, also refers to the importance of urban landed landownership.

54 Arnould, "Impot", p. 11. The original text of the ordinance is edited in F.M. Grapperhaus, *Alva en de tiende penning*, [s.l.] 1982, pp. 341–361.

55 For a general evaluation of this source, see: N. Maddens, "Zestiende-eeuwse fiskale bronnen ter bestudering van de sociaal-economische toestanden op het Vlaamse platteland" in *Historie economique de la Belgique*, pp. 21–30.

56 For example, Peter Verberth had to pay a fine of 51 pounds 4 shillings (4 x 12 pounds 16 s.) for the park in Hoboken that he had leased from Costen van Halmale because he had not declared it in the original register. ARA Aud. 618 /1 (Hoboken, quadrupel).

only the royal domain, the properties of some privileged individuals, a few so-called *terres franches* (franchised lands), churches and abbeys (but not their landed property), castles that were not leased out, and the communal land were exempt.[57] Finally, the registers also could be incomplete in other ways. While the taxation officers were very strict as far as the estimated value of the holdings was concerned, the precise size was not always indicated. As a result, many landowners declared only the lease value of their farms, but not the size. This lack could be overcome by calculating an estimated size through analogous lease prices.

A final disadvantage of the tax registers is that most of those pertaining to the surroundings of Antwerp are lost. Only two useful documents remain in the archives of the central administration in Brussels: those concerning the villages of Schoten and Onze-Lieve-Vrouw-Waver.[58] The latter is situated 20 km from Antwerp and belonged more to Mechelen's sphere of influence. In community archives and other local archives, however, we were able to retrieve three more registers concerning villages in the surroundings of Antwerp: Edegem, Boechout, and Duffel ter-Elst. While Edegem and Boechout, situated ca. 10 km southeast of Antwerp, were predominantly agrarian, Duffel ter-Elst – the part of Duffel that belonged to the abbey of Tongerlo – is interesting because of the proto-industrial character of the village. Schoten, Edegem and Boechout therefore form a small but convenient sample for the closer surroundings of Antwerp, while Duffel ter-Elst can serve as a control sample on one hand and as an example of the indirect influence of Antwerp via proto-industrial activities on the other hand. Unfortunately, the villages immediately adjoining Antwerp are not covered by this sample.[59]

10.4.2 The Social Distribution of Landed Property

There was a very similar pattern to the distribution of the landed property in three of the four villages we analysed. There was a strong concentration of land ownership at the top of the social hierarchy, while the distribution was relatively even among the lower classes. In Schoten, Boechout and Duffel ter-Elst, the richest 10% of the landowners held no less than 60 to 65% of the land, whereas 50% of the small landowners had a combined share of no more than 9 to 10% – in Schoten it did not even exceed 7.5%. The only village that clearly did not follow this pattern was Edegem. There, the accumulation at the top was far less accentuated than in the other places: the top 10% owned 40% of the land. At the lower end of the hierarchy, the share of the small landholders was slightly higher than it was in the other places.

As in the fifteenth century, we find mainly abbeys and other ecclesiastical institutions at the top of the hierarchy. The ecclesiastical institutions therefore retained the position they had held in the late Middle Ages as the major landowner. In Schoten and Duffel ter-Elst, where the abbeys of Villers and Tongerlo moreover held part of the manorial rights, such institutions prevailed among the landowners, with almost 52% and 45% of the landed property, respectively. This predominance was due almost exclusively to the large properties

57 ARNOULD, "Impot", pp. 26–31.

58 ARA, Aud. 618/1. See also: VAN DER WEE, *Growth*, vol. I, p. 509, Appendix 42/2.

59 The register of Berchem, for example, which J.B. STOCKMANS mentions – without providing a precise reference – in his *Geschiedenis van Berchem* from 1886 (p. 15), has been searched for in vain. It seems to have disappeared in the meantime.

of the two ecclesiastical landlords. Villers owned no less than 354.5 *bunders* (460.85 ha.) or 42% of the total area of Schoten. Similarly, the abbey of Tongerlo held 91.75 *bunders* or 40% of the total area of Duffel ter-Elst. While there were numerous other institutions in both villages, these all held much smaller properties. In Schoten, the Beguines of Antwerp had a farm of 22.5 *bunders* and the chantry of Our Lady had 7 *bunders* of land in small plots, but the holdings of the other fourteen institutions with landed property were insignificant in size. In Duffel, the parish church, with its 2 *bunders* of land and meadow, was the only institution besides Tongerlo that held any property worth mentioning (graph 8).

Graph 8: Distribution of Land by Social Group, 1570

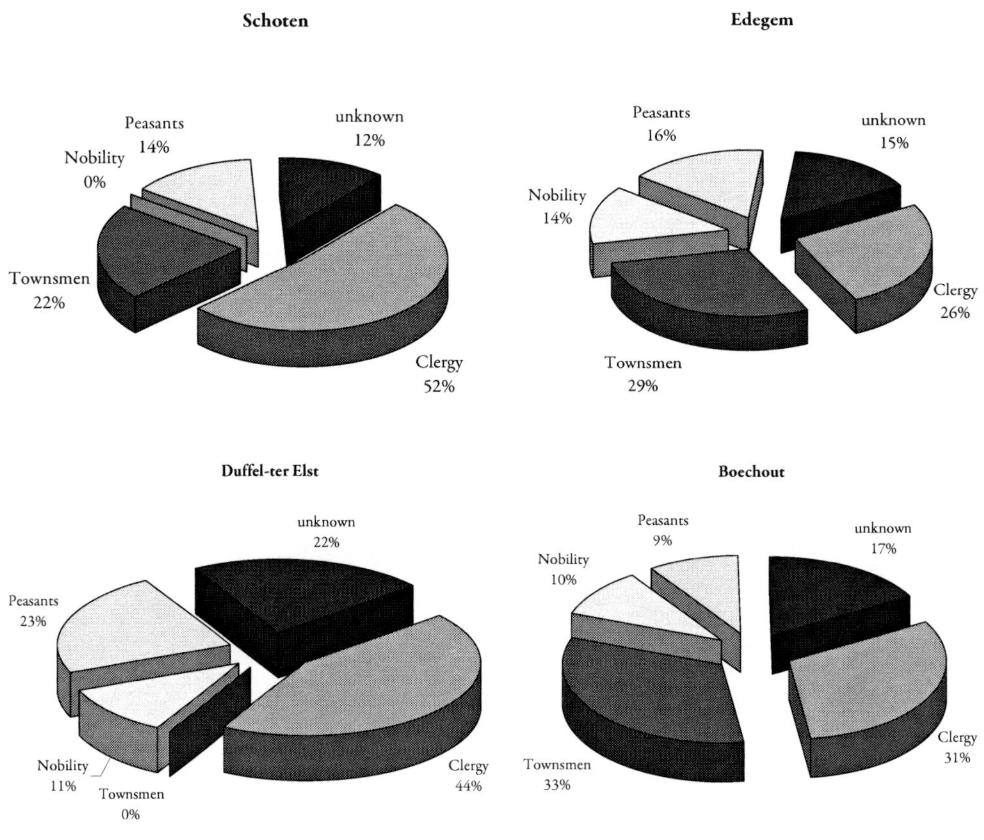

Sources: ARA, Aud. no. 618 /1, SAA, VG, no.14, RAA, OG Boechout, no. 93.

In the other villages, the predominance of the large ecclesiastical landowners was less pronounced. In Boechout, the abbey of St. Bavo in Ghent was only the second largest landowner, its four large farms and a mill comprising 158 *bunders* or 19% of the village area. St. Bavo was followed immediately by another major ecclesiastical landowner, the abbey of St. Bernard in Hemiksem. The latter held two farms with an estimated total size of 55 *bunders*. The rest of the 26 institutions with property in Boechout, nine of which were based in Antwerp, five in Lier and five in Boechout itself, had much smaller holdings.

The distribution of the property among the different social groups was most even in Edegem. There was no predominance of a single institution or individual. The Commandery of Pitsemburg in Mechelen, belonging to the Teutonic Order, held 39 *bunders*, which was only a few *bunders* more than the second, third and fourth largest landowners there: the Antwerp lawyer Gielis Gerardi, Willem van Immerseel and the St. Elisabeth hospital, respectively. Consequently, the ecclesiastical institutions' share in the total landed property was only 26%. The group with the largest share were the townsmen, who held 28.5% of the land.

In general, the proportion of land belonging to townsmen was almost as high as that belonging to ecclesiastical institutions. According to the tax rolls, their share varied between 22% in Schoten and 33% in Boechout. This is comparable to the figures for Holland at the beginning of the sixteenth century.[60] Nevertheless, we have to take into account that the proportion of landed property in Holland increased further during the sixteenth and seventeenth centuries, and that the surroundings of Antwerp form a much smaller research area than the province of Holland. However, if we keep in mind that these numbers include only those individuals who are clearly identified in the sources as coming from Antwerp, the actual share of the townsmen must have been notably higher.

In fact, a whole group of landowners remains unidentified in terms of being either townsmen or locals. Only four townsmen, all of them named in the tax roll of Boechout, were identified as such through explicit references to the town from which they came. Only two of them came from Antwerp: "seigneur Doncker, canon in Antwerp", and "*Master* Seger 's Hertogs, notary in Antwerp". The two others came from Lier and Breda, respectively. The term "master" (*meester*) referred to people with an university degree, which in effect is an indirect way of identifying townsmen, albeit without reference to the specific town: in total, 11 people were described in this way. Finally, a third method of identifying landowners as townsmen is via secondary literature and other sources. While a considerable number of rich merchants, members of the town magistrate and other prominent persons could be identified in this way, this method is not exhaustive and will always leave room for doubts. The results thus obtained probably understate the real number of townsmen. Many of the unidentified persons may have been townsmen, but unfortunately there is no criterion distinguishing them from inhabitants from other places. If the numbers of positively identified townsmen are therefore minimum numbers, the maximum numbers can be obtained by simply adding the unidentified persons to the group of townsmen. In the case of Duffel, for example, none of the landowners could actually be identified as townsman. Not only was no one explicitly mentioned as coming from Antwerp, Mechelen or Lier, but our knowledge of the names of citizens from Lier and Mechelen was also insufficient for recognising individuals via the literature as we could for many Antwerp merchants. While some of the non-residents were probably citizens of Lier or Mechelen, there was no group of substantial merchants or patricians buying land in great quantities in Duffel, as we have seen in the case of Schoten or Edgem. The richest merchant we could identify was Matheus

60 J. de Vries, & A.M. van der Woude, *Nederland 1500-1815, De eerste ronde van moderne economische groei, Amsterdam, 1995*, p. 611, cited " in Van Bavel, *Transitie en continuïteit*, p. 386.

van den Steene, a cloth merchant from Duffel. Another cloth merchant was Cornelis Crets, who figures in the tax register as the owner of two houses.

In Schoten, the townsmen's share of the landed property was about 22%. Among them were the merchants Diego de Ayala, Peter van Coppemaal and Jan vander Eggen, the wine merchant's widow Catarina Schuurmans, and members of ancient Antwerp families, such as Peter van Cantelbeke, Martin van Ranst and Adrian van Zevendonk.[61] Moreover, the lord of Schoten and Rumst, Melchior Schets, and his brother Coenrad can be considered as Antwerpers, although I listed them under members of the gentry, because they had been knighted shortly before.[62] By adding the Schets brothers and half of the unidentified persons, this percentage would reach ca. 30%, which is still far below the share of the ecclesiastical institutions. The tax rolls also confirm what we said about the types of landed property that townsmen preferred. They owned primarily large and medium-sized farms and woods. Some of them had also country residences, which were exempted from taxation.

In Boechout and Edegem, townsmen held the largest share of the landed property. In Boechout, the largest landowner was the above-mentioned Antwerp merchant Francois vanden Cruyce, whose five farms and an independent plot of land will have comprised about 183 *bunders* or 22% of the total village area. In total, twelve owners of land in Boechout could be identified as inhabitants of Antwerp. Among those were the merchants Cosimo dell' Affaitadi and Francois Schot, as well as the members of the town magistrate: Jan vander Meere, Jacob vander Heyden and the heirs of Jan vander Rijt. Some of them owned farms of up to 30 *bunders*, although none of their holdings compared with that of Vanden Cruyce. Together, their share in the landed property was ca. 33%.

In Edegem, the urban landowners were not so much merchants, but rather patricians and high officials. Master Willem van Immerseel, who owned a country house with a garden, a large farm, and a tithe, was a descendant of a noble Antwerp family for example, while Cornelis van Mechelen, esquire, who owned 21.5 *bunders* of land in separate plots, belonged to the Antwerp patriciate. Among the officials, Cardinal Granvelle, a member of the central government and the owner of a 26-*bunder* farm, was the most famous. Master Peter van der Noot was also important as a member of the Council of Brabant and as lord of Watermaal, near Brussels. Van der Noot's property was untypical. Instead of having just one or few large holdings, he held thirteen individual plots of farmland, meadows and wood, with a total size of ca. 14 *bunders*. Other officials were the lawyer Gielis Gerardi and the secretary of Antwerp Frederik Steudelin.[63] Gerardi was the second greatest landowner with his four farms and a country house with garden, with a total size of 30 *bunders*. Taken together, the total share of townsmen in the landed property of Edegem was 28.5%.

A group whose share was equally weak in all four villages was the gentry. As discussed in Chapter 8, the boundary between the gentry and the urban patriciate is difficult to draw. The scion of a noble family, Martin van Ranst was called *meester* in the tax roll of Schoten, for example, while the Van Mechelen brothers, likewise members of the Antwerp patriciate with properties in Edegem, bore the title "esquire". The same difficulty exists for the merchants and other townsmen who became lords of a village and were therefore titled

61 Most of these persons are identified in Baetens, *Schoten*, pp. 6–9 and 97–107.

62 See Marnef, *Antwerp*, p. 16.

63 Van Passen, *Edegem*, pp. 120–128.

heer in the registers, as in the case of Francois Schot or the Schets brothers. Even if they were also in fact townsmen, we counted all knights, seigneurs (*heren)* and esquires (*jonkers*) among the gentry. Their share in the total landed property varied between 6.15% in Duffel ter Elst and 13.2% in Edegem.

The weak position of the gentry and the almost total absence of the nobility among the landowners are striking. While it is possible that this is the consequence of their having been exempt from the tax, only very few privileged individuals were subject to such an exemption according to the ordinance itself. Moreover, some particularly privileged personalities were actually included among the taxpayers, such as the Cardinal Granvelle or Willem van Merode, lord of Duffel.

The absence of nobility and gentry in the tax roll could also be the result of the increasing presence of townsmen among the landowners in the Antwerp surroundings. As we have shown in the previous sections, the great merchants were especially interested in large demesnes, including castles and country houses, which they often bought from noblemen or members of the gentry. It is also true that the landed property of the nobility proved to be already relatively limited in the fifteenth century. This means that the weak position of the gentry and nobility among the landowners of the Antwerp countryside didn't have to be the result of any recent development. The purchases of land by the Antwerp bourgeoisie will nonetheless have further diminished their presence.

Finally, the rest of the land, was held by inhabitants of the villages themselves. The tax rolls do not explicitly indicate whether or not a person was an inhabitant. We therefore had to deduce their status from whether or not they were the immediate holders of one of the taxed houses or farms of the village. The term "inhabitant", as we use it in this analysis, therefore includes people who either leased a farm or a house or who owned one without leasing it out. Thus defined, the inhabitants made up 40-60% of the total number of landowners, but their share in the total village area was only 15-20%. Only about 10% of them, three or five persons per village, had property of more than 5 *bunders*, the size of a full-size farm.

This group of wealthy inhabitants was the largest in Schoten, with six persons or 14% of the local landowning population. Some of them even owned more than one farm, working one of the farms themselves and leasing out the others, which were usually relatively small. Abraham de Knaepe, the greatest landowner from Schoten, had two mid-sized farms of 6 and 5 *bunders*, for example, one of which he held himself, while he leased out the other. Another wealthy inhabitant of Schoten was Jan Gijsels, owner of the inn called "The Crown" at the main square of the village, four houses and some barns. The Gijsels seem to have been one of the richest families of Schoten. Besides Jan, there were two other members with considerable landed property: Peter, the owner of a farm of 6 *bunders*, and Jacob, who owned a smaller farm of 2.5 *bunders*.

In the other villages, the number of residents who owned large farms was smaller. In Edegem, for example, there was only one: Peter Backaerts, who apparently worked his farm of 15 *bunders* himself. In Boechout, two inhabitants had property of more than 5 *bunders*: Jan de Winter, whose farm had ca. 18.5 *bunders* of land, and Jan Hendricx, who owned 6.75 *bunders*. The position of both these men within the village community can only be understood if one also considers the properties they held in lease, however. Indeed, Jan de

Winter was not only the owner of a farm of significant size in Boechout, but he was in the first place the lessee of that village's largest farm, comprising 50 *bunders*, which was the property of the abbey of St. Bavo in Ghent. Jan Hendrickx, for his part, was lessee of the windmill that belonged to the same abbey.

Clearly, then, the group of local tenants who held landed property of more than 5 *bunders* was very limited. Indeed, the great majority of the inhabitants of the villages had less than 5 *bunders*. The percentage of owners of small farms with one to 5 *bunders* differed between Schoten and Boechout, on one hand and Edegem, on the other. Some 35% of the local population had landed property of between 1 and 5 *bunders* in Schoten and Boechout while in Edegem nearly 50% had such holdings. In contrast, this group of small peasants was almost absent in the weavers' village of Duffel, where only 14% of the local population of landowners had between 1 and 5 *bunders* of land. There, the majority (82%) had even less than 1 *bunder* of land. These were generally the owners of a house with a garden, and occasionally some separate plots of land. In Schoten, this group of essentially landless labourers made up 56%, in Boechout 58%, and in Edegem 40% of the people mentioned as owning land. These cottars could not live exclusively from their holding, but were dependent on wage labour, weaving (particularly in Duffel), or leasehold. In the following section we will investigate on the role that leased farms and farmland played in the agrarian economy of the villages of our sample.

10.4.3 The Distribution of Land among the Local Farmers and Tenants

While the landed property of great landowners could comprise hundreds of *bunders*, the tenants who worked their own lands had to make do with considerably less. In practice, however, the holdings of the large landowners consisted of various individual farms that were leased out and hence available to the local tenants. Indeed, the individual farms formed the basic units of agrarian operations. The size of the farms, their price and their availability were decisive for the farmers and the landowning tenants in terms of their farming activities. In what follows, we will therefore be looking at the distribution of the farm size in the above-mentioned villages, as well as at the social distribution within the local populations. Graph 9 shows the distribution of the farm size in the four villages of our sample, enhanced with data for Onze-Lieve-Vrouw-Waver that H. van der Wee has collected.[64] These five villages had one general feature in common: the fact that the very small holdings of less than 1 *bunder* of land (which cannot be considered as full-size farms, but rather as cottages), made up for ca. 40-50% of the total number of holdings. The share of large farms of more than 10 *bunders* differed between the villages in the closer surroundings of Antwerp on one hand and the two villages situated further to the south on the other. While the share of farms larger than 10 *bunders* was higher than 13% in Schoten, Edegem and Boechout, it was less than 9% in the other two villages.

64 Van der Wee, *The Growth*, vol. I, p. 509, Appendix 42/2.

GRAPH 9: Distribution of Farm-Size, 1570

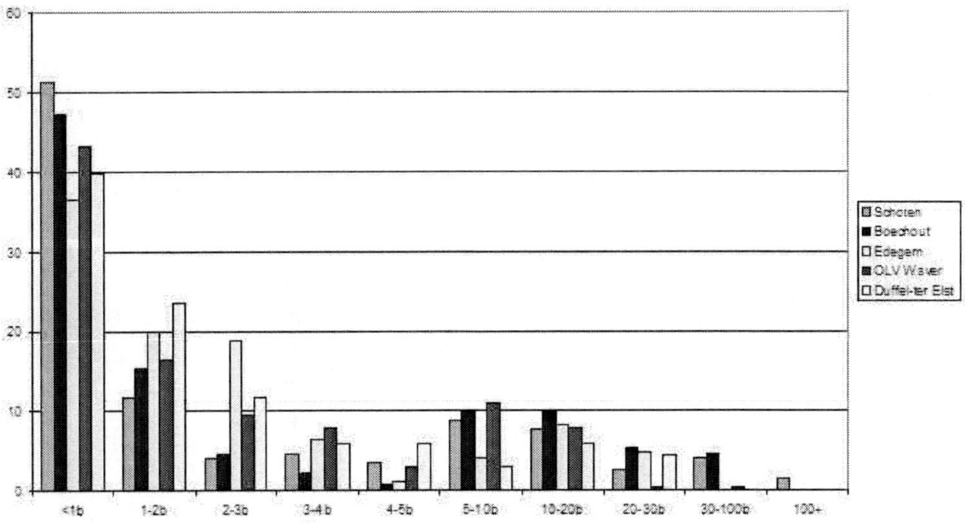

SOURCES: ARA, Aud. no. 618 /1, SAA, VG, no.14, RAA, OG Boechout, no. 93.

Beneath these general patterns, there were some significant differences between the individual villages. Schoten had the greatest polarisation between very large farms and very small holdings. It had three farms with more than 100 *bunders* and eight that were larger than 30 *bunders*, while more than 50% of the holdings were smaller than 1 *bunder*. In contrast to these extremes, the proportion of the small and mid-sized farms was very low, especially in comparison with the other villages. In particular, farms between 1 and 4 *bunders* were underrepresented.

In Boechout, too, the polarisation between large farms and smallholdings was strong, although there was a major difference with the situation in Schoten. The share of very small holdings was also high, with 41% of the total for Boechout. The share of the large farms, the so-called *hoeven*, was the greatest of all five villages, with 39 farms or 30% of all holdings. While there were no extremely large farms as in Schoten, five farms were larger than 30 *bunders*. But it was the farms of between 5 and 30 *bunders* that were the most numerous in comparison with the other villages. A category that was especially well represented there was that of farms between 5 and 10 *bunders*. In contrast, holdings of between 1 and 3 *bunders*, the typical small farms, were not very frequent, although still a bit more common than in Schoten.

In contrast, the very small holdings with less than 1 *bunder* were relatively less important in Edegem and Duffel ter-Elst than they were in Schoten and Boechout. Both villages had a considerable number of small farms with 1 to 3 *bunders*, while the largest farms did not exceed the 30 *bunders*. In Edegem, small farms of between 2 and 3 *bunders* were particularly frequent, while in Duffel ter-Elst, the share of the holdings of less than 2 *bunders* predominated. Hence, while there was a great polarisation of farm size between large farms and very small holdings in Schoten and Boechout, the proportion of small farms of between 1 and 3 *bunders* was relatively high in Edegem and Duffel ter-Elst.

While the number of smallholdings was considerably higher than that of large farms, the share of the land of the different kinds of farms was distributed quite differently. In Schoten, Edegem and Boechout, between 75 and 90% of the land belonged to farms larger than 5 *bunders* (see graph 10). Hence, although the greatest number of farms was small or very small, the greatest share of farmland belonged to large farms. As a result, the economic importance of large lease farms was quite considerable. Farm size was closely related to the method of farming. Small peasant farms were more likely to be labour intensive and capital extensive, while large farms that were worked by means of wage labour tended rather to be labour extensive.[65] This picture of the predominance of large farms confirms the qualitative indications concerning the economic conditions of the Antwerp surroundings around 1570, as presented in the declarations of the village aldermen, which were discussed in Chapter 6.

Graph 10: Distribution of Land by Farmsize

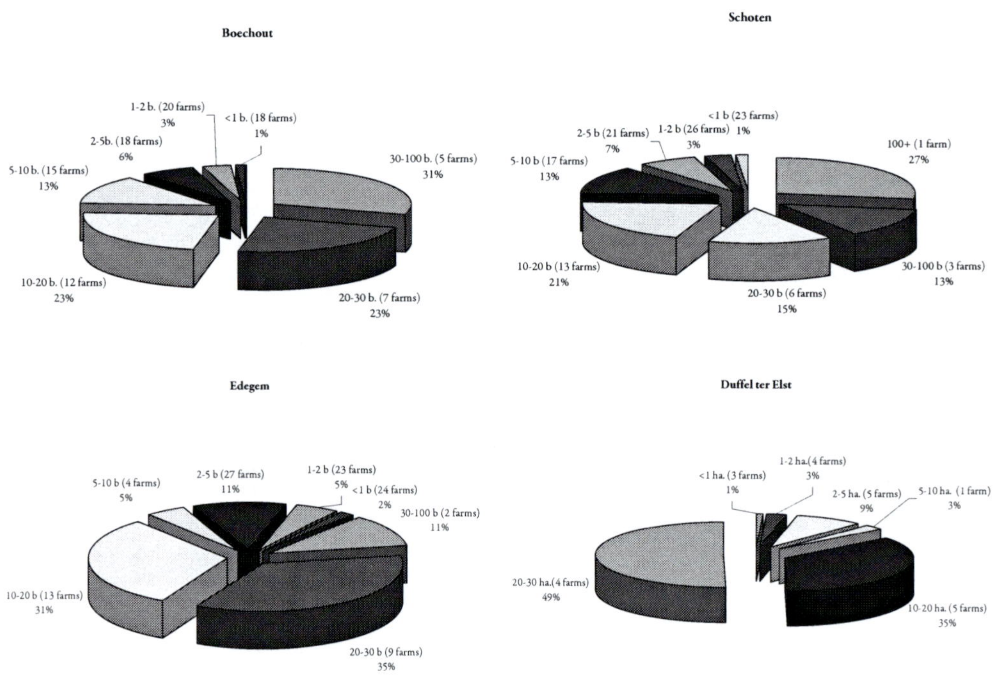

Sources: ARA, Aud. no. 618 /1, SAA, VG, no.14, RAA, OG Boechout, no. 93.

65 Cf. Van Bavel, *Transitie*, pp. 573–619.

The analysis of the distribution of the landed property among the social groups in the previous sections showed that 70-80% of the land was owned by people or institutions from outside the village communities who were not directly involved in the working of the land. Most of this land was leased as separate plots or farms to inhabitants of the villages or to farmers coming from outside the village. Hence, temporary lease was the predominant form of agrarian landholding in all of the villages that we analysed. It was applied, depending on the village, for 70 to 80% of the holdings. In Schoten, 72% of the holdings were lease holdings, and in Edegem and Boechout even 82%. In Duffel, in contrast, the percentage was only ca. 50%. Large and mid-sized farms were almost all leased out; this held to a lesser degree for separate plots and small farms. The typical holding that remained in the hands of the proprietor, on the other hand, was a little house with a garden and hardly any farmland attached to it.

The leaseholders were not necessarily landless. At a closer look, a considerable share of the landowning village population did not work their own land, but rather leased a farm, while at the same time leasing out their own holding. These could be tenants of mid-sized farms or their family who leased one of the large farms of the substantial landowners, but also others who chose for a more fitting farm by leasing it. While in most cases, the tenants leased out their own small farm in order to lease a large one, also the opposite happened: Merten Jacobs, for example, who owned a small farm of 2 *bunders*, leased that out and then leased an even smaller one of 1.25 *bunders* for himself. We can only guess Merten Jacobs' motivation for changing his farm for a smaller one. Maybe it was his age or perhaps his financial or physical capacities were insufficient for maintaining a larger farm.

In any case, the system of temporary lease offered a high degree of flexibility. According to the possibilities of the lessee, he could lease a larger or smaller farm, without having to sell his own property. Temporary lease was therefore not only the form of landholding that prevailed for holdings of non-residents, but also for holdings belonging to local landowners. The de facto distribution of farmland among the agrarian producers was therefore not only determined by their own landed property, but also by size of their holdings in lease. Both factors contributed to the socio-economic position of an individual within the village community.

The lessees of the largest farms often came from outside the village in which the farm was situated. In all four of the villages analysed, some of the largest farms were held by such "outsiders". The other large leaseholders were generally relatively wealthy tenants with mid-sized holdings, or their relatives. If they had a farm of their own, they generally leased out their own holding to a third person. These tenants hence became lessees and lessors at the same time. For example, Peter vanden Wijngaarde, lessee of Cardinal Granvelle's 26-*bunder* farm in Edegem, leased out two small farms of 0.75 and 3 *bunders*, respectively, in the same place. In Schoten, 22 of the lessees of large farms were local tenants or members of a local family, whereas 23 did not own any farm or land within Schoten. Among the local lessees of large farms, three had holdings of more than 4.5 *bunders* themselves and were therefore among the ten tenants with the largest amount of landed property. Another, Willem Brants, lessee of one of the farms of the abbey of Villers, was a relative of the second largest local tenant, Peter Brants, who owned 14.25 *bunders*.

The other major leaseholders were generally owners of 1 or 2 *bunders*. In the other villages, the proportion of the leaseholders of big farms who came from outside the village was a bit lower than half. In Boechout, where there was but little sizeable landed property within the local population, only one of the big leaseholders had a large holding of his own: Jan de Winter, whom we mentioned earlier as the greatest local tenant. The other lessees of large farms had only very modest holdings of their own. The situation was similar In Edegem: only one local leaseholder had a large holding of his own. Two more lessees of large farms apparently had family with considerable property.[66] In Duffel, finally, there were only two lessees of large farms who were among the top rank of the local tenants. Both of them leased their farm from the abbey of Tongerlo.[67]

In contrast to the large farms, the smaller farms were mostly held by lessees without landed property in the village. These may have been inhabitants of surrounding villages or former tenants who had to sell their own property. Among this group, we can distinguish a number of members of local families. These individuals had no holdings themselves, although their respective families were relatively well off. This was for example the case for Gielis Schilleman from Boechout, the lessee of a farm of 2 *bunders*. Although he had no landed property of his own, other tenants called Schilleman held two small farms, a house and some land. Moreover, a certain Lucas Schilleman was the lessee of a 40-*bunder* farm. Some of these members of local families even leased farms from relatives. Similarly, in case of an inheritance shared among several brothers and sisters, one may have leased the farm from the others.[68] There were few lessees of small and mid-sized farms who owned their own farm and leased it out, however.

Owners of small farms probably chose to expand their own holding by leasing additional land instead. In Boechout, this strategy can be observed for various tenants of relatively small farms who obtained considerable holdings by leasing separate plots from different landowners. Michiel van Sent was the most remarkable of these collectors of leased land. He expanded his own holding of ca. 2.5 *bunders* by leasing seven plots of land with a total size of 7 *bunders* and thus obtained a farm of 9.5 *bunders*. Another tenant who extended his holding in that way was Dirk Verstrepen, who initially held a farm of 1.5 *bunders*. He leased four more plots from different owners – mostly from Antwerp – and thus attained a holding of the considerable size of 5.5 *bunders*. Jan van Ganssele had a farm of 2.5 *bunders* and extended his holding to 5.4 *bunders* by leasing three more plots. This strategy was particularly widespread in Boechout, which meant that the proportion of mid-sized farms (of between 5 and 10 *bunders*) was significantly higher there than in the other places of our sample, where it was only the holders of small farms who expanded their holdings with leased plots.

66 Gielis van Campe was the lessee of a 16.5-*bunder* farm and the owner of a meadow of 6 *bunders* that he leased out. Roeland Verbert, lessee of a farm of 21.5 *bunders* of the commandery of Pitsenburg, was probably a relative of the second largest tenant of Edegem, the widow of Hendrik Verbert, owner of a farm with 6.75 *bunders* of land. Peter van Bauwel, lessee of a 24.5-*bunder* farm seems to have been a relative of Hubrecht van Bauwel, owner of 2.5 *bunders* of land.

67 Merten Zomer, the lessee of a farm of 28 *bunders*, had somewhat less than 5 *bunders* of his own, while his relatives Willem and Gerard Zomer owned smaller farms. Hendrik de Grove, who leased a farm of 24 *bunders*, had only half a *bunder* of land of his own. However, the brewer Cornelis the Grove, whom we suppose to be a relative of Hendrik was among the five most highly taxed tenants.

68 In Edegem, for example, the heirs of Anthonis de Vos leased a farm of 1.5 *bunders* to Cornelis de Vos.

As for the very small holdings, i.e. those of less than a *bunder*, these were held by their owners in between one fourth and nearly half of the cases (35% in Boechout, 26% in Edegem and Schoten and 44% in Duffel). The others were leased either from ecclesiastical institutions or from the wealthier local tenants. Townsmen and members of the gentry hardly ever leased out such smallholdings without land. To what extent these very small holdings can even be considered agrarian holdings is difficult to say. The documents distinguish between small farms (*steden*) and houses with gardens. In Edegem and Schoten, about the half the smallholdings were farmlets with some farmland, however tiny. One such farmlet in Edegem was said to have measured 0.025 *bunders* or ca. 325 m^2. In Boechout, on the other hand, 80% of the smallholdings were defined as houses with gardens, although some had some plot of land connected to them. In Duffel, as much as 90% of the very small holdings consisted of such houses without farmland.

We have observed a series of local differences among the villages we considered in the preceding analysis. They seem to have been the result of the prevailing property structures and other local preconditions, in combination with the impact of the expansion of urban landed property. In Schoten, this led to the strongest polarisation between large farms and small peasant holdings. The same tendency can be observed in Boechout, although to a lesser degree. There, many small farmers extended their holdings by leasing additional land and thus attained holdings of a considerable size. The situation in Edegem, located next to Boechout, tended rather towards a multitude of very small farms. In Duffel ter-Elst, a typical weavers-village that was also significantly further away from Antwerp than the other villages that we analysed, the size of farms held by the small tenants was even smaller than those in Edegem. Moreover, a large share of the peasants there held only houses without any farmland.

The foregoing overview shows that the purchases of land made by townsmen had a visible impact on the property structures of the surrounding villages. Around 1570, they held a considerable share of the total landed property: between 20 and 30%. Townsmen, ecclesiastical institutions and the gentry accounted for 80 to 85% of the land, leaving only very little for the local population. As a result, temporary lease became the predominant way of holding land among the local tenants. Temporary lease superseded the traditional forms of landholding, although without replacing them. For the tenants, having now become farmers, this signified a higher land rent (the lease price plus in most cases the original feudal land rent) that could fluctuate according to the market price. Furthermore the farmers ran the risk of losing the farm at the end of the lease period. On the other hand, leasing a farm had the advantage of more flexibility in terms of the adequate farm-size and a reduction in terms of investments in the necessary farm buildings and other infrastructure. Furthermore the lessee could profit from credit facilities consisting mainly in delayed payments of the lease. Hence, Gomaer Seldenslag, the farmer of a 14-*bunder* farm in Kontich, was 248 guilders in arrears in 1561, which was almost the lease of five years. Nevertheless, the owner renewed his lease for another term.[69] Hence, relatively wealthy tenants could afford to lease farms that

69 SAA, SR 286, fo. 107r: "Philippus Michiels coopman verhuurde Gommar Seldenslach x Margriet Noulaets een hoeve met huis groot 14 bunder gestaen onder Contich in diversche perchelen elck jaar elck bunder omme 5 carolus gulden en 10 stuyvers (6-2-1561); and 107v: Gommar Seldenslagh x Margriet Noulaets debent Philippus Michiels x Berbele Hellemans 348 gulden 16 stuyvers ten cause van achterstelle en huere van goederen gelegen oder Contich' (6-2-1561).

far exceeded the dimensions of their own landed property, often by leasing out their own holdings to smaller tenants.

We can therefore pose the question: Who were the losers in terms of the purchases of land made by townsmen? Among the so-called lords, the nobility and the gentry seem to have lost ground in favour of merchants, who bought both seigniorial titles and large landed property, including large country residences and castles. The ecclesiastical institutions, on the other hand, maintained their position quite firmly. Te great abbeys in particular remained the leading landowners in the villages that we analysed. The question is more difficult to answer with regard to the villagers. The local upper class, the greater tenants and those who held small feudal tenures may have lost some of their properties to townsmen, but they still maintained their dominant position within the village both as lessees of the largest farms and as lessors of their own tenures. As farmers, they were employers of landless labourers. As lessors of small and medium-sized farms, on the other hand, they reinforced their role as a local elite, becoming almost like local landlords. They levied leases from those who farmed their holdings and they gave credit to the smaller tenants. In many cases these members of the local upper class might ultimately even buy the farms of the smaller tenants. On the other hand, a large share of the small tenants ended up as small-scale farmers, who either managed to lease enough land to produce a regular surplus or were forced to make a living through wage labour on one of the larger farms or through other types of supplementary income.

Returning to the general question about the extent to which urban capital was able to transform the local property structures, we have the impression that the participation of townsmen on the rural land market caused a significant change in the rural property structures in the closer surroundings of Antwerp. I use the term "impression" cautiously, because of the unstable basis of our knowledge concerning the proportion of leaseholds in the late Middle Ages. This transformation from tenure-holding to temporary lease took place in several stages, however. Large-scale merchants did not primarily buy small farmlets from local peasants. Their main objective to purchase significant holdings, like large farms or even castles with a surrounding park. Small plots might eventually serve to augment their holdings but were not bought for their own appeal. Other townsmen had more modest ambitions, however, and larger tenants sometimes bought smaller farms and separate plots of land. One of the most obvious reasons for tenants to sell their farm was debt. The easy availability of credit, whatever the advantages for the tenants may have been, could easily lead to debts and, in the long run, may have forced many landowners to sell their holdings. Craftsmen from Antwerp, but also a local brewer or baker, could lend money to a tenant in return for an annuity on the latter's farm and even end up buying it.

In terms of economic change, the predominance of lease farming can be seen as an incentive to market-oriented agriculture. Farmers of leasehold farms were exposed to the forces of the market more strongly than landowning peasants. In order to pay their lease in cash, they had to sell part of their surplus at the market. If the lease payments were due in kind, however, they had to produce whichever products the lessor demanded, which in the most cases was rye. This argument applies in principle to all lessees of a farm, hence to ca. 40-50% of the village population. The only ones who were excluded were tenants with their own holding and those who held insufficient land for farming. For large farmers, the wages of their farmhands formed an additional market-dependent factor. On the other hand, the purchase of farms by townsmen provided an investment in agriculture. Farms were mostly leased out with the existing farm buildings, fences, dikes and sluices, whereas the farmer had to provide the livestock, the crops and the farming gear and to pay for the regular repairs.[70] In fact, many farms were enlarged and adapted at the owner's expense during the first half of the sixteenth century.[71] An example of this can be seen in the farm that the chapter of Antwerp's Our Lady cathedral owned in Edegem. The chapter took out a mortgage of 6 guilders in order to repair the farmhouse.[72] Hence, townsmen buying farms contributed a considerable share of the necessary capital for their exploitation. In some cases, the merchants' policy of enlarging their holdings by purchasing adjoining plots had an effect on the size – and thus also the labour productivity – of the farms. At first sight, however, townsmen owning a farm did not stimulate the application of new agrarian techniques or specialisation. Such "top-down" innovation may have occurred in some cases, but at least during the sixteenth century, it had no far-reaching impact on the local agrarian system. Rather, the initiative was generally on the side of the farmers, who were relatively free to apply whatever technique or crop rotation they liked.

70 LINDEMANS, *Landbouw*, vol. I, pp. 214–216 remarks that by the sixteenth century in the province of Brabant and in the Campine, a large part of the farm buildings were the property of the lessor, while in most other parts of Belgium they were the property of the lessee. In the polder area, the farm buildings remained the property of the lessee until the eighteenth century.
71 LINDEMANS, *Landbouw*, I, p. 225.
72 R. VAN PASSEN, *Geschiedenis van Edegem*, p. 140.

Conclusion

Rural Brabant in the Fifteenth Century: A Peasant Economy?

At the end of the Middle Ages, the southern part of the duchy of Brabant was a highly urbanised area with four major urban centres and a number of secondary towns. The ducal residence, Brussels, was the largest with about 33,000 inhabitants, followed by Mechelen, Leuven and Antwerp, each with about 20,000 inhabitants. The population density in the countryside was also extremely high. In fact, the south of Brabant was among the most populated regions in the whole of Europe. This high concentration of people and towns was limited to the southern part of the duchy, however. North of the rivers Rupel and Nete, the population density gradually diminished and was even very low in the northern part where the soil was sandy and navigable rivers were almost absent. Similar differences can be observed in terms of the agrarian system. western Brabant was a very productive farming area with cereal yields that were among the highest in Europe. In fact, agrarian techniques were very advanced in this area, as the analysis of lease contracts has shown.

Antwerp was situated at the margin of this Brabantine core area. Its rise as a commercial centre during the Middle Ages was due to its location on the Scheldt, which made it a river port that was accessible for large sea-going vessels. Large parts of its agrarian hinterland were characterised by sandy soils, however. Only within a small area to the south was the land favourable to intensive husbandry. The polders along the Scheldt to the north of Antwerp served as pasture for cattle, sheep and – especially near the town – oxen.

This geographic duality of the environs of Antwerp is reflected by the internal differences in population density there. South of Antwerp, it was relatively high, while in the sandy Kempen, the average figures were about 20 inhabitants per square kilometre. The agricultural profile of the Antwerp area corresponded with the natural conditions. South of the town, relatively demanding crops such as wheat could be cultivated, and productivity was considerable, though inferior to the area around Brussels. In contrast, to the east and northeast of Antwerp, the farms were worked in extensive husbandry. In fact, the Kempen was a region of extensive sheep farming, and many farms contained large areas covered with heath.

The economic structure of western Brabant was in many respects similar to that of Flanders. Agriculture was based on an intensive but "traditional" farming system of mixed grain and cattle farming, with the addition of some alternative crops. A large share of the peasants held their land in copyhold, whether from the duke, a lay landlord or one of the great abbeys. Lease holding was also a very important form of landholding, however, due to the fact that most ecclesiastical and urban institutions leased out much of their property and a considerable group of individual landowners sublet their holdings. Peasants were either the owners of mid-sized farms or smallholdings or they were leaseholders. Between half and two-thirds of the peasants held less than 2 *bunders* (ca. 2.6 ha.) of land and can therefore be characterised as cottars. Indeed, peasants rarely owned large farms. Those were usually held in lease. As in Flanders, the extra-economic power of the landlords was relatively weak. Peasants could rely to a strong degree on customary law. In contrast to the northern provinces, however, lordly power and manorial structures were not insignificant in the duchy of Brabant. Peasants still had to pay various manorial fees and other dues, in some cases also including corvées. The high degree of urbanisation in Brabant meant that, just as in Flanders, the rural economy was strongly oriented towards the urban market. Land rents were to a large extent payable in money, which implies that peasants generally sold some of their surplus at the market – indeed, peasants *had* to sell their surplus at the market in order to be able to pay their rent. Furthermore, the fact that many landlords, including noblemen and abbeys, had a residence in town forced the tenants to come to town to deliver their land rents and lease payments in kind. Besides agriculture, there were also highly organised rural industries and trades in several places, especially along the rivers Scheldt and Rupel, and in the textile area between Mechelen and Lier.

The rural economy of western Brabant therefore had many features of a peasant economy at the end of the Middle Ages, such as the predominance of peasant households, the importance of subsistence farming, and the relatively unspecialised character of agriculture. On the other hand, it deviated in a major way from the classical peasant model, namely in terms of market opportunities. The Brabantine peasant economy was strongly monetised and highly commercialised. Another point of debate involves the significance of lease farming. Can we consider lease farmers as peasants if they had no holding of their own on which they could fall back in case of economic failure? And if we cannot, then to what extent was lease farming a significant feature in the rural economy of Brabant – and for that matter of Flanders? Our data do not enable us to quantify exactly the extent of lease farming in the areas around Brussels and Antwerp. However, considering the high proportion of ecclesiastical property (more than 20% in the case of Kontich) and the general tendency of great landowners to lease out large farms, lease farming must be considered to have been of great significance during the fifteenth century.

The Significance of the Rise of Antwerp

Our analysis of the economic relationship between the Brabantine towns and their surroundings during the fifteenth century has shown that the urban impact on the rural economy was already very strong in the late Middle Ages. The demand for agrarian products was already higher than the agrarian potential of the rural economy, the towns already attracted many immigrants from the surrounding villages, and textiles from Duffel, Walem and Kontich were exported via the Brabantine fairs. In the opposite direction, the large towns served as distributors of industrial goods and "imported" goods for the countryside, including things like salt and herring. Hence, market integration had already achieved a high level. So did the extraordinary expansion of Antwerp around 1500 actually lead to a qualitative change in the urban impact on the rural economy, or did it merely spur further developments that had already started in the late Middle Ages? The main characteristics of the economic rise of Antwerp, in terms of town-country relationship, can be summarised as a) an explosive population growth leading to an increase in the demand for rural produce, b) a strong accumulation of capital in Antwerp that was invested partly in the countryside, and c) an increase of the economic activity in the town that offered opportunities for employment there and in the surrounding area.

The Impact of the Demographic Growth of Antwerp on the Rural Economy

The economic rise of Antwerp led to a five-fold increase in the number of inhabitants and, as a result, a corresponding increase in the demand for food and other rural products. This increase in demand took place on two different levels. Besides the demand for products for mass consumption for the lower class (e.g. rye, dairy products, wood, beer, cheap textiles), there was also a demand for high quality products for the wealthy middle and upper classes (e.g. wheat, meat, wine, fruit, quality textiles, luxury products). The demand for bread grain remained a dominant feature of urban supplies also during the sixteenth century. The imports from the Baltic region could alleviate this problem to some extent but did not replace the Brabantine countryside as the major supplier of grain for the metropolis.

Meat was imported in the form of oxen from Denmark and the northern Low Countries. This trade offered opportunities for cattle merchants and butchers in Antwerp and its more immediate environs to make considerable profits by fattening meagre oxen over the summer and then selling them at the urban market. The polders north of Antwerp were the preferred location for grazing. Another form of meat farming involved the fattening of pigs by millers and brewers. Besides fattened oxen and pigs, a variety of different types of meat of local origin were sold in Antwerp as well. Hence local peasants could not only sell their surplus in grain, but also some lambs, poultry, etc. In the case of dairy products, too, the imports from Holland and Flanders probably left a sufficient share of the market for the local producers. Nevertheless, the Antwerp area did not specialise in any particular products that would have been comparable to Dutch and Flemish dairy or Danish oxen.

Intensive gardening is one of the few sectors in which real specialisation did take place. Around Antwerp, two particular areas of market gardening can be distinguished in the sixteenth century. These were the area outside the Rodepoort stretching until Borgerhout and the area outside the St. Jorispoort extending to "Het Kiel". Hence, while we could not observe any overall agrarian specialisation, there nevertheless does seem to have been a tendency towards agrarian intensification. The production of bread grain was increased by growing winter crops instead of summer crops and, in part, by reducing the fallow. Such an increase in the production of wheat or rye was dependent on a sufficient use of fertiliser, however. The latter was supplied by increasing the efficiency of traditional manuring through stable feeding and in some cases through the application of up-and-down husbandry. Stable feeding also allowed an increase in the amount of livestock through the use of industrial waste products like mash as fodder. Furthermore, the town provided great quantities of domestic and industrial waste, which was systematically sold to farmers.

The Investment of Antwerp Capital in the Countryside

The strong accumulation of capital was characteristic of large cities with a wealthy elite. In the case of Antwerp, the degree of capital accumulation in the hands of the rich merchant class was exceptionally high. This capital was invested in the countryside in different ways: first, through the purchase of seigniorial titles; second, by buying agricultural land and farms; and third, by providing credit to peasants or other landowners. The purchase of seigniorial titles and manorial rights did not have any direct influence on the agrarian economy; it simply redirected the flow of land rents and other peasant dues from the traditional groups of lords (i.e. the duke, the nobility and patricians) to a new group of lords. Besides enhancing the social status of the merchants, it also increased their influence on a local level, which could be an advantage if they owned landed property or had commercial interests in "their" village, as in the case of Jacob van Hencxthoven in Hemiksem.

In comparison, the purchase of land and farms was more frequent and had more far-reaching consequences for the local economy. The purchase of large farms and the expansion of holdings by means of systematic land purchases were ways of increasing farm outputs and, as a result of economies of scale, increasing the marketable surplus. At the same time, these purchases usually went hand in hand with investments by the owner in the infrastructure of the farm in question. The castles or country residences that Antwerp citizens owned in the surroundings of Antwerp, with their large pleasances, were often combined with a large lease farm that served to provide basic foodstuffs and fuel for the owner's household. This does not seem to have brought about any revolutionary innovations in the operation of these farms in the short run. The regular presence of the owner on or near the farm may have led to a certain involvement in the agrarian activities of the farmer, but as yet we have found no evidence of any direct interference in the production process.

In contrast, the massive purchases of land by merchants and other urban citizens did change the property relations in the countryside. While the economic impact was limited as long as such purchases took place at the level of landlords, the consequences became far-reaching as soon as it concerned purchases from peasants. By 1570, merchants and other citizens had acquired no less than 20 to 30% of the land in the surroundings of Antwerp. At the same time, the peasants' share in the landed property was reduced to a meagre 15%, which was again concentrated in the hands of the local top. If lease holding was already an important characteristic of the rural economy of western Brabant during the fifteenth century, it became the dominant feature in the environs of Antwerp during the sixteenth century. Lease farming was not limited to large farms and separate plots of land owned by non-peasants; it also was applied for small farms and cottages, which were sublet by their owners who in turn leased a larger farm for themselves.

Finally, the providing of credit to peasants and other landowners had an ambiguous character. While offering the peasants opportunities to invest in their holdings, and hence to increase their productivity, it represented at the same time a great risk of accumulating arrears. The frequency of holdings pledged with multiple annuities shows the considerable dimensions of this phenomenon in the countryside near Antwerp. About half the deeds in the registry of the city's aldermen concerned the sale of annuities. The success rate among peasants who had borrowed money is not known. In the event of economic misfortune, however, indebted peasants easily lost their property rights to their creditors or were forced to sell their holding. But besides helping to accelerate the transfer of land from the peasantry to the merchant class, credit issued in the form of mortgages augmented the social polarisation within the village community. Small peasants generally did not lend money from large-scale merchants, but rather from the wealthier tenants in the same community. It was this latter group that accumulated much of the land that remained peasant property.

Antwerp and the non-agrarian sector

The economic expansion of Antwerp provided labour for many thousands of workers from the countryside, both within and beyond the city walls. Many people were busy providing fuel and building materials for the metropolis, whether as brick-makers or woodcutters; others were active in the transport sectors as carters, wagoners or boatmen. Brewers, millers, butchers and bakers from the surrounding villages worked for the urban market, and tavern keepers in Borgerhout, Berchem, Het Kiel and Wilrijk received thirsty townsmen for a cheap drink. In addition to those located in the town's immediate surroundings, the villages along the major traffic routes provided a broad range of services for merchants and other travellers. In comparison with these sectors, which were directly related to the urban economy, the rural textile industry, a typical "proto-industrial" sector, was relatively underdeveloped in the Antwerp area. The great exception was Duffel in the traditional weavers' district north of Mechelen. Probably due to the relative advantages it enjoyed in comparison with the other drapers' villages nearby, it established itself as a modest centre of export in the first half of the sixteenth century. After 1550, the production of serges gave a new impulse to the textile industry of Duffel, making it a well-known provider of cheap textiles. Non-agrarian labour was therefore an alternative source of income for many villagers, although not all of these occupations were accessible for those who typically suffered most from the social changes of the sixteenth century: the poor peasants.

The social analysis of the non-agrarian activities in the surroundings of Antwerp showed that rather than the two groups commonly presumed to have been the main actors, that is, the urban merchants and rural labourers, a third group appears to have played the major role: the local merchants and entrepreneurs. They were the main protagonists in the development of the brick-industry of the Rupel area, although they temporarily had to cope with competition from the building trust of the Antwerp entrepreneurs Gilbert van Schoonbeke and Jacob van Hencxthoven. They were also the ones who organised the substantial wood trade in the area south of Antwerp. And, finally, they also played a leading role in the organisation of the cloth industry of Duffel. While merchants from Antwerp did interfere in these trades, especially around the middle of the sixteenth century, they evidently failed to get a firm grip on them in the long run. The local merchants and entrepreneurs had either the special skills or the considerable capital required for a broad range of village crafts. They could afford to lease a brewery or mill or purchase a *pleitschip* or *heude*, for example, while those things would have been inaccessible to a landless peasant. And while these local merchants and entrepreneurs could attain a leading position in the village economy, the cottars and poor labourers remained on the lowest scale despite their non-agrarian incomes.

The Case of Antwerp in Light of the Theoretical Concepts of J. de Vries and R. Brenner

Finally there remains the overall evaluation of the impact of Antwerp's economic growth on its surrounding countryside in light of the theoretical concepts discussed in the introduction. The rise of Antwerp as the commercial focus of Western Europe did not turn the economy of its rural surroundings into one with specialised agriculture comparable to that of seventeenth-century Holland. The agrarian system remained predominantly based on grain farming, with rye as the main crop and livestock farming as a subordinate activity. In comparison with the northern provinces, the cultivation of rye gave good results, and the high demand – and hence high prices – made it very profitable as well. Although Antwerp had access to Baltic grain, this does not seem to have had any negative effects on the market for local grain. On the contrary, the production of rye actually increased as a result of a higher percentage of the land being cultivated with it. However, it should be noted that the Dutch case was exceptional because of its particular geographical circumstances. As the Antwerp surroundings had very different geographical and economic patterns, the economic response of the urban impact can hardly be expected to have been the same as in Holland. Although this did not signify any radical change in the agrarian structure of the area, intensive farming was nevertheless a response to the market opportunities. This "positive" response to the market opportunities was limited to large and mid-sized farms, which produced a marketable surplus, however. Although few in number, they constituted a large share of the farmland and were therefore economically significant.

On the lower end of the social hierarchy, the situation has more in common with the peasant model than with the specialisation model. Many peasants lived on very small holdings which were insufficient even for subsistence farming. Rather than having a homogenous middle class of capitalist farmers, the Antwerp countryside was characterised by a strong social differentiation. If the difference between Brabant and Holland in terms of agrarian specialisation was determined to a large extent by their different natural and economic preconditions, the social aspect must be explained by differences concerning the peasants ties to their land, or at least to village life. The more feudal character of property relations in Brabant did not prevent the poorer peasants from losing their property rights to a richer neighbour or to an urban citizen. By the end of the sixteenth century, very few peasants in the surroundings of Antwerp had the full ownership of their land. The strong demand for land among townsmen and the local elite led many peasants to sell their land and choose for leasehold instead. This resulted in property relations that corresponded in many points to the classical definition of capitalist class relations. Leasehold replaced copyhold as the dominant form of landholding, and instead of a duality between lords and peasants, there was now a relationship between landowners and tenant farmers, also for very small holdings. Instead of breaking the constraints of the feudal system, the leasehold system extended *beyond* the feudal property structures as Kriedte has suggested.

The survival strategy of the small-scale tenants in the villages near Antwerp was mainly a combination of intensive farming and wage labour. The proximity to Antwerp and the great variety of labour opportunities may therefore have been decisive for the survival of these expropriated tenants in a rural surrounding that was dominated by large lease farms and a large tenant class with little or no land. In a certain sense, the case of Antwerp contradicts Brenner's hypothesis that market structures by themselves could not change the feudal property structures and separate the peasants from their landed property. In fact, the Antwerp case has shown that the impact of the urban economy, and especially of urban capital, could transform the property relations of the surroundings into capitalistic ones. And yet it would be hazardous to speak of a capitalist rural economy in the surroundings of

Antwerp. Although market oriented and partly market dependent, farmers still remained subsistence-oriented, rather than profit- oriented. Changed property relations and the prevalence of lease farming may have been a precondition for capitalist farming, but it cannot be equated with capitalist farming.

These findings concerning the Antwerp area must nevertheless be qualified. These changes only took place in a small area around the greatest commercial metropolis of the sixteenth century and did not affect Brabant, let alone the southern Low Countries as a whole. On the other hand, a comparative study of land values in Brabant shows that the urban influence on the rural economy was not a phenomenon that was limited to Antwerp. The Brussels area experienced a similar development, and other urban spheres of influence will no doubt have been impacted by some of the same forces. In an area with such a concentration of large towns as the Low Countries, the urban influence was sufficiently important to consider it a major factor in the development of the rural economy.

Bibliography

Archival Sources

Brussels, Algemeen Rijksarchief/ Archives generaux du royaume

Audiëntie(Aud.)
No. 618 /1: Kohieren van de honderdste penning, 1569-1570.

Familiearchieven
Merode de Westerlo (MW)
No. 327, Cijnsboek Walem ca.1480 en 1500.
G 674, Schenking van de heerlijkheden Duffel en Walem aan Jean de Merode, 1525.
O 910: Rekening land van Duffel'8-6-1527- 8/6/1528.
Rekeningen van de heerlijkheid Grimbergen (onder Nassau)
I 796: 1434/35 –1462/63
I 797: 1466-1467 -1474/75
Rekeningen van de heerlijkheid Grimbergen (onder de Glymes)
M 113: 1464-1465.

Feudal court of Brabant (Leenhof van Brabant/Cour féodale de Brabant (LB))
no. 7 Dénombrements van lenen, kwartier van Brussel, 1440
no. 8 Dénombrements van lenen, kwartier van Antwerpen, 1440

Raad van Beroerten
no. 164: Confiscaties

Chamber of accounts (Rekenkamer/ Chambre des comptes (Rk))
Register 4175: Rekening van het hertogelijke domein Brussel 1448/49
Register 4762: Rekeningen van het hertogelijke domein *Tervuren-Vilvoorde* 1449/50.
Registers 11897-11915: Rekeningen van het hertogelijke domein *Land van Mechelen* 1464/65-1589/90.
Register 22739: Tolregister ‚het wiel' near Rupelmonde okt. 1541 -sept. 1542.
Register 22740: Tolregister Rupelmonde okt. 1541 -sept. 1542.
Register 24660: Rekening van ammortisatie kerkelijke goederen (nieuwe aanwinsten) 1474-1476.
No. 44830 Cijnsboek van het hertogelijke domein Brussels
No. 44914 Cijnsboek van het hertogelijke domein Overzenne,
No. 45583, Cijnsboek van Aartselaar, Kontich, Reet, Duffel, Schrieck, Waarloos, ca. 1440-1460
No. 45597, Cijnsboek van Aartselaar, Duffel, Kontich, Waarloos, 1516
No. 45599, Cijnsboek van Zellaar, Putte, Rijmenam, St. Katelijne-Waver, Beersel 1516

No. 45601. Cijnsboek van Niel, Schelle, 1519
Ecclesiastic archives of Brabant (KA)
No. 8108 Pachtboek van de abdij Groot Bijgaarden, derde kwart 15e eeuw.
No. 8264. Pachtboek van de abdij Grimbergen, derde kwart 15e eeuw.

Antwerp, City Archives (Stadsarchief
Collectanea(Coll.)
No. 3-4.

Schepenregisters(SR).
No. 43, 1450

Privilegiekamer(Pk)
No. 2428: Correspondence of the Antwerp representatives at the Estates of Brabant, 1664-1669.

Tresorij(T) No. 584: Process between Mechlin, Antwerp and Brussels, 1433.

Vreemde Gemeenten(VG)
No. 2: Schepenbrief van10 nov. 1563 betreffende goederen van Fernando der Bernuy in Oorderen.
Nos. 4-5: Toestand der dorpen van het markgraafschap in 1593.
No.14:
– Toestand van Mortsel and Luithagen, 17 sept. 1593.
– Tax list of the 100th penny Edegem, 1569.

Antwerp, National Archives (Rijksarchief)

Kerkelijke Archieven, St. Bernards 10
Oud Gemeentearchief Boechout, No. 93: Kohier van de honderdste penning, 1569

Antwerp, Archives of the Public Assistance (OCMW)
St.-Elisabeth Gasthuis
Register 4: Rekeningen 1502/1503 - 1504/1505
Doos 30: Pachtcontracten 16e – 18e eeuw
170: Pachtboek 1464-1557
172: Cohier van de zeven kwartieren van Antwerpen 1686,
178: Inkomsten uit pachten,1557-ca.1580

Printed sources

De Momper, B. (after Frans Huys), *Panoramic view on Antwerp (1557)*, Paris, Bibliotheque Nationale.

Guicciardini, L., *Descrittione di tutti i Paesi Bassi, altrimenti detti Germania inferiore, Antwerpen*, W. Silvius, 1567.

Guicciardini, L., *Descrittione di tutti i Paesi Bassi, altrimenti detti Germania Inferiore, Antwerp*, C. Plantin,1588.

Multifarium casularum, Antwerp, H. Cock, 1559.

Marchionatus Sacri Romani Imperii (J.C. Visscher, 1587-1652)" in N. Visscher, *Kaert-Boeck van de XVII Nederlandstsche Provinciën...etc.*, Amsterdam 1684, reprinted in D. R. Duncker and H. Weiss, *Het hertogdom Brabant in kaart en prent: zijn vier kwartieren Leuven, Brussel, Antwerpen*, „s-Hertogenbosch, Tielt, 1983, pp. 86–87.

"*Praediorum villarum*", Antwerp, H. Cock, 1561.

Weston, R., *A discours of Husbandrie used in Brabant and Flanders shewing the wonderfull improvement of Land there, and serving as a pattern for our practice in this commonwhealth*, London, William Du-Gard, 1650.

Edited sources and repertories

Antwerpse Poortersboeken, 1533 - 1608, 3 vols., Antwrpen, 1977.

Asaert, G., Berger, R., Delmaire, B., e.a., *Valleien van Schelde en Scarpe*, Brussel, 1991 (Albums de Croÿ, 25).

Beterams, G., *Antwerpse schepenbrieven bewaard op het Rijksarchief te Antwerpen 1300-1794*, Brussel, 1959.

Cuvelier, J., *Les dénombrements de foyers en Brabant (XIVe - XVIe siècle)*, Brussels, 1912.

De Cuyper, A., *Coutumes de la ville de Bruxelles* (Coutumes du pays et duché de Brabant. Quartier de Bruxelles, tome premier) Brussels 1869.

De Longé, G., "Coerboek de la ville d'Anvers (14th c.)" in *Coutumes de la ville d'Anvers*, Brussels, 1870 (Coutumes du pays et duché de Brabant. Quartier d'Anvers; 1), p. 22-26.

De Longé, G., *Coutumes du Kiel, de Deurne et de Lierre*, Brussels, 1875 (Coutumes du Pays et Duché de Brabant: Quartier d'Anvers, 5).

De Nave, F., "De oudste Antwerpse lijsten van nieuwe poorters (28 januari 1390-28 december 1414)" in *Handelingen van de Koninklijke Commissie voor Geschiedenis* 139 (1973), pp. 67–309.

De Ridder, P., *Inventaris van het oud archief van de kapittelkerk van Sint-Michiel en Sint-Goedele te Brussel*, 3 vols., Brussel, 1987-1988.

Denucé, J., *Inventaire des Affaitadi, banquiers italiens a Anvers de l'annee 1568*, Antwerp, 1934.

Doehaerd, R., *Etudes anversoises. Documents sur le commerce international à Anvers, 1488-1514*, 3 vols., Paris, 1963.

Galesloot, L., *Inventaire des archives de la Cour Feodale de Brabant*, 2 vols., Brussel, 1870-1884.

Génard, P., ed., "Boek van dagvaerden," in *Antwerpsch Archievenblad*, 19-21 1882-1884.

Génard, P., "De rekening der stad Antwerpen van het jaar 1549-1550," in *Antwerpsch Archievenblad*, 1(1864), p. 17-104.

Génard, P., "Index der gebodboeken 1489-1620" in *Antwerpsch Archievenblad* 1 (1864), p. 120-464.

Kocken, M., *De gekochte poorters van Mechelen* (1400-1795), Handzame, 1975 (Poorterboeken van de Zuidelijke Nederlanden, 7).

Mertens, J. and Vandewalle, P., *Metrologisch Vademecum voor Vlaanderen*, Brugge, 2003.

Pergameni, C., *Les archives historiques de la ville de Bruxelles: notices et inventaires*, Brussels, 1943.

Prims, F., "Het 'denombrement' van de zeven kwartieren van Antwerpen van 1686," in Bijdragen tot de Geschiedenis 37 (1954) p. 108-122.

Prims, F. and Dierckx H., *Atlas der Antwerpsche stadsbuitenijen van 1698. Fac-simile van de kadastrale plattegronden van C.J. Van Lyere vergeleken met den tegenwoordigen toestand*, Antwerpen, 1933.

Scholliers, E., "Prijzen en lonen te Antwerpen (15e en 16e eeuw) - Prix et salaires à Anvers (15e -16e siècles)" in C. Verlinden e.a, *Dokumenten voor de geschiedenis van prijzen en lonen in Vlaanderen en Brabant (Xve -XVIIIe eeuw)*, vol. I, Gent 1959, pp. 241–480.

Spelkens, E., "Les bourgeois de Bruxelles, notés par J.B. Houwaert, depuis le début XIVe siècle jusqu'au milieu du XVIIe siècle" in *L'intermédiaire des généalogistes* XI (1956), pp. 14, 79, 261, 335; XII (1957), pp. 12, 76, 143, 210, 279; XIII (1958), pp. 155, 229, 314, 543.

Stabel P. and Vermeylen, F., *Het fiscale vermogen in Brabant, Vlaanderen en in de heerlijkheid Mechelen: de Honderdste Penning van de hertog van Alva (1569-1572)* (Commission royale d'Histoire/Koninklijke commissie voor Geschiedenis), Brussel, 1997.

Strieder, J., *Aus Antwerpener Notariatsarchiven: Quellen zur deutschen Wirtschaftsgeschichte des 16. Jahrhunderts*, Berlin, 1930, (Deutsche Handelsakten des Mittelalters und der Neuzeit, 4).

Thys, O.H., "Lenen van het leenhof van Mechelen te Aartselaar en Reet, 1473," in *Vlaamse Stam* VIII (1972), pp. 441–447.

Thys, O.H., "Lenen van het Leenhof van Mechelen te Kontich, 1473," in *Vlaamse Stam* IX (1973), pp. 628–638.

Unger, W.S., *De tol van Iersekeroord. Documenten en rekeningen 1321-1572*, The Hague, 1939 (Rijks geschiedkundige publicatiën, kleine serie, 29).

Van Havre, G. ed., *Chronijck der stadt Antwerpen* [attributed to G. Bertrijn], Antwerp, 1879 (Uitgave der Antwerpsche Bibliophilen, 5).

Van Passen, R., "Het cijnsboek van Helmont (Kontich) van 1431" in *Bijdragen tot de Geschiedenis*, 49 (1966), pp. 139–156.

Vandewalle, P., *Oude maten, gewichten en muntstelsels in Vlaanderen, Brabant en Limburg*, s.l.,1984 : (Centrum voor landelijke geschiedenis, 82).

Verstrepen, C., *Stadsarchief Antwerpen Schepengriffie. Antwerpse schepenbrieven betreffende de dorpen van de Rupelstreek. Aartselaar, Boom, Boechout, Hemiksem, Kontich, Niel, Reet, Rumst, Schelle, 1384-1565*, 7 vols, Brussel, 1990-1996.

Verstrepen, Ch., *Schepengriffie, Vrijheid van Rumst 1536-1547*, Brussel, 1989.

Wauters, A., *Documents concernant le canal de Bruxelles à Willebroeck précédés d'une introduction contenant un résumé de l'histoire de ce canal*, Brussels, 1882.

Literature

AERTS, E., and CLARK, P., eds., *Metropolitan Cities and Their Hinterlands in Early Modern Europe* (Proceedings Tenth International Economic History Congress Leuven, August 1990, Session B-6), Leuven, 1990.

AERTS, E., and DAELEMANS, F., "Sociaal economische aspecten van het 16de-eeuwse Brussel" in *Tijdschrift voor Brusselse Geschiedenis* 1/ 1984 no.1-2, pp. 9–38.

AERTS, E. and VAN CAUWENBERGHE, E., "Die Grafschaft Flandern und die sogenannte spätmittelalterliche Depression" in F. SEIBT ed., *Europa 1400. Die Krise des Spätmittelalters*,, Stuttgart, 1984, pp. 221–232.

ARNOULD, M.A., *Les relevés de feux* (Typologie des sources du Moyen Âge occidental 18, A-IV.1), Turnhout, 1976.

ARNOULD, M.A., "L'impot sur le capital en belgique au XVIe siècle" in *Le Hainaut économique,* 1 (1946), pp. 17–45.

ASAERT, G., "Antwerp and the Sea" in J. VAN DER STOCK, ed., *Antwerp, Story of a Metropolis*, Ghent, 1993, pp. 33–35.

ASAERT, G., *De Antwerpse scheepvaart in de XVe eeuw (1394-1480). Bijdrage tot de ekonomische geschiedenis van de stad Antwerpen*, Brussels, 1973 (Verhandelingen van de koninklijke Academie voor Wetenschapen, Letteren en Schone Kunsten van België, Klasse der Letteren, XXXV (1973), 72).

ASAERT, G., "Handel in kleurstoffen op de Antwerpse markt tijdens de XVe eeuw" in: *Bijdragen en mededelingen betreffende de geschiedenis der Nederlanden* 88 (1973), pp. 377–402.

AUGUSTYN, B., "Traces of a Protoindustrial Organization of the Medieval North Flemish Peat Region. Test Case Kieldrecht, a Peat Diggers Village ca. 1400" in H.J. NITZ (ed.), *The Medieval and early modern Rural Landscape of Europe under the impact of the Commercial Economy*, Göttingen, 1987, pp. 61–73.

BAELDE, M., *De domeingoederen van de vorst in de Nederlanden omstreeks het midden van de zestiende eeuw (1551-1559)* Brussel 1971 (Verzameling van onuitgegeven Belgische kronieken en van onuitgegeven documenten betreffende de geschiedenis van België: reeks in-8°, 85).

BAELDE, M., "Financiële politiek en domaniale evolutie in de Nederlanden onder Karel V en Filips II (1530 - 1560)" in *Tijdschrift voor Geschiedenis*, 76/1963 pp. 14–33.

BAERTEN, J., "Brussel, hoofdstad van een hertogdom: politieke en economische aspecten" in J.STENGERS, ed., *Brussel, Groei van een hoofdstad*, Antwerpen, 1979, pp. 56–67.

BAETENS, R. "Omvang en produktie van de baksteennijverheid in de Rupelstreek(16e – 20e eeuw)" in: *Bijdragen tot de Geschiedenis,* 62 (1979), pp. 103–183.

BAETENS, R., "De lokale markten te Antwerpen (16e-18e eeuw)" in *Antwerpenin de XVIIde eeuw*, Antwerpen, 1989, pp. 169–199.

BAETENS, R., *De nazomer van Antwerpens welvaart. De diaspora en het handelshuisDe Groote tijdens de eerste helft der 17e eeuw*. 2 vols., Antwerpen, 1976.

BAETENS, R., "De reacties van Antwerpen op de stormvloeden van 1530 en 1532 in Zeeland" in *Onder de koepel van het Pantheon. Liber Amicorum Jacques Claes*, Kapellen, 1994, pp. 244–262.

BAETENS, R., "La "villa rustica", phénomène italien dans le paysage brabançon au 16ème siècle" in *Aspetti della vita economica medievale: atti del Convegno di studi nel 10 anniversario della morte di Federigo Melis*, Firenze-Pisa-Prato, 10-14 marzo1984, Firenze, 1985, pp. 171–191.

Baetens, R., "La ‚Bellezza' et la ‚Magnificenza'. Symboles du pouvoir de la villa rustica dans la region anversoise aux temps modernes" in Id. and B. Blondé, B., eds., *Nouvelles approches concernant la culture de l'habitat/ New Approaches to Living Patterns. International Colloquium 24-25 10 1989, University of Antwerp, Antwerp 1993*, pp. 159–180.

Baetens, R. 1979. "Omvang en produktie van de baksteennijverheid in de Rupelstreek (16e - 20e eeuw)" in *Bijdragen tot de Geschiedenis,* 62, pp.103–183.

Ballaux, B., "Molenstenen voor de Kempen: landvervoer en transportkosten in de vijftiende en zestiende eeuw" in *Bijdragen tot de Geschiedenis* 82 (1999) pp. 269–280.

Bartier, J., "De Bourgondische adel" in Broeckx J.L., De Clercq C., Dhondt J., Nauwelaerts M.A., eds., *Flandria Nostra: ons land en ons volk, zijn standen en beroepen door de tijden heen*, vol. IV (1959), pp. 319–344.

Bartier, J., "Un document sur les prévarications et les rivalités du patriciat bruxellois au XVe siècle" in *Bulletin de la commission royale d ‚histoire/handelingen van de koninklijke commissie voor Geschiedenis*, CVII (1942), pp.337–365.

Beltrami, D., *La penetrazione economica dei veneziani in terraferma. Forze di lavoro e proprietà fondiaria nelle campagne venete dei secoli XVII e XVIII*, Venice-Rome, 1961.

Bergmann, A., *Geschiedenis der stad Lier*, Lier, 1973[3].

Berlière, U. e.a., eds., *Monasticon Belge IV, Province de Brabant*, 6 vols., Liege, 1964-1972.

Billen, C., "Problèmes de méthodologie autour de l'untilisation des censiers du bas moyen age" in *Histoire économique de la Belgique*. traitement des sources de état des questions. Actes du colloque de Brussels, 17-19 novembre 1971, pp.439–471.

Bindoff, S.T., "The Greatness of Antwerp" in *The New Cambridge Modern History II. The Reformation*, ed. G.R. Elton, Cambridge, 1958, pp. 50–69.

Bloch, M., *Les caractères originaux de l'historie rurale française*, vol. I, Paris 1952.

Blockmans, F., *Het Gentsche stadspatriciaat tot omstreeks 1302*, Bruges, 1938.

Blockmans, W.P., "Die Niederlande vor und nach 1400. Eine Gesellschaft in der Krise?" in F. Seibt, ed., *Europa 1400. Die Krise des Spätmittelalters*, Stuttgart, 1984, pp. 117–133.

Blockmans, W. P., Pieters, G., Prevenier, W., Van Schaik, A.W., "Tussen crisis en welvaart: sociale veranderingen 1300 -1500" in *Algemene geschiedenis der Nederlanden* IV, (Haarlem, 1980) pp. 42–86.

Blockmans, W.P., Prevenier, W., "Armoede in de Nederlanden van de 14de tot het midden van de 16de eeuw: bronnen en problemen" in van den Eerenbeemt, H.F.J.M., Jansen, P.C., van Uytven, R., eds. *Armoede en armenzorg*, special issue of *Tijdschrift voor Geschiedenis,* 88 (1975), pp. 501–538.

Blondé, B., *Een economie met verschillende snelheden, Ongelijkheden in de opbouw en de ontwikkeling van het Brabantse stedelijke netwerk (ca. 1750- ca. 1790)*, Brussel, 1999 (Verhandelingen van de Koninklijke Vlaamse Academie van België voor Wetenschappen en Kunsten, Klasse der Letteren, Jaargang 61, 1999, no. 166).

Blondé, B. and Limberger, M., "De gebroken welvaart" in: R. van Uytven, e.a. eds., *De geschiedenis van Brabant van het hertogdom tot heden*, Zwolle 2004, p. 307-330.

Blondé, B. and van Uytven, R., "De smalle steden en het Brabantse stedelijke netwerk in de Late Middeleeuwen en de Nieuwe Tijd" in *Lira Elegans* 6 (1996), pp. 129–182.

Blondé, B. and van Uytven, R., Langs land- en waterwegen in de Zuidelijke Nederlanden. Lopend onderzoek naar het preïndustriële transport“ in *Het transport en het stedelijke netwerk in de Zuidelijke Nederlanden,* special issue of *Bijdragen tot de Geschiedenis*, 82 (1999) pp. 135–158.

Bois, G., *Crise du féodalisme*, Paris, 1981.

Boone, M., "La terre, les hommes et les villes. Quelques considérations autour du thème de l'urbanisation des propiétaires terriens“ in *La ville et la transmission des valeurs culturelles au bas moyen âge et aux temps modernes: actes* (Crédit communal. Comité d'histoire. Colloque international 17: 1994: Spa) (*Historische uitgaven: reeks in-8°* = Collection histoire: série in-8°; 96), Brussels, 1996, pp. 153–173.

Bousse, A., "De verhoudingen tussen Antwerpen en het platteland“ in *Bijdragen tot de Geschiedenis*, 58 (1975) pp. 139–150.

Bousse, A. *Geschiedenis van Schilde. Van heidenschommig dorp tot woonforensengemeente*. Schilde, 1983.

Braudel, F., *Le temps du monde*, Paris, 1979 (Civilisation matérielle, économie et capitalisme, XVe - XVIIIe siècle, vol. 3).

Braudel, F., *The Structures of Everyday Life. The Limits of the Possible*, London, 1981. *(Civilization and Capitalism 15th - 18th Century*, vol. I.)

Brenner, R., "The Agrarian Roots of European Capitalism“ in *Past & Present,* 97 (1982), pp. 16–113.

Brenner, R., "Agrarian class structure and Economic Development in Pre-industrial Europe“, in *Past & Present,* 70 (1976), p. 30-75.

Bril, L., *De handel tussen de Nederlanden en het Iberisch Schiereiland (midden XVIe eeuw.). Een kwantitatieve peiling*, Ghent, unpublished MA-thesis, 1962.

Britnell, R.H., *The Commercialisation of English Society, 1000-1500* (Manchester, 1996).

Brouette, E., "Abbeye de Villers, à Tilly“ in *Monasticon Belge IV, Province de Brabant*, deuxième fascicule, Liege, 1968, p. 341-405.

Brulez, W., "De economische kaart van de Nederlanden in de 16e eeuw volgens Guicciardini“ in *Tijdschrift voor Geschiedenis* 83 (1970) pp. 352–357 (reprint: *Studia gandensia*, 152).

Brulez, W., *De firma Della Faille en de internationale handel van Vlaamse firma's in de 16e eeuw*, Brussel, 1959 (Verhandelingen van de Koninklijke Vlaamse Academie voor Wetenschappen, Letteren en Schone Kunsten van België. Klasse der Letteren, 35).

Brulez, W., "De handel“ in *Antwerpen in de XVIe eeuw*, Antwepen, 1975, pp. 109–125.

Brulez, W., "De handelsbalans der Nederlanden in het midden van de 16e eeuw“ in *Bijdragen voor Geschiedenis der Nederlanden* XXI (1966/67), pp. 278–310.

Bruneel, C., "Bijdrage van de poortersboeken tot de historische demografie. Kritische bedenkingen bij het voorbeeld van Antwerpen“ in *Gemeentekrediet van België. Driemaandelijks tijdschrift*, 44 (1990), pp. 101–110.

Bruneel, C., "Les migrations entre ville et campagnes. L'exemple des pays-bas méridionaux“ in *Le migrazioni in Europa secc. XIII-XVIII. Atti della "Venticinquesima Settimana di Studi" 3-8 maggio 1993*, Prato, 1994, pp. 501–532.

Bush, M.L., "Tenant Rights and the Peasantries of Europe under the Old Regime“ in Idem, ed., *Social Orders and Social Classes in Europe since 1500: Studies in Social Stratification*, London, 1992, pp. 136–157.

Campbell, B.M.S., Galloway, J.A., Keene, D., Murphy, M., *A Medieval Capital and its Grain*

Supply: Agrarian Production and Distribution in the London Region, c.1300, London, 1993 (Historical Geography Research Series, 30).

Carlier, C., "Migration trends in the towns of Flanders and Brabant (15th-18th century)" in *Le migrazioni in Europa secc. XIII-XVIII. Atti della "Venticinquesima Settimana di Studi" 3-8 maggio 1993*, 1994, pp. 355–370.

Cerutti, F.F.X., "De schepenbank in de Brabantse stad en de overdracht en bezwaring van onroerende goederen" in *De Brabantse stad. Tweede colloquium, 23-24 nov. 1968*, 's-Hertogenbosch, 1969, p. 47-87.

Chartier R. and Neveux, H., "La ville dominante et spoumise" in: E. Le Roy Ladurie, *La ville classique*, Paris, 1981 (Histoire de la France urbaine, ed. G. Duby, vol. III), pp. 15–286.

Christaller, W., *Die zentralen Orte in Süddeutschland*, Jena, 1932.

Clark, P. and Lepetit, B., eds., *Capital Cities and their Hinterlands in Early Modern Europe*, Aldershot, 1996 (*Historical Urban Studies*, 1996:1).

Coornaert, E., "Draperies rurales, draperies urbaines. L'évolution de l'industrie flamande au moyen âge et au XVIe siècle" in *Belgisch Tijdschrift voor Filologie en Geschiedenis* 28 (1950), pp. 59–96.

Corrijn, F., "Het schippersambacht te Gent (1302-1492)" in *Handelingen van de Maatschappij voor Geschiedenis en Oudheidskunde te Gent*, 1 (1944), p. 165-204,

Cosemans, A., "Het uitzicht van Brabant op het einde der XVIde eeuw" in *Bijdragen tot de Geschiedenis* XXVII (1936) 285-351.

Craeybeckx, J., "Les Français et Anvers au XVIe siècle" in *Annales E.S.C.*, 17/1962, pp. 542–554.

Daelemans, F., "Pachten en welvart op het platteland van belgish Brabant (15e - 18e eeuw)" in *AAG Bijdragen*, 28 (1986), pp. 165–184.

Daelemans, F., "Peiling naar de evolutie van de landbouw te Grimbergen aan de hand van enkele pachtcontracten (13e-18e eeuw)" in: *Eigen Schoon en de Brabander*, 11-12 (1971), pp. 409–427.

De Boer, D.E.H., "VandenCorencopers". Veertiende-eeuwse graan-speculatie door een dichterlijke bril" in *"Proeve 't al, 't is prysselyck". Verbruik in Europese steden (13de - 18de eeuw). Consumption in European Towns (13th -18th century). Liber Amicorum Raymond van Uytven* (*Bijdragen tot de Geschiedenis*, 81 (1998)), pp. 127–143.

De Brabantse stad. Colloquium Brussel 29-30 maart 1974, in *Bijdragen tot de Geschiedenis* 58 (1975), pp. 5–166.

De Commer, P. and Soly, H., "De zestiende eeuw. Harde Tijden voor zusters en zieken (1490-1585)" in *Het St.-Elisabethziekenhuis te Antwerpen. 750 jaar Gasthuis op't Elzenveld 1238-1988*, Brussel, 1988, pp. 65–89.

De Groote, H.L.V., "De vermogensbalans van Melchior Schets en zij vrouw Anna van Stralen met hun testament van 1 juli 1596" in *Bijdragen tot de Geschiedenis* 55 (1972), pp. 226–263.

Dejongh, G. and Thoen, E., "Arable Productivity in Flanders and the Former Territory of Belgium in a Long-Term Perspective (from the Middle Ages to the End of the Ançien Regime)" in: B.J.P. van Bavel and E. Thoen, eds. *Land Productivity and Agro-Systems in the North Sea area. Middle Ages – 20th Century. Elements for Comparison*, Turnhout 1999 (Corn Publication Series, 2), pp. 30–46.

De Laet, M., "Mechelen versus Antwerpen. De strijd om het bezit en het behoud van de stapel voor vis, zout en haver (1233 - 1467)" in: *Handelingen van de Koninklijke Kring voor Oudheidkunde, letteren en Kunst van Mechelen* 90(1986), (Symposium De sociaal- economische geschiedenis van Mechelen in de Bourgondische tijd (1384 - 1530)) pp. 57–90.

De Nave, F., *Antwerpen, stad en land (1394-1402). De innerlijke vervlechting van stedelijk en landelijk milieu in de late middeleeuwen op basis van het privé bezit aan gronden en renten en andere soorten van goed*, 5 vols., (unpublished thesis, VUB), Brussels, 1978.

De Nave, F., "De vrijheid van Antwerpen (vanaf de middeleeuwen tot de tijd van Rubens)" in L. Voet, e.a., *De stad Antwerpen van de Romeinse tijd tot de 17de eeuw: topografische studie rond het plan van Virgilius Bononiensis, 1565*, Brussels, 1978, p. 59-94.

De Schepper, L., *Hemiksem*, Antwerpen, 1953.

De Smedt, F., een nieuw altaar in 1495" in *Ascania* 36 (1993), pp. 59–63.

De Smedt, O. *De Engelse natie te Antwerpen in de 16e eeuw (1496-1582)* 2 vols. Antwerpen, 1950-54.

Despy-Meyer, A. and Gérard, C. "Abbaye de Affligem, à Hekelgem", in *Monasticon Belge*, vol. IV, fasc. 1, Liège, 1964, pp. 48–50.

De Vries, J. & van der Woude, A.M., *Nederland 1500-1815, De eerste ronde van moderne economische groei,* Amsterdam, 1995.

De Vries, J., *European Urbanization 1500 - 1800*, London, 1984, pp. 179–198.

De Vries, J., *The Dutch Rural Economy in the Golden Age, 1500 - 1700*, New Haven, 1974.

De Waha, M., "Het landelijke leven" in A. Smolar-Meynart and J. Stengers, *Het Gewest Brussel: van de oude dorpen tot de stad van nu*, Brussel, 1989 (*Historische uitgaven: reeks in-4°* = Collection Histoire: série in-4°, 16), pp. 80–109.

De Waha, M., *Recherches sur la vie rurale à Anderlecht au moyen age* (pro civitate serie in 8°, 57,) Brussels, 1979.

De Win, P., "Adel en Stadspatriciaat in het Hertogdom Brabant in de 15de eeuw" in *Spiegel Historiael*, 16 (1981), pp. 407–411.

De Zeeuw, J.W., "Peat and the Dutch Golden Age; the Historical Meaning of Energy Attainability", in *A.A.G. Bijdragen* 21, p. 3-31

Deligne, C., *Bruxelles et sa rivière. Genèse d'un territoire urbain (12e - 18e siècle)* (Turnhout, 2003), (Studies in European Urban History (1100-1800), 1).

Derville, "Le rendement du blé dans la région lilloise (1285-1541)" in: *Buletin de la Commission historique du Département du Nord*, XL (1975-1976), pp. 23–39.

Des Marez, G., *L'organisation du travail à Bruxelles au 15e siècle*, Brussels, 1904.

Dewald, J., *The European Nobility 1400-1800,* Cambridge, 1996.

Dewald, J. and Vardi, L., "The Peasantries of France, 1400-1789" in T. Scott, ed., *The Peasantries of Europe from the Forteenth to the Eighteenth Centuries*, London and New York, 1998, pp. 21–48.

Dijksterhuis, E.J., *Archimedes*, Princeton, 1987.

Domsta, H.J., *Geschichte der Fürsten von Merode im Mittelalter*, Düren, 1981, (Beiträge zur Geschichte des Dürener Landes, 15-16).

Donet, F., "Les Anversois aux Canaries" in *Bulletin de la Société de Géographie d'Anvers*, 19 (1896), pp. 284–310 and 20 (1895), pp. 206–363.

Dufflea. Bijdragen tot de geschiedenis van Duffel, s.l., 1960-1962.

Duplessis, R.S., *Transitions to Capitalism in Early Modern Europe*, Cambridge, 1997 (New Approaches to European History, 10).

Ehrenberg, R., *Das Zeitalter der Fugger, Geldkapital und Kreditverkehr im 16. Jahrhundert,* vol. II: *Die Weltbörsen und Finanzkrisen*, Jena, 1922.

Enno van Gelder, H., "Coins and Accounts in the Eastern Netherlands" in N.J. Mayhew, ed., *Coinage in the Low Countries* (880-1500). Oxford Symposium on Coinage and Monetary History; 3, Oxford, 1979 (BAR International Series, 54), pp. 203–215.

Epstein, S.R., "Cities, Regions and the Late Medieval Crisis: Sicily and Tuscany Compared" in *Past & Present* 130 (1991), p.3-50.

Epstein, S.R., "Town and Country: Economy and Institutions in Late Medieval Italy" in *Economic History Review*, XLVI, 3 (1993), pp. 453–477.

Epstein, S.R., ed., *Town and Country in Europe, 1300-1800,* Cambridge, 2001.

Everitt, A., "Country Carriers in the Nineteenth Century" in D. Gerhold *Road Transport in the Horse-Drawn Era*, Aldershot, 1996, pp. 1–24.

Farmer, D.L., "Marketing the Produce of the Countryside", in E. Miller, ed., *The Agrarian History of England and Wales*, 3: 1348-1500 (Cambridge, 1991), pp. 324–420.

Fisher, F.J., The Development of the London Food Market. 1540-1640" in *The Economic History Review*", V (1934-1935), pp. 46–64.

Fourquin, G., "La population de la région parisienne aux environs de 1328" in *Le Moyen Age,* 1956, 1-2, p. 63-91.

Fourquin, G., *Les campagnes de la région parisienne a la fin du Moyen Age (du milieu du XIIIe siècle au début du XVIe siècle)*, Paris, 1964.

Galloway, J.A., Keene, D., and Murphy, M., "Fuelling the City: Production and Distribution of Firewood and Fuel in London's region, 1290-1400", *Economic History Review*, 49 (1996), pp. 447–72.

Ganshof, F.L, Verhulst, A., Medieval Agrarian Society in its Prime: France, The Low Countries, and Western Germany" in *The Cambridge Economic History of Europe, Vol.I: The Agrarian Life of the Middle Ages,* Cambridge, 1971², pp. 291–339.

Gascon, R., *Grand commerce et vie urbaine au XVIe siècle. Lyon et ses marchands*, 2 vols. (*Civilisations et sociétés* 22) Paris, The Hague, 1971.

Génicot, L., *L'économie rurale namuroise au bas moyen âge*, Louvain-la-Neuve, 4 vols., 1960-1985.

Geudens, E., *Le "Peerdsbosch" ou le domaine rural du Bremdonck*, Antwerp, 1908 (Annales de l'Académie royale d'archéologie de Belgique).

Gillisjans, M., "De uutpachter van het hof te Pamel", in *Ascania,* 37 (1994), pp. 115–116.

Goblet d'Alviella, F., *Histoire des bois et forêts en Belgique*, 4 vols., Paris, 1927-1930.

Godding, Ph., "Impérialisme urbain ou auto-défense: Le cas de Bruxelles (12e - 18e siècles)" in: *Bijdragen tot de Geschiedenis,* 58 (1975), (De Brabantse stad. Colloquium Brussel 29. - 30. march 1974) p. 117-138.

Godding, Ph., "La bourgeoisie foraine de Bruxelles du XIVe au XVIe siècle" in *Cahiers Bruxellois*, VII/1 (1962), pp. 1–78.

Godding, Ph., *Le droit foncier à Bruxelles au moyen âge*, Brussels, 1960.

Godding, Ph., *Le droit privé dans les Pays-Bas méridionaux du 12e au 18e siècle*. Palais des académies: Brussels, 1987 (*Verhandelingen: verzameling in-4°* = Mémoires: collection in-4°, 2:14).

Goetschalckx, P. and Prims, F. "Lillo en Zandvliet in de Xvde eeuw" in *Bijdragen tot de Geschiedenis,* reeks III, V (1953), pp. 65–103

Goris, J.A., *Etude sur les colonies marchandes méridionales (portugais, espagnols, italiens) à Anvers de 1488 à 1567. Contribution à l'histoire des débuts du capitalisme moderne*, Louvain, 1925.

Goris, J.M., "Het abdijgoed" in Id., *Een kaartboek van de abdij Tongerlo. 1655-1794*, Brussels, 2001, p. 19-39.

Goubert, P., *Beauvais et le Beauvaisis de 1600 à 1730: contribution à l'histoire sociale de la France du 17e siècle*, 2 vols., Paris, 1960.

Grapperhaus, F.M., *Alva en de tiende penning*, s.l. 1982.

Guns, P., *De Antwerpse Noorderpolders in de 16de en 17de eeuw*, Antwerpen 1972.

Gutmann, M.P., *War and Rural Life in the Early Modern Low Countries*, (Assen, 1980) (Maaslandse monografien, 31).

Gysels, H., *De landschappen van Vlaanderen en Zuidelijk Nederland. een landschapsecologische studie*, Leuven, Apeldoorn, 1993.

Hagen, W., "Capitalism and the Countryside in Early Modern Europe: Interpretations, Models, Debates" in *Agricultural history*, 62 (1988), pp. 13–47.

Hatcher, J. and Bailey, M., *Modelling the Middle Ages. The History and Theory of England's Economic Development*, Oxford, 2001.

Hilton, R., *The English Peasantry in the Later Middle Ages*, Oxford, 1975.

Hodges, R., *Primitive and Peasant Markets*, Oxford, 1988.

Hoffman, Ph., *Growth in a Traditional Society. The French Countryside, 1450-1815* Princeton, 1996.

Hollestelle, J., De steenbakkerij in de Nederlanden tot omstreeks 1560, Arnhem, 1976[2].

Hoppenbrouwers, P.C.M., *Een middeleeuwse samenleving. Het Land van Heusden (ca.1360 - ca. 1515)*, (Historia Agriculturae, 25), 2 vols., Groningen, 1992.

Hoppenbrouwers, P. and Van Zanden, J.L. eds., *Peasants into Farmers? The Transformation of Rural Economy and Society in the Low Countries (Middle Ages -19th Century) in Light of the Brenner Debate,* Turnhout, 2001 (CORN Publication Series, 4)

Hoyle, R.W., "Redefining Copyhold in the sixteenth Century: the Case of Timber Rights" in P. Hoppenbrouwers & B. van Bavel, eds., *Landholding and Land Transfer in the North Sea Area (late Middle Ages - 19th Century*, (CORN-Publication Seeries, 5), Turnhout, 2004, 250-264.

Hoyle, R.W., "Tenure and the Land Market in Early Modern England: or a Late Contribution to the Brenner Debate" in *Economic History review*, XLIII, pp. 1–20.

Irsigler, F., "L'approvisionnement des villes de l'Allemagne occidentale jusqu'au XVIe siècle"in: *L'approvisionnement des villes de l' Europe occidentale au Moyen Age et aux Temps Modernes. Centre Culturel de l'abbaye de Flaran. Cinquièmes Journées internationales d'histoire 16-18 septembre 1983.* (Auch, 1985) pp. 117–144.

Jacquart, J., "L' endettement paysan et le crédit dans le campagnes de la France moderne" in M. Berthe, ed., *Endettement paysan & crédit rural dans l'Europe médiévale et moderne: actes des 17es Journées internationales d'histoire de l'Abbaye de Flaran, septembre 1995*, Toulouse, 1998, p. 283-298.

Jacquart, J., *La crise rurale en Ile-de-France. 1550-1670*, Paris, 1974 (Publications de la Sorbonne : nouvelle série : recherches, 157).

Jacquart, J., "Paris: First Metropois of the Early Modern Period" in P. Clark and P., Lepetit, eds., *Capital Cities and their Hinterlands in Early Modern Europe*, Aldershot, 1996, pp. 105–118.

Jansen, H.P.H., *Landbouwpacht in Brabant in de 14e en 15e eeuw*, Assen, 1955.

Janssens, F. and Van Cauwenberghe, E., "Stedelijke bevoorradingspolitiek en graanwetgeving in crisistijd te Antwerpen ond het midden van de zeventiende eeuw", in *Bijdragen tot de Geschiedenis*, 62 (1979), p. 231.

Jodogne, P., ed., *Lodovico Guicciardini (1521-1589): actes du colloque international des 28, 29 et 30 mars 1990*, Louvain, 1991 (Travaux de l'Institut interuniversitaire pour l'étude de la Renaissance et de l'Humanisme, 10).

Kaplan, S.L., *Provisioning Paris, Merchants and Millers in the Grain and Flour Trade during the Eighteenth Century*, Ithaca, 1984.

Kerremans, C., *Etude sur les circonscriptions judiciaires et administratives du Brabant et les officiers placés à leur tête par les ducs, antérieurement à l'avènement de la Maison de Bourgogne(1406)*, Brussels, 1949.

Kerridge, E., *The Agricultural Revolution*, London, 1967.

Klep, P.M.M., *Bevolking en arbeid in transformatie. Een onderzoek in Brabant 1700 - 1900*, Nijmegen, 1981.

Klep, P.M.M., "Regional Disparities in Brabantine Urbanization Before and After the Industrial Revolution 1374-1970. Some Aspects of Measurement and Explanation" in P. Bairoch, M. Lévy Leboyer, eds., *Disparities of Economic Development since the Industrial Revolution*, London, 1981; pp. 259–269.

Klep, P.M.M., "Urban Decline in Brabant. The Traditionalization of Investments in Labour (1374 -1806)" in H. Van der Wee, ed., *The Rise and Decline of Urban Industries in Italy and in the Low Countries (Late Middle-Ages – Early Modern Times)*, Leuven, 1988, pp. 261–286.

Klep, P.M.M., "Urbanization in a Pre- Industrial Economy. The Case of Brabant, 1374 -1930" in *Belgisch Tijdschrift voor Nieuwste Geschiedenis*, 7 (1976), pp.153–168.

Kriedte, P., *Spätfeudalismus und Handelskapital. Grundlinien einer europäischen Wirtschaftsgeschichte vom 16. Jahrhundert bis zum Ausgang des 18. Jahrhunderts*, Göttingen, 1980.

Langton, J., and Hoppe, G., *Town and Country in the Development of Early Modern Western Europe*, Norwich, 1983 (Historical Geography Research Group. Research Paper Series, 11).

Leenders, K.A.H.W., "De Antwerpse polder in de Middeleeuwen. Ontginning, bedijking en overstromingen" in: *Tijdschrift van de Belgische Vereniging voor aardrijkskundige studies,* 1985/1, pp. 43–77.

Leenders, K.A.H.W., *Van Turnhoutervoorde tot Strienemonde: ontginnings- en nederzettingsgeschiedenis van het Noordwesten van het Maas-Schelde-Demergebied, 400-1350: een poging tot synthese*, Zutphen, 1996.

Leenders, K.A.H.W., *Verdwenen venen,* Een onderzoek naar de ligging en exploitatie van thans verdwenen venen in het gebied tussen Antwerpen, Turnhout, Geertruidenbergen Willemstad 1250-1750, s.l. 1989.

Lefèbvre, S., "The City and the Forest: a Privileged Relationship? Some Remarks on the Case of the Soignes Forest, 16th-18th Centuries" in B. Blondé, E. Vanhaute, M. Galand, eds., *Labour and Labour Markets between Town and Countryside (Middle Ages -19th Century)'* (Corn Publication Series, 6), (Turnhout 2001), pp. 236–249.

Limberger, M., "Credit, Land Market and the Connection between Rural and Urban Economy. The Use of Perpetual Annuities in Aartselaar (Brabant), 14th - 16th centuries" in T. Lambrecht and P. Schoffield, eds., *Credit and the Rural Economy in Europe, c.1100-c.1800. (CORN Publication Series)(forthcoming).*

Limberger, M., "De prijs van het water- en wegtransport in de vijftiende en zestiende eeuw. Het vervoer van molenstenen in de rekeningen van het hertogelijke domein Tervuren-Vilvoorde (1450-1572)" in *Het transport en het stedelijke netwerk in de Zuidelijke Nederlanden,* Bijdragen tot de Geschiedenis 82 (1999), p. 215-234.

Limberger, M., *Die Metropolenstellung Antwerpens im 16. Jahrhundert. Aspekte der Antwerpener Zentralität auf verschiedenen Wirtschaftsebenen: Weltwirtschaft, nationaler und regionaler Markt* (unpublished M.A. thesis, University of Vienna, 1990).

Limberger, M., "Feeding Sixteenth-Century Antwerp. Food Imports, Local Supply, and the Agrarian Structure of the Town's Rural Surroundings" in P. van Cruyningen and, E. Thoen eds. *Food: Production, Demand and Trade. Aspects of the Economic Relation between Town and Countryside (Middle Ages-19th Century)* (CORN Publication Series no. 9, forthcoming).

Limberger, M., Merchant Capitalism and the Countryside: Antwerp and the West of the Duchy of Brabant – (XVth – XVIth centuries) in: P. Hoppenbrouwers, J.L. van Zanden, (eds.), *Peasants into Farmers? The Transformation of Rural Economy and Society in the Low Countries (Middle Ages -19th Century) in Light of the Brenner Debate, Turnhout, 2001* (CORN Publication Series no. 4), p. 158-178.

Limberger, M., "Periferie urbane e processi di sub-urbanizzazione ad Anversa nel XVI secolo. "Forze di mercato" e "mano visibile" in: *Società e Storia* 112 (2006), pp. 267–284 (special issue: P. Lanaro, G.M. Varanini, eds., Perieferie e spazi periferici nella città europea del medioevo e dell' età moderna (secoli XIV-XIX) : le trasformazioni indotte dall'economia).

Lindemans, P., *Geschiedenis van de landbouw in Belgie,* 2 vols., Antwerpen, 1952.

Maddens, N., "Zestiende-eeuwse fiskale bronnen ter bestudering van de sociaal-economische toestanden op het Vlaamse platteland" in *Economische geschiedenis van België: behandeling van de bronnen en problematiek: handelingen van het Colloquium te Brussel, 17-19 nov. 1971,* Brussel 1972, pp. 21–30.

Marnef, G., *Antwerp in the Age of Reformation: Underground Protestantism in a Commercial Metropolis, 1550-1577,* Baltimore, Md, 1996 (The Johns Hopkins University studies in Historical and Political Science; 114:1).

Martens, M., *L'administration du domaine ducal en Brabant au moyen âge, 1250-1406,* (*Mémories: collection in –8°,* 2e série), Brussels, 1954.

Masschaele, J., *Peasants, Merchants and Markets. Inland trade in Medieval England, 1150-1350,* New York, 1997.

Masure, T., *De stadfinanciën van Antwerpen 1531-1571. Een poging tot reconstructie,* 2 vols., MA. thesis Univ. Ghent, 1986.

Mendels, F.F., *Industrialization and Population Pressure in Eighteenth-Century Flanders,* New York, 1981.

Merrington, J., "Town and Country in the Transition to Capitalism" in R. Hilton, ed., *The Transition from Feudalism to Capitalism*, London, 1976. pp. 170–195.

Mertens, J., *De laatmiddeleeuwse landbouweconomie in enkele gemeenten van het Brugse platteland, (Historische uitgaven: reeks in –8°)*, Brussel, 1970.

Mertens, J.F. and Torfs, K.L., *Geschiedenis van Antwerpen sedert de stichting der stad tot onze tyden*, 7 vols., Antwerpen, 1845-1853.

Musgrave, P. *The Early Modern European Economy*, Basingstoke, London, New York, 1999 (European History in Perspective).

Nauwelaers, J., *Histoire de la ville de Vilvorde*, Paris, Brussels, Kortrijk, 1941.

Neveux, H., *Les grains du Cambrésis. Vie et déclin d'une structure économique: (fin du 14e-début du 17e siècle)*, Paris, 1980 (*Civilisations et sociétés*, 64).

Nicholas, D., *Town and Countryside: Social, Economical and Political Tensions in Fourteenth-Century Flanders*, Bruges, 1971.

Noordergraaf, L., "Het platteland van Holland in de zestiende eeuw. Anachronismen, modelgebruik en traditionele bronnenkritiek" in *Economisch en sociaalhistorisch Jaarboek*, 48 (1985) pp. 8–18.

Nooyens, F., *Geschiedenis van Deurne I (tot 1648)*, Deurne, 1981.

Overton, M., *Agricultural Revolution in England: the Transformation of the Agrarian Economy, 1500-1850*, Cambridge, 1996 (Cambridge Studies in Historical Geography, 23).

Peeters, J.P., *Bloei en verval van de middeleeuwse stadsvrijheid Vilvoorde*, Tielt, 1975.

Peeters, J.P., "Een spiegel van de binnenscheepvaart op het einde de middeleeuwen: het proces omtrent de bouw van een nieuwe sluis op de Zennerivier te Heembeek (tussen Brussel en Vilvoorde) (1434)" in: *Eigen Schoon en de Brabander*, LVII (1974), pp. 203–221, 349-363, 477-493.

Petri, F., "Das Verhältnis von Stadt und Land in der Geschichte der Niederlande" in *Stadt- Land-Beziehungen und Zentralität als Problem der historischen Raumforschung*, Hannover, 1974, pp. 103–122.

Pirenne, H., *Histoire de Belgique*, vol.III, Brussels, 1923.

Piuz, A.-M., "Les rélations économiques entre les villes et les campagnes dans les sociétés préindustrielles" in *Revue européenne des sciences sociales*, XV (1977), pp. 195–231.

Ploegaerts, G., "L'abbaye cistercienne de Villers pendant les cinq derniers siècles de son existence" in *Annales de la société archéologique de l'arrondissement de Nivelle, XI (1913-26)*, pp. 93–673.

Postan, M., *The Medieval Economy and Society. An Economic History of Britain 1100-1500*, London, 1972.

Pounds, N.J.G., "Population and Settlement in the Low Countries and Northern France in the Later Middle Ages" in *Belgisch Tijdschrift voor Filologie en Geschiedenis/Revue Belge de Philologie et d'Histoire, XLIX* (1971) pp. 369–402.

Prevenier, W. and Blockmans, W., *De Bourgondische Nederlanden*, Antwerp, 1983.

Prims, F., "Antwerpen in het 'land van Oosterweel'" in: *Antwerpiensia 21* (1950) pp. 25–28.

Prims, F., "De schippers en hun ambachtskamer inhet oude Antwerpen" in *De binnenscheepvaart* I, 1945-1948, pp. 10–13

PRIMS, F., "Historische teksten II. Hoven en hoveniers te Antwerpen in 1338" in *Bijdragen tot de Geschiedenis*, 23 (1932), pp. 150–156;

PRIMS, F., *Geschiedenis van Antwerpen*, vol. III, pp. 85–88.

PRIMS, F., "Polderstudiën: Wilmarsdonk Dalenhof" in *Antwerpiensia,* 1950 (21e reeks)" Antwerpen, 1951, p. 65-68.

RINGROSE, D. R., *Madrid and the Spanish Economy, 1560-1850*, Berkeley, 1983.

ROMBAUT, H. and DE NIEL, P., "De kleinijverheid in de Rupelstreek (13de - 20ste eeuw): een kort overzicht van het steenmaken, dak-pannen en plaveien" in *Ons Heem*, 53, 1999, p. 135-165.

RUSSEL, J. C., "Population in Europe 500-1500" in C.M. CIPOLLA, ed., *The Fontana Economic History of Europe*, vol I, chapter 1, London, Glasgow, 1971.

SABBE, E., *Anvers. Metropole de l'Occident (1492 - 1566)*, Brussels, 1952.

SACRÉ, M., *Geschiedenis der gemeente Merchtem*, Rousselare, 1904.

SCHNAPPER, B., *Les rentes au XVIe siècle, Histoire d'un instrument de crédit*, Paris, 1957.

SCHOLLIERS, E., *Loonarbeid en honger. De levensstandaard in de XVe en XVIe eeuw te Antwerpen*, Antwerpen, 1960.

SIVÉRY, G., "Les profits de l'éleveur et du cultivateur dans le Hainaut à la fin du moyen age" in *Annales E.S.C.*, 31 (1976), p. 604-630.

SIVÉRY, G., *Structures agraires et vie rurale dans le Hainaut à la fin du moyen-âge*, 2 vols., Lille, 1977-1980.

SLICHER VAN BATH, B., *De agrarische geschiedenis van West - Europa (500 -1850)*, Utrecht,1960.

SLOOTMANS, C.J.F., *Paas- en koudenmarkten te Bergen op Zoom*, 3 vols., Tilburg, 1985 (Bijdragen tot de geschiedenis van het zuiden van Nederland, LXIV-VI).

SMOLAR-MEYNART, A., STENGERS, J., *Het Gewest Brussel: van de oude dorpen tot de stad van nu*, Brussel, 1989 (Historische uitgaven: reeks in-4°/Collection Histoire: série in-4°,16).

SNOOKS, G.D., "The Dynamic Role of the Market in the Anglo-Saxon Economy and Beyond, 1086-1300" in R.H. BRITNELL and B.M.S. CAMPBELL, eds., *A Commercialising Economy: England 1086-c. 1300* (Manchester, 1995), pp. 27–54.

SOLY, H., "De brouwerijonderneming van Gilbert van Schoonbeke (1552 - 1562)" in *Belgisch Tijdschrift voor Filologie en Geschiedenis* 46/1968, 337 – 392, 1166 - 1204.

SOLY, H., "De economische betekenis van Zuidnederlandse brouwindustrie in de zestiende eeuw. Problematiek" in *Economische geschiedenis van België: behandeling van de bronnen en problematiek: handelingen van het Colloquium te Brussel, 17-19 nov. 1971*, Brussel 1972, pp. 97–117.

SOLY, H. "Een Antwerpse Compagnie voor de levensmiddelenbevoorrading van het leger in de Nederlanden in de zestiende eeuw" in *Bijdragen en Mededelingen betreffende de Geschiedenis der Nederlanden*, 86 (1971), pp. 350–362.

SOLY, H., "Social Relations in Antwerp in the Sixteenth and Seventeenth Centuries" in J. VAN DER STOCK, ed., *Antwerp, Story of a Metropolis*, Gent, 1993, pp. 37–48.

SOLY, H., "The ‚Betrayal' of the Sixteenth Century Bourgeoisie: A Myth? Some Considerations of the Behavior Pattern of the Merchants of Antwerp in the Sixteenth Century" in *Acta Historiae Neerlandica,* 18 (1975), pp. 31–49.

SOLY, H., *Urbanisme en kapitalisme te Antwerpen in de 16e eeuw. De stedebouwkundige en industriële ondernemingen van Gilbert van Schoonbeke*, Brussel, 1977 (Historische uitgaven: reeks in-8°/Collection histoire: série in-8°; 47).

Sosson, J.P., Les travaux publics de la ville de Bruges 14e-15e siècles, Brussels, 1977 (*Historische uitgaven: reeks in-8°* /Collection histoire: série in-8°; 48).

Stabel, P., *Dwarfs Among Giants: the Flemish Urban Network in the Late Middle Ages*, Leuven, 1997.

Stabel, P., *De kleine stad in Vlaanderen: bevolkingsdynamiek en economische functies van de kleine en secundaire stedelijke centra in het Gentse kwartier (14de-16de eeuw)*, Brussel, 1995 (Verhandelingen van de Koninklijke Academie voor Wetenschappen, Letteren en Schone Kunsten van België: Klasse der Letteren, 156).

Stadt-Land-Beziehungen und Zentralität als Problem der historischen Raumforschung, Hannover, 1974 (Veröffentlichungen der Akademie für Raumforschung und Landesplanung: Forschungs-und Sitzungsberichte vol. 88, Historische Raumforschung, 11)

Stockmans, J.B., *Geschiedenis van de gemeente Berchem*, Brussel, 1975² (orig. 1886).

Thijs, A.K.L., "Een ongeziene commeriele bloei" in K. van Isacker and R. van Uytven (eds.), Antwerpen. Twaalf eeuwen geschiedenis en cultuur. Antwerpen, 1986, pp. 93–102.

Thijs, A.K.L., "Weemoes, weemoesputten en weemoesvelden: kanttekeningen betreffende de invloed der stedelijke lakenververij op de ontwikkeling van de landbouw in het Antwerpse" in *Bijdragen tot de Geschiedenis*, 57 (1974), pp. 189–202.

Thijs, A., "The river Scheldt Closed for Two Centuries, 1585-1790" in Asaert, G., De Vos, A., Thijs, A., Veraghtert, K., *Antwerp, a Port for All Seasons,* Antwerpen, 1986, pp. 165–212.

Thoen, E., "A ‚Commercial Survival Economy' in Evolution. The Flemish Countryside and the Transition to Capitalism (Middle Ages – 19th Century)" in: Hoppenbrouwers and van Zanden (eds.), *Peasants into Farmers?,* pp. 102–157.

Thoen, E., "Driesch" in *Lexikon des Mittelalters*, vol. III, München, Zürich, 1984-1986, kol. 1399-1400.

Thoen, E., *Landbouwekonomie en bevolking in Vlaanderen gedurende de late middeleeuwen en het begin van de moderne tijden. Testregio: de kasselrijen van Oudenaarde en Aalst* (Publications du Centre Belge d'Historie Rurale, 90), 2 vols., Gent, 1988.

Thoen, E., "Technique agricole, cultures nouvelles et économie rurale en Flandre au bas moyen age" in *Plantes et cultures nouvelles en Europe occidentale au Moyen Age et à l'époque moderne* (Centre culturel de l'abbaye de Flaran. Douzièmes Journées internationales d'histoire, 11,12,13 septembre 1990), Auch, 1992. p. 51-68.

Thoen, E., "Warfare and Countryside: Social and Economic Aspects of the Military Destruction in Flanders during the Late middle Ages and the Early Modern Period" in: *Acta Historia Neerlandica* XIII (1980), pp. 25–40.

Tits-Dieuaide, L' évolution des techniques agricoles en Flandre et en Brabant du XIVe au XVe siècle" in *Annales E.S.C.,* 36 (1981), p.362-381.

Tits-Dieuaide, M.J., *La formation des prix céréaliers en Brabant et en Flandre au XVe siècle*, Brussels, 1975.

Unger, R. W., "Feeding Low Countries Towns: the Grain Trade in the Fifteenth Century", in *Revue belge de philologie et d'histoire*, 77, 1999, pp. 329–358.

Urbain, Y., "La formation du réseau des voies navigables en Belgique. Développements du système des voies d'eau et politique des transports sous l'Ancien Régime" in *Bulletin de l'iinstitut de recherches économiques et sociales* 10 (1938-1939), pp. 272–314.

Van Bavel, B.J.P., "Land Lease and Agriculture: the Transition of the Rural Economy in the Dutch River Area from the Fourteenth to the Sixteenth Century" in *Past & Present*, 172 (2001), p. 3-43.

Van Bavel, B., *Transitie en continuïteit: de bezitsverhoudingen en de plattelandseconomie in het westelijk gedeelte van het Gelderse rivierengebied, ca. 1300-ca. 1570*, Hilversum, 1999 (*Werken uitgegeven door Gelre, 52*).

Van Bavel, B.J.P., and Hoppenbrouwers, P., eds., *Landholding and Land Transfer in the North Sea Area (late Middle Ages - 19th Century)*, Turnhout 2004, (Corn Publication Series, 5).

Van Beylen, J., *Schepen van de Nederlanden. Van de late middeleeuwen tot het einde van de 17de eeuw*, Antwrpen, 1970.

Van Cauwenberghe, E., *Het vorstelijk domein en de overheidsfinancien in de Nederlanden (15de en 16de eeuw) Een quantitative analyse van Vlaamse en Brabantse domeinrekeningen* (Gemeentekrediet van Belgie, Historische Uitgaven Pro Civitate r.8°, 61,) Brussels, 1982.

Van der Stock, J., ed., *Antwerp, Story of a Metropolis* (Exhibition Catalogue, Antwerp, Hessenhuis, 25 June -10 October 1993), Ghent, 1993, pp. 37–48.

Van der Wee, H., Antwerp and the New Financial Methods of the 16th and 17th Centuries" in *The Low Countries in the Early Modern World*, (Aldershot: Variorum, 1993), pp. 145–166. (orig. "Anvers et les innovations de la technique financière au XVIe et XVIIe siècles" in *Annales*, E.S.C., XXII (1967), pp. 1067–1089).

Van der Wee, H., "Industrial Dynamics and the Process of Urbanisation and De-Urbanisation in the Low Countries from the Late Midle Ages to the Eighteenth Century. A Synthesis" in *The rise and decline of urban industries in Italy and in the Low Countries (late middle ages – early modern times)*, Leuven, 1988, pp. 307–381.

Van der Wee, H., *The Growth of the Antwerp Market and the European Economy (fourteenth - sixteenth centuries)*. 3 vols. Den Haag, 1963.

Van der Wee, H., "The Agricultural Development of the Low Countries as Revealed by the Tithe and Rent Statistics. 1250-1800" in Idem and E. Van Cauwenberghe, eds., *Productivity of Land and Agricultural Innovations in the Low Countries (1250 - 1800)*, Leuven, 1978, pp. 1–23.

Van der Wee, H. and Aerts, E., "The Lier Livestock Trade in the Low Countries from the 14th to the 18th Century" in: E. Westermann (ed.), *Internationaler Ochsenhandel (1350-1750). Akten des 7th International Economic History Congress Edinburgh 1978*, Stuttgart, Bamberg, 1979 (Beiträge zur Wirtschaftsgeschichte, 9), pp. 235–254.

Van der Wee, H, and Van Cauwenberghe, E., eds., *Productivity of Land and agricultural Innovations in the Low Countries (1250 - 1800)*, Leuven, 1978.

Van der Woude, A., "Demografische ontwikkeling van de noordelijke Nederlanden, 1500-1800" in *Algemene Geschiedenis der Nederlanden* 5, Haarlem, 1980, pp. 102–168.

Van der Woude, A.M., "Large Estates and Small Holdings. Lords and Peasants in the Netherlands during the Late Middle Ages and Early Moden Times" in: P. Gunst and T. Hoffmann (eds.), *Large Estates and Small Holdings in Europe in the Middle Ages and Modern Times.* National reports Budapest 1982.

Van Ermen, E., *De landelijke bezittingen van de heren van Wezemaal in de middeleeuwen*, 2 vols., Leuven, 1982 (Belgisch Centrum voor landelijke Geschiedenis, 68).

Van Ermen, E., *Feodaal-heerlijke verhoudingen en territoriale patronen in het middeleeuwse hertogdom Brabant (12de - 14de eeuw) met bijzondere aandacht voor de regio Leuven*, 6 vols., (PhD dissertation, KUL) Leuven, 1989.

Van Gerven, J., "Antwerpen in de veertiende eeuw. Kleine stad zonder toekomst of opkomend handelscentrum ?" in *Revue belge de philologie et d'histoire*, 76, 1998, pp. 907–938.

Van Houtte J.A., "Anvers aux XVe et XVIe siècles. Expansion et apogée" in *Annales E.H.C.*, 16 (1961), pp. 248–278;

Van Houtte, J.A., "La genèse du grand marché international d'Anvers à la fin du Moyen-Age" in *Belgisch Tijdschrift voor Filologie en Geschiedenis/Revue Belge de Philologie et d'Histoire*, *XIX* (1940), pp. 87–126;

Van Houtte, J.A. and Verhulst, A., "L' approvisionnement des villes dans le Pays-Bas (Moyen Age et Temps Modernes)" in: *Troisième conférence internationale d'histoire économique*. Munich, 1965, Paris, The Hague, 1968, vol. I, pp. 73–77.

Van Houtte, J.A. and van Uytven, R., "Nijverheid en Handel 1300-1482" in *Algemene geschiedenis van de Nederlanden IV*, Haarlem, 1980, pp. 87–111.

Van den Nieuwenhuizen, J., "Abbaye de St. Michel à Anvers", in *Monasticon Belge* vol. VIII, 1, pp. 195–262P.

Van Passen, R., *Geschiedenis van Edegem*, Edegem, 1974.

Van Passen, R., *Geschiedenis van Kontich*, Kontich, 1988[2].

Van Passen, R., *Geschiedenis van Wilrijk*, Wilrijk, 1982.

Van Tielhof, M., "Grain Provision in Holland, ca. 1490- ca. 1570" in Hoppenbrouwers & van Zanden, eds., *Peasants into Farmers...*, p. 202-219.

Van Tielhof, M., *De Hollandse graanhandel, 1470-1570: koren op de Amsterdamse molen*, Den Haag, 1995, (*Hollandsche historische reeks*, 23).

Van Uytven, R., "Brabantse en Antwerpse centrale plaatsen (14de-19de eeuw)" in *Het stedelijk netwerk in België in historisch perspectief (1350-1850). een statistische en dynamische benadering/le reseau urbain en Belgique dans une perspective historique (1350-1850), une approche statistique et dynamique*, (Handelingen 15de Internationaal Colloquium / Actes 15e Colloque International, Spa, 4-6 sept. 1990), Brussels, 1992, pp. 29–79.

Van Uytven, R., "Crisis als cesuur, 1482-1494" in *Algemene geschiedenis der Nederlanden V*, Haarlem, 1980, pp. 434f.

Van Uytven, R. "De premonstratenzerabdijen en de politiek in de Nederlanden" in *De glans van Prémontré. Oude kunst uit Witherenabdijen der Lage Landen*, Heverlee, 1973, p. 47.

Van Uytven, R., "De Premonstratenzers in het sociaal-economisch leven der Nederlanden", in *De glans van Prémontré*, pp. 63–74.

Van Uytven, R., "De sociale krisis der XVIe eeuw te Leuven" in *Belgisch Tijdschrift voor Filologie en Geschiedenis/Revue Belge de Philologie et d'Histoire* XXXVI (1958), p. 356 - 387.

Van Uytven, R., "Die ländliche Industrie während des Spätmittelalters in den südlichen Niederlanden" in H. Kellenbenz (ed.), *Agrarisches Nebengewerbe und Formen der Reagrarisierung im Spätmittelalter und 19./20. Jahrhundert* (Bericht über die 5. Arbeitstagung der Gesellschaft für Sozial- und Wirtschaftsgeschichte, (Stuttgart 1975), pp. 57–78.

Van Uytven, R., "Het sociaal economisch leven" in Idem, ed, *De geschiedenis van Mechelen: van heerlijkheid tot stadsgewest*, Tielt, 1991, pp. 41–57.

Van Uytven, R., "In de schaduwen van de Antwerpse groei: het Hageland in de zestiende eeuw" in *Bijdragen tot de Geschiedenis*, 57 (1974), pp. 171–188.

van Uytven, R., "La draperie Babançonne et Malinoise du XIIe au XVIIe siècle: grandeur éphémère et decadence" in *Produzione, commercio e consumo dei panni di lana (nei secoli XII-XVIII)* Firenze, 1976, p. 85-97 (reprint in: van Uytven, *Production and Consumption in the Low Countries...* chapter VIII).

Van Uytven, R., "Landtransport durch Brabant im Mittelalter und im 16. Jahrhundert" in F. Burgard, A. Haverkamp, *Auf den Römerstraßen ins Mittelalter. Beiträge zur Verkehrsgeschichte zwischen Maas und Rhein von der Spätantike bis ins 19. Jahrhundert*, Mainz 1997, p. 471-499.

Van Uytven, R., "L'approvisionnement des villes des anciens Pays Bas au Moyen Age" in: *L'approvisionnement des villes de l' Europe occidentale au Moyen Age et aux Temps Modernes.* Centre Culturel de l'abbaye de Flaran. Cinquièmes Jornèes internationales d'histoire 16-18 septembre 1983, Auch, 1985, pp. 75–116 (reprint in: Van Uytven, R., *Production and Consumption in the Low Countries...* chapter XI).

Van Uytven, R., "Le combat des boissons en Europe du moyen âge au XVIIIe siècle in: S. Cavaciocchi (ed.), *Alimentazione e nutrizione secc. XIII-XVIII, Atti della "Ventottesima Settimana di Studi" 22-27 aprile 1996*, Firenze, 1997, pp. 53–88 (Istituto Internazionale di Storia economica "F.Datini" Prato, serie II – Atti delle "Settimane di Studi" e altri Convegni, 28).

Van Uytven, R., "Politiek en Economie. De crisis der late XVe eeuw in de Nederlanden" in *Belgisch Tijdschrift voor Filologie en Geschiedenis/Revue Belge de Philologie et d'Histoire,* 53 (1975), pp. 1097–1149.

Van Uytven, R., *Production and Consumption in the Low Countries, 13th-16th Centuries*, Aldershot, 2001.

Van Uytven, R., *Stadsfinanciën en stadseconomie te Leuven van de XIIe tot het einde der XVIe eeuw*, Brussels, 1961 (Verhandelingen van de koninglijke Academie voor Wetenschapen, Letteren en Schone Kunsten van Belgie /Klasse der Letteren Jg.XXIII/1961, no. 44).

Van Uytven, R., "Vroege inbreuken op de braak in Brabant en de intensieve landbouw in de Zuidelijke Nederlanden tijdens der 13de eeuw" in: *Tijdschrift van de Belgische Vereniging voor aardrijkskundige studies,* LIII 1984/1, pp. 63–72.

Van Uytven, R., "Wereldelijke overheid en reguliere geestelijkheid in Brabant tijdens de Late Middeleeuwen" in *Bronnen voor de religieuze geschiedenis van België/ Middleeuwen en Moderne Tijden*, Leuven, 1968, pp. 48–134.

Van Uytven, R., "What is New Socially and Economically in the Sixteenth-Century Netherlands?" in *Acta Historiae Neerlandicae. Studies on the History of The Netherlands* 7, (1974), p. 18-53; (reprint in van Uytven, R., *Production and Consumption in the Low Countries...* chapter I).

Van Uytven, R., and De Puydt, J., "De toestand der abdijen in de Oostenrijkse Nederlanden, inzonderheid der Statenabdijen, in de tweede helft de 18de eeuw. Het verslag De Kulberg en de proceverbalen der abtskeuzen" in *Bijdragen tot de Geschiedenis*, 48 (1965), pp. 5–80

Van Werveke, H., "La banlieue primitive des villes flamandes" in *Miscellanea Mediaevalia in memoriam Jan Frederik Niermeyer,* Groningen, 1967, pp. 313–325.

Van Zanden, J.-L, "A Third Road to Capitalism? Proto-Industriaization and the Moderate Nature of the Later Medieval Crisis in Flanders and Holland, 1350-1550" in Hoppenbrouwers and van Zanden, (eds.), *Peasants into Farmers?*...p. 85-101.

Van Zanden, J.-L., *The Rise and Decline of Holland's Economy*, Manchester, 1993.

Vandenbroecke, C., "De Proto-industriële Ontwikkeling van België in het Kader van de Internationale Historiografie" in *Belgisch Tijdschrift voor Filologie en Geschiedenis/Revue Belge de Philologie et d'Histoire*, LXIII (1985), pp. 310–323.

Verbeemen, J., "Immigratie te Antwerpen" in *Mededelingen van de Geschied- en Oudheidkundige kring voor Leuven en omgeving* (1965), pp. 81–100;

Verbesselt, J., "Inboedel van het hof te Boutersbrugge in 1436" in *Eigen Schoon en de Brabander*, p. 450-451.

A. E. Verhulst, *De Sint-Baafsabdij te Gent en haar grondbezit, 7de-14de eeuw: bijdrage tot de kennis van de structuur en de uitbating van het grootgrondbezit in Vlaanderen tijdens de middeleeuwen*, Brussel, 1958 (Verhandelingen van de Koninklijke Vlaamse Academie voor Wetenschappen, Letteren en Schone Kunsten van België. Klasse der Letteren; 30).

Verhulst, A., *Het landschap in Vlaanderen in historisch perspectief, Antwerpen, 1956.*

Verhulst, A., The 'Agricultural Revolution' of the Middle Ages Reconsidered" in B.S. Bachrach and D. Nicholas, eds., *Law, Custom and the Social Fabric in Medieval Europe, Essays in Honor of Bryce Lyon*, Kalamazoo 1990, pp. 17–28.

Verhulst, A. and Vandenbroeke, C., eds., *Landbouwproductiviteit in Vlaanderen en Brabant, XIVe-XIXe eeuw*, Gent 1979.

Voet, L. "De Vorsten: de middeleeuwse vorst" in Broeckx J.L., De Clercq C., Dhondt J., Nauwelaerts M.A., eds., *Flandria Nostra: ons land en ons volk, zijn standen en beroepen door de tijden heen*, vol. V, Antwerp, 1960, pp. 33–98.

Von Thünen, J.H., *Der isolierte Staat im Beziehung auf Landwirtschaft und Nationalökonomie*, Stuttgart, 1842[3].

Wallerstein, I., *The Modern World System. Capitalist Agriculture and the Origins of the European World-Economy in the Sixteenth Century*, New York, 1974.

Wauters, A., *Histoire des environs de Bruxelles ou description historique des localités qui formaient autrefois l'ammanie de cette ville*, 10 vols. Brussels, 1855 (new edition, Brussels, 1975).

Wildiers van der Wee, K., "De Geschiedenis van het Lierse veemarktprivilegie" in *Land van v Rijen*, XVI, pp. 124–136 and XVII, pp. 33–52.

Woolf, S. J., "Venice and the Terraferma: Problems of the Change from Commercial to Landed Activities" in B. Pullan, ed., *Crisis and Change in the Venetian Economy in the 16th and 17 Centuries*, London 1968, pp. 175–203.

Wrigley, E.A., "A Simple model of London's Importance in Changing English Society and Economy 1650-1750" in P. Abrams and E.A. Wrigley, eds., *Towns in Societies: Essays in Economic History and Historical Sociology, Cambridge, 1978 (Past and Present Publications, 10)*, pp. 215–309.

Wrigley, E.A., "Metropolitan Cities and their Hinterlands: Stimulus and Constraints to Growth" in Aerts and Clark, *Metropolitan Cities*...p. 15,

Zoete, A., *De beden in het graafschap Vlaanderen onder de hertogen Jan zonder Vrees en Filips de Goede* (1405-1467), (Verhandelingen van de Koninklijke Academie voor Wetenschappen, Letteren en Schone Kunsten, Klasse der Letteren, 56 (1994), no. 149), Brussel, 1994.

Appendix

Appendix 1: Fifteenth-Century Lease Contracts

a) Antwerp area SAA - SR 43:
No. 1: SR 43, fo. 84:
Owner: Willem van Riethoven (receiver of the ducal domains of Antwerp and Herentals)
Lessee: Wouter de Vos
Description: farmland 0.6 ha. (1/2 b) + house inc. 0.24 ha. land
'met grachten en ale toebehoorten' Antwerpen, buiten Sint Joris-poorte langs de steenweg
Size: 0.84 ha.
14 years, from christmas
Lease: 6 lb. 12 s. gr.Br.
+ 1 basket of bakingpears and apples

No. 2 SR, 43 fo. 87 r.
Owner: Gielis Sanders
Lessee: Peter van Loeke, brother in law
Description: hoeve te Hemixem, ca. 48 b.?, zo verre als hij ze besaeien zal.
helftwinning, voor weie, die daartoe behoort, elk bunder voor 11 s. gr.
& 4 b. maeybeken alsoe sij binnen dezelfde hoeve gelegen zijn, voor 4 lb. Br. gr.
Size: 48 b., + meadow +4 b. hayland
Term: 12 years.
Lease: halfwinning, meadows for 11 s. per bunder, 4 lb. Br. for hayland

No.3 SR 43 fo. 212: 10.10. 1450;
Owner: Jan van Berchem & Jan van Emmerhoven
Lessee: Peter ? + Gertruid + brother
Description: hoeve, Vremde, Hagenbroek
Term: 14 years (~~9~~ deleted)
Price: 16,5 lb. (18 lb. deleted)
+ 12 capons
+ 4 geese

No. 4: SR 43, fo. 259 vo.: 9 january 1451 Peter Reyner (alderman)
Lessee: Jan Abts
Description: hoeve onder Berchem en Wilrijk (met land aarde ende beemde)
Lease: 14 lb. gr.
14 zisters rye
8 capons, 4 hens
1/2 money bamis, rest christmas
to be delivered in Antwerp

No. 5: SR 43, fo.278: 6 maart 1451
Owners: Jan Vander Heyden son of Jacob (the tanner) + Jacob Roemans, Jan Manaert, Jacob vander Heyden, mercer
Lessee: Jan Jacobs & wife
'goed der kinderen vander heyden "toud steden" met huizingen, aerden, binnen Schoten; int Goer
from past 1 march: 10 years
Lease: 20 lb. gr.
11 zister rye
2 vt. buckkwheat
12 capons
7 gelten buttter
2 geese
100 eggs
1200 woods, faggots or bark

No. 6: SR 43, fo. 336: 17 augustus 1450
Owner: Godevaert Sanders
Lessee: Peter Hendricszoon from Zandvliet
hoeve, 47.9 hectar (48.5 gemeten = 36.4 bunder)
Ossendrecht, Nieuwland
6 years (from 21 march)
Lease: halfwinning: 'als de vruchten gebonden staan ende de tiendenaar yijn tiende wech heeft' grassland: 2 s. gr. Br. gemet.

No. 7: SR 43, fo. 403 - 404: 18 dec. 1450
Owner: Lady Katelijne van Limale - superior St. Elisabeth hopsital
Lessee: Jan vander Tangen
Gasthuisgoed 'zadelroede' te Mortsel & bredevelde daarnaast, met huizingen etc.
3 years (1 may)
Lease: 22 zister 2 vt. wheat
22 zister 2 vt. rye
25 zister rough oats
15 zister oats
60 golden crowns of 21 stuivers

No. 8: SR 43, fo. 433 vo.: 15 dec. 1450
Owner: Broeder Jan Rav(n)ens, provost van Sint Michiels
Lessee: Jan de Raet, gezeten te ranst
hoeve te Wommelgem
Term: 9 y. (joh. bapt.)
Lease: 6,5 zister rox
12,5 zister evene

14 phls. penninge 'rijders'
12 geese
8 lb. wax
100 eggs in 2 terms
2 corveys 'diensten opte kempene' or one Rhine-Guilder

No. 9: SR 43, fo.433vo.-434 ro. 18 dec. 1450
Owner: St. Elisabeth hospital
Lessee: Zamen van Hoernick
Description: Goed ter Bist in Sint Laureis, te Hove
Term: 10 years (5 may)
Lease: farmland: 4 zister rye
3 zister wheat
12 zister rough oats
meadows: 24 gouden ouden Reynaldus gilders
14 capons
7 hens
1 stuc boter van 14 lb.
100 eieren
4 lb. gt. eens

No.10: SR 43, fo. 434 vo. 18 dec.1450
Owner: Sint Elisabeth gasthuis
Lessee: Jan Balleken
Description: hoeve met huis en hof, beemde en aarde Merxem
Term: 6 years, 5 may
Lease: 5 zister rox
3 lb. 10 s. gr.Br.
1 fat lamb
4 capons
4 hens
1 peace butter (12 lb.) "pachter betaalt herencijns ende alle anderen commeren zonder mindernisse van huer Jonkheer Jan van Assche 4 hoenderen yearlijks"

No. 11: SR 43, fo. 445
Owner: Claus Vander Heyden, at Gierle, in the name of meester Peter Vander Heyden, living in Brussels,
Lessee: Matheeus de Bye te Massenhoven
Description: alsulcke percelen van beempde land en aarde metten wasse van houte etc. binnen Massenhoven ende Voorschoten
Term: 12 years

Lease: 14 vrt. rye
11 Rijnsche Gulden
6 capons
4 gelten butter à 7 lb.

No. 12: SR 43, fo. 462: 20 feb. 1451,
Owner: Vrouw Lijsbeth Stormelijns, priorinne des godshuis van Sint Margeritendale buiten Antwerpen
Lessee: Henrik van Aekle, Hendriksz;
Description: hoeve te klein Zundert
12 y. begin mid-march
Lease: 6,5 zister rye to be delivered in Antwerp in measure of Breda
2 wethers (custbaere hamelen)
without reduction of landrent

No. 13 SR 43, fo. 572: 19 oct. 1450
Owner: Heer Peter Stroebaert (Stoccaert) en meester Lambrecht van Overtrecht(?) cannunieken v. OLV als meyeren vanden cappittel
Lessee Lijsbeth Rath, weduwe
Description:
*1/4 34 r. land te Boechout bij het veldeken vander hoeve vanSint Baafs
* 3/4 31r. tussen Aard Tsermeys ende tsgodshuis erve van Sint Lijsbeth Antwerpen
* 1 b. min 32 r. tussen Jan vander Tangen en Peter de Pote
* 1/4 28 r. op hoverveld tussen godshuiserve Sint Michiels en Bouden sroyen erfg.
* 1/2 b. 52 r. naest tcapittelland
* 1/2b.min 22 r. opt hoverveld tusssen hl. geest v. Boechhout en Aerd Tsermeys
* 1/4 aldaer Jan Tsherhermans en Bouden Bettens
* 1b min 17r. Jan Tsertogen / Ard Tsermeys
* 3/4 b. min 13r. Jan Woyts en wed. Heeno. Quintens
* 1/2b. in wouters s'leeuwen goed ten vicaris OLV
Term: 9 years
Lease: 3 lb. 18s. gr. To be delivered in Antwerp

No. 14: SR 43, fo. 576 vo. 7 nov. 1450
Owner: Gheert van Eyck (schepen)
Lessee: Jan Francke van Bladele
Description: nederhof van zijn hof te Zandvliet met huizingen met hoegenlande ettinge en hoeymaden met zuythoeven
6 gemeten land int Nieuwland van Berendrecht
Term: 9 years beginning may last year 'met mogelijkheid van afstaen binnen 1e 6 jaren met 1 jaar termijn'

No. 15: SR 43, fo. 593 r.: 19 november 1450
Owner: Heer Peter Stoccaert (Strobbaert) + meester Lambrecht van Overdrecht cannuniken OLV als meyeren v.d. kappittele
Lessee: Gielis Besselen, Gheert de Visser
Description:

* 5/4 land Oosterwiel inden eersten hoeck inden oude land
* 3 1/2 b. toeb. Daneels wive van Ranst
* 6 1/2 gemeten land den gemeyn cappitel OLV
* 3 1/2 gemeten toeb. Wijnand van Geele
* 1/2 gemet bij s'hertogen v. Brabants erve
* 1/2 gemet heer Jan de Leeuw (cap.)

3/4+1/2 gemet
7/4 land +1 1/2 gemet
3 1/2 vd. land
8 1/2 vd.
1 gmet/ 50 r. 1 gemet/ 200 r./ 200 r. 1 gemet, 1 gemet
Term: 9 jaren durende
Lease:6 lb.

No. 16 SR 43, fo. 595vo.: 28 nov. 1450
Owner: Broeder Claus van Wesele voor Sint Michiels abdij
Lessee Anthonis Hendricszone en Jacoppe&Laureys zijn sonen
Description: godshuishoeve, land & beemden 46,3 ha.(ca. 47 gemeten)
Zandvliet, noordland te moershoode
& (13,8 ha.) 14 gemeten land - 27 roeden aldaer, & 41.5 ha. (42 gemeten)+75 roeden land Ossendrecht waarts
total: 102.3 ha.
Term: 8 years
Lease: 94 goude salute ad valorem
12 capons
100 schoven cruyts
2 zister haver
100 eieren to be delivered in Antwerp

No. 16a SR 43, fo. 605: 2 januari 1451
Owner: Willem vanden Broecke (Antwerp alderman)
Lessee: Gielis Bouwelmans alsias Wilbouts
Descritption: hoeve (9,15 ha.) 7,5 b.
Zandhoven
Term: 6 years
Lease: 13 gouden overlandsche gulden
4 zister rye

8 capons -to be delivered at Antwerpen

No. 17 SR 43, fo. 653:
Owner: Wouter Minnelade
Lessee Henric vande Wiele
stede (12,8 ha.) 13 gemeten (daaraf 6 gemeten toebehoren Willem de Gortere)
9 years (vanaf kerstmis)
Lease: 6 lb. 7 s. gt.
18 vt. rye
4 wethers

b) nos. 18- 55 (D1-D37): see. F. Nooyens Geschiedenis van Deurne, I, pp. 417-457.

c) nos. 56-63 Leases in Kontich and Edegem (see: van Passen, Kontich, and Id. Edegem... passim)
No. 56: SAA, SR 94, 155v-156r.
Owner: Sint Baafs-abdij Gent
Description Hoge Beke te Lint (Kontich) 1478
lating: goed in drie lagen laten liggen naar hofrecht.

No. 57: SAA, SR 71, 50v-51r
Owner: Abbay St. Salvator, Antwerp
Description hoeve Moensgoed (Kontich) (10b.)

No. 58: SR 82, 254r-255r. (1472):
Owner: Peter de Meere
Description Hoeve ter Beke (Kontich) 15 b.

No. 59: 1449, SR 41,346r-v, (s also SR 52,324v, SR116 53rv)
Description Vrijselhoeve Kontich

No. 60: 1478, SR 93, 26v°-27 r°
Description Goed ter Zalen op Lint 4 b. "besaeijt in zyn mes oft in zijn weemoes"

No. 61: 1494 (Kontich): SR 105, 57 r°-v°
Description alle jaren 2 last weemoes op zijn land leggen..

No. 62: SR45, 460r.(1452),
Owner: Commandery Pitsemburg Mechelen
Lessee: Jan Vuesel
Description: Crockenroede (Edegem) 15.5 b. (+3 b eeusel)+2b bos en hooitienden, + 1/6 van tiende van Edegem (owner farm = owner1/2 of tithe)
Term: 6 y.,
Lease: 5b. wintercoren

5b. zomervruchten
5 b. braak; geploegd voor zomergraan

No. 63: 1455:
Owner: Pitsemburg
p: hendrik raet + katline vander stoct (verlenging),
Description: hoeve in het dorp (Edegem)
15 b. land + 3 b. eusel
Term: 7 y.
Lease:40 vt. rye, 40 vt. evene, 12 lb overlandse rijnse gulden, 2 lb payments, 4 kapuinen, een korf appelen;
+ 1/2 van grote tiende voor natura betaling: tarwe, rogge, gerst haver ev afslag bij misoogst.

Appendix 2: Farm Leases Near Antwerp Payable to St. Elisabeth Hospital (1501-1560)

The lease registers of St. Elisabeth hospital contain information concerning 72 different plots of land situated in the closer surroundings of Antwerp, with a total size of 228 ha.[1] On the basis of these documents a sample of 613 lease prices payable in money was assembled for the period between 1501 and 1560. The disadvantage of this sample is its aggregate character. Rather than a continuous series involving a well-defined area of land, it comprises multiple individual price annotations or short-term series covering several years. It is nevertheless possible to situate each of the plots and to calculate its rent per hectare. The sample consists of 40 plots of farmland and gardens at Willibrordus' field towards Borgerhout and in the villages of Deurne, Wommelgem, Wijnegem, Hove, Borsbeek,and Berchem, with a total size of 108 ha., and of 31 plots of river meadows (waterland) and farmland, with a total size of 127 ha, situated just outside Antwerp, north of the town, between Antwerp and Oosterweel. Most of these plots were relatively small, and only one plot in Deurne had 10 *bunders* (13 ha). These data were grouped in two series: one containing plots of farmland and the other containing land situated in the polders (land and waterland). The lease value per hectare was calculated for both.

1. Farmland near Antwerp

Description	Size	Hectare	Period
Hoeve Borsbeek	18 bunder	23,4	1545-1550
Land Deurne	10 b.	13	1510-1530, 1541-1549, 1556
Land Ettenhoven	8 gem.	8	1524-1529, 1545-1550
Land	7.5 gem.	7,5	1536-1541
Land Wommelgem		4,3875	1556
Land St. Willebroortsveld	3	3,9	1507-1512, 1516-1521, 1525-1531
Land Wommelgem	2,5	3,25	1505-1510, 1524-1529, 1540-1545, 1551-1557
Land+groes Ettenhoven		3,15	1551-1580
Land St. Willebroortsveld	2,25	2,925	1503-1514
Land Deurne	2	2,6	1532-1536, 1538-1562
Land Edegem de Cuyte	2b.	2,6	1551-1580
Land Hoogboom	2.5 gem.	2,5	1547-1552, 1556
Land en beemden bijvank Lier	7 plots	2,5	1556-1580
Land Nonnenveld	2 gem.	2	1551-1556, 1570
Land	1,375	1,7875	1546-1551
Land St. Willibrortsveld	1,25	1,625	1540-1551

1 OCMW EG 170 and EG 178.

Description	Size	Hec-tare	Period
St. Willebrords	1,25	1,625	1543-1548, 1556
St. Willebrords		1,625	1548-1556
Land Wommelgem	1	1,3	1508-1513
Land Borsbeek	1	1,3	1508-1513
Land St. Willebroortsveld	1	1,3	1509-1514, 1525-1531
Land	1	1,3	1524-1529
Land St. Willebroort, Lazare	1	1,3	1539-1544
Land St. Willebroorts	1	1,3	1540-1545
Land St. Willebrords	1	1,3	1544-1580
Land St. Willebrord	1	1,3	1548-1580
Land Ettenhoven		1,3	1551-1576
Land St. Willebrordus	1 b.	1,3	1556-1564
Land St. Willebrordsveld	1 b.	1,3	1556-1569
Land Berchem	1 gemet	1	1502-1507
Land Hove	1 gemet	1	1551-1556
Land Hove	0,75	0,975	1539-1544, 1556-1561
2 aardekens Hove	Jan Vleminck	0,65	1501-1506 and 1557-1579
Beemd Schilde	0.5 b.	0,65	1506-1511
Land Deurne	0,5	0,65	1540-1545, 1556, 1569
Land Wijnegem	0,5	0,65	1543-1548, 1556, 1569
Land St. Willebrord	0,125	0,1625	1535-1547

2. Waterland in the Polders North of Antwerp

Description	Size	Hectare	Period
Waterland	9 gemeten	9	1556-1576
Land Slijkpoort	8 gem.	8	1510-1515, 1524-1547
Waterland Coestalle	7.5 gem.	7,5	1522-1527, 1544-1549
Biesmaade en Vinckemaede	7.5 gem.	7,5	1523-1544, 1555-1580
Waterland buiten cruiphol	7 gem.	7	1509-1514
Waterland	7 gem.	7	1527-1532
Waterland Oyvaarsnest en Quade Sesse	7 gem.	7	1550-1576
Land Oorderen+Ettenhoven	6 gem.	6	1551-1566, 1570
Waterland		5,225	1549-1580
Waterland Steenborgerweert	5 gem.	5	1550-1580
Waterland	4.5 gem.	4,5	1545-1550
Waterland	3,25	4,225	1539-1544
Waterland	4 gem.	4	1556
Waterland Schijnbroek	4 gem.	4	1538-1543
Waterland, biesmaad	4 gem.	4	1539-1550, 1556-1580
Land Slijkpoort "De Wilge"	4 gem.	4	1549-1580
Land Steenborgerweert	2 gemeten	2	1505-1510
Waterland	2,75	3,575	1523-1528
Land Schenkeldijk	2,5	3,25	1524-1531
Waterland	3 gem.	3	1502-1507
Waterland buiten cruiphol	3 gem.	3	1509-1514
Waterland	3 gem.	3	1542-1547
Waterland	2,25	2,925	1508-1516, 1519-1525
Waterland		2,75	1556-1576
Waterland	2 gem.	2	1520-1525
Waterland	1 gem.	1	1502-1513
Waterland	1 gem.	1	1508-1513
Schoorken Ekersche weg	1 gem.	1	1523-1544
Land Coestalseweg	1 gemet	1	1506-1517
Land Steenborgerweert	1 gmet	1	1505-1510, 1527-1533, 1556-1579
Land Schijnbroek	1 gemet	1	1504-1509
Waterland	1 gem.	1	1539-1551
	1 gem.	1	1509-1514

APPENDIX 3: REFERENCES TO BRICK OVENS IN THE REGISTERS OF THE ANTWERP ALDERMEN, 1491-1563

Source: VERSTREPEN, Antwerpse schepenbrieven.

Year	Name owner	From	Description	Place	Source
1491	Joos van der Vliet		kalkoven	Boom	SR 99 fo. 44r.
1493	Jan Pluym	Boom	tichelbakker	Boom	SR 103 fo. 229 v.
1496	W. Vander Eycken (pachter G. De hagen)	Hoboken	steengeleg met oven en 2 logies	Hoboken	SR 110 fo. 131 r.
1497	Jan Galopijn	Callebeek	steengeleg	Callebeek	SR 110 fo. 148 r.
1498	Joos van der Vliet		sttengeleg +huizing en calkoven 7 vd.	Boom	SR 113 fo. 5r.
1498	Jan Wyckmans		steengeleg 3/4	Niel	Verstrepen no. 722
1498	W. Vander Eycken	Reet	steengeleg	Hoboken	SR 113, fo. 131 v.
1500	Willem vander Eycken	Reet	steengeleg met 2 logien + 1 B; bos	Hoboken	Verstrepen no. 1121.
1501	Gillis vander Heyden	Callebeek	steenbakker	Callebeek	SR 120 fo. 46 v.
1502	Jacob de Hont		de hoge bosch met logien en hove	Hemiksem	SR 123 fo. 55v.
1502	Andries vander Heyden en Adriaan Goessens		2 kalkovens	Callebeek	SR 121 fo. 210 r.
1503	J. Robbijns	Hemiksem	steenbakker		SR 124 fo. 6r.
1504	Jan Robbijn	Hemiksem	steenbakker		SR 125 fo. 17 v.
1504	Hendrik Pluym	Boom	1/3 steengeleg	Boom	SR 125 fo. 27 r.
1504	Jacob Pluym		2/3 steengeleg, koopt 1/3	Boom	SR 125 fo. 27 r.
1504	Jan Pluym	Boom	2 steengeleg +tichelgeleg 2 b.	Boom	SR 125 fo. 36 r.
1504	Jan Robbijns		steengeleg huis logie heve	Hoboken	SR 125 fo. 152 r.
1507	Jan Robbijns		steenbakker	Hoboken	SR 132 fo. 10 v.
1508	Jan Bal, steenbakker	Hoboken	steengeleg met huis	Hoboken	SR 134 fo. 33 r.

Year	Name owner	From	Description	Place	Source
1510	Joos de Vliet	Boom	steengeleg 7b.+1/2 kalk-oven 9 vd.	Boom	SR 137 fo. 70 r.
1511	Jacob vanden Wouwer, metser		steengeleg 2 logien 1 b.	Hoboken	SR 140 fo. 91 r.
1512	G. Meeus+M. Possemiers	Rupel-monde	1/2 steengeleg	Hoog-boom	SR 142 fo. 63 v.
1513	Jacob Florens	Rumst		Rumst	SR 143 fo. 184 r.
1515	Jan van der Eycken		steengeleg incl. 2 kalkovens	Hemiksem	SR 148 fo. 99r.
1517	Antoon van Kerkhoven	Boom	1/2 steengeleg	Boom	SR 152 fo. 232.
1518	Antoon Pinte		steengeleg	Callebeek	SR 154 fo. 174 r.
1518	Antoon van Kerkhoven en Cornelis Wouters		2-3 b. met steenoven en kalkoven	Boom	SR 153 fo. 329 v.
1520	Martin van Wijnegem		steengeleg	Hemiksem	SR 157 fo. 173r.
1521	Antoon Peeters	Callebeek	owes 12 ships of bricks to mason		SR 159 fo. 2r.
1521	Antoon Peeters	Callebeek	steengeleg met 4000 rouwe steen	Callebeek	SR 159 fo. 136 v.
1523	Kerstiaan van Asse	Rumst	1/2 steengeleg	Rumst	SR 163 fo 203r.
1523	Jan en Corne-lis Wyckmans	Hemik-sem	steengeleg	Callebeek/ Hemiksem	SR 164 fo. 90 r.
1523	Jan Thoen		steengeleg	Callebeek	SR 164 fo. 90 r.
1523	Kerstiaan Matheeus		tichelgeleg	Boom	SR 168 fo. 85 r.
1525	Antonis Goessens	Hemik-sem	steengeleg met huis	Hemiksem	SR 168 fo. 247 r.
1528	Kerstiaan van Asse	Rumst	1/2 steengeleg	Rumst	SR 174 fo. 399
1537	erfg. Jan Sanders		steengeleg	Callebeek	SR 192 fo. 443 v.
1537	Jan Wyckmans		steengelegmet huis en hove	Callebeek	SR 192 fo. 499
1537	Corneis Wyckmans		steengeleg	Callebeek	SR 192 fo. 499
1544	Adriaan van Boom		steengeleg	Callebeek	SR 214 fo. 210 r.
1545	Claes Wyck-mans		steengeleg	Callebeek	SR 215 fo. 45

Year	Name owner	From	Description	Place	Source
1548	Katelijn van Kerkohoven en Michiel Cruyt		oud steengeleg	Boom	SR 229 fo. 256 r.
1548	Bertelmeeus Karels		steengeleg	?	SR 229 fo. 256 r.
1550	Laureis Wyckmans		steenbakker	Hemiksem	SR 238 fo. 290
1551	Adriaan Pinten	Hemiksem	stenbakker		SR 241 fo. 573 r.
1552	Jan Heyman		steengeleg	Hellegat	SR 245 fo. 190 r.
1552	Geert Wils, metser		1/2 steengeleg	Hoboken	SR 246 5 v.
1556	erfg. Martine van der Eycken		steengeleg	Callebeek	SR 258 fo. 4r.
1556	Antoon van Boom				SR 258 fo. 232
1558	Aart Wils, mason		steengeleg	Hoboken	SR 267 fo. 98 v.
1559	Jan Seldenslag, steenbakker				SR 273 fo. 353 r.
1560	Antonis van Boom		steengeleg	Hemiksem	SR 278 fo. 57 v.
1560	Peter Pinte, steenbakker	Hemiksem			SR 280 fo. 222 v.
1561	Aart Wils, mason		steengeleg	Hoboken	SR 286 fo. 441 v.
1563	Cornelis Wouters		steengeleg	Boom	SR 295 fo. 137 v.
1563	Daneel Berckelaar		steengeleg	Boom	SR 295 fo. 137 v.
1564	Peter Pinte, steenbakker	Hemiksem			SR 297 fo. 456 v.

Appendix 4: References to Woodcuts in the Registers of the Antwerp Aldermen 1436-1446 and 1536-1545

Source: Verstrepen, Antwerpse schepenbrieven.

1. 1436- 1446

Year	Cutter	From	Owner of Wood	Location of Wood	Price (lb. Brab.)	Bunders
1436	Aert Steylaert + Peter Claus			Schelle		
1437	Peter Vinck			Hoboken		6
	Calmtyn Blomaert					
1438	Geert Reckemast		heer Aart van Immerseel	Boom	160	22
1438	Jan van Oerle					
1438	Jan van der Donk					
1438	Floris van den Beemde					
1441	Willem en Michiel Cop	Schelle	heer Jan van Witthem		21	
1441	Peter van der Eycken	Schelle	heer Jan van Witthem	Aarts, Hemiksem	19	
	Jan Reckemast	Schelle				
1441	Willem Cops	Schelle	stad Antwerpen		19	
1441	Gillis de Doncker, al. de bakker		Jacob Kerreman	Kontich	12	
1441	Willem en Machiel Cops	Schelle		Schelle	13	
1441	Bertel Wielancs		Cornelis de Herde	Schelle Reet	20	
1442	Jan Sincval	Schelle		Schelle	19	
1442	Jan Mys, al. de Kerelaar	Kon-tich	kartuizers Ant-werp	Kontich	14	
1442	Willem de Laet	Kon-tich	Willem vande Werve		12,24	
1442	Jan van Loock		Claus Wielancs	Aartselaar	10	
1443	Jan vander Donck	Rumst	heer Aart van Immerseel	Boom		28
			Jan van Bout-ersem			

			Willem van Sompeke			
1443	Hendrik Cop	Schelle	Claus de Herde	Hemiksem	28	
1444	Jan Reckemast & Hendrik Cop	Schelle		?	27,56	
1444	J. Vandenboome			Schelle	24	
1444	P. vander Eycke		L. Volckaert	Schelle	40	
1444	L. vander Eycken	Schelle		Schelle	44	
	Peter Reckemast					
1445	G. Reckemast	Schelle		Reet	42	6
1446	J. Reckemast & Michiel Cop	Schelle		Reet	22	

2. 1536-1545

Year	Cutter	From	Owner of Wood	Location of Wood	Price	Bunders
1536	Jan van Boome	Schelle	Mr. Ruysch Mertens	Reet	66	
	Jan van Stalbeemde	Schelle				
	Bertelmeeus van Santvoort	Hemiksem				
1536	Jan van Boome	Schelle	kartuizers Antwerp	Kontich	64	
	Jan van Stalbeemde	Schelle				
	Bertelmeeus van Santvoort	Schelle				
1537	Jan van Stalbeemde	Schelle	St. Michiels	Aartselaar	95	7
1538	Peter Baeck and Margarete Rycke		kartuizers Antwerp	Reet, Lint, Waarloos	137,5	9
1539	Peter de Schoesitter al. Claeys	Aartselaar	Peter Pinte, coopman	Aartselaar	80,5	5
	Margarete Bal	Aartselaar				
1543	Peter Baeck and Margarete Rycke		kartuizers Antwerp	Kontich	76	
1543	Gillis Schoesitter	Wilrijk	kartuizers Antwerp	Kontich	43	
	Merten Hermans	Broechem				

1544	Merk Sanders	Hemiksem	kartuizers Lier	buiten Antwerpen	30,5	1,75
1545	Lenaert Bal, smit	Aartselaar	Lenaert van de Werve	Hemiksem	50	3

Appendix 5: Boatmen and Ship-Carpenters along the Rivers Rupel and Scheldt

1. Boatmen along the Rivers Rupel and Scheldt

Year	Name	Place
1470	Pauwel Bertels	Boom
1471	Hendrik Pluym	Boom
1474	Peter vande Voorde	Rumst
1503	Hendrik Pluym	Boom
1505	Bertelmeeus Fleurens	Boom
1505	Hendrik Pluym	Boom
1510	H. Peeters	Schelle
1518	Joos Bertels	Boom?
1525	Antonis van de Voorde	Rumst
1525	Hendrik van der Eycken	Rumst
1530	H Van Assche	Rumst
1536	Jos Drossate	Boom
1546	Cornelis van Pee	Boom
1546	Jan Pluym	Rumst
1546	Gillis Schaerborch	Schelle
1546	Lieven Steven	Schelle
1556	Damiaan van Schoonwinkel	Schelle
1556	Simon van Damme	Schelle
1557	Adriaan Segers	Hingene
1557	Jan Melis	Schelle
1557	Gillis Laureis	Wintham
1558	Jan van den Beemde	Hemiksem
1558	Jan van Raamdonk	Hingene
1558	Joos van Raamdonk	Hingene
1559	Jan Berens	Wintham
1559	Jan van der Molen	Wintham
1560	Jan Melis	Schelle
1561	Adriaan Joos	Bornem
1561	Jan Coleman	Bornem

1561	Jan Verheyden	Bornem
1561	Jan van den Beemde	Hemiksem
1562	Gillis van Vercler	Boom
1562	Jacob Magnaert	Rumst
1563	Lieve vanden Eedt	Willebroeck

2. Ship-Carpenters along the Rivers Rupel and Scheldt

Year	Name	Description	Place	Type of transaction	
1471	Jan Roelants	Schipmaker	(Hemiksem)		
1471	Peter Bertels	Schipmaker	Rumst	transaction with brother in Law from Maastricht	
1500	Gillis Bertels	scheepstimmer-man	Rumst	leases out little farm	
1503	Gillis Bertels	scheepstimmer-man	Rumst	sells annuity to brother (Mechelen)	
1505	Gillis Bertels		(Rumst)	sale pleitschip	11 £ Fl.gr.
1520	Cornelis Wouters	Schipper	Boom	sale pleitschip	4 £ 10 s. Fl.gr.
1530	Jan Roelants	schiptimmerman	(Hemiksem)	sale pleitschip	31 Car. Gld.
1536	Jan Roelants+Lijsbeth Pluym	Schipmaker	(Hemiksem)	sale pleitschip to Antwerp boatman	
1536	Lieve Lammens	Schipmaker			
1537	Lijsbeth Pluym wed. Jan Roelants		(Hemiksem)	sale pleitschip	43 £ Fl. gr.
1537	Hendrik Smit	Schipmaker	Schelle	sale pleitschip to Rupel-monde	30 £ Fl. gr
1537	Gillis Bertels	schipstimmerman	(Rumst)		
1537	Lieve Lammens			sale pleitschip to boatman from Antwerp	34 £ 10 s. Fl.gr.
1540	Lijsbeth Pluym wed. Jan Roelants	schipstimmerman	(Hemiksem)	sale pleitschip	31 Car. Gld.
1541	Lijsbeth Pluym wed. Jan Roelants		(Hemiksem)	sale pleitschip	23 £ 10 s. Fl. gr.

1542	Jan Roelant de jonge		Hemiksem	sale big ferryboat	20 Car. Gld.
1547	Anthonis Brogelmans	Scheepsmaker	Rumst	buys former brewery 'rode Leeuw' at the ferry	
1556	Jan Witharts	schipstimmerman	Hemiksem	sale pleitschip	6 £ Fl. gr.
1558	Cornelis Wouters	Schipper	Rumst	sale pleitschip	8 £ Fl. gr.
1559	Ad. Saerle	scheepsmaker	Rumst	sale schuit to Brussels boatman	14 £ Fl. gr.
1559	Cornelis Wouters	scheepsmaker	Rumst	sale huede	37 £ Fl. gr.
1560	Ad. Saerle	scheepsmaker	Rumst	sale pleit Antwerpen	
1560	Ad. Saerle		(Rumst)	sale pleitschip	50 £ Fl. gr.
1562	Jan Roelants	scheepstimmerman	Hemiksem	sale pleitschip	49 £ Fl. gr.
1562	Gomaer Struyf	scheepstimmerman	Schelle	sale huede	15 £ Fl. gr.
1564	Gomaer Struyf	scheepstimmerman	Schelle	sale pleit to Brussels boatman	395 Car. Gld.
1565	Cornelis Saerle		Schelle	sale pleit to Lier boatman	21 £ Fl. gr.

Appendix 6: Owners of Fiefs in the Surroundings of Antwerp, 1440

Source: Brussels, ARA, Lb. 8, fol. 19-328.

Name	Place	Bunders	Description
Van Immerseel Aert	Wommelgem, Deurne	99,5	lord, hoeve 59 b., hoeve 24 b. land, grote tiende, 81 tenants, +achterleen in Deurne 16,5 b.+cijns 12 laten
Sanders Gillis	Aartselaar	97	lord van Vaelaer, 42 tenants, 97 bunders
Van Mechelen Jan	Kontich	90	
Van Lier Jan	Berchem	80	lord, owner goed van Berchem, 80 b. cijns
Van Sompeke Hendrik	Boechout, Bevel	30	owner of 30 b. in Boechout and a fief in Bevel
Pot Pieter	Wommelgem	26	owner of farm, 26 b.in Wommelgem (under Art van Immerseel)
Van de Werve Claus	Berchem	25	owner farm Valkenputte 20 b. + 5 b. land
Van den Berghe Kathelijne	Deurne	24	owner house and 11 b. land, 10 b. meadow, 2 b heath, 1 b forest, tenure
Van Brecht Jan	Wilrijk	23	owner farm Venstote? 12 b.inc. tenure, and Steffenyen, 10 b. + 1 b. bos
Thijk Jan	Lier	22	Owner 22 b.
Van Mechelen Hendrik	Wijnegem?	20,5	20, 5 bunder Hoeve Diedegem
Keerle Wouter	Bevel	17,5	owner goed van Wayenberg, 17-18 b., 7.5 in cijns, 5 tenants
Van Helmont Hendrik	Boechout	16,5	lord, 28 fiefholders, 29 tenants, goed ten broecke, 4.75 b meadow,10 b land+1.75 b elst
Van Emeren Lijsbeth	Brochem	16	owner fief, ca.16 b.
Van den Wouwe Bouden	Boechout	13,25	owner 13 bunder 1 dw. Land

Name	Place	Bunders	Description
Van Zevenbergen Geert	O.L.V. Waver	13	owner hof Battenbroek, tenure, seignieurie, lease, 13 b. Meadow
Keerle Willem	Boechout	12,5	owner fief ten dijke, 12-13 b.
De Blabbenaer Mathijs	Deurne	12	owner subfief, 7b meadow, 5b land, tenure 15 tenants (15s.)
Symaert Lijsbeth	Oosterwiel	11	Owner 1/2 fishing rights Schijn, 1/8 toll,7 b. land, 4 gemeten leased, annuities
Van de Werve Willem	Deurne	10	owner 2 fiefs 10 b land in herditary lease : 10 zisters rogge + annuity in Lillo
Van Rotselaar Anthonis	Kontich	10	owner fief 10 b., 25 tenants
Van Kets Berbele	Oorderen	9,75	scutterie van Oorderen and Wilmarsdonk,+ 13 gemeten land leased for 18 peeters
Raet Jan	Lillo, Lier	7,25	9 gemeten land+1/2 b. in Lier
Allayn Clare	Lier	6,5	owner farm Lier and Kessel, 6.5 b. + more land
Van Ijzendijk Margriet	Duffel	3,5	owner fief, 3.5 b. inc. 10 fiefholders
Van Heesbeen Clare	Broechem	2,5	owner fief, 2.5 b.
Van den Wouwe Gillis	Boechout	1,7	owner house + 1.7 b. land
Van Cruyningen Jan, heer	Wilmarsdonk	1,5	owner Schenkeldijk, owner 1/2 4 gemeten land
Van Gottengijs Lancelot	OLV Waver	1,25	owner fief (achterleen) beemde Swaen 5/4
Van Immerseel Hendrik	Lier	1,25	esquire, owner hof van Deurne, 10 - 11 houses + 5/4 meadow
Wycman Jan	Wommelgem	1	owner fief (under Art van Immerseel) 1 b.
Van der Stoct Gielis	Hove	0,75	owner meadow 3 vd.
Raet Wouter	Massenhoven	0,5	owner land, ½ b.

Name	Place	Bunders	Description
Bau Jan, ridder	Halle		owner fief
Colibrand Willem	Lier		wife owns fief
De Helt Reyner	Oelegem		from Mechelen, owner fief goed te Oelegem, (under Art van Immerseel)
De Keyzer Wouter	Lier		owner fief in surroundings of Lier
Drake Walraven	Kessel		owner fief
Korsendonk priorij	Lier		owns many fiefs in Lier and surroundings
Musse Aert	OLV Waver		subfief goed den doncker (g.v Zevenbergen)
Ridder Richard	Duffel		owner seignieurie, part of tithe, cijns, 13 tenants, seignieur de Myrode and Vriensche
Sint Bernaerts abdij	Schoten		owner tithe (under Art van Immerseel)
Van Berchem Roeland	Oelegem, Lier		owner of fiefs
Van Berchem Arnd	Baarle		owner fief
Van den Broecke Wouter	Oelegem		owner fief, inc. 5 tenants
Van Diest Gijsbrecht	Berchem		owner fief
Van Eekhove Wouter	Vreemde		lord Vreemde Millegem,16 keurmannen, tenure, pontgeld
Van Ijzendijk Margriet	Lier		owner fief
Van Lier Jan	Zandhoven		fief hof te Schoten, (under Art van Lier)
Van Lille Margriet	Lille		Seignieurie
Van Luxemburg Jean	Rumst		lord inc. toll

Name	Place	Bunders	Description
Van Molle Jan	Oelegem		owner meadow
Van Oyenbrugge Joos	Borgvliet		owner broekland
Van Ranst Clare	Ranst		onwer fief, farm, tithe, 13 tenants
Van Ranst Jan	Mortsel, Wijnegem, Wommelgem		lord, 22 fiefholders, 25 tenants, tenure Boechout, 14 tenants, mill, tithe.
Van Sompeke Wouter	Wommelgem		holder of fief in Wommelgem (under Art van Immerseel)
Van Wezele Liesbeth	's Gravenwezel		Lord
Van Wezemaal Jan	Lier		owner fiefs in Lier, Kessel, Itegem, Emblem, Beverle, Berlaar, land + cijns, 116 man
Van Wezembeke Jan	Schoten		owner fiefs in Schoten, Zoerzel etc.
Van Wittham Jan	Kontich		owner 10 fiefs, lord of Boutersem, Antwerpen, Lier, Zandhoven, Waterland etc.
Van Wittham Jan	Boutersem		seignieur
Van Zandhoven Margriet	Lier		wife Roeland van Berchem, owner fief in Lier

Appendix 7: Landed Property in 1570

1. Boechout

Source: RAA, Oud Gemeentearchief Boechout, no. 93 (Boechout).

Nr.	Owner	Plots	Type	Bunders	Bunder estimated	Total lease
1	Abbey of St Baafs, Ghent	14	4 farms, mill+land	158,07	158,7	972
2	Francois vanden Cruyce	6	4 farms, 1 stede +land	44,5	182,6	582,75
3	Abbey of St. Bernards, Hemiksem	3	2 farms+land	30	55	295,8
4	Heer Jacob van Herbeys	4	2 farms, stede+aard	35	49	291,5
5	Mr. Jan Valckenborch	2	farms	32	32	285,8
6	Jan de Clerck	4	3 steden+house	20,25	20,25	172
7	Sr. Cosmas de Affaydati		farm	27	27	155
8	Andries de Haze	1	farm	26	26	123
9	Heer Jacob van Reymerswale		farm	18	18	110
10	Wed. Adriaenssens		farm	23	23	109
11	Jan de Winter	4	farm (e)+land (e)	18,5	18,5	108,75
12	Jf. Dijckx	4	farm+land	19	19	107,65
13	Jan vander Meere		farm	11,5	11,5	90
14	Hendrik vanden Velde	5	2 steden, 2 houses+land	6,75	6,75	77
15	Mr. Jan Fouwillems		farm	7,5	7,5	67,5
16	Chapter of Antwerp	2	land	8,5	8,5	59
17	Jan hendricx	3	stede, house +land	6,75	6,75	51
18	Anthon Nuyens	1	farm	6	6	50

19	heirs of Peter Baeck	2	stede+aard	5,5	5,5	50
20	Michiel van Sent	4	stede (e)+house+land(e)	4	4	50
21	Jonker Ambrosio van Baussele	3	land+aard	7,75	7,75	41,85
22	Gielis Wittocx		stede (e)	2,5	2,5	40
23	Gommaer Gielis		stede	3	3	40
24	Jh. Willem van Erp		land+aard	7	7	39,35
25	heirs Simon Noulaet	3	stede+2 houses			38
26	Anna Braeckmans	1	stede	2	2	36
27	Gommaer van Dievelt		stede	2	2	35,8
28	Jan Verstockt	4	3 houses+land	1	1	33
29	Andries van Santvoort	1	stede	3	3	32
30	Hendrik Smet		stede	2,5	2,5	32
31	Merten Seldeslach	2	2 steden	1,5	1,5	32
32	Lansloot van Campe+consorten		stede	3,5	3,5	31,6
33	broeders Verstrepen		stede	1,5	1,5	30,5
34	heirs Niclaes Noots		inn de bijle	1	1	30
35	Margret en Fijnken Hendricx		farm	5	5	30
36	Bernaerd Struyve	2	stede+land	0,25	0,25	29,5
37	Heer Jacob vander Heyden	4	land (4 prcelen)	4,5	8,25	29
38	Lucas Dom		stede	2,5	2,5	29
39	heirs Peter Verhaeghen		house and garden			28
40	Peter Haghe		stede	2	2	28
41	Hl. geest Lier	2	land (5 percelen)	0,5	0,5	27,35

42	Peter der Kinderen en cons.(e)		stede(e) 'de Cutsheye'	4	4	27,2
43	Anthoni Daems	2	stede+house	1	1	27
44	Adriaan Goorman	1	stede	2	2	26
45	Adriaen Bruynkens	1	house and garden (e)	1,625	1,625	25
46	Jan van Houte cum suis	2	stede+land	2	2	25
47	Jan van ganssele		stede (e)	2,5	2,5	24
48	heirs wed. Swinters		stede	1,25	1,25	22,04
49	Jf. Johanna Smangeleren		stede	1	1	22
50	Nazareth	4	land	3,75	3,75	21
51	Bastiaen van Ganssele	2	stede+land	0,5	0,5	20
52	Cornelis Hennicx		house and garden	1,25	1,25	20
53	Jacob Haghe		stede	1,75	1,75	20
54	Mr. Jan de Pauw		stede	1,5	1,5	20
55	Wouter van Regemorter		stede (e)	1,75	1,75	20
56	Hl. Geest Boechout	6	house+land	2,125	2,125	19,75
57	Michiel van Schore	2	stede+land (e)			18,5
58	Alijt Capprijns	1	house and garden			18
59	heirs Adriaan Schilleman		stede	0,75	0,75	18
60	heirs Hendrik de Belze		stede	1	1	18
61	heirs Jan vander Rijt		house and garden	0,75	0,75	18
62	Jan Cousijn		house and garden	0,5	0,5	18
63	heirs Adriaen Horckmans		stede	1	1	16
64	wed. Simoen Noulaet		house and garden (e)			16
65	heirs Jacob de Bakker		stede	1	1	15,5

66	Jan van Eeussele		stede	0,5	0,5	15,35
67	Dierick de Wilde		house and garden (e)			15
68	heirs Elisabeth Smits		house and garden			15
69	heirs jan Cautereels, al. Wuyts		stede	0,75	0,75	15
70	Lansloot vanden Wijngaerde	2	2 houses			14,5
71	heirs Willem Hock-mans		house and garden			14,05
72	heirs Anna Schuyts		land	1,5	1,5	14
73	Gommaer van Mierop		house and garden (e)	0,75	0,75	14
74	Melchior van Goorle	2	land+weide	1,75	1,75	14
75	Peter van Regemorter Laureiss.		house and garden (e)	0,75	0,75	14
76	wed. Geert Smet		smisse+veldeke	0,25	0,25	13
77	Adriaen Schilleman	1	house and garden			12
78	Bertelmeeus Schille-man		stede (e)	1	1	12
79	Gasthouse Lier		land	1,75	1,75	12
80	Willem van Male		house and garden (e)	0,75	0,75	12
81	Elizabeth Keersmak-ers		stede			11,5
82	Capelrie Millegem		land	1,75	1,75	11
83	Hendrik Pijpelinck		house and garden			11
84	Niclaes Noulaet	1	stede	0,5	0,5	11
85	Wed. Peter Baeck		land	1,25	1,25	11
86	Jan van Dijcke		house and garden			10,5
87	Jan Horckmans		house and garden (e)	1,25	1,25	10,25
88	capelrij st. Amelber-ghe Santhoven		aard	1,25	1,25	10

89	heer Francois de Schot		land	2	2	10
90	Joos van Campe		house and garden	0,25	0,25	10
91	Partners Michiel van Sent		house and garden	1,25	1,25	10
92	capelrij St. Niclaes Altaer Boechout	3	land+aard	0,5	0,5	9,9
93	Hendrik Waghemans		house and garden (e)			9
94	Lucas Meys		house and garden			9
95	Aert verheerstraten en cons.	1	land	1	1	8,5
96	Capelanen Antwerpen	2	land	2	2	8,5
97	Cornelis van Passchele		house and garden (e)			8,5
98	Capelrij in St. Joris kerk Antwerpen		land	0,875	0,875	8
99	Jonker Roeland de Boluere		land	0,75	0,75	8
100	St. Michiels		land, 3 pc.	1,25	1,25	8
101	Vicaris Antwerpen		farm	14	14	8
102	Capelrie OLV Boechout		land	1,25	1,25	7,6
103	Coralen tAntwerpen		land	1	1	7
104	Cornelis Stuyck		house and garden			7
105	Heer Doncker, cannuniek te Antwerpen		land	0,75	0,75	7
106	Roeland de Bevere		land	0,75	0,75	7
107	Lucas Schilleman	2	land	1,125	1,125	6,5
108	Cornelis Meys		house and garden (e)			6
109	Heer Gregorius Zeghers, priester		house and garden (e)			6

110	Heer jan goedemaet		land	1	1	6
111	Hendrik Schilleman		house and garden			6
112	Jan van Eynde Balthzaarsz.		land (e)	1	1	6
113	Jan Verstockt de jonge		house and garden (e)			6
114	jf. vanden Wenne tot Breda		land	1	1	6
115	Willem Vervorst		house and garden (e)			6
116	Parochiaen v. gasthouse v. Antwerpen		land	1	1	5,8
117	Capelrie st. Claes altaar Boechout		aard			5,5
118	Anthuenis van Horcke	2	land (e)	0,75	0,75	5,25
119	Hendrik Goetheyns		house and garden (e)			5
120	Peter van Beempde		house and garden (e)			5
121	Peeter de Keersmaker		house and garden (e)			4,75
122	Adriaan en Anthonis van Horcke	1	land	0,5	0,5	4,5
123	Cornelis van Eynde		house and garden (e)			4,5
124	Peter van Hecke		house and garden (e)			4,5
125	Begijnen Antwerpen		land	0,75	0,75	4
126	heirs Willem Braeckmans		land	0,5	0,5	4
127	Kerk van Vremde		land	0,5	0,5	4
128	kinder Francois de Somere		land	0,5	0,5	4
129	Anthonis van Sent		aard	0,5	0,5	4
130	notaris Mr. Seger shertogs, Antwerpen		rente			4
131	Capellanen St. Gommaers Lier		land	0,75	0,75	3,75

132	Adam Vermijlen tot Liere+consorten	1	aard	0,375	0,375	3,5
133	Francois de Pape		land	0,25	0,25	3
134	kerk en hl. geest v. Boechout	2	land	0,25	0,25	3
135	Jacob Smet		house and garden (e)			2,5
136	Jan Kegels		land (e)	0,25	0,25	2,25
137	Bartelmeeus van Hecke		land	0,25	0,25	2
138	Abbey of Roosendael		land	0,5	0,5	2
139	Chapter of Ghent		land	0,25	0,25	1,8
140	Costen Verbiest+neven		land (e)	0,25	0,25	1,3
141	Parochiaen van Mortsel		land			1,2
142	Chapter of Lier		land	0,07	0,07	0,6

2. Edegem

Source: SAA, VG 14.

Rank	Owner	Plot	Description	Size/b	Total
1	Commandry of Pitsemburg, Mechelen	2	2 farms+tithe	39	324,1
2	Mr. Gielis Gerardi	5	2 farms, 2 steden+speelhof	31	338,2
3	Mr. Willem van Immerseel	4	farm, speelhof, aard, tithe	30,75	263,5
4	St. Elisabeth-hospital	4	farm, stede, meadow	30	109,1
5	Cardinal Granvelle	1	farm	26	163
6	Jonker Anthonis Cole	1	farm	24	190
7	Jan Carels	1	farm	23	145
8	heer van Kersbeeke	1	farm	21,5	170
9	Jonker Cornelis van Mechelen	7	land+beemd+aard+wood	21,5	222
10	Capelrie Antwerpen	6	farm+tithe+land+beemd	21,25	147,75
11	Hendrik Pijpelinks	1	farm	20	140
12	Heer Jaspar Crox	1	farm	16	91
13	Olv.-altaar borchtkerk	1	farm	15	100
14	Peter Backaerts	1	farm	15	120
15	Peter van Pulle	1	farm	15	82,6
16	Abbey of St Bernards	1	farm	14	93,4
17	Mr. peter van der Noot	13	land, beemd, aard, wood	13,75	104,15
18	Frederik Steudelin	1	farm	13,5	159,7
19	Jonker Marten van Mechelen	1	farm	12	115,35
20	Lijsbeth van Velthoven	3	farm+land+speelhof	11,75	82,5
21	Mr. Jan Servilen	1	farm	11	100
22	curen van Edegem	4	farm+tithe+land	10,75	111,5
23	Christoffel Thijs	1	farm	10	110
24	Marten Martens	6	4 steden, wood, speel-houseken	8,25	107,5
25	Loots		farm	8	61,35
26	Chartreuzen Lier	3	land	7,25	63,5
27	Wed. H. Verbert	5	stede, beemd+aard	6,75	77
28	Capitel Antwerpen	1	land	6	39

29	Gielis van Campe	1	meadow	6	58
30	Balthazar de Nayer	3	stede	5,25	88,2
31	Peter Verbraken	1	farm	5	55
32	Hubrecht Verlinden	2	land+wood	4,5	19,8
33	Laureis Bellens		stede 1/2	4,5	27
34	Nicolas Bellens	1	stede 1/2	4,5	27
35	Hendrik Adriaensz.	3	land	4,25	35
36	Begijnen Antwerpen	1	land	4	26
37	Mathijs van Beemde	3	stede+land+beemd	3,75	17,5
38	kerk van Edegem	5	land+beemd	3,5	13,85
39	Cloister of Thabor	2	beemd+wood	3,5	25
40	Peter van Boome	2	land+wood	3	34,3
41	Roeland Verbert	1	aard	3	23
42	Willem Aerts		stede	3	26,65
43	Peter van den Wijngaerde	3	2.5 steden	2,6	40,5
44	Hans Matheus	1	wood	2,5	14,55
45	Hubrecht van Bouwel	1	land	2,5	20
46	Jan van Campe tot Aartselaar	3	house+stede+land	2,5	30,25
47	capelrij van Edegem	3	2 steden+land	2,25	43,5
48	Jan Bal	1	stede	2,25	35,85
49	Cornelis Reys		land	2	23
50	Cornelis Stuyck tot Boechout	3	stede+house+wood	2	41,2
51	heirs Anthonis de Coninck	1	land	2	15
52	heer en mr. Andries vander Rijt	1	stede	2	27
53	Jan de Kessele	1	land	2	14
54	Janne Gaveceles	1	stede	2	25,1
55	Janneken Cruyts	1	land	2	15
56	Jonker Haesdonk	1	beemd	2	30
57	Peter de Bock	1	stede	2	24
58	Peter Wegge	1	land	2	18
59	wed. H. van Berckelaar	1	stede	2	21,45
60	Peter Schoezittere	1	bleekwood	1,75	18,7
61	Hl. Geest Edegem	2	land+aardekens	1,5	12,5

62	Olivier Stuyck	1	land	1,5	8
63	Peter Cornelis	1	1/2stede	1,5	18,5
64	St. Michiels	1	land	1,5	9
65	Willem Vuesels		stede	1,5	24,425
66	Dirk Cuiseleers	1	stede	1,25	21
67	Kinder Fierens	1	land	1,25	9
68	kinderen Vuesels	1	stede	1,25	27
69	Adriaen Abels	1	stede	1	14
70	Jacob Steymans	1	stede	1	18
71	Jan de Bisschop	1	stede	1	21,75
72	Philipp Verbiest	1	stede	1	19
73	St Jans-hospital Antwerp	1	land	1	9
74	Adriaen mennekens	1	land	0,75	8
75	erf. Anthonis de Vos	1	stede	0,75	17
76	heirs Matheus van Putte	1	stede	0,75	11,65
77	Hendrik Verbert	1	aard	0,75	5,5
78	Jan Batens	1	stede	0,75	19
79	Kerk van Deurne	1	beemd	0,75	12
80	Mr. Merten van Ranst	1	beemd	0,75	10
81	Peter Dijkstrate	1	land	0,75	6
82	vicarissen Antwerpen	1	aard	0,75	6
83	heirs Jan Achergem	2	stede+house	0,525	15
84	Adriaan Avonds	1	land	0,5	3,5
85	Adriaen de Welde v. Luithagen	1	beemd	0,5	6
86	Claas vanden Bogaert	1	land	0,5	5
87	Erfgen. Meester Jan Servilens	1	speelhof met graff, 1/2 bunder	0,5	
88	Lenaert van Viersel		herberge+boomgaart	0,5	20
89	Andries de Roye	1	stedeken	0,375	8
90	Anthonis de Bock	3	stede+2 houses+boomgaart	0,375	34
91	Nicolaes de Meyer	1	stede	0,375	8
92	heirs Matheus van den Wijngaerde	1	stede	0,25	9
93	LijskenTheus		stede	0,25	8

94	H+P Vertongen	1	house+boomgaart	0,125	12
95	Jan de Bock	1	house+boomgaart	0,125	17
96	Anthonis de Clecrck		herberge 'de locht'	0,07	10
97	Andries de Backer	1	boomgaart	0,055	2
98	Peter van Dapel	1	stedeken	0,025	5
99	Jan van Woensel	1	land+tithe	0	50
100	Andries van Nieuwenhuize, parochiaen	1	tithe		92
101	Jan Calluys	2	house+kamer		6,75

3. Schoten

Source: Brussels, ARA, Aud., nr. 618/1.

	Owners	Plots	Description	Size bunders	Lease value guilders
1	Abbey of Villers	30	7 farms, jursidiction, fiefs, wood, land, meadow, house	354,5	1926,35
2	Melchior Schets, lord of Rumst and Schoten	22	3 farms, land, meadows, wood		488
3	Marten van Ranst	11	3 farms, 2 steden, land, heath, meadows	68,75	423
4	Our-Lady's Chapter Antwerp	3	tithes		336
5	Jacob Ghijsels	7	3 farms, 1 stede, wood	30,5	224
6	Abraham de Cnape	11	3 farms, 6 steden, land	28	189,6
7	Peter van Coppemael	9	2 farms, 5 houses, heath, wood	29,5	179
8	Diego de Ayala	6	farm, house, land		169,5
9	Francois de Fever	4	farm, house, wood	13,5	130
10	Hendrik Vinckt smitts	1	heath	14	128
11	St. Bernards	2	land, meadow	20	125
12	Cappelrie OLV-Schoten	10	farm, tithe, land	7	120,5
13	Begijnen Antwerpen	2	farm, wood, heath	22,5	111
14	Peter Brandts	10	2 steden, 3 houses, land	14,25	89,75
15	Elisabeth Lemmens	1	farm with heath	20	88,9
16	Jan Bonnecroy	7	stede, 3 houses on the square	4,5	83,35
17	Jacob Huygen	1	inn	7,5	82
18	Mr. Jan van Asselbergs	1	wood	14	80
19	St. Anthonis Capelle	1	farm	21	73
20	Jan vander Eggen	3	farm	30	71,3
21	Jan de Wolf	3	farm, stede, wood	8,5	64,15
22	Aert van Tijl	1	farm	5	64
23	Wed. Schuermans	5	farm, 3 steden	8	60,5
24	Peter Aerts	1	farm		60

25	Jan Ghijsels	6	inn, 2 houses, chamber,	14	59
26	Roeland van Berge	2	inn, house		57
27	Jan de Greve	3	farm, land	12,75	53
28	Heer Peter Kerstiaens	8	4 houses, land, meadow,wood		50,5
29	Jan van den Broecke	1	farm	6	48
30	Jan de Schoenmaker	3	stede, 2 houses	2	44
31	Gasthuis (St. Elisabeth)	2	wood peerdsbos		43,45
32	Machiel de Keyzer	4	stede, land, house	6	41
33	Heer van Renesse	1	house		40
34	Henrik van Hulshout	1	2 steden	1,5	39,35
35	Geert Verbeke	1	inn den binckelstap	1	37
36	Cornelis Janssen	1	stede	3	34,9
37	Jan Blijleven	1	stede	2	33,4
38	Peter Gijsels	1	farm	6	32
39	Chaplain of Schoten	2	2 houses at the chu-rhyard		30
40	Engel Reiners	3	inn, house		29
41	Hendrik Gijsels	4	2 steden, land, bos	2,5	28,2
42	Jan Tulpen	1	inn de helm at the square	2,5	28
43	Holy Spirit Schoten	3	land	1	27
44	Geert Bogaerts	1	stede	2	25,3
45	Peter van Cantelbeke	1	plantation of wood		25
46	Heer Coenrad Schets	1	wood		24
47	Jan van Baerle	5	5 houses		24
48	Jan Verleent	1	chamber		24
49	Denijs de Coster	1	stede	1	22
50	Jan Vileet	1	stede	1	22
51	Jan Vijsens	1	1,5 steden	3,5	20,9
52	Jan Geens	1	stede	2	19,2
53	parochian of Schoten	3	land		19
54	Margerite Alekens	1	stede	5	18,5
55	Jan Bueckeleer	1	stede	1	18,3
56	Geert van Massenhoven	1	stede, plantation of wood	3	17

57	St Jans Chapel	1	wood		17
58	Anna Soffens	1	stede	1	16,5
59	Claes van Hulshout	1	stede	3,75	16
60	Peter de Greve	1	stede	3	16
61	Merten Coels	1	stede, wood	4,1	15,6
62	Jacob de Cnape	1	stede	0,75	15,15
63	Cornelis Boots	1	house		15
64	heirs of P. Ghielens	1	stede, land	1,25	15
65	Henrik Mortelmans	1	stede	1,75	15
66	Lenart Janssen	1	stede	1	15
67	Meester Jan van Asselmans	1	wood	2,75	15
68	St. Vincent	1	plantation of wood		15
69	Jasper de timmerman	1	stede		14
70	Nicolaes de Deken	1	chamber	0,75	12,4
71	heirs of Andries Bosschaerts	1	stede	0,5	12
72	Henrick Ghijs	1	stede	0,5	12
73	Jan Bessels	1	stede	1	12
74	Jan Ghijs	1	stede		12
75	Joris Joris	1	stede	0,5	12
76	Peter de la Gaingne	1	wood		12
77	heirs of Jan de Deken	1	stede	0,5	11
78	Jan Daelmans	1	stede		10,35
79	Heilke Sconinks	1	stede		10
80	Peter de Deken	1	stede	0,125	10
81	Francois van Massenhoven	1	stede	0,5	9
82	Jan Dierickkx	1	house		9
83	Church Schoten	1	house		7
84	heirs of P. Ghijsels	1	land	1	6,5
85	Jan Mortelmans	1	house		6,5
86	Adriaen Hellaerts	1	house and garden		6
87	Nicolaes de Wever	1	stede	0,25	6
88	Cornelis Mannekens	1	house		5,5
89	High Bailiff of forests	1	plantation of wood		5

90	Jacob Vijsens	2	house		5
91	Mr. Adriaan van Zeven-donk	1	stede		4,1
92	Jan de Bruine	1	house		4
93	Adriaen Bogaerts	1	wood		3,6
94	Adriaen Bernaerts	1	land	0,5	3
95	Dirik de Schoenmaker	1			3
96	Huibrecht Vleems	1	house		3
97	Jan de Deken	1	land	0,5	3
98	Kosterij van der capelle inde horst	1		0,5	3
99	Holy Spirit Merksem	1	meadow	0,5	2
100	Paschijn Conincks	1	land	0,125	1
101	Archers of Schoten	1	shooting yard		0,2

4. Duffel ter-Elst

Source: Antwerp, ARA Inv. 35: Duffel Nr. 400.

	Owner	Plots	Description	Size	Value
1	Abbey of Tongerlo	24	5 farms, wood, land, meadow, tithe	91,75	1230
2	Vanden Steene heirs Matheeus	8	Farm+stede+ house, wood...	21,25	222,1
3	Den Klerken van Halen Hendrik	1	Farm +house and garden	20	108,4
4	Priest of Duffel	8	Land + tithe	6,25	96,27
5	Vincke Jan	6	1/2 farm, house+land+wood	8	80,6
6	Van Merode Willem, esquire	1	Farm house and garden	11	70
7	Lord van Eekhoven	4	Farm	12	60
8	Van Tolhuisen Charles	2	1/2 farm, house and garden	7	54,3
9	Parlognes Anthonis	4	house and garden		50
10	Zomer Willem	4	house and garden+meadow		46,5
11	Abbey St. Bernards	1	Tithe		46
12	De Grove Cornelis	1	house and garden + brewery		35
13	Stelmans Catelijne	1	stede+ 6 plots of land	4	34
14	Zomer Merten	4	pasture+land	4,75	57
15	Passchuer Aerts	2	stede+house and garden+wood	3	32,9
16	Van Gotengijs, lord Lancelot	3	stede+land and meadow	1,5	26,45
17	Diercicx Adriaen	4	?	0	24,5
19	Van Dijke Augustijn	1	house and garden		24
20	Van Keerbergen Jan	3	house and garden		31
21	Crets Cornelis	2	houses		20
22	Kaerls heirs Jan	2	wood	2,25	22,7
23	Wouters Jan	1	house and garden		20

24	De Herde Anna	1	stede, house and garden+ land	1,5	18
25	Marien Hendric	2	house and garden		30
26	Vervaren Rombout	1	meadow		16
27	Eliaes Catelijne	2	stede+ house and garden+wood	1,25	15,25
28	Van Halen heirs jf Anna	2	wood	1	15
29	Van Tuist heirs Ctelijne	2			15
30	Goirhoven Wouter	1	house and garden		15
32	De Laet heirs Jan	2	houses		14
33	Wouters heirs Rombout	1	2 plots od land	2	14
34	Charle Jacob	1	house and garden		14
36	Van Tolhuisen Digna	1	house and garden		12,5
37	Van Tolhuisen Elisabeth	1	house and garden		12,5
38	Verbiest Digne	1	house and garden		12,5
39	Colaerts Wouter	1	house and garden		12
40	Henstmans Adriaen	1			12
41	Verspouwen Aert	1	house and garden		12
42	Boedts Jan	1	house and garden		11
43	Van Hincxthoven Jan	1	meadow 1/2 b.	0,5	11
44	Meeus Anthonis	1	house and garden		11
45	Copmans Gomaer	2	houses		10,6
46	Zomer Gheraert	1	stede	0,75	10,5
47	Bosmans Mertens	1	house and garden		10
48	De Reigher Jan	1	house		10
49	Van Tolhuisen Jan	1	2 parc. 3/4 b beemreets	0,75	10
50	Van Briele Henderic	1	house and garden		10

51	Van Hove Peter	1	house and garden		10
53	Van Schore Francois	1	house and garden		10
54	De Laet Digna	1	Land	1	9,5
55	Sgroven Merten	1	Land	1,25	9,25
56	Church of Duffel	2	Land+meadow	2	23,5
57	Holy Spirit Duffel	2	meadow, land	1,25	12
58	Nolaet Hendrik	1	Land	1,5	9
59	Van Hoeye Cleerken	1			9
60	Meels Bertel	1	meadow		8
61	Van Rijmenam Anna	1	house and garden		8
62	De Herde Berbel	1		1,25	7,5
63	Monastery of Nazareth	2	land	1	7
64	Van Bonnecroy Lisbeth	1	stede	0,25	7
65	Van Tolhuisen, heirs Catelijne	1			7
66	Wijts, heirs of Laureis	1			7
67	Goris Gomaer	1	1/2 b. beemrets	0,5	6
68	Aerts Berbel	1	house and garden		6
69	Eliaes Wouter	1	house and garden		6
70	Inden NegelentuerLaureis	1	house and garden		6
71	Joos Jan	1			6
72	Smolders Catelijne	1			6
73	Stuevers Dominicus	1	house and garden		6
74	Huissens Jan	2	land+wood	0,25	5,3
75	De Snijder Anthonis	1	meadow	0,75	5
76	Wandelaerts Joos	1			4,5

77	De Malder Andries	1	meadow	0,75	4
78	De Grove Hendric	1	1/2 b. land	0,5	3
79	Wellens Peter	1	garden		2
80	Sellenslach Adriaen	1	1/8 beemreets	0,125	1,25
82	Van Bentick heer Laureis	1	wood	0,1	1
83	Hees Digna	1	stede+house and garden	5	1
84	De Bisschop Merten	1	stede	4,5	1
85	Van Halen Fransois	1	wood	1,75	
86	Van Halen Jan	1	wood	1,75	